PRAISE FOR ALICE
LEG

CW00701608

"This is so much more than a ve., detailed biography of Alice
Ann Bailey; it is also a very comprehensive review of the many
interesting groups and people throughout the history of theosophical thought and the continuing impulse of the Ageless
Wisdom teachings. At every turn we feel like we are on intimate
terms with the lives and events of this span of time, and the
overall view is awesome and inspiring."

– Gail Jolley, *School for Esoteric Studies*

"Our thanks to Dr Blackthorn for her insights into the life of
one of the most influential esoteric teachers of the twentieth
century. As scribe for the Tibetan Master, Alice Ann Bailey
provided a body of teachings unrivalled in their importance at
the dawn of the Aquarian Age."

– John F. Nash, PhD *www.uriel.com*

"A really enjoyable read! A clear light shining on a very
important spiritual scribe of our age, and that to come. The
inclusion of historical context gives great flavor and understanding of AAB's challenging life, and clears up many misun-
derstandings of her views. An erudite explanation of living
theosophy for general consumption – no mean feat!"

– Brenton Phillis *www.heartforchange.net*

"As a long-time student of the blue books and someone who
deeply admires AAB I couldn't have asked for a better biography. A pleasure to read. Many clues are drawn together to

provide a fuller picture of AAB. New information is given. Key periods in her life are given new light – such as the Ascona period. Alice Bailey and her writings are made more accessible and put into historic and esoteric context. It is high time the myths and misconceptions about AAB and her writings be dispelled and she takes her place as one of the greatest esoteric thinkers of the 20th Century. Isobel Blackthorn has done a great service to Alice Bailey's legacy and provided a gateway for a new generation of Alice Bailey students."

– Patrick Chouinard, *theosophical scholar and teacher*

"This remarkable, deeply researched book on Alice Bailey is a fascinating read for anyone who has an interest in the occult, Theosophy, the origins of the New Age movement, spirituality or the esoteric. Isobel Blackthorn has done an extraordinary job of writing an accessible biography of a unique woman whose ideas and writings have inspired generations, yet remains obscured and half-forgotten in history."

– Right Worshipful Master K. Crombie, 18° Freemason.

"I don't think you will find a more thorough and documented treatment of Bailey's life. Extremely well researched."

– Dr Lisa Love

"A MUST for any Bailey student, a MUST for anyone at all interested in the 'New Age' movement and wondered where it all came from, and a MUST for all those who wonder, amidst our confused and divided world, where it will all end?"

– Steven Chernikeeff, author of *Esoteric Apprentice*

"This is a remarkable biography for its sheer scope and level of detail, placing Alice Bailey clearly amid her spiritual contemporaries. One of the many strengths of Alice A. Bailey: Life and Legacy is the way it enables the reader to follow the maturation of Bailey's teachings, and to witness how through Bailey's unique spiritual guidance, she arrived at such a large vision for humankind."

– Maggie Hamilton, author of *The Secret World of Fairies*

"Blackthorn´s study is a treasure trove of new data on the life and work of Alice Bailey This biography is an important and ground-breaking contribution to our understanding of, not just Alice Bailey, but also the Esoteric Tradition, the third intellectual force or pillar in cultural history alongside science and religion. Isobel Blackthorn is to be commended for an excellent work of interest to all serious students of esotericism."

– Håkan Blomqvist, *Sweden Librarian and co-founder of Archives for the Unexplained (AFU)*

"Isobel Blackthorn's thorough research and compelling style present the polarity of experiences of Alice Bailey: admiration and antagonism, leadership and service, devotion and betrayal, and the accumulation of wisdom that underpins, without acknowledgement, much of our modern belief systems. Lovers of enlightenment and esoteric philosophy will treasure this book."

– Veronica Schwarz, *author and editor*

ALICE A. BAILEY

LIFE & LEGACY

Isobel Blackthorn

For World Servers

CONTENTS

AUTHOR'S NOTE

The first thing that struck me when I came across Alice Bailey's writing was the austere, formal look of the books themselves, with the lack of the author's name on the front cover. Instead, the covers all feature a curious triangular symbol containing a series of lines which I would later know to be the initials L U X: Latin for light. Then there was the Edwardian tone of the teachings and of course, the woman herself; presented in the few photographs that exist of her in the public domain as unassuming, benevolent and kind. I succumbed to an immediate trust.

Yet how could I trust so wholeheartedly and immediately someone I had never met, who had died in 1949, thirteen years before my birth, a woman I could only see in an old photograph? I was making a judgement based on a quick impression. Perhaps ill-founded, although at the time I was certain it was not. Could that kindly visage belie forces of absolute evil, as the Christian fundamentalists would have it? Could the thoughts scribed by this homey figure provide the foundation for a new dystopian World Order, as the conspiracy theorists claim? Was she a maverick, an imposter, plagiarising pre-existing works, as some Theosophists argue? Or was she simply a deluded crank, a view harboured by scholars? These were questions far from my mind when I stared into the face of Alice Bailey in 1994, poised to read her unfinished autobiography.

Alice Bailey came into my life in a curiously ceremonial fashion. I was living in Perth, Western Australia, as a practicing astrologer studying for a diploma in Transpersonal Counselling, and I had a crush on a rather fine young man who had recently left his life in Adelaide, packed up his things and driven the long distance across the desert-dry Nullarbor Plain. There wasn't much space in his car, and he had left many possessions behind, yet he'd felt compelled to bring with him a book in which he had no particular interest. He'd found it in a second-hand bookstore, and it was called *Esoteric Astrology*. One day, while I was visiting him at his new home, he asked me to wait while he fetched something from his bedroom and reappeared with the book on upturned palms. 'Before we met, I had no idea why I packed this book,' he said, all formal and sombre, 'but now I do. It's meant for you.'

I took the book, a thick and heavy tome, and thanked him. I soon devoured that book and over time purchased every other book Alice Bailey had written. I had no clear idea what I was going to do with them, but every time I moved house, and I moved a lot at the time, I boxed them up and took them along.

It was in 2001, just after the twin towers fell, that another series of events occurred which led me to set about a serious study of Alice Bailey's texts. I was working at the time as a high school teacher of history and religious studies. My job fulfilled me immensely, yet I began to make inquiries to undertake a doctorate. At first, my ideas were vague, and The Open University, best suited to my need for distance education, kept losing my emails.

In January 2002, I took a party of high school students to a university campus to research their A Level coursework essay. They'd all decided to study the New Age. As we were leaving the campus, I found a textbook in the university bookshop which looked like it would provide my students with all they needed to complete their essays. I purchased the book and took it home. There, I read the editorial introduction by a Dr Marion Bowman of the University of Bath. I thought nothing of it. Later that same afternoon, I checked my emails. To my astonishment, a Dr Marion Bowman, the same Marion Bowman only now working for the Open University, had responded to my doctorate query! She asked me to re-send my email because somehow the original content was lost. I did, and this time, by way of a postscript that I regarded more to be a throwaway line, I mentioned Alice Bailey. Dr Bowman replied instantly and followed up moments later with a phone call.

Personal circumstances meant I didn't study Alice Bailey under Dr Bowman. Instead, I secured supervision in the School of Social Ecology at the University of Western Sydney. With its holistic, ecological and communitarian values and its emphasis on transpersonal psychology, Social Ecology proved a fitting home for a thesis on Alice Bailey.

I recall my first research residential on campus, the hundred or so students taking the Bachelor's and Master's degrees, and the expressions of impressed astonishment on the faces of inquirers when they discovered what I was about to undertake.

I received my doctorate in 2006. At the time, as far as I could ascertain, I was the world's only scholar of Alice Bailey, a matter I found puzzling since to me, she seemed to have contributed so much to world thought.

Ten years and another string of addresses went by before Alice Bailey re-entered my life for a third time. I'd purchased a 1970s bungalow and the kitchen was in dire need of a kitchen renovation. When the old wall oven's electronic time display flashed 'HELP' in digital green – a feature of the model, I have since discovered, but I did not know that at the time – I felt I had to act. After the renovations were complete, I found I had a high shelf in a prominent place at the end of a kitchen cupboard. From that purview, you could survey all the living areas. I dusted off my old photocopy of Alice Bailey's portrait featured in her autobiography, which I'd put in a frame. I had no idea why I put her portrait up there on that high shelf, but I sensed, dimly, the significance.

She smiled down at me.

A month later, and completely unexpectedly, I was writing her biography.

I used the original version – which I felt was incomplete and insubstantial due to a paucity of research material – to compose *The Unlikely Occultist: A biographical novel of Alice A. Bailey*, which complements this non-fiction version and tells the known story of Alice. On the strength of the positive response from the Bailey community to that novel, I resumed work on the biography.

I could not have written this biography without Steven Chernikeeff, whose wholehearted support, encouragement and guidance enabled me to understand the unknown story of Alice and the history of the Bailey community. I am indebted to Stephen Pugh who talked me through a complex and difficult period in that history and supplied me with open access to The Polaris Project. Warm thanks to Lynda Vugler, Cynthia Ohlman, M. Temple Richmond and Geoffrey Logie, all of whom responded to my questions and provided much clarity. My gratitude to Rose Bates for her willingness to talk to me at length and provide me with some key resources and photographs, and to Patrick Chouinard, Murray Stentiford, Kenneth Sørensen and Håkan Blomqvist for their valuable feedback. I am grateful to Gvido Trepsa of the Agni Yoga Society, who assisted me with vital research. My heartfelt thanks to Gail Jolley at The School for Esoteric Studies for providing me with a significant cache of unpublished material. And to Christine Morgan and Steve Nation of the Lucis Trust who delved into their small archives to supply photos and furnished me with useful resources. Finally, a warm thank you to Mindy Burge and Veronica Schwarz for casting their critical eyes over the manuscript and making it shine.

Note: I have broken with convention and chosen the full name of Alice Bailey when referring to the public figure, and Alice when presenting her life.

INTRODUCTION

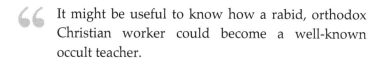 It might be useful to know how a rabid, orthodox Christian worker could become a well-known occult teacher.

[and]

One of the things that I seek to bring out in this story is the fact of this inner direction of world affairs and to familiarise more people with the paralleling fact of the existence of Those Who are responsible (behind the scenes) for the spiritual guidance of humanity, and for the task of leading mankind out of darkness into Light, from the unreal to the Real and from death to Immortality.[1]

If there was a single word to sum up the character of Alice Bailey it would be devotion. Devotion in standing firm and acting with skill and strength when beyond her edifice of spiritual teachings and organisations attackers and detractors were armed and ready. That a woman and a body of work fundamentally spiritual should be subject to a whole century of vilification, derision, condemnation and dismissal is not surprising. What Alice Bailey set out to achieve was a complete global transformation of consciousness, a transformation of the way we think and act in the world. Little wonder then, that people would and will resist.

Alice Bailey was a leading occultist of the 20th century, well known and highly regarded in freethinking circles during her lifetime, although controversy surrounded her even then. The moment she began writing her corpus, she endured accusations of plagiarism and fraud, purists in the Theosophical milieu regarding her as a third generation Theosophist, a neo-Theosophist, or worse, a pseudo-Theosophist. These early attacks were harbingers of the blistering condemnations her work would later receive.

After her death, Alice Bailey drifted into obscurity, known beyond her own milieu only amongst Theosophists, some New Age adherents, the odd fundamentalist Christian, and more recently, conspiracy theorists. In the academic community, she has been overlooked, if not altogether snubbed by historians of religion.[2] As a result, outside of her sphere of influence, her teachings are largely unheard of, misunderstood or misrepresented. Yet her body of work continues in various ways to influence seekers far and wide. Van Morrison's entire album *Beautiful Vision* is a celebration of the Bailey teachings, especially *Glamour: A World Problem*. The Velvet Underground's song 'White Light White Heat' is said to have been inspired by *A Treatise on White Magic*. And progressive rock instrumentalist Todd Rundgren's album *Initiation* is an homage to *A Treatise on Cosmic Fire*. The album's second side carries the same title. How many artists, writers, poets and other creative and critical thinkers have learnt from, drawn inspiration from and applied the Bailey teachings in their own fields is not known. Many prefer to keep their esoteric beliefs to themselves.

In her autobiography, Alice Bailey describes herself as a shy and intensely private woman who hated publicity. Yet she was an excellent public speaker, having honed her skills in her twenties leading Gospel meetings. She hailed from the British aristocracy. As a child and young adult, she endured immense loss and hardship. Around the age of thirty-five, she found Theosophy was for her an epiphany, one that aroused commitment second to none. She espoused her newfound wisdom just as she had her former Christian beliefs. She wrote every day for over thirty years as an amanuensis for the Tibetan, or Djwhal Khul, a Master in Theosophy's Spiritual Hierarchy, a group of Masters of the Wisdom overseeing the evolution of consciousness of humanity. The result is an extraordinarily detailed and comprehensive outpouring of the Ageless Wisdom.

The Bailey teachings are thought to be the second of three outpourings, the first that of founder of the Theosophical Society Helena Blavatsky. Alice Bailey's version serves to guide aspirants and disciples of the spiritual path into the twenty-first century. A third outpouring is predicted around 2025 along with the externalisation, or physical plane appearance of the Hierarchy in some form, along with the much-anticipated re-appearance of the World Teacher.

In the last months of her life, after much cajoling, Alice Bailey began to write her autobiography. She never finished it. Little has been written about her life since. Alice Bailey's *The Unfinished Autobiography* remains the central source of information and insight into her life. It is an inspiring work and depicts honestly the tragedies and the triumphs of a woman dedicated to world service.

Alice Bailey was a contemporary of influential esoteric luminaries Rudolph Steiner, George Gurdjieff and P. D. Ouspensky who, along with a raft of notable figures including Indra Devi and Carl Gustav Jung, made significant contributions to the development of the New Age, a term Alice Bailey appropriated and made her own. Her contribution to the movement is outstanding. She'd reached the middle of her life when she took up the challenge and embarked on thirty years of work, for which she has been described as 'the mother of the New Age'.[3]

Her writings, translated into many languages and read world-wide, remain in print. Among her organisations, she founded: The Arcane School, an esoteric school delivering training by correspondence for disciples on the spiritual path; World Good-will, an organisation hosting regular seminars and conferences with the objective of spreading loving understanding and well-being for all; the global meditation network Triangles; The Beacon magazine; and her publishing house, the Lucis Trust. All are still active today.[4]

One of the difficulties with Alice Bailey's body of work is its inaccessibility. Pure esoteric knowledge is hard for the non-esoteric reader to grasp and even those esoterically inclined are known to find parts of her work challenging. The other is that Alice Bailey claims to have written most of her output in tele-pathic rapport with the Tibetan Djwhal Khul, an arrangement difficult for the sceptic to accept.

The Bailey texts are intended to serve as advice and teachings for aspirants and disciples of the spiritual path. The canon is vast, amounting to around eleven thousand pages of text, enough to fill a bookshelf, and includes slim volumes to weighty tomes such as *A Treatise on Cosmic Fire*, a work of pure esoteri-cism that is impossible to grasp unless the reader has an appetite for it.

Before travelling along with Alice Bailey's life and works, it's worth pausing to put the teachings into context and gain a partial understanding of the terrain. The following concepts provide a frame through which to view the content of the following chapters.

THE ESOTERIC SENSE

Esotericism opens a door on an inner reality which lies behind the world we can see and hear and feel. Its primary aim is the creation of a unity between our inner or subjective reality and the outer world in which we find ourselves (extramental reality).

To achieve this, esoteric practitioners cultivate within the self an intuitive way of knowing termed the esoteric sense – the ability to recognise and understand a metaphysical reality that can only be known or seen subjectively. This new reality to some extent displaces the ordinary, pre-existing inner life, reshaping the practitioner's worldview. Through esoteric training, thoughts and actions begin to cohere with this metaphysical realm. An astrologer, for example, through many years of immersion, training and application, conjures in her imagination an entire cosmology of planets and signs of the zodiac and their complex interactions. The astrologer sees into and through this cosmology, derives meaning from it, and communicates what she finds in the form of storytelling. She sees in symbolic images another's personality traits and foibles, talents and attributes, difficulties and challenges. She may even predict a thing or two. It is through these processes of immersion, absorption and interaction that hidden knowledge is transferred.

The main purpose of the training Alice Bailey offers in her spiritual school, the Arcane School, and in the bulk of her body of work, is the development of the esoteric sense, or 'the power to live and function subjectively, to possess a constant inner contact with the soul and the world in which it is found".[5] Cultivating the esoteric sense involves continuous meditation and spiritual orientation until the individual lives in the seat of the observer, the soul. It is akin to the Buddhist practice of mindfulness but at a much more advanced level.

An active, open and responsive consciousness is required to interact in a synthetic way with metaphysical realities. In the process of interaction, the esotericist is practising gnosis. Leading scholar of Western Esotericism Wouter Hanegraaff is one of a small group of intellectuals concentrating their efforts on demystifying esotericism and affording the field of study some academic standing. Hanegraaff draws on Dutch theologian Gilles Quispel's definition of gnosis as a third orientation towards meaning and reality. While faith finds truth in revelation as found in holy scripture, and reason in what can be rationally known and what can be discovered through science, gnosis relies on inner personal experiences often expressed in images, and is oriented 'towards secret knowledge of the hidden coherence of the universe'.[6]

The typical gnostic is an intellectual and a radical. Luminaries of a gnostic orientation include: abstract artist Wassily Kandinsky; designer of Canberra Walter Burley Griffin; poet W.B. Yeats; philosophers Gottfried Leibniz and Francis Bacon; composers Erik Satie and Claude Debussy; author and playwright Johann Goethe; physician Robert Fludd; and mathematician and physicist Isaac Newton. How their individual gnostic ways of knowing and approaches to knowledge influenced their ideas and creativity would form an interesting discussion.

Alice Bailey's aim was not only to foster the esoteric sense – an inner contact with the soul – in those with a gnostic disposition, but also to make esoteric activists out of armchair enthusiasts, to steer her students away from the allure of esotericism as a form of knowledge per se, and towards esoteric practice in group formation oriented towards the betterment of humanity.

WESTERN ESOTERICISM

The keynote of esotericism is inaccessibility. Esotericism goes out of its way *not* to be understood. Knowledge is kept secret, there only for the few prepared to undergo specialised training.[7] Western Esotericism refers to those variants emerging in the West, including Astrology, Gnosticism, the Kabbalah, Alchemy, Rosicrucianism, Illuminism and Freemasonry. Each variant carries its own unique style but shares similar views on the existence of unseen or metaphysical realities inhabited by energies, forces and spiritual entities. All variants involve: the practice of correspondence, based on the belief that everything in the universe is interconnected; belief in the existence of the soul and its evolutionary journey back to the Source; a commitment to personal transformation; transmission of an Ageless wisdom; and the use of the imagination as the point of entry into esotericism.

Esotericism resides on the margins of mainstream culture and society and this is mirrored in the type of personality drawn towards esoteric practice. Yet marginality does not denote powerlessness. Esotericism is far from ineffectual. It's a powerful shadow player, more likely to influence particular kinds of intellectually gifted individuals located at the centre of society and culture. A good example of such influence can be found in Nicholas Goodrick-Clarke's *Hitler's Priestess*, which explores the influence of occult thought upon Adolph Hitler. More uplifting examples can be found in art, literature, music, science, and psychology as noted above. Within Bailey's circle of influence are: prominent New Age precursor Vera Stanley Alder; renowned American philosopher David Spangler; and eminent psychiatrist, Roberto Assagioli.

THEOSOPHY AND THE THEOSOPHICAL SOCIETY

Alice Bailey's writings belong to the variant of Western Esotericism known as Theosophy. The notion of 'theosophy' predates the fifteenth century, the term first used by Neoplatonist Porphyry (234-305 C.E.) to describe a combination of the capacities of the philosopher, the artist and the priest. The term was later adopted in the late sixteenth and seventeenth centuries by Christian mystic and theologian Jacob Boehme who created a theosophy rooted in Judeo-Christianity, inspired by the writings of Paracelsus (1493-1541 CE).[8]

Theosophy emerged again in the late nineteenth century English-speaking world, especially amongst free thinkers. The period witnessed a growing disenchantment with Christian doctrine, with its institutionalized structures and fundamentalist interpretations. There was a concomitant need to respond to a new wave of scientific discoveries, particularly Darwin's evolutionary theory which not only undermined the Christian creation story but also threatened the very foundations of any faith in a non-material reality. This led many seekers to pursue esoteric interests as a new spirituality. Or, in the words of author and scholar Peter Washington, 'spirituality itself was not in question, so much as a secure source of spiritual authority...the search for a single key that would solve the mysteries of the universe'.[9]

Western science confines itself to understanding the physical universe. Eastern science has a broader scope, placing religion, history, philosophy and psychology within its reach. Uncovering the laws of nature is one thing. Learning how to live harmoniously with those laws is another. Drawing upon Eastern mystical notions of karma and reincarnation allowed Theosophists to propose their own evolutionary theory, in contrast to both the biblical Genesis of Christianity and scientific Darwinian theory. Theosophists claimed that their belief system transcended the cleavage between science and religion through its return to an Ageless Wisdom. The mysteries of the universe were explained in theosophy through an elaborate cosmology, which had the potential to become the spiritual authority sought by individuals distanced from Christianity.

The Theosophical Society was founded in New York in 1875 by occultist and Russian aristocrat Madame Helena Petrovna Blavatsky (1831-91), along with lawyer and journalist Colonel Henry Steel Olcott (1832-1907), and Anglo-Irish mystic William Quan Judge (1851-96). The trio shared a prior interest in Spiritualism, with its belief in life after death and the ability, through the role of a medium, to contact and receive messages from the spirit world.

Blavatsky devoted her life to the pursuit of esoteric knowledge. Eventually, she responded to what she felt was the call of the Masters of the Wisdom – many of whom were located in the border region of India and Tibet, near Darjeeling – to serve as a transmitter of the Ageless Wisdom to a world in dire need of it.

The result was *Isis Unveiled,* followed about a decade later by her most well-known work, *The Secret Doctrine.*

Blavatsky and Olcott travelled extensively in India in the early years of the society, and their vision was well received among both English and Indian communities. It was while they were in India that allegations of fraud were instigated – with the wholehearted support of some Christian missionaries – by Emma and Alexis Coulomb after their dismissal from the centre in Adyar, Bombay, in what is known as the Coulomb Affair.[10] These allegations concerned Blavatsky's claim that her writings were transmitted to her by a Master in the Spiritual Hierarchy. From that moment the Theosophical Society was the subject of criticism, both from within, borne out in internal power struggles and accusations of fraud and deception, and from without, the reliance on Eastern mystical ideas arousing annoyance from adherents to the more Western-centred esoteric currents of the day.[11]

Controversy continued into the second generation of the Theosophical Society, involving scandals, schisms and crises of authority over claims made by prominent leaders that they were operating under the direct guidance of spiritual masters.[12] Alice Bailey did not escape embroilment.

The existence of the Masters of the Wisdom has proven contentious. The reader should consider the Spiritual Hierarchy to be a '"society of organised and illumed minds" – illumed by love and understanding, by deep compassion and inclusiveness, illumed by knowledge…'[13]

It is also worth noting that the Masters' emphasis is always on humanity as a whole and world service, and they are never concerned with individual teachers and their groups. Always and uppermost is not any single individual's claimed connection with this Master or that, but rather how they themselves are World Servers, oriented towards human and planetary betterment, and not towards any form of self-aggrandisement, no matter how subtle that might be.

This biography begins with the tragedies of Alice Bailey's childhood as an aristocratic orphan shunted about the stately homes of her aunts and ends with the legacy of a world teacher and her oeuvre that would inaugurate, not so much a new age, but rather the New Age movement. It is a story of one woman's journey of faith, from orthodox Christian beginnings, through a protracted spiritual crisis, to a newfound belief in Theosophy. It is the story of a mystic and a seeker, and the life she came to lead as the founder of a number of global organisations that continue to this day to carry on her work. It is also the story of one woman's struggle to overcome adversity, fend off her adversaries and find fulfilment in her service to humanity.

Threaded throughout the narrative is the remarkable story of her output. Alice Bailey's cosmology in *A Treatise on Cosmic Fire* can be considered an esoteric theory of everything, replete with planes of existence, cosmic rays, radiating spheres and solar fires. Numerous volumes contain instructions to aspirants and disciples of the spiritual path, with insightful depictions of initiatory events along the way. Eventually, the seeker faces the Dweller on the Threshold, the sum total of all that stands in the way of spiritual advancement, and Alice Bailey provides the necessary means to dispel it.

After her death, her husband Foster Bailey took full organisational control. Tensions grew as others felt entitled to certain responsibilities. A co-worker broke away to form a splinter group, taking a small group with her. A few years later, another split occurred right at the heart of the headquarters in New York. Both splits went on to scar the Alice Bailey community, creating disunity where unity should have been.

Key figures furthered the Bailey teachings. Pioneering Italian psychiatrist and founder of Psychosynthesis Roberto Assagioli was instrumental in the formation of Transpersonal Psychology and headed his own global meditation group along Ageless Wisdom lines. Devoted student Vera Stanley Alder wrote a number of books that rendered the teachings more accessible, books that inspired future New Age practitioners of esoteric healing. With the help of such students, Alice Bailey left a remarkable legacy as the mother of the New Age movement. From enthusiastic crusader Benjamin Creme to trailblazer David Spangler, Alice Bailey's work has influenced a raft of thinkers and their organisations. Alternative, and perhaps utopian, visions of a global, spiritual awakening continue to be advanced by her followers in the hope of fostering a paradigm shift. The teachings undergird the vision, the aspiration and the hope for a better world.

The teachings have inspired pursuits in esoteric psychology, or the psychology of the Seven Rays, and the closely related esoteric astrology, as students endeavour to understand and develop the ideas and put them into practice. Individuals and small and large groups dotted around the globe continue to study, follow, practice and apply the Ageless Wisdom. It is through all these groups that the Ageless Wisdom is kept alive and will inspire many generations to follow.

SOME NOTES ON THE UNFINISHED AUTOBIOGRAPHY

Alice Bailey's *The Unfinished Autobiography* has been the primary source for those interested in knowing something of the life of the occult figure. The early chapters of the current work rely heavily on and substantially embellish Bailey's own words wherever possible. The lack of complementary sources in the form of letters or other corroborating materials is problematic. All autobiographies are prone to bias, including omissions, emphases and modifications of the truth, and should be regarded more as expressions of feeling and remembering in the form of vignettes than as demonstrations of historical fact.

Alice Bailey had a particular premise in mind when she put pen to paper in 1949 in the final months of her life, an agenda, things she wanted said and other things she chose to omit. There is very little said of her mother's family. Perhaps there was little to tell, Alice Bailey ignorant of her maternal heritage. The pain she felt over her only sister's rejection of her is evident through the lack of mention of her name, Lydia, as though Alice Bailey had chosen to subtly deny her full existence between the covers. Alice Bailey chose to be elusive when it came to her relationship with Foster, not bothering to quell rumours she had most likely heard that their marriage was unconsummated. There is also no detail at all of Foster's family. Some friends are mentioned but scores of others are not. She is tight-lipped when it comes to her split from the Theosophical Society and to the upsetting situation with Olga Fröbe. She does not mention Helena Roerich or Rudolph Steiner, neither of whom she held in especially high regard.

Alice Bailey is naturally keen to show herself in a good light, and she does so with humility and wit, providing scores of entertaining vignettes. Yet she is defensive too when it comes to affirming the integrity of her daughters and her relationship with the Tibetan. Uppermost, behind the words, is a keen intention to portray herself with dignity as an authentic world disciple, and distinguish herself from the cranks and mediums operating on the lower psychic level who abounded in her lifetime.

Final note – It is my sincere wish that this book will stimulate as much as inform and entertain and that by the end of it, readers will choose to do much more than wonder at the mysteries of the universe and consider acting to promote human and planetary betterment. To paraphrase Alice Bailey, remaining mentally quiescent in the face of life is a disaster.

AN EMERGING EVANGELIST

*T*he child who would become the controversial occult figure Alice A. Bailey began her life as Alice Ann La Trobe-Bateman in Manchester, England, on 16 June 1880. She was born under the zodiacal sign of Gemini, the sign of the twins, the one mortal, the other divine. It's the zodiacal home of the planet Mercury who, in his psychopomp role, is the conductor of souls between this world and the next. For some, Gemini is the symbol of the duality of the shadow and the self. The esoteric ruler, Venus, the highest aspect of mind, unites these pairs of opposites and offers a relationship with the divine brotherhood. All of which provides, in astrological terms, a symbolic echo of a kind of dual consciousness that was to be the hallmark of an extraordinary life.

Alice was born in late-Victorian Britain, at a time when the landed gentry were undergoing a period of considerable adjustment to the new economic conditions emerging in post-Industrial-Revolution Britain. A downturn in farming revenues on the great country estates, partly due to cheap imports of grain from the United States of America, caused many to sell off parcels of their land. Others began to take an interest in the affairs of business and trade. It was a time of lavish investment in public works and civil engineering, most significantly for the pioneering engineers of the La Trobe-Bateman family, in bridge building and water supply.

In her autobiography, Alice Bailey makes much of her father's side of the family, with a liberal sprinkling of names and places mentioned. She grew up within the folds of British aristocracy and confesses to having been an outright snob. As a child, and again in later life, she moved in privileged circles. Her social standing had much bearing on the manner in which she fashioned her organisations, the people she was associated with and the legacy she has left humanity. Her cultured pedigree shaped the way she viewed the world, the attitudes and beliefs she held dear and above all, her Edwardian morality. Yet this illustrious lineage represents only one half of Alice Bailey's heritage and the other, her mother's line, tells a different story.

In her autobiography, Alice Bailey misspells her mother's maiden name. On her mother's side, Alice refers to herself as a Holinshed. She claims her family members were descendants of Raphael Holinshed, the notable chronicler who inspired Shakespeare. She makes no other mention of her maternal heritage other than stating:

 As far as I know none of my [maternal] ancestors did anything particularly interesting. They were worthy but apparently dull. As my sister once put it, "they sat among their cabbages for centuries." It was good, clean cultured stock but none of the people attained any famous or infamous notoriety.[1]

THE IMPRESSION ALICE BAILEY gives is one of a lazy landed gentry living off the fat of the land.

Alice La Trobe-Bateman's mother was Alice Harriet Hollinshead (6 August 1856- 3 October 1886), born to William Hollinshead and Jane Hollinshead (Wrathmell), in Birkby, Huddersfield.[2] The family appears, minus Alice Harriet, on the 1861 census in Brushfield, a hamlet of three farms in the Peak District in what is now Derbyshire.[3] The region is known for its bucolic beauty – rolling green hills, rushing rivers and quaint villages – and for its water mills which first milled corn and then later, during the Industrial Revolution, cotton. Some mills, including Bamford Mill, maintained their own gas works and William Hollinshead was at that time an ironfounder/inventor. It would have been for the purposes of William's employment, that the family was living in Brushfield.

William hailed from middle-class parentage, the third youngest of eight children. His parents, Alice's great-grandparents, were Joseph Hollinshead and Elizabeth Hollinshead (Swetmore), who came from and were married in the Potteries region of Staffordshire, known since 1910 as Stoke-on-Trent. Joseph was a linen draper or dry-goods merchant. Among William's siblings were a schoolteacher, a governess, a bonnet maker and a railway clerk. William himself started out as a bookkeeper before taking up gas engineering.[4]

Alice Harriet was the second eldest of ten children. After an early childhood nestled in Brushfield, the family moved to the market town of St Neots in Cambridgeshire (then Huntingdonshire) sometime between 1860 and 1863, where four of Alice Harriet's siblings were born. St Neots was by then a thriving industrial town, containing breweries, the Paxton paper mill and a gas works. Here, William continued working as a gas engineer/inventor. Industrialist and gas-appliance developer George Bower had just established Vulcan Iron Works in the town, a foundry making gas equipment and appliances, and farm machinery. William was employed to invent 'improvements in apparatus for the production and transmission of gas or other fluids', with two of his inventions receiving patents with George Bower, one in 1863, the other in 1868.[5]

The move to St Neots did not prove entirely successful. Bower was not known for wise business practice and he was declared bankrupt in 1887. Perhaps his imprudence rubbed off on William, who was himself declared bankrupt in London twelve years earlier, on 21st June 1865, presumably after garnering investment for an unsuccessful patent.[6] Whatever had occurred, William continued working for Bower. The family remained in St Neots, but sometime before 1871 they also took up residence in Hill Street, Peckham, where Alice Harriet's youngest sister Louise was born.[7]

Alice Harriet enjoyed relationships with her aunts and uncles. In 1871, at age fourteen, she visited her father's siblings – Ann, Hannah and Joseph – for Easter in the family home in George Street, Huddersfield. Ann was by then fifty-two and working as a governess. She had assumed the role of head of the household, Alice Harriet's grandparents having died.[8] Alice Harriet may have also enjoyed a close relationship with her father. Five years later, at the age of just nineteen, she was at his bedside in St Neots when he passed away.[9] William died from consumption (tuberculosis), at the age of forty-six.

Around this time, Alice Harriet's fortunes underwent a radical change. Within two years, she married Frederic Foster La Trobe-Bateman (1853-1889) in St Margaret's Church, Westminster, in what can only be described as a significant leap in social standing from her middle-class origins into the bosom of the British gentry.[10]

It was no ordinary wedding. Founded by Benedictine monks in the twelfth century, rebuilt and later restored and renovated in the seventeenth century when it was encased in Portland stone, St Margaret's sits in the grounds of Westminster Abbey and serves as the parish church of the Palace of Westminster. Notable weddings include those of Winston Churchill, Lord Louis

Mountbatten and members of the extended British royal family. It was the sort of church befitting Frederic Foster and not Alice Harriet.

It is likely the couple met through business networks. George Bower, an ambitious man, had an interest in Buenos Aires in the years prior to 1876 when he was contracted to light the city with gas, a contract that led to his bankruptcy.[11] Working in his father's business and proving his worth as an engineer, Frederic was at that time installing drainage and water supply in the same city. Perhaps Frederic and William met in Buenos Aires and William, eager to find a match for his eldest daughter, contrived an introduction.

Frederic might not have gained his parent's immediate approval to marry a young woman from the middle classes, albeit the daughter of a modestly successful inventor and engineer. No doubt it came as a small disappointment to his parents when they discovered their second son had chosen Alice Harriet for a wife. Perhaps when his father acknowledged that his own father and manufacturer John Bateman was also an unsuccessful inventor and therefore of no particular eminence, his sympathy for William Hollinshead and, by extension, his daughter Alice Harriet, was aroused and he granted permission. Most likely Frederic Foster, an ardent and passionate man, wore his father down.

Frederic's father John Frederic La Trobe-Bateman (1810-1889) was the first son of John Frederic Bateman (1772-1861) and Mary Agnes La Trobe (1773-1848). The union of the Batemans with the La Trobes can only be described as fortuitous for the manufacturer husband, Mary hailing from a family of high achievers.

The La Trobes were of Huguenot origin and had moved to Ireland some centuries before when Henri Bonneval La Trobe left France in 1688 to join the army of William of Orange, arriving in Dublin after being wounded in battle.[12] Mary's father Reverend Benjamin Bonneval La Trobe was a leading Moravian minister, and Mary's siblings included the accomplished composer, musician and Moravian leader Christian Ignatius La Trobe, who fathered Charles La Trobe, first governor of Victoria, Australia. Another brother was Benjamin Henry La Trobe, the renowned architect who made his name after migrating to the United States.

The trend continued into the next generation. John Frederic's younger brother and Alice's great uncle was Edward La Trobe-Bateman, the renowned watercolourist and book illuminator.[13] John Frederic furthered the achievements of his family by gaining eminence in his chosen profession of water engineering, constructing reservoirs and water works and devising water supply systems for numerous British cities and others around the world. In Britain, he was president of the prestigious Institute for Civil Engineers in 1878 and 1879, and he stood in close proximity to the governing power of the day.[14]

Following in his father's footsteps, John Frederic married to his advantage, his wife Anne Fairbairn (1817-1894) being the only daughter of the distinguished Scottish engineer and scientist Sir William Fairbairn.[15] Fairbairn was a pioneer in bridge building, ship building and railway locomotives. In 1844, he invented the Lancashire boiler. While still in his mid-twenties, the ambitious John Frederic worked with Fairbairn in the construction of reservoirs in Ireland, an association which led on to the young man's success. Both men were highly regarded in the science and engineering community, and both were elected without ballot to the Athenæum Club, a private members club for those who have attained distinction in their field.[16]

In the light of so much achievement, Frederic Foster's parents would have held high aspirations for their son. His older sisters had married advantageously and it seems Frederic bucked the trend. Was Frederic, the second youngest sibling, an impulsive and fixated young man? Hot-headed, perhaps? Stubborn? Or just hopelessly in love? In her autobiography, Alice Bailey hints that he might have been all those things.

As a child, Frederic had not enjoyed good health and was removed from Westminster College and tutored at home. His health did not prevent him from seeking to achieve some stature in the field of engineering. After working in his father's business on water engineering projects in Manchester and Buenos Aires, he was made a business partner in 1880 and supervised the construction of large additions to waterworks around Manchester. His wife Alice Harriet had married into familiar circumstances with regard to her husband's profession if not his wealth and social standing, giving birth to a daughter within a year.

Alice Ann La Trobe-Bateman was born at home at Holly House, Hollins Lane, Greenfield, Saddleworth, on the rural outskirts of Manchester.[17] Greenfield is a wealthy area situated on the southern edge of the Southern Pennines just below Saddleworth moor. The old stone farmhouses dotted around date back to the 1600s, many of them grade II listed. Holly House is a beautiful mansion in a charming rural setting up Hollins Lane, enjoying sweeping views of the wide valley below. A bucolic location, safe, traditional, wholesome and homey.

In those early months of her life, Alice benefited from contact with at least one of her maternal aunts. At nine months, baby Alice was left at home with her mother's sister Sarah Hollinshead, aged seventeen, along with a nurse and various servants, while her parents visited Frederic's parents at the family's London house in Great George Street, Westminster.[18] In his memoir, *Memories of Grave and Gay*, Frederic's older brother William Fairbairn La Trobe-Bateman talks warmly of the house on the corner of Great George Street, with its large front garden and veranda overlooking Westminster Bridge and the Houses of Parliament.[19]

The La Trobe-Bateman family enjoyed considerable social advantage. When Alice was born, her grandfather John Frederic sat at the pinnacle of his field and moved in the upper echelons of British society. It is only possible to imagine what Alice

Harriet made of her newfound privilege, but it was an indulgence that was to be short-lived. Frederic whisked away his little family to Montréal in the autumn of 1881, where he drafted plans for an extension of the Victoria Bridge over the St Lawrence River.[20] His report, dated 18 January 1882, was lodged with the local authorities, but nothing came of his design. The Jacques Cartier Bridge stands in its stead. It is not clear if Frederic persisted with his plans for the extension of the Victoria Bridge during his time in Montréal, but presumably he did as the family remained in the city and Alice's sister Lydia was born there, also in about 1882.[21]

It was an exciting time to be in Montréal. Mark Twain visited in the same year and a special banquet was held in his honour. Thanks to the Victoria Bridge, the city was fast becoming Canada's industrial and railway hub, the 1880s witnessing a phase of rapid expansion. About half the population at that time was French. To celebrate its thriving economy, the city had its first winter carnival in 1883. Alice would have been about three and a half. Perhaps she went. Alice Bailey has few recollections of this period of her life, other than getting into serious trouble for shutting herself and Lydia in a trunk full of toys and nearly suffocating them both.[22]

As with others of their standing, the La Trobe-Batemans benefited from the era's burgeoning rail and steamship networks, and travel became a keynote of Alice's childhood, imbuing her with a lifelong love and appreciation of it. Yet despite the adventures of a new land, reflecting back on those early childhood years, Alice Bailey recalls only a maudlin sense growing within her that 'things were futile' and life was scarcely worth living. Even at that early age, she didn't like the 'feel' of life. 'I did not appreciate what the world seemed to be or had to offer.'[23] She attributes her episodic states of misery as evidence of a mystical disposition, a view certainly borne out by her later experiences.

The unhappiness of her formative years in Canada worsened

dramatically when her father hurried them back to Britain. It wasn't until the family had made the return that five-year-old Alice found out why they'd left Montréal; her mother had become gravely ill with tuberculosis. The family went first to Switzerland to the renowned Davos sanatorium, where it was believed the high altitude would affect a cure. A confusing and upsetting time for a little girl old enough to understand that her mother was ill and too young to make much sense of it. They remained in Davos for several months, but the treatment proved of no benefit, and they returned to England. Her mother passed away soon after. She was thirty. She was buried in Torquay, Devon, where Alice's paternal aunt Mary Dorothy La Trobe-Bateman resided with her husband Admiral Sir Brian Barttelot and their four children.[24]

Due to the early death of her mother, it is doubtful Alice Bailey knew much about her maternal heritage. She never mentions her maternal aunts and uncles, and it is likely she never saw any of them again. All she recalls of her mother in her autobiography is her golden hair.[25]

Losing a mother at an early age is traumatic and known to have lingering consequences. How young Alice handled her loss is unclear. There is no indication in her autobiography that she was especially close to her mother. It's as though she had shut her out of her life altogether, not because she had no affection for her, but rather, at the time of writing, when her own lifetime had all but passed, the loss was perhaps too distant and possibly also a touch poignant. There is much contained in that sentimental memory of her mother's golden hair. It might also be the case that she knew nothing about her mother or her mother's family because the La Trobe-Batemans never related to her the little or the much that they knew. The humble Hollinsheads were written off, although Alice was certainly led to believe they were of good social stock.[26]

After the death of his wife, Frederic took his daughters to live with his parents at Moor Park, their country residence in Farnham, Surrey. It was to be a very different life to the one Alice would have led if she had been passed on to her mother's sisters.

Built in the 14th century as Compton Hall, Moor Park was redesigned in the 1680s by diplomat and essayist Sir William Temple, and renamed after his other Moor Park mansion in Hertfordshire. Temple laid out five acres of magnificent formal gardens on the property. John Frederic had purchased the property in 1859 and immediately established a hydrotherapy spa, run by physician and hydrotherapist Dr Edward Lane. Among those in regular attendance was Charles Darwin, who had his fiftieth birthday at Moor Park and finished working on *The Origin of the Species* during this period. The seminal text was published on 24 November 1859.[27]

The luxurious setting didn't escape Alice's notice. 'I remember vividly…the beauty of the countryside and the flowery lanes and the many woods through which my sister and I drove our little pony carriage.'[28]

Life for Alice during this period was far from halcyon. Despite the obvious luxury, the daily routine at Moor Park for the little La Trobe-Bateman girls was punishing and Alice Bailey recalls every detail. The girls were forced to adhere to a rigorous daily routine under the strict control of governess, nurse and maid. Discipline and obedience were the order of the day, as was typical of the times and social background, although perhaps somewhat more austere in the Moor Park household. 'I can see the chart hung on the wall of our schoolroom, indicating the next duty. How well I remember going over it and asking myself: "What now?"'[29]

Little wonder: Up at six, an hour of scales and a schoolroom breakfast at eight followed by family prayers, lessons till noon, a walk followed by lunch in the dining room, then an hour spent lying on a sloping board while her governess read aloud, another walk and lessons until five. The girls were then dressed in silk and sashes and taken to the drawing room where the house party of the day were seated to tea. There the girls curtsied and stood as the others observed and picked them over, until they were taken away for a schoolroom supper followed by more lessons until eight, then off to bed.[30]

This regimentation was echoed in the household's daily worship. Every morning the entire household, including the servants, would gather around Alice's grandfather, who would lead prayers from the head of the dining room table. In this manner, the La Trobe-Batemans carried forth an austere and duty-bound faith. The denomination of this faith is unclear. The aristocracy of Victorian Britain observed the High Church of England, and there is no indication the La Trobe-Bateman household was any different. Although as the grandson of Reverend Benjamin La Trobe, John Frederic had been raised in a Moravian settlement and attended Moravian schools, and this unconventional upbringing must surely have influenced his beliefs and religious observances.

Founded in Moravia, Central Europe, in the early fifteenth century by breakaway Catholic priest Jan Hus, the denomination is considered to be the oldest of all Protestant faiths. The faith centres around a deep belief in Jesus Christ and places a strong emphasis upon values of love and respect for others rather than commitment to religious doctrine. Moravians are known for communal living and missionary work. In his biography of John Frederick's cousin, scholar John Barnes identifies the influences of the faith in the choices and decisions Charles La Trobe made as first governor of Victoria.[31] Was John Frederic's domestic sermonising borne of his Moravian upbringing? Certainly, this faith strikes a distant note in Alice Bailey's own belief system, particularly her commitment to the value of love and good works over doctrine.[32]

At Moor Park, Alice and Lydia were taught to care for the poor and the sick. Several times a week, they 'had to go to the housekeeper's room for jellies and soup for some sick person on the property, for baby clothes for the new baby at one of the lodges, for books for someone who was confined to the house to read.'[33] Such acts are in keeping with the Moravian faith with its strong sense of duty and community. It was the result of such deeds that young Alice was imbued with a sense of responsibility and duty to others typical of the paternalism of her social class, yet perhaps more intently expressed at Moor Park. This dedication to serve others, inculcated in the impressionable child that she was, went on to become a keynote in Alice Bailey's body of work, not only shaping her notion of goodwill but becoming the primary motivational force for human and planetary betterment, to be instilled in the minds and hearts of every spiritual disciple in the form of world service.

A shadow of illness hung over the Moor Park household when it became apparent that Frederic himself had succumbed to the same disease as his wife. In this atmosphere of bereavement and illness, Alice was to endure a difficult few years. In her autobiography, she states that her father had never liked her and seemed to blame her very existence for the death of his wife.[34] It was a shocking thing for a little girl to be told, and one has to wonder at the character of a man given to such a cruel attitude. Perhaps grief and illness had affected his manner. Whatever the reason, the anguish Alice must have been feeling over the loss of her mother was compounded, seared in her memory by this brutal condemnation. It was a harbinger of another punishing rejection Alice Bailey was later to suffer from her sister.

As a young, impressionable child, Alice might have internalised her father's attitude and privately blamed herself for her mother's death, an ill-founded guilt that was perhaps at the root of a strong sense she carried throughout her life that she'd let someone down and needed to make amends. It was guilt culminating in an at times crippling fear of failure.

Throughout her childhood, Alice suffered from pervasive melancholia. In her self-reflections of that time, Alice Bailey is harsh on herself, attributing her 'rather inchoate unhappiness' to her standing amongst the La Trobe-Batemans. 'I was the plainest of an exceedingly good-looking family and I am not plain. I was always regarded as rather stupid when in the schoolroom and as the least intelligent of an intelligent family.'[35] Such remarks allude to the maudlin self-pity that had Alice in its grip, the product of intense loneliness and a profound lack of belonging.

Lonely and miserable, Alice watched her father's decline. In 1888, his condition deteriorated, and it was decided the English climate was hampering his health. In a desperate attempt to improve his symptoms, the family arranged for him and the girls to move to Pau in the French Pyrenees, a location heralded by well-known Dr Alexander Taylor as having a curative climate and waters. Finding Pau of no help shortly after their arrival, and in a final bid for survival, the girls were returned to Moor Park while their father embarked on a voyage to New Zealand in the company of a nurse. He died near Hobart, Tasmania, on 5 February 1889.[36] By then Alice was eight and a half.

After their father's death, Alice and Lydia remained with their paternal grandparents at Moor Park until their grandfather also died. He passed away four months after the death of his son on the 10 June 1889, six days before his granddaughter Alice's ninth birthday. Moor Park was then sold and the girls moved to London to reside with their grandmother, who was so strict she once made Alice sit for an entire luncheon in the dining room with her elbows in saucers, punishment for gazing out the window with her elbows on the table.[37]

The girls remained with their grandmother in London intermittently, as they were also farmed out to various paternal aunts. If they'd been boys, they would have been sent to boarding school. Alice's grandmother died in May 1894, when Alice had almost reached her fourteenth birthday. She writes little of those five years, other than that she recalls that life with her grandmother was 'so dull and so monotonous'.[38] She refers here only to the attitude of a girl in her mid-teens. There is no doubt that she carried a great closeness and affection for both her grandparents.

Upon the death of their grandmother, the girls came under

the joint guardianship of their father's older sisters, Aunt Dora (Mary Dorothy Barttelot) in Torquay, and Aunt Agnes Elizabeth Parsons, whose husband, 'hard and stern Uncle Clere', was the son of renowned Anglo-Irish astronomer William Parsons, Third Earl of Rosse, famed for setting out to build the world's largest telescope. The Parsons had six sons of their own, a happenstance of greater import to Alice's sister Lydia, who went on to marry one of those boys, prominent ecclesiast of the Church of England Lawrence Edmund Parsons (1883-1972), one-time Commissary to the Archbishop of Cape Town, South Africa.[39] Alice and Lydia also stayed with their Aunt Margaret Maxwell in Scotland.

Despite much upheaval as the teenaged girls were shunted back and forth from the Galloway region of the Scottish Borders to Devon, Switzerland and the French Riviera, between the various homes of their guardians and other family members, these were undeniably years spent in the greatest physical comfort and luxury of the British aristocracy. Alice was surrounded, she says, by much beauty and many interesting people. She wanted for nothing and yet she remained sullen and miserable.

Reflecting on her life, Alice Bailey admits to having no good cause for her misery, yet there is much in her circumstances to render her unhappy. No one can claim to be unaffected by the loss of both parents at an early age and both grandparents not long after, and it is well known that stability and continuity in childhood foster a sense of belonging. Alice, the eldest child, would have borne the greater burden. Lydia could at least look to her older sister for comfort. Who did Alice have to turn to?

Of all the influences of various family members, it was the summers spent in Scotland with Margaret Maxwell that had the greatest bearing on Alice's life. Widowed before Alice was born, Margaret Maxwell was the wife of David Maxwell, who died in 1874. David was the eldest son and heir of Sir William Maxwell, sixth baronet of Cardoness Castle, Kirkcudbrightshire. David having died prematurely, his father provided for widowed Mrs

Maxwell, who resided at Castramont House, an elegant manor perched on a knoll on the banks of the River Fleet north of Gatehouse of Fleet, in the rolling wooded lowlands of Scotland's southwest.

It wasn't the idyllic if isolated setting or her aunt's social standing that impressed Alice. Mrs Maxwell was a leading philanthropist, both president of the Scottish arm of the Young Women's Christian Association (YWCA), and founder of her own cottage hospital, accomplishments that made a deep and lasting impression on her young charge. A great affection grew between them. 'She gave me a keynote for living so that I feel to this very day that any achievement which I may have had can be traced back to her deeply spiritual influence.'[40]

Another influential figure in her life at that time was her 'Uncle Billie', or Sir William Gordon, sixth baronet of Earlston, known for being one of the leaders of the charge of the light brigade at Balaklava, Ukraine, during the Crimean War. In accordance with the spirit of the man, he encouraged Alice to go off and follow her own path in life and not bow to the wishes and strictures of her social class. She says he always stood up for her, telling her: '"I bank on you, Alice. Go your own way. It will be all right with you."'[41] With those words, Uncle Billie helped give Alice the endorsement to be different, an endorsement she badly needed in the light of the expectations of conformity that were no doubt coming from others.

The greatest stabilising influence in her life at that time came via her governess, Miss Godby. Alice Bailey recalls her as, 'plain, quite ordinary in background and equipment, but sound and sweet'.[42] Miss Godby loved and believed in Alice from the first. She would travel with Alice and Lydia from one family estate to another in Scotland, with autumns spent in Devonshire and winters – due to the girls' less than robust health – on the French Riviera. Miss Godby's presence bestowed upon Alice feelings of continuity, belonging and confidence. 'She was the one person to whom I felt "anchored".'[43] Alice Bailey would remain in contact with Miss Godby until her death around 1934.

Despite her dark and introspective moods, Alice Bailey admits she was an especially hot-tempered teenager. Once, in a fury over something Miss Godby had done, she took all of her jewellery and flushed it down the toilet. About that time, Alice had taken to sneaking into her governess's room to read her diary, in which Miss Godby wrote her reflections on her own behaviour throughout the day in the form of self-examination. In the days that followed, Alice read there that Miss Godby knew what Alice had done with her jewellery. When the pressure of the misdeed became unbearable and Alice confided all, Miss Godby's reaction astonished her. It wasn't the material loss that hurt her governess, but the betrayal of confidence. Miss Godby's reaction made a lasting impression. Reflecting back through the lens of her own beliefs, Alice Bailey sees it as a highly significant lesson in the importance of spiritual over material values.

Like so many children, throughout her childhood Alice was in the habit of comparing herself unfavourably to her sister, although as the elder sibling, this is a reversal of the usual tendency; such resentments are more commonly held by the younger child. She describes Lydia as, 'one of the most beautiful girls I have ever seen and her brains are superlative'.[44] A simple remark of admiration belying the simmering teenage jealousy she felt at the time. Perhaps Lydia stole the attention and affection of the extended family. She may have been outgoing, confident and popular, an extroverted child with an abundance of charm, gaining the approval of all. She was certainly a smart and ambitious child who would obey the expectations of her social class in at least one respect, by marrying her cousin. A staunch adherent to social mores, Lydia also remained an orthodox Christian her whole life.

Cast in the perhaps self-created shadow of her sister, Alice was convinced no one much liked her, so she hated just about everyone as a result. She describes herself as a morbid and exceedingly self-absorbed child brimming with jealousy and self-pity. From the outside, it appears that she was sensitive, wounded and lost, estranged from most of her family even while a part of it.

Those feelings were deeply held. She made three attempts to take her own life before she reached fifteen, once when she was five and threw herself down a flight of stone steps; another when she was eleven and tried to smother herself in sand, only to find 'sand in one's mouth, nose and eyes is not comfortable and I decided to postpone the happy day'; and the last when she tried to drown herself in a Scottish river.[45]

Alice Bailey would be the first to admit we are not here on this planet to be comfortable. There is no motion without friction, no change or growth without suffering. Perhaps a psyche such as Alice Bailey's should be understood on its own terms. As her testimony shows, the mystical disposition is prone to extremes of mood, almost pathological introspection, and a kind of interior churning that requires much forbearance and is certainly not for the fainthearted.

Christianity had been drilled into Alice from an early age and by fifteen, she was nothing short of a zealot. She saw the world in black and white, as ever the young are wont to do, humanity divided into two groups: savers of souls and heathens. Perhaps her fundamentalism provided a much-needed anchor, a constant in an ever-changing life and a replacement for lost loved ones. Believing made the alienation easier. She drew God close to her for comfort, a sort of existential crutch. Yet how much of a person's character is innate, left over from a past life, if that is what you choose to believe, and how much formed through conditioning? Whatever the case, in her heart, Alice Bailey carried until her death a form of missionary zeal. Although her religious mindset in its current Christian form was about to receive a gentle but firm knock.

On Sunday 30 June 1895, during one of her stays with Margaret Maxwell at Castramont, while the rest of the house was attending church, Alice had a strange visitation. She was alone in the drawing room, reading, when a tall man in European clothes, his hair hidden beneath a turban, entered the room and sat down beside her. Terrified at the sight of this man sporting a turban, she didn't speak. The man had much to say. He told her important work lay ahead for her, her Master's work, work that would take her to many countries, but she would not be given this work if she did not drastically change her poor manner. She needed to exercise self-control and learn to be pleasant, and she needed to make this change straightaway. He was emphatic about it. He went on to tell her he would be in touch every few years and then he departed the room, pausing in the doorway to give her a look, 'which to this day I remember very distinctly'.[46]

Once the initial terror wore off, doubts flooded in. Alice thought she might have been dreaming or going insane. These thoughts soon gave way to feelings of self-satisfaction. There was special work ahead for her. She'd been singled out. All she needed to do was change her manner. For once, she was not in her sister's shadow.

The visit was an extraordinary occurrence and one Alice Bailey imbues with a particular meaning. In her autobiography, she is adamant that she hadn't been asleep and dreamt the encounter. That it wasn't any sort of vision. It was a real event. A man walked into the drawing room, spoke to her directly, then he left.

There are alternative explanations. Some might argue she was having a lucid dream, one in which she sincerely believed she was completely awake. She may have been unwell that day. After all, why wasn't she with the others at church? She may have drifted to sleep in the middle of reading her book, dreamt the scene and woken up, still dreaming, just as the strange man was leaving the room. In her disoriented state, she would have thought she had been awake the whole time. Or perhaps her testimony is accurate. That man really did walk in with his message. To engage with the teachings offered to the world through Alice Bailey, the student must either accept this view or suspend judgement.[47] The man in the drawing room was Koot Hoomi, a Spiritual Master high up in the ranks of the Spiritual Hierarchy overseeing the evolution of humanity. That visitation was an early sign for Alice Bailey that she was a disciple called for World Service.

Around the time of this visit and reinforcing the view she would later develop that a Spiritual Hierarchy does indeed guide the evolution of humanity, she had two identical visionary experiences she describes as waking dreams. On each occasion, she found herself participating in a ceremony in the Himalayas at the time of the Full Moon in May:

 I found myself (whilst wide awake) in this valley and forming part of a vast, orderly crowd – mostly oriental but with a large sprinkling of occidental people. I knew exactly where I stood in that crowd and realised that it was my correct place and indicated my spiritual status.

The valley was large and oval shaped, rocky and with high mountains on either side. The people, crowded in the valley, faced towards the East and towards a narrow, bottle-necked passage at the end. Just before this funnel-shaped passage, there stood an immense rock, rising out of the floor of the valley like a great table, and on top of the rock was a crystal bowl which looked as if it was three feet across.[48]

Standing in front of the rock were three figures in the form of a triangle. The one at the apex of the triangle she knew as the

Christ. The crowd was in motion, forming first one symbol then another: a Cross, a circle with a point in its centre, and a five-pointed star. She describes the whole process as a solemn rhythmic dance, both dignified and silent. The three figures stretched out their hands to the heavens and the crowd froze. A figure appeared in the sky above the bottleneck and approached the rock. She knew the figure to be the Buddha. The vision in its entirety she retrospectively took to be a ceremony of the unity of all things, material and spiritual, Eastern and Western.[49]

At the time, Alice didn't know what to make of her mystical experiences. Her limited theology was challenged in light of this new understanding. Before her, a new subjective world of meaning flickered into being, an inner spiritual realm she could scarcely make sense of. It would be another twenty years before she found a satisfactory explanation, one that would form the essence of her esoteric worldview.

It is not without a measure of caution that the mature Alice Bailey provides her testimony. 'It is said that one's deepest and most intimate spiritual experiences should never be discussed or related.'[50] She acknowledges that such testimony is often discredited. In her day, she was known, at least in her own circles, as a sane, intelligent woman of good standing, and in her autobiography, she chose to add for the record her 'certain knowledge and conviction to the witness of many others down the ages'.[51]

Those visions, coupled with her strange turbaned visitor, had a profound effect. Fifteen-year-old Alice pulled herself up and made a resolute effort to change. The transformation precipitated a search for meaning and answers for her sorrows. Her journey of self-improvement was a process of intense purification, and initially, the result was perhaps not what the Master quite had in mind. Alice had gone from being a self-absorbed, sulky and sometimes volatile teenager, into an astonishingly virtuous young woman. On one occasion, her Aunt Margaret came to her and said, '"Good Lord, Alice, lose your temper."'[52]

It was a transformation that fostered a reorientation. No longer sucked inwards by her misery, she began to reach out into the world around her. She joined her Aunt Margaret doing good works for the YWCA. Ironically, this change of orientation brought with it an over-enthusiastic desire to convert others as she herself had been converted, into an authentically good Christian. She did so indiscriminately. In her late teens, she would spend much time attending parties in large houses, endeavouring to save the souls of all those she encountered.

Meanwhile, she says she took long walks or lay down in a field in Scotland, the south of France, or by Lake Geneva, and she would 'try to listen to the silence' and 'hear the Voice':

 I knew that behind all that I could see and touch there was a Something that could not be seen but which could be felt and which was more real and more truly essential than the tangible. I had been brought up to believe in a God Transcendent, outside His created world, inscrutable, unpredictable, often cruel...loving only those who recognised Him and accepted Him...Innately I criticised this presentation of a loving God, but automatically accepted it. But He was far away, distant and unapproachable.

Yet all the time, something within me, inchoate and indefinable, was reaching out after God Immanent, after a God behind all forms, Who could be met everywhere and touched and really known, Who truly loved all beings...[53]

THIS DIVISION in her religious views would not resolve for two decades.

Holding her faith fast inside her, Alice completed finishing school and then, after the terms of guardianship were over, she resided with her sister and a chaperone in a rented house near St Albans. She was a well-travelled, French-speaking society girl with a good classical education. She was known to be very attractive with good taste in clothes. The trouble was she had a deep knowledge of the Bible and knew absolutely nothing about the facts of life. She was a self-described religious fanatic of the naïve and earnest sort. Hers was the kind of superior holiness that lent no favours when it came to finding acceptance in her social milieu. It would certainly not find her a husband.

When Lydia came of age, she chose to undertake a medical degree at the University of Edinburgh, an impressive opportunity at the time and for which she received 'some months of coaching'.[54] Medicine was a rare path for a woman at the turn of the twentieth century. Few were permitted to study the discipline. There were only two hundred women doctors in Britain in 1900. Lydia became one of the first to win a university distinction. She became a doctor. She went on to write *Life, How it Comes: A Child's Book of Elementary Biology* and later took up cancer research. She was also a poet, writing under the pen name Stephen Reid-Heyman. *A Vagabond's Wallet* was published in 1916. Her seventy-two-page poem, *A Vision of Immortality*, published in 1917, was re-released in 2011 and considered by scholars to be of cultural significance.[55] When she was around thirty, Lydia had one daughter, Mary Alice Parsons (1912-), born in the same year as Alice's middle child, Mildred.[56] There is no indication that Alice Bailey ever met her niece, but she certainly knew of her existence, despite making no mention of this in her autobiography.

Back in St Albans, Alice needed to find her own way in life, and she had no appetite for tertiary education.[57] She was in receipt of a small allowance from the family estate, as was her sister, enough to afford her a measure of financial independence. All she needed was a direction.

She would spend much of the first two decades of her adult-hood learning many tough lessons, lessons of humility and common goodwill, undoing the snobbish attitudes instilled in her by the La Trobe-Batemans and perhaps re-claiming some of the character of her maternal Hollinshead heritage along the way.

ELISE SANDES' SOLDIERS' HOMES

$\mathcal{A}$t the age of twenty-two, Alice La Trobe-Bateman stood poised to break away from the bonds of her family, shun her society girl lifestyle and set off into the world with 'the sure touch of complete inexperience'.[1] If only she could figure out how. She had never been alone before, yet any fears and uncertainties she had were eclipsed by an unwavering resolve. She had in her sights a life spent saving souls, carried out in a fashion commensurate with her social standing. It was a choice that must have come as a great disappointment to her family. Through their eyes she would have appeared an extremist, an extremist doomed to pay a high price. Despite three seasons, she had failed to find a husband. She was incapable of interacting socially with her party-loving contemporaries, her upright temperance and piety too off-putting for the milieu. No one in the aristocratic society scene was interested in being saved. Worse, the La Trobe-Batemans upheld the Protestantism of their class and Alice had developed strong evangelical leanings, more commonly associated with the lower classes. Or, in her own words, she had become a 'dyed-in-the-wool Fundamentalist', albeit one who was 'exceedingly narrow-minded and very class conscious'.[2]

The year was 1902 when Alice sought her life direction. King Edward VII had taken the throne after the passing of Queen Victoria and society was changing, imperial expansion and moral propriety giving way to a new era of peace, social flexibility and prosperity. Philanthropy continued to thrive as the Protestant upper classes like the La Trobe-Batemans saw it as their duty to help the poor and disadvantaged. Evangelism had also greatly expanded during the nineteenth century, with its emphasis on service over doctrine. The status of women started to improve. It was considered respectable for middle and upper-class women to engage in social work. Charitable roles enabled women to find fulfilment beyond the bounds of domesticity and motherhood, whilst viewed as an extension of the very same. Ladies of good standing participated in this groundswell of charity and philanthropy through fundraising: organising dinners, banquets and fetes.[3] None of these roles appealed to Alice. While admitting to having a talent for needlework, she had little interest in or regard for feminine pursuits.

Neither did she hold an interest in feminism. As Alice searched for a fulfilling role in life, women in Britain still lacked the right to vote. The Suffragette movement, that had been campaigning for decades around the world and had been taken up in Britain at that time by Emmeline and Christabel Pankhurst, was in full swing.[4] Alice Bailey would have been well aware of the Suffragettes, but she makes no mention of the movement in her autobiography, other than to describe herself as not a feminist.[5] Her silence on feminism is notable in the light of her strong opinions on matters of race, equality and human rights peppered throughout the body of work. Perhaps these strident women were an affront to her sensibilities. Perhaps she found political activists as distasteful as she did evangelists 'yelling and ranting on platforms':

The evangelists I had met (and they were many) had not impressed me much. They seemed a badly educated bunch of people; they wore cheap and badly cut clothes and their hair seemed to need brushing; they were too good to be well-groomed.[6]

AN OPPORTUNITY for a life direction arose when it was suggested she visit Elise Sandes' Soldiers' Homes, located in garrison towns throughout Ireland. Alice warmed to the idea, and once she had settled her sister at university in Edinburgh, she took whatever talents she had, hoping to do good works out in the field.

Britain had been at war in various countries in Africa and Asia throughout the nineteenth century, with the Second Boer War (1899-1902) seeing the largest force Britain had ever sent overseas, amounting to about half a million soldiers. Away from the battlefield those soldiers were corralled in garrisons such as those dotted about Ireland. For an upright Christian like Elise Sandes, the result was a social and moral disaster. Bored and restless, the soldiers sought entertainment in pubs and brothels; and drinking, gambling and illicit sex were vices sure to lead straight to hell. An evangelist and philanthropist from Tralee in Ireland's southwest, Elise Sandes was a childhood playmate of Lord Kitchener. In 1868, Sandes responded to a request to befriend a single soldier. Out of that friendship grew a life's work. Sandes established her first soldiers' home in Cork in 1887, with others opening in Belfast, Dublin, Dundalk, Queenstown and the Curragh. By 1913 there were twenty-two homes attached to barracks in Ireland and another nine in India. The homes provided recreation and promoted the welfare of young soldiers in the British Army. 'She introduced the element of home life into the camp' for many thousands of soldiers.[7]

Each home contained a large dormitory for overnight accommodation, a coffee shop with food served at low cost, and a recreation room for letter writing, games, and areas to sit and read. Two ladies were assigned to each home, housed in separate quarters. Their role was primarily to talk to the lonely, fed up and homesick. Each home also had a Gospel room, complete with harmonium, hymn books, Bibles and chairs, and 'someone who could expound the Scriptures and plead with the men for their soul's salvation'.[8]

It was work that befitted a woman of Alice's background. Elise Sandes sought out ladies of refinement and good standing to work in her homes, the separation of class thought to provide enough distance to avert impropriety. Upon first meeting, Alice found Miss Sandes to be 'a very exquisite, charming, cultured woman'.[9] It was an impression that must have been both a relief and a delight to a timid and snobbish young woman eager to do good.

Alice was installed at the Belfast home. She fitted in nicely, quickly making friends and acquiring the skills needed for the work. Part of her role involved circulating tables in the recreation room and the cafeteria, each often filled with hundreds of soldiers. 'There were rooms where they could write letters, play games, sit around the fire and read the current papers, play chess and checkers and be talked to by us if they were feeling lonely, fed-up and homesick.'[10] All the while she was expected to retain her reserve. It was hard work and Alice 'loved every bit of it'. She had suddenly found a marvellous outlet for saving souls.

In her own account, Alice Bailey is keen to emphasise the struggle she faced taking her first Gospel meetings. This was no wonder, given the naivety and youthful arrogance of her initial approach. She could have had no idea just how challenging her first serious public speaking event would be. At the time she thought she had the equipment for the job. After all, she had led Bible study and spoken at prayer meetings in the past. But this was different. This was standing up in front of a few hundred soldiers, not exactly a sympathetic audience of well-wishers and religious devotees.

The meetings were held on Sundays. When it was her turn, she went and stood on the platform filled with misguided self-assurance. She didn't get far into her speech. As she faced that sea of expectant faces, panic took hold, and her mind emptied. She fled the platform in tears. A few weeks later, she made a second attempt. This time, in the hope of averting another cata-strophe, she had assiduously memorised her speech. About mid-way in, as she was attempting to recite a poem, she suffered a sudden lapse in memory. Again, she bolted from the stage.

Alice wouldn't give up, but it took quite a few more attempts and an inordinate amount of anxiety before she gained confi-dence Looking back, Alice Bailey remarks it wasn't until she realised the root of her problem was self-centredness that she was able to forget about herself and focus her attention on the group.[11] It was an important and much-needed lesson that would go on to serve Alice Bailey as a public speaker.

Word went around that Alice was good at her job. Impressed, Elise Sandes invited her to the Artillery Practice Camp in Kildare, central Ireland. Alice Bailey writes favourably of this time, of how she shared a bedroom with Miss Sandes in 'the funny little house' in which they lived. Still vulnerable and somewhat adrift in her early adulthood, Alice adored Miss Sandes. 'I loved her for her beauty, her mental strength, for her knowledge of the Bible, for her understanding of humanity and also for her rippling sense of humour. I loved her most, I believe, because I discovered that she really loved me.'[12]

It was a powerful sentiment, one that suggests Alice had found in Miss Sandes a mother figure, along with the endorse-ment and approval she craved. She admits her time in Ireland, while short, was one of the happiest periods in her life. In Elise Sandes, Alice had found not only a friend and role model, but a profound sense of belonging along with it. Thirty years her senior, Sandes offered much-needed guidance and direction. Her influence began to broaden Alice's narrow and absolutist version of Christianity, softening her conviction that *her* way to salvation was the only way, and that it was her duty to save the soul of every single person she encountered.

In her chapter on the soldiers' homes, Alice Bailey reflects on how it was through her relationships with the men that she began to temper her upright manner. In learning to be the subject of teasing and good-natured ridicule, she also learned a lesson in humility, although she would retain a certain prudish quality throughout her life and would always be a woman of upright moral opinions.

She went on to spend time at homes in Dublin and Curragh, where there were five thousand soldiers stationed. A dedicated worker, she kept accounts, wrote letters for the soldiers and took endless Gospel meetings and prayer meetings.

Her time in Ireland came to an abrupt end when a letter arrived for Elise Sandes from Miss Theodora Schofield in India, announcing she was not well. The harsh climate and heavy workload had taken its toll on her health. A woman of great character and strength, Theodora Schofield had taken over from pioneer Anna Ashe and had been in charge of the homes in India for some years.[13] Miss Sandes faced a dilemma. There was no one available at the time to replace Miss Schofield. She decided Alice would have to do, telling her, '"even if you aren't much good, you would probably be better than no one at all."'[14]

Funds materialised days later in the form of an anonymous letter containing five hundred pounds. Alice then gained permission from her aunt Agnes Parsons who, together with Lydia, saw Alice off at Tilbury Docks.

Alice had no idea what she was walking into when she disembarked at Bombay. She would have appeared to others just as she was, a young, attractive and especially inexperienced Edwardian woman, vulnerable and naïve, alone in India: a fool in every sense of the word.

India was at that time enduring a phase of industrial expansion as Britain sought to maintain its manufacturing position in the face of advances in America and Germany. Investment in infrastructure was considerable. In 1900, the British Raj boasted the largest irrigation system in the world, and all was far from peaceful. Lord Kitchener's reforms – beginning in 1903 – concentrated the British Army in the north of the subcontinent, primarily to defend the North-West Frontier. Under Kitchener, fighting divisions were arranged along the Lucknow-Peshawar-Khyber axis and the Bombay-Mhow-Quetta axis.[15] The soldiers' homes were concentrated along these lines.

Alice was initially to spend two years at the home in Quetta, situated in an elevated valley of some five thousand feet and known for its exceptional beauty, about fifty miles from the Afghan border in what is now Pakistan.[16] From there, she would make the long journey back across the Thar desert and then on through northern India to reach the other homes scattered to the north of Delhi as far east as Lucknow.

India made a powerful impression; Alice Bailey says she was 'stunned by the Orient':

 It was all so new, so strange, so utterly different to anything I had imagined. Colour, beautiful buildings, dirt and degradations, palm trees and bamboos, lovely little children and women (in those days) carrying water-pots on their heads; water buffaloes and queer carriages, such as gharries and ekkas... crowded bazaars and streets of native shops, silverware and beautiful carpets, silent-footed natives, Moslems, Hindus, Sikhs, Rajputs, Gurkhas, native soldiers and policemen, an occasional elephant with his mahout, strange smells, unfamiliar language, and always the sun, except during the monsoon—always and ever the heat....I loved India.[17]

THE MOMENT ALICE arrived at the Quetta home and faced having to tame out-of-control soldiers running amok in the canteen, she realised she was too young and ill-equipped for her new responsibilities. She managed to quell the fracas, which proved to be just one in all manner of challenges.

It was in Quetta that she developed a lifelong fear of the dark. Her co-worker became ill with typhoid and was moved to a hospital. Alice remained in her quarters alone. At night, before she retired to bed, the managers of the home checked her rooms to ensure they were empty and then locked all the doors. Fighting on the frontier was fierce, and it was a time of year when the guards were doubled as members of the hill tribes were allowed down into the cantonment. At two in the morning, she awoke to find the sitting-room door handle 'being twisted and turned'. She knew the safe in the sitting room contained many hundreds of rupees and that if whoever it was did manage to break in she would receive a knife in the heart because 'it was a great virtue to kill a white woman'. Stricken with terror, she sat on the edge of her bed and watched the door handle. Forty-five minutes passed. 'I discovered then that there comes a point in fear when you are so desperate that you will take any chance.' She walked across the room and opened the sitting room door. She had no idea who was behind that door and fully anticipated the worst. Instead, there stood her two managers.[18]

There were many highs and little triumphs during her time in India but overall, Alice Bailey describes her time there as demanding:

 I went from one Home to another, attending to the accounts, interviewing the managers, holding endless Gospel meetings, talking to the soldiers about their souls and their families, visiting in the military hospitals and dealing with the many problems which naturally arise when hundreds of men are stationed away from home and are faced with the problems of life in a hot climate and an alien civilisation.[19]

IGNORING her own wellbeing and the limitations of her constitution, which was not robust, she went far beyond the duties required of her. She would not only keep the men entertained playing checkers but would also sit at the piano and play the favourite songs of the day, or take to the harmonium and sing hymns. She had a 'very good mezzo soprano voice with a wide range and exceedingly well trained'.[20] No one had seen anything like it, at least, not from a Gospel preaching evangelist. On one occasion, as she was about to launch into the hymn 'Shall We Gather at the River', a General, along with his adjutant and his staff, walked in. They were confronted with 'a somewhat religiously flippant young woman in a white dress and blue sash who resembled no evangelist they had ever pictured'.[21]

She was shockingly different, perhaps a touch vaudeville in tight fundamentalist skin, but her songs were highly appreciated by soldiers and officers alike, and she was repeatedly saluted as she went about her business. She was having a marvellous time. She was well known and much loved by all. The soldiers called her 'granny', or 'benevolent old lady' or 'mother' – names given to all of the ladies at the homes – but one regiment had a special name for her. They called her 'China'. In her own account this last name puzzled her. It was an abbreviation of Cockney rhyming slang. A 'china plate' is a 'mate'.

The affection was reciprocal. She enjoyed the company of the men. Yet all those musical performances were adding to a growing fatigue. The pressures of an overloaded work schedule were building. The homes were feeding five or six hundred men each evening in the coffee shops. 'I was put in charge of six soldiers' homes. I had the catering to do for these six homes, with 600 men in each, every day of the week. I conducted fifteen prayer meetings and gospel meetings a week...I went to forty British regiments. I had a Sunday Bible class of 600 men each Sunday: I got thousands of letters. They were all eulogistic.'[22] She was called for 'constantly' to sit with men who were dying. She suffered migraines that would incapacitate her for days, yet still she continued to fulfil her duties. Compounding the strain of her heavy schedule, the managerial decisions she made often filled her with doubts and self-recriminations. To cap it all, she found she had to deal with the mental breakdowns of staff members who had 'succumbed to the climate, to the loneliness, to the general discomfort of life in India in those days'. [23]

This endless stream of problems and heavy responsibilities and her inability to self-regulate had a dire effect on her health. Her migraines worsened. She was on the brink of physical, emotional and mental exhaustion. Exacerbating an already precarious situation, while the work pressures were mounting, she underwent a spiritual breakdown as well, the result of an unfolding of existential doubt deep within her. Life experience was to free Alice from her overzealous fundamentalism, only it was so intensely felt and psychologically shattering, it was to leave her shaken for a decade.

The seeds of collapse of her internal religious edifice were planted when she was in her early teens and staying with her aunt in Scotland. She had spoken at a Gospel meeting at her local church, and upon her return, her cook Jessie Duncan – an ally at the time – came into the room, took Alice by the shoulders and said '"Will you ever learn, Miss Alice, that there are twelve gates into the Holy City and everybody in the world will come in by one or other of them. They will all meet in the market-place but not everybody is going in by your gate."'[24]

Telling was Duncan's allusion to a habit, Alice's indiscriminate acts of salvation as she sought to convert the soul of every person she encountered. At the time, she had no idea what Duncan meant, but the words of her cook made a lasting impression and would be recounted to thousands in Alice Bailey's public lectures.[25]

Two experiences in India compounded Jessie Duncan's early censure. The first was when Alice arrived at Ambala in the Himalayan foothills to open a new soldiers' home. She was accompanied by her personal bearer Bugaloo. They were standing on the compound veranda, looking out at the road beyond, a road filled with passers-by, 'countless hordes and throngs of Indians'. Bugaloo came up to her, put a hand on her arm and said, '"Missy Baba, listen. Millions of people here. Millions, all the time long before you English came. Same God loves me as loves you."'[26]

It was a brave and assertive thing to say. After all, Bugaloo was her servant. Why he felt compelled to say this to Alice, and in a manner that suggested she really needed to hear it, was most likely in response to ceaseless ministrations and voiced opinions on her part. Bugaloo's remark carried a note of challenge to the imposition of any form of Christianity on those of the Hindu faith. He meant for her to understand a keynote of all religions: the universality of God.

His comment darted into her mind, penetrating the essence of her faith. She started to wonder what God had done about the millions of people on the planet before Christ came. How were all those people saved? Were they saved? Or had they all gone to hell? She just couldn't fathom how God, even her vengeful and punishing God, could have condemned the whole of humanity to damnation for so long.

The third experience Alice recounts was to undo the religious dogmatism in her heart. She was staying in Quetta and had it in mind to give her first lecture on hell. As a saved and therefore heaven-bound Christian, she didn't know much about the place where God deposited undesirables. For an entire month:

> I saturated myself with the thought of hell and, glowing with information and forgetting that nobody had ever come back from hell to tell us whether any of it was true or not, I stood up that afternoon on the platform before five hundred men prepared to terrify them into the courts of heaven.[27]

SHE DELIVERED her lecture in 'an immense room, with long French windows opening out into the rose garden'. The roses were in full bloom. A pretty setting, and in a symbolic sense, one that could not have been further from the words she was to utter. As she 'declaimed vociferously', lost inside herself like a true fire and brimstone pastor, she failed to notice as one by one her audience stood up and left. At the end, she saw only a small group of religious soldiers remaining in their seats. One of them drew her aside and told her, '"Now, Miss, just so long as you speak the truth we will sit and listen to anything you have got to say, you know that, but the moment you start telling lies most of us will up and go. And we did."'[28]

It was a 'drastic and violent lesson' and one it took her some time to understand. Yet hearing the sincerity of the soldier's explanation and having suffered the devastating humiliation of not only losing an entire audience but failing to even notice until it was too late to change course, caused her to question the veracity of the foundations of her beliefs:

> I believed that the Bible taught the fact of hell and all my values were being shaken. If teaching about hell was untrue, what else was false?...I knew there were a lot of nice people who did not think as I did and hitherto I had only been sorry for them...A tiny fermentation had started which was basic in its

results and agonising in its application. I was thoroughly worried and began to sleep badly. I could not think clearly and did not dare ask anyone about it.[29]

In 1906, about three years into her time in India, Alice was 'worn to a frazzle'. Her migraines increased in both frequency and intensity. Migraines that would render any sufferer incapable of raising the head from the pillow, yet still she would drag herself around to fulfil her tasks. Then, compounding the strain and the suffering, she fell in love with a private in the Hussar regiment: Walter Evans. It was this love that would ultimately be her undoing.

Alice Bailey describes Walter Evans as 'exceedingly good looking' and 'highly educated'. He had a 'brilliant mind' and through her ministrations at the soldiers' homes was 'soundly converted'.[30] She also calls him a 'gentleman ranker', a term usually reserved for those who, through misfortune or misadventure, fail to secure a commissioned officer rank or have been stripped of it. His class background was not suited to the officer class, so presumably, it was his education that merited such a rank. None of this mattered to Alice at the time. Her love for him was ardent, and yet it was a love forbidden. The ladies working at the soldiers' homes hailed from aristocratic backgrounds to ensure many degrees of separation between them and the soldiers. Marriage, as far as Alice knew, was forbidden. Believing this, she became 'utterly frantic'. She was at that time so physically and mentally exhausted, little wonder she was incapable of a single rational thought. Her heart was pulling her in one direction, her head, filled as it was with rules that must not be broken, in another.

It was while she was in this feverish state that she received another message from her Master Koot Hoomi. She was staying at the soldiers' home in Lucknow. It was a hot night and she was unable to sleep:

 I walked up and down my room and felt entirely desolate. I went out on to the broad veranda shrouded in flowering bougainvillaea (sic) but found nothing there but mosquitoes. I returned to my room and stood by my dressing table for a minute. Suddenly a broad shaft of light struck my room and the voice of the Master Who had come to me when I was fifteen spoke to me....He told me that things were planned and that the life work which he had earlier outlined to me would start, but in a way which I would not recognise.'[31]

BY THIS TIME, Miss Schofield had returned to India. Escaping the monsoon, Alice joined her on the long journey up to Ranikhet in Uttarakhand, the location of a hill station and military hospital and headquarters of the prestigious Kumaon Regiment, the most decorated infantry regiment in the Indian Army. The ladies travelled there to open a new home.

With an elevation of over six-thousand feet, Ranikhet was also used by the British Army as a retreat station during the summer heat, which explains why Walter Evans arrived with his regiment at the same time. He was discreet about his affections, but when he, along with some others, offered to help Alice improve her riding skills, any hopes she held that her love would be kept from Miss Schofield were dashed.

Months passed and at the end of the monsoon, Miss Schofield instructed Alice to attend to the closure of the home and left ahead of her. This decision brought the illicit love affair to a head. Walter Evans was still at the hill station and Alice was alone in the house. Perhaps it was this extraordinary trust Miss Schofield had placed in her young colleague – leaving her alone with her conscience – that caused Alice to end the affair and cut off all ties with Walter. With all the melodrama of the over-wrought, she pledged herself 'to a spinster's life and tried to go on with the work'.[32]

Alice's health had by then deteriorated dramatically. Her migraines became both severe and constant. She became so unwell Miss Schofield arranged to take her back to Ireland. She was too ill to protest. 'I had reached the point where I did not care whether I lived or died.'[33]

When she left Ranikhet, she was taken straight down to Bombay for the passage home. Her memories of that passage reveal the extent of her malaise. Alice Bailey recalls sleeping for an entire seventeen hours while they waited to board the ship, much to the alarm of her carers, then crying for the entire journey home, a whole three weeks of tears.

What happened when she finally spent time with Elise Sandes was so unexpected Alice couldn't help but be arrested by it. Instead of validation and approval for the immense personal sacrifice she had made, she faced a most disappointed and anxious Miss Sandes. Alice had worked herself into the ground, going far beyond what was expected of her and as a result Miss Sandes' hopes that she would go on to work for the homes for many more years were in jeopardy. She had even wanted to appoint Alice a trustee of her work.

Looking back, some sort of breakdown was inevitable given Alice Bailey's psychology. She carried an ingrained fear of failure and had a 'profound inferiority complex', both qualities driving her to excel, bringing her to the brink of the very failure she was so desperately trying to avoid.

Alice also came to realise she had let Miss Sandes down in another way, and her 'gallant sacrifice' of her beloved Walter Evans had been unnecessary. Miss Sandes made it clear that Alice was free to marry him if she wished. One way or another, arrangements could be made. 'She loved me and petted me and told me not to worry. I was too tired to care much in any case…I was aghast…I felt let down. I faced a major anti-climax…I felt a fool or an idiot.'[34]

Chastened and filled with renewed if cautious hope, Alice dashed off to Edinburgh to discuss the matter with her Aunt Margaret, who was staying there at the time. Alice was there for only one week. In those seven days, she received offers of marriage from two other men, one by post from an army officer, and another from one of the doctors who had cared for her when she contracted measles while at one of the soldiers' homes, 'a very charming and delightful man' who had followed her 'all the way from India'.[35] Alice didn't mention either proposal to her solicitous aunt and concentrated instead on explaining her predicament.

Her aunt's response proved inadequate, so Alice went on to seek the advice of her 'Aunt Alice', the head of the Church of Scotland deaconesses and Margaret Maxwell's father-in-law Sir William Maxwell's sister. 'I adored her for there was no narrowness or stupidity in her.'[36]

Her confession landed on sympathetic ears.

Walter Henry Evans (1880-1935) was born in Brotton, an ironstone mining village in the county of Redcar, Yorkshire, into a lower-class family with no servants.[37] He was about to be discharged from the army. Aunt Alice arranged for him to travel to the United States and take a theology course. He was to become a clergyman of the Episcopal church, rendering him an acceptable match for Alice in the eyes of her family, and positioning the couple far enough away from the attention of her social set, for whom the marriage would have been viewed a scandal, subjecting the family to gossip.

Equally in love, Walter was agreeable. While he underwent his training, Alice returned to India. She went first to Umballa for the winter then to Chakrata in the Himalayan foothills during the monsoon. Still exhausted, it wasn't long before her health took another turn for the worse, and eventually, she became so ill she was incapable of functioning. It was only with the assistance of two colonels that she made it back down to Bombay and on to England, bringing to a sudden and dramatic end an important phase of her life.

In the six years Alice had worked for Miss Sandes, she acquired essential skills in managing and running projects, everything from managing staff to handling correspondence to keeping the accounts. She became accustomed to addressing large audiences. All of which she would put to use later in life, and without which she would not have been equipped to actualise the esoteric work that was to come. A woman of passion and drive, Alice Bailey never did learn from those breakdowns to accommodate the frailties of her constitution and slow down.

DARK TIMES AS MRS EVANS

*F*or the first twenty-eight years of her life, Miss Alice La Trobe Bateman had not moved beyond the bounds of her social class. Despite all her work with the many thousands of soldiers in the British Army, she remained set apart. Her personal dealings were with various men of the officer class, with her co-workers, and with ladies from aristocratic backgrounds, including her close friends Edith Arbuthnot-Holmes and Catherine Rowan-Hamilton, and Elise Sandes' successor after 1934 Eva Maguire.[1] It was a narrow and sheltered existence, despite the daily encounters with the soldiers. Her life lessons were personal, centred on her various strengths and weaknesses, particularly her physical health. She had enjoyed her work, travelled back and forth across India on a First Class rail ticket and experienced no financial worries.[2] She had endured a crisis of faith but cut off as she was from her maternal family's more modest background, she had yet to embrace the core values that would form the moral basis of her worldview: common humanity, the idea of a shared belonging to a single human family, one that means we are all equal and all worthy.

Alice convalesced for six months at Castramont House. When she wasn't in bed or walking through the small fields and woods on the estate, she spent much time at needlework. Her pursuits did nothing to cure the tenacious longing in her heart. Walter Evans kept the flame alight with his letters, which arrived every few days.

When she was well, her supportive 'Aunt Alice' made the arrangements and paid for Walter to come to Scotland so they could marry. Unlike the illustrious wedding of her parents at St Margaret's of Westminster, Alice Bailey describes her wedding as a small ceremony held in a private chapel at a friend's house. They were married by the Bishop of Ripon, Right Reverend William Boyd Carpenter, and her father's eldest brother William gave her away.[3]

Everyone but the couple concerned could see it was a mismatch. It wasn't just Walter's background that had aroused the La Trobe-Batemans' misgivings, although that alone would have been shocking enough; they seemed to see something in Walter that Alice was blind to. Even the servants were concerned. The old coachman Potter, who took the newlyweds to the station, stood in his livery and reached for her hand and said, '"Miss Alice, I don't like him and I don't like to say this to you, but if he doesn't treat you right—you come right back to us."'[4]

Determined to ignore the disapproval and follow her heart, Alice set off for Cincinnati filled with optimism for her new future.

The Lane Theological Seminary was situated in Cincinnati in the neighbourhood of Walnut Hills, about a kilometre from the Ohio River and northeast of the city's centre. Organised along Presbyterian lines, the seminary was established around 1829, named in honour of donors Ebenezer and William Lane and most known for an abolitionism controversy of 1834, in which the school's board of directors tried to ban students from supporting the abolition of slavery. Many students left as a result.[5]

The seminary campus was large and comprised several

impressive buildings. The last was demolished in 1956 to make way for residential construction. Existing on the site today is a car yard. Remaining is a row of two-storey weatherboard dwellings on Seminary Place, a narrow street that runs behind the former seminary grounds. All could have been built in the late 1800s. The Evanses may have boarded in any one of those homes, taking a room on the top floor.[6]

Alice arrived in Cincinnati at a vibrant time in its history. Formerly a border town between the southern slave states and the north, in 1908 Cincinnati was a bustling industrial and emerging cultural hub with a specialty, thanks to its large German population, in brewing beer, boasting thirty-six breweries around that time.[7] It wasn't the beer or the buildings that left their mark on Alice. She was struck by the city's multicultural atmosphere and by the lingering racism she confronted among the white people she encountered. In her autobiography, it is in the passages concerned with her time in Cincinnati that she is at pains to stress her views on race, her belief in equality of opportunity and in the need for civil rights. She says she was appalled by the racism she found in America. 'I have been shocked, amazed and frightened by the attitude of many Americans to their fellow-Americans, the Negro minority.'[8]

These words do not sit comfortably with passages on matters of race found elsewhere in her writings. The inclusion of commentary on race and racism in her autobiography is a defensive move designed to exonerate herself from such accusations.

Theosophy has long been accused of racism. Trevor Ravenscroft's *The Spear of Destiny: The Occult Power Behind the Spear which pierced the side of Christ* – released in 1973 and known for its poor scholarship – claims that Blavatsky's root race scheme gave the Nazis their rationale to exterminate the Jews.[9] Dubious scholarship or not, Ravenscroft expresses a popular and deeply held misconception of the root races.

In Theosophy, evolution occurs in vast schemes, informed by the great cycles of constant renewal found in Hinduism. In Alice

Bailey's words, in these vast schemes 'race after race of human beings had appeared and disappeared upon our planet and that each civilisation and culture had seen humanity step forward a little further upon the path of return'.[10] There are seven root races in all: The first is known as Polarian, the second Hyperborean and the third Lemurian. The fourth, Atlantean root race began over four thousand million years ago in Africa. Currently, humanity as a whole is said to be the fifth or Aryan root race, which is said to have emerged out of the Atlantean root race about a hundred thousand years ago in Atlantis.

For some, Blavatsky's use of the word 'Aryan' was not meant to refer to an actual race of people, but to a macrocosmic notion denoting a certain stage in the evolution of consciousness, the term 'race' referring only to a 'state of thinking'.[11] Yet there is no escaping the pro-Indo-European flavour of the word, which has made it vulnerable to abuse by Nazi and right-wing esotericists.[12]

Any idea can be twisted to suit the aims of another group. It is spurious, backward logic, logic inherent in presentism, to argue that since Blavatsky's Aryan root race idea was adopted by the Nazis, the original idea must of itself be racist. Theosophical ideas can be difficult to unpack; they need to be considered within the overall argument, understood from an esoteric perspective and situated in the context of the times in which they were written. Presentism, and indeed far-right antagonists then and now, would do well to take note of this.

However, when Blavatsky asserts that indigenous Australians, the 'Australoids', along with various African peoples and others, are descendants of the semi-animal Lemurian root race, the metaphoric or 'state of thinking' argument is undermined and it becomes difficult for Theosophists to defend allegations of racism.[13] Although this is a gross oversimplification and for Theosophists, the root races are both an expression of physical evolution and a state of thinking, forming one part of an elaborate macro-cosmology. Each root race is comprised of seven sub-races, adding further complexity. We are the fifth sub-race of the fifth root race, known as Teutonic. Crucially, the sixth sub-race is said to be coming into incarnation in the twenty-first century and will be known for having highly developed pineal glands, lending greater psychic abilities and a developed capacity for intuitive knowing or holistic perception.[14] Setting matters of race aside, the root race scheme is one of advancement, of the evolution of consciousness. The larger challenge in all such models is to avoid the tendency to create hierarchies of superiority.

Allegations of racism move a step beyond the root races in the Bailey teachings. In *Problems of Humanity*, a collection of pamphlets Alice Bailey penned under her own name during the Second World War between October 1944 and December 1946, there is one titled 'The Problem of the Racial Minorities'. In this pamphlet, Alice Bailey is at pains to explain the 'Negro' problem from the point of view of human evolution and the tendency of the personality to separate itself from others. Adopting Blavatsky's idea of human evolution, Alice Bailey asserts that those nations that have advanced in industry, technology and complexity in social, cultural and economic fashion are examples of evolutionary progress, whereas nations relying predominantly on traditional practices have, in effect, marked evolutionary time. Consequently, she describes Africans as tribal, primitive, warlike, and constantly fighting among themselves.[15] Such remarks are those held by many of her social class at the time. It would be another thirty years before this attitude, borne of empire, would begin to give way to progressive thinking evident in academic circles in new disciplines such as Development Studies. To her credit, Alice Bailey also sees among African belief systems a 'fundamental and pure mysticism...and an esoteric understanding which may someday make Africa the seat of the purest form of occult teaching and living'.[16] The comment would not appease those determined to condemn her for her opinions.

Alice Bailey is something of a paradox. She upheld, perhaps

tacitly, perhaps not, the core values and attitudes of her class and, at the same time, proposed progressive ideas that would undermine those values and attitudes if followed through. In the same pamphlet, she recognises the complexities involved in dealing with issues of racial discrimination and the need for cool-mindedness on the part of all involved in addressing the matter. She talks of the need for self-governance and autonomy, and the need to end discrimination. She talks of ending cleavages and promoting a spirit of goodwill. Her tone is at times inescapably superior, yet the trajectory of her argument is that of goodwill. She seeks to persuade her readers to train to become problem solvers, mediators, negotiators and peacemakers, not adversaries. She comes from a space of love, not hatred.

There was to be no peace for Alice in Cincinnati, but there was goodwill. Her first friendship in America was with Mrs Snyder, an African-American woman who ran the boarding house where the Evanses stayed. No doubt, Mrs Snyder saw in Alice a vulnerable, somewhat delicate and cultured English-woman, and she took to her immediately, fast becoming Alice's staunch ally.

Alice needed her.

Difficulties in the marriage presented early and were borne out in the battlefield of financial hardship. Alice used her small income from the family estate to pay for all of their weekly expenses in America. Walter received a small stipend from the seminary, which, it appears, he squandered. It became quickly apparent that the couple had nothing in common apart from their religious views, and that was only the case because it was she who had converted him. Her natural enthusiasm and drive must also have been challenging for Walter's ego. Not content with the traditional role of a wife, she took the opportunity to pursue her own interest in theology. 'I immediately set in and took his various courses with him.'[17] Her attendance would certainly have threatened his intellectual pride, but that doesn't excuse the way he chose to respond. An apparently physically, mentally and spiritually gifted man, he reacted with the basest form of male assertion: violence.

At first, his temper exploded in tirades of words. Fortunately for Alice, Mrs Snyder afforded her some protection. Mrs Snyder loathed Walter Evans, 'and took pleasure in telling him so'.[18] When Alice fell pregnant, it was Mrs Snyder who cared for her. She even arranged for her own doctor to attend the birth when Dorothy Margaret Matilda Evans came into the world on 24 February 1910.[19]

Alice's friendship with Mrs Snyder was short-lived. A few months after Dorothy's birth, the young family moved to a small apartment. It was here that Alice had her first taste of childcare and housewifery. She had a young baby, and she had never done a stroke of housework in her life. Despite all those years in the soldiers' homes, she didn't know how to boil an egg or even make a cup of tea. The weekly washing was her 'Waterloo'. She hadn't a clue how to launder delicates and managed to ruin all of the baby clothes she'd brought with her from Britain. After witnessing Alice's poor attempts, Mrs Schubert, an English servant in the flat below, offered to assist, saying, 'I can't stand it any longer...I'll teach you how to launder clothes.'[20] And so she did.

In her autobiography, Alice Bailey focuses on these basic acts of kindness she encountered from strangers throughout the duration of her disastrous marriage. Through such vignettes, she demonstrates her lifelong conviction that basic goodwill is humanity's salvation. To a large extent, she downplays the horrors she was living through and focuses instead on her own inner questioning and growth. Adopting this stance is integral to the way of the soul: to transcend, to forgive and let go. Yet so vicious was Walter Evan's violence that from the perspective of Alice Bailey, the woman and historical figure, it is worth pausing to dwell further on what she went through and the ensuing ramifications that must have influenced future life choices and decisions.

The domestic abuse Alice endured occurred at a time in history when there was little awareness of the damaging effects of family violence on victims, and there was no provision in society for battered wives. The expression 'sweep it under the carpet' best describes the response of many women who found themselves in Alice's situation, and victims commonly experienced enormous shame associated with the yelling and the beatings. Families would turn a blind eye, and neighbours, while perhaps concerned, often pulled back from involvement for fear of repercussions. In the early twentieth century, the man was the head of the household and the woman was to know her place. Police would intervene, but arrests were rare, and the courts were generally not interested, the violence occurring in the private sphere.[21]

In the seclusion of their apartment, Walter frequently let loose his rage. Behind his verbal tirades was the menace of physical attacks. Terrified, Alice would run and take refuge in Mrs Schubert's small apartment.

Respite came when, leaving Walter to finish his training and become ordained, Alice took Dorothy to Britain to visit the family. It was not a happy time. During their stay and presumably why they went, on 22 July 1911, Lydia married their cousin Lawrence Parsons in the All Saints Church in Ascot, Windsor, Berkshire.[22] Seeing her younger sister marry within her station must have exacerbated Alice's anguish but she wouldn't divulge it, not to her sister or to Lawrence's mother Aunt Agnes, or even her favourite aunt, Margaret Maxwell. She simply couldn't bring herself to talk of her husband's terrifying temper. 'My pride would not let me, but they undoubtedly guessed it though they asked no questions.'[23]

For reasons of happenstance, she wasn't to return to Britain for another twenty years and spent two decades without the benefit, or indeed the judgement, of her extended family. Indicative of her reduced circumstances, she travelled back to Boston on a Cook's Tourist ticket in, 'a small, dirty boat, four in a cabin, and meals at long tables where the men kept their hats on'.[24]

When she arrived in New York, she felt 'tired, ill, miserable and homesick'. She went to Gotham Hotel on Fifth Avenue for lunch and sat in the lounge 'feeling very blue and depressed'. To occupy herself she picked up a magazine. She opened it at random and there, to her amazement, was a portrait of her grandmother Anne Fairbairn, her grandfather John Frederic La Trobe-Bateman, and her great-grandfather Sir William Fairbairn, all looking back at her. She was so overcome, she wept.[25] It must have been a punishing moment of realisation that, through her marriage, she had created a great distance from her family. It would be one that was never resolved. In her two decades of absence from Britain, she lost her Aunt Dora in 1899, her Aunt Agnes and Uncle Clere in 1923, and her much loved Margaret Maxwell, also in 1923.

While she was in Britain, Walter Evans was sent to work as a rector under the Bishop of San Joaquin in Reedley, central California. Tired and depressed, Alice made her way across America by train with a restless Dorothy on her lap, arriving at a town – unnamed in her autobiography – containing at the time a population of about fifteen hundred. In 1910, Reedley had, 'shops with false fronts, hitching posts where surreys and buggies tied up (for automobiles were still a scarcity) and the village post-office from which all the gossip and talk emanated.'[26]

Mrs Alice Evans was clearly not impressed.

Photos of Reedley dating back to that time convey a different impression, one of a thriving small town with a smattering of large houses for the wealthier residents. A large German Mennonite colony had built a fine church there in 1906 to champion the equally fine Catholic church, and the Baptist and United Brethren churches were also grand. Not so the Methodist-Episcopalian church where Walter had been sent, a rather plain weatherboard affair capped with a simple A-frame roof, resembling a village hall. Beside it, sat the rectory where presumably the Evanses lived.[27] No wonder Alice felt demoralised.

It was there that Alice learned to be a clergyman's wife. She had to contend with the 'strictly feminine aspect of congregations'. 'I had to hold Mothers' Meetings and I always had to go to church and, ceaselessly and endlessly, I had to listen to Walter's sermons.'[28]

She found fulfilment in none of it. The town of Reedley might have been god abiding, with its eleven churches of various denominations – although with tiny congregations according to Alice Bailey – yet amongst all those worshippers Alice felt, 'completely isolated, culturally and mentally and spiritually'. Her only friends at the time were the bishop and his wife, Ellison. Locals' concerns were for their children and their crops. 'For months I stuck my snooty little nose up in the air and decided there was nobody good enough for me to associate with.'[29] Alice wasn't to know it then, that among the locals – tradespeople, railroad workers, fruit pickers and schoolteachers – was a groundswell of good neighbourliness.

Alice's one positive experience was Bible class which soon outnumbered her husband's Sunday morning congregation, a matter Walter couldn't have liked. Through it, the mistake the couple had made in their choice of each other became strikingly apparent. Alice didn't suit the stereotype of the devoted wife content with a supportive role in her husband's life. She never had an appetite for feminine duties or pursuits, other than needlecraft. She was an achiever, a woman brave enough to set off for India alone, capable of running soldiers' homes, a passionate and intelligent woman educated enough to be a preacher in her own right. There was a mission inside her, inchoate but dearly felt, one she could scarcely contain. She was a woman in her early thirties, strong-willed and dominant, albeit not in an overbearing manner, and old enough to know her own mind. She would have known by then she had fallen foul of obsessive romantic love, and that her own desire, stubborn as it was, had latched on to Walter with all the tenacity of desperation. Perhaps she had clung to him during her convalescence because deep down she couldn't have tolerated the loss of his love, one that would have compounded her earlier losses of her parents and grandparents. Perhaps she was blinded, despite all of her assets of beauty and a cultured education, by low self-esteem, the result of a childhood lived in her younger sister's shadow. Perhaps she was following in her father's footsteps in marrying beneath her.

Walter had married far above his station. Being handsome, intelligent and 'spiritually gifted', he would have had much to prove. His wife may privately have been for him a bitter disappointment. She was not the trophy he had hoped for. Alice was trapped. Walter was trapped as well. Trapped in an unhappy marriage with an incompatible mate, but the way he continued to choose to respond to the situation was abominable.

Privately, Alice was suffering a twin terror. Terror of her husband's temper and a 'constant terror that members of the congregation would discover it, and that he would lose his post'.[30] She was unwilling to face the humiliation and destitution that would have entailed. In her own account, Alice Bailey is careful to praise Walter's attributes. 'As a clergyman, he was greatly liked and was an impressive figure in his surplice and stole. He was a very good preacher.'[31] She doesn't blame herself directly, although she acknowledges that her very strategy of coping, her 'attempted patience' as she calls it, may have aggravated him. 'Nothing, however, that I could manage to do would please him and after destroying all the photographs and books which he thought I might value, he had taken to knocking me about.'[32] It was a typical pattern of escalation.

He never harmed Dorothy directly, and Alice Bailey states he was 'always lovely to children', but as is now well known, children who live in a domestic battlefield, one in which their mother is being beaten black and blue, don't tend to come out of it undamaged. Perhaps that is why Dorothy never bore children of her own.

Much of the time Alice was enduring the beatings, she was pregnant. Her second daughter, Mildred Kathleen, was born on 3 August 1912.[33] It was a difficult birth, 'Mildred was ten days overdue; the temperature was 112 degrees on my porch; the twelve children next door were terribly noisy; I had been very ill for days; and then the cesspool fell in.'[34] Dorothy was just two and a half at the time, and Alice worried she might fall in. Walter had disappeared 'about his parochial duties', and the doctor was late coming. Alice only had a nurse in attendance, a nurse becoming increasingly frightened. The next thing Alice knew, the saloonkeeper's wife marched in and took charge. She rounded up the doctor, tucked Dorothy under her arm and disappeared. Alice didn't see Dorothy again for two days.

Mildred was 'an instrument baby', and Alice suffered two haemorrhages as a result. She almost died. News of her plight quickly spread and the community rallied. 'Custards, pies, port wine, fresh fruit poured in.' Women took turns to clean the house, do the washing, sew and mend. They sent the nurse away and for days they looked after Alice's every need. The kindness landed in her mind like a revelation. 'I suddenly woke up to the fact that the world was full of lovely people and that I had been blind all my life.'[35]

Ten days later, without any assistance, she was up doing the washing. The churchwarden's wife discovered her, and 'sought out Walter Evans and read him the riot act'. After that, folk were suspicious and watchful. By then 'his tempers were assuming serious proportions'. Alice felt in danger of her life. Yet she could find no explanation for his behaviour, no rationale. He had no vices. He didn't drink, gamble, or even swear. As the violence worsened he became, 'quite impossible to live with and eventually it became dangerous to be in the same house with him'.[36]

On one occasion, the churchwarden's wife came in to find Alice's face badly bruised. She was feeling so wretched she disclosed that he'd thrown a pound of cheese at her and it had hit her square in the face. The churchwarden's wife immediately contacted the bishop whose solution was to move Walter Evans and his family to Fowler.

Alice was happy with the move. She was in a larger community closer to her good friend and the bishop's wife Ellison Sanford. Her health began to improve, and she gained in strength.

In 1913, Alice fell pregnant again, and in the autumn of that year, when she was nearing her term, her health again declined. Walter's temper declined along with it. One day, in a savage fit of rage, he hurled his heavily pregnant wife down the stairs.

Ellison was born on 24 January 1914 with a leaking heart valve.[37] Alice Bailey attributes the defect to the trauma Ellison suffered before she was born.

After Ellison's birth, the violence continued. The yelling and banging must have been intense because the community all knew about it. Again, people rallied. A 'very nice' girl offered to move in as a paying guest so that Alice had someone in the home. The girl soon became scared to be there, but she stayed put. A group of farmers took turns to plough the field next to the rectory every day, so that Alice had 'somebody within call'. The women at the telephone exchange took to calling the rectory at intervals to check that she was all right. The doctor who took care of Ellison's birth made Alice promise 'every night to hide the carving knife and the axe' under the mattress. People even began to question Walter's sanity. Adding to the bruises, and the constant battlefield that was her domestic life, Alice found the whole experience deeply humiliating, and her pride was 'very sorely wounded'.[38]

Walter's sanity was so much in question that one day, Alice and the girls were invited to spend the day with a friend and while they were out, Walter was sent to San Francisco for a thorough psychiatric assessment. No evidence of mental illness could be found. Instead, he was diagnosed with an uncontrolled

temper. Although he did have other failings, a certain irresponsi-
bility, manifesting in an inability to manage money. 'He would
leave the home to pay the monthly grocer's bill and return with
a gramophone.'[39]

Alice's tribulations didn't end. While Walter was away,
Ellison became ill with infantile cholera. Alice was advised to
take her to the Children's Hospital in San Francisco while her
friend Ellison Sanford minded Dorothy and Mildred. The prog-
nosis was not good. Alice was sent back home and told to care
for her other two children. She never expected to see Ellison
again.

Miraculously, Ellison made it through. She was discharged at
the same time as Walter was 'dismissed from observation with a
clean bill of health'.[40] They returned home together.

Their homecoming might have marked a turning point, and
in a sense it did, for Alice was suddenly forced by circumstances
to rise up and take charge of her husband. Walter's appalling
violence had rendered him unemployable within the church and
they were forced to exist on her small income which, owing to
the First World War, had begun to arrive intermittently, if at all,
and at a much-reduced rate.

Alice Bailey remarks that if it were not for the kind generosity
of the local Jewish grocer, Mr Jacob Weinberg, who ignored her
mounting debt – a debt Alice would eventually pay back in full –
and even slipped in some cash with the grocery order, they
would have been destitute.

Alice Bailey takes the opportunity of this vignette to go to
considerable lengths to clarify her attitude to the Jewish people,
taking a four-page digression in her autobiography to explain
her views. She begins by stating that she never came across any
anti-Semitic attitudes in Britain and believed there to be no anti-
Jewish feeling there, matters many would dispute. Neither was
there any anti-Jewish sentiment in her heart, at least none that
she could see. Three of her closest and loyal associates, Roberto
Assagioli, Regina Keller and Victor Fox, were Jews. She states

she was 'officially on Hitler's "blacklist"' because of her defence of the Jews whilst lecturing up and down western Europe'.[41] Yet what she describes as 'the Jewish problem' remains a controversial aspect of her oeuvre.

In her depiction of the Jewish community, she re-paints the stereotype, making generalised comments about Jewish customs – 'hanging clothing out of windows' and 'sitting in groups on the sidewalks' – which she casts in the light of their ancient 'tent dwelling' history.[42] She also acknowledges the millennia-long history of persecution. To her credit, she makes an effort to elevate the Jewish people from her macrocosmic evolutionary perspective, describing them as members of an ancient and highly developed root race.

For Alice Bailey, the Jews are a unique group with a very special role to play in the evolution of humanity and the planet. In her esoteric language, the Jewish people represent the solar plexus chakra of the planetary Logos, and the resolution of the Jewish problem will cause a 'great transmutation'.[43] Yet she also states that part of the problem of the Jewish people is their inability to assimilate and their demand that 'Gentiles and Christians make all the concessions'.[44]

Elsewhere in her comments, when writing during the build-up to the founding of Israel, she criticises Zionist attitudes and their claims of special entitlement. For Alice Bailey, any act or policy that separates one group from another is evil, and wherever she saw such attitudes, she pointed them out. There is no doubt that her thoughts would have upset many in the Jewish community, then, as now.

When she wrote her opinions, the Jewish people had become a major concern for many intellectuals and commentators. Animosity towards the Jews was growing after the Treaty of Versailles (1919) forced Poland to protect its own Jewish minority, while no other nation was required to take similar action. Anti-Semitism soon gathered pace in Austria, with calls to have Jews expelled from Vienna. Discrimination remained rife for decades, continuing after the end of the Second World War, with pogroms occurring regularly in Poland. The rise of Zionist and nationalist protest movements was hardly surprising in the light of such recent, systematic and heinous persecution.

Again, Presentism will do nothing but condemn Alice Bailey's views. Some historical empathy is required, a sound awareness of the historical and esoteric contexts of her remarks. In her defence, she was writing for a specific audience, and her argument was straightforward. In her writings, she cites numerous outward manifestations of the forces of separation, including those operating within and through the Jewish people, whom she believed were actively undermining progress towards spiritual unity and common humanity. In her worldview, the idea of unity-in-diversity only works if the diverse elements cooperate with each other. Any selfish motive from any group, whether Christian, Jewish, that of a nation, state or political group or individual, will create divisions, polarise thought and inflame emotions. Political correctness has since required thinkers and writers to take care with how they phrase such ideas, making some topics almost completely off-limits.

Alice Bailey was well aware of the contentious nature of her statements, which was why she took great pains in her autobiography to praise Jewish contributions to history, cite her Jewish friends, and state, 'no matter what the race or nation, basically we are all alike'.[45]

Perhaps in an effort to clarify and defend her views, she tied herself up in knots and there is no escaping that at times, she was prone to unfortunate phrasings. Her followers and co-workers have striven to understand the meaning behind the words and not taken them at face value or as literally true. Aware of the potential harm her writings on the Jews may cause, today her core organisation the Lucis Trust is at pains to explain the situation on their website, acknowledging that the matter remains unresolved:

We would stress the Tibetan's statement, "Through the Jewish people throughout the world, feeling…is being gathered…" implies that the feeling nature of all human beings, not just those currently incarnated in Jewish bodies, is being stimulated through their reaction to the problems centred in the situation of the Jews. We have all had a hand in the creation of this problem over the millennia, and it is up to all people of goodwill to solve it by right thinking, loving attitudes, and an unwavering identification with the fact of the one humanity.[46]

THE ISSUE for the trust is less that opponents use such words to vilify Alice Bailey, and more that parts of her teachings may be off-putting to those who may otherwise be sympathetic to her ideas. Given that such opinions do not constitute the core of Alice Bailey's teachings, but rather serve as examples of what she perceived was wrong with the whole of humanity, the reader is invited to keep an open mind.

Back in California, facing mounting bills with no means of paying them, Alice was left with little choice but to give Walter an ultimatum. After a long talk with Bishop Sanford, she told her savage husband that if he stopped the physical abuse and proved himself a changed man, then she could report his improved behaviour in due course and he would receive another posting. If he didn't stop knocking her about, then she had plenty of grounds and evidence for divorce and his career as a clergyman would be over.

In a fashion, her ultimatum worked. Duly censured and succumbing to his own sense of pride, Walter responded by reining himself in and instead of hitting her, 'he sulked and would not talk for days on end'.[47] In a typical passive-aggressive manner, he also turned idle, leaving her with all the work.

They could no longer remain at the rectory, and in keeping with their near destitution, they moved to a shack in the pine-forested hinterland of Pacific Grove.

A coastal city south of San Francisco, Pacific Grove was founded in 1875 and renowned for its historic Victorian homes. Rich in natural beauty, the town became an artist's haven and around the time Alice was there, the locale had attracted many notable artists, including Charles B Judson and Eugen Neuhaus. Later, author John Steinbeck, son of Monterey's County Treasurer, lived there in his father's cottage, his inspiration culminating in *Cannery Row*.

It was in the back blocks of this salubrious setting, that Alice became a chicken farmer. She kept hens, several hundred of them, and managed to feed the family by selling the eggs.

Times were hard, and Walter kept right on sulking. 'I used to go out in the surrounding woods with a wheelbarrow, the children trotting after me, and collect the wood for the fires.'[48] Life was 'humdrum' and she grew enormously dissatisfied. 'I felt I was of no use to anybody.' Her 'morbidly conditioned' fundamentalist conscience played the role of inner critic and kept telling her she was 'paying the penalty' for having 'questioning doubts'. And that if she'd held onto her faith, she 'wouldn't be in this pickle'.[49]

About six months later, Alice saw the bishop and told him Walter 'had behaved himself'. In response, and after some searching around for a suitable post, the bishop sent him away to a mining village in Montana. The couple were separated. Part of his stipend was to be sent to her for the children. 'This was in 1915 and it was the last time I ever saw Walter Evans.' Unsurprisingly, she received little from him, other than abusive letters, 'filled with threats and innuendo'.[50]

After he'd gone, Alice moved into a three-roomed cottage in Pacific Grove (address unknown). At the age of thirty-five, when the First World War was in full swing, she became an impoverished single parent. Ellison was one, Mildred three, and Dorothy five. Alice's small income from Britain arrived irregularly. None of her friends was in a position to help, and she was 'not at all a believer in squealing and crying and wailing to one's friends'.[51] She also refused to seek assistance from her relatives. Adopting the prevailing attitude of the times, she decided she had made her bed and must lie in it. Besides, the humiliation of admitting to her family that they had been right about Walter all along and that she had made a dreadful mistake in giving up her life to him would have felt like defeat. It was a typical response of a survivor of family violence, then, as now. Around that time, she began to receive 'helpful and understanding letters' from her Uncle Clere – her sister Lydia's father-in law – letters demonstrating to Alice that she was not forgotten. In her autobiography, she is convinced her sister knew nothing of the 'friendly and happy relationship' that existed between her and her uncle.[52] It was, at least in Alice's mind, a secret affection, and one that must have been sustaining.

A stoic survivor, Alice shored herself up on the conviction that God helps those who help themselves. The trouble was, she had no skills other than needlework, for which there was no demand at that time of war and shortages. To compound an already dire situation, her ongoing spiritual crisis wouldn't leave her alone. Her search for answers as to which spiritual truths could be believed, a search that had begun in her teens and hit a high-water mark in Quetta with her failed talk on hell, could not be found in theological texts. 'Theologians never seem to face up to the basic issues; they fall back upon the trite statement that, "God said."'[53] She started to question the veracity of the Bible in its entirety, deciding that, since the sacred book had undergone numerous translations and consequent interpretations, all of them in all likelihood unreliable, the entire work might be regarded as untrustworthy. Her pressing question 'Why did God speak only to Jews?' couldn't be answered by the Scriptures, yet she knew nothing of the teachings of other faiths. The final blow came when she discovered that the symbol of the cross, that quintessential metaphor of suffering and human sacrifice, of Jesus Christ and all he stood for, long preceded its use in Christianity. 'I was, therefore, completely disillusioned by life, by religion with its orthodox presentation and by people, particularly my own husband whom I had idealised.'[54]

No one needed her other than her three young daughters, and she was used to being needed by 'hundreds and thousands'. She felt 'absolutely useless' and 'knew the meaning of complete despair'. In truth, the needs of her children kept her going. She may have been 'tired of washing diapers and cutting bread and butter', but hidden in those routine tasks was her strength. Yet her frustration was intense. She was, after all, an intelligent, passionate woman with a strong sense of purpose.

She went off into the woods one day and pleaded with God to release her into a more useful life. She thought she might have a vision, hear a voice, something, anything to give her a sense of purpose, direction and hope, but there was 'absolutely no response'. God had forsaken her. Christ seemed 'very far away. I felt deserted by God and man.'[55]

She was lost in a metaphoric and a literal wilderness, one of intense hardship and financial insecurity, but she didn't mope. Instead, with extraordinary resolve she went downtown to the only industry in the district and, 'rather than let the children starve', she applied for a job as a factory hand at one of Monterey's sardine canneries. Securing work proved easy as the sardine industry was booming in 1915, brought about by the war.[56]

The work was hard and the workplace crude, and Alice couldn't hide her fears. 'I was down among the people; I was just nobody and I had always thought I was somebody. I was holding down the kind of job that anybody could hold down.'[57] It was piecework. Half her wages went to a neighbour who minded her daughters. Alice would go down to the cannery at seven in the morning and return home at four. At first, she worked in the labelling department, but she couldn't earn enough to meet her needs, so she joined the packing department.

She applied herself to the task of packing sardines with dogged resolve to earn enough to get by, and she proved good at it too, gaining the respect of her co-workers. 'I handled an average of ten thousand sardines a day and packed hundreds of cans.'[58] Yet with her cultured voice and her refined manners, she was vulnerable. Visitors to the factory, who were brought in to observe her remarkable packing skills, were less than kind. Rather than admire her efforts, many visitors aspersed her with, 'she must have done something to have brought herself down to this kind of work' and, 'better not be taken in by appearances, she's probably a bad egg'. Once, a foreman at the factory over-heard the comments, and he came up to her afterwards and said that on the factory floor, she was known as 'a diamond lost in the mud'.[59]

She packed sardines for about two and a half years. When she could, she filed for divorce only to discover Walter had left Montana and entered the war. 'He did most distinguished work and was given the Croix de Guerre.'[60] Seeking a divorce from a husband on the battlefield was disfavoured. Alice withdrew proceedings to avoid the disgrace. Even though she was fully aware heroic acts on the battlefield do not automatically make a man good at home.

Life was demanding of Alice, but she persisted. 'I was still in the dark, spiritually, but was too busy earning money and taking care of the three girls to have time to wonder about my soul.'[61] That darkness was about to lift.

AN ESOTERIC CONVERSION

*L*ife in Pacific Grove settled into a rhythm of hard work and domestic duties. In her neighbourhood and at the sardine factory Alice was surrounded by good, hardworking women and men. It was an enriching time in a physical sense, and free of Walter, her emotions and her nerves had a chance to settle. This allowed the inner spiritual quest that had always been a part of her nature to unfold. She was no longer the rabid Christian of her formative years. She became aware of her mind, its powers of reflection, both inwardly and outwardly on the world around her, but her innate mystic disposition was left with no guidance or creed. Because of this, and despite her busy work life and her children, she was lonely. She would always be an upper-class British woman of Edwardian virtue, one with an inquisitive mind, and she craved intellectual stimulation and likeminded company. There was plenty around in the artistic and freethinking community of Pacific Grove. Alice just needed to find a way in.

She knew of two other English women of a similar background she was keen to meet. She had seen them in the streets, and they aroused her curiosity. When she heard a rumour that the women were hosting a lecture in their drawing room on 'some peculiar subject', Alice secured an invitation through a mutual friend.

She wasn't impressed. 'I found the lecture very dull and the lecturer very poor. I can imagine no worse lecturer anywhere.'[1] It was an introduction to Theosophy. '"Nineteen million years ago the Lords of the Flame came from Venus and planted the seed of mind in man,"' the man said.[2] He'd said it as a statement of brute fact. Such an absolutist view landed in Alice's mind as an affront. She was facing in another form her own tendency to do the same, borne out in her lingering Christian views. After all, she still took the date of Creation to be 4004 BC. She'd read with much guilt and disloyalty the theory of evolution Charles Darwin developed under her own grandfather's roof at Moor House. Seated in that lecture in Pacific Grove, she met this new idea with incomprehension, deciding the very notion that the world began nineteen million years ago was 'sheer blasphemy'. The rest of the lecture proved impenetrable. 'The lecturer wandered all over the world of thought...I registered a resolve at that time that if I ever found myself lecturing I would endeavour to be everything that this Theosophical lecturer was not.'[3]

Despite the tedium, the evening was not wasted, Alice becoming friends with the two English women, who took her 'immediately in hand' and gave her books to read. She says after that evening she was 'in and out of their home, talking and asking questions, a great deal'.[4]

Alice couldn't have known that in walking through the front door of those English women's home, she was entering into a new and exciting hall of wisdom, and that she would live in that hall for the rest of her life. The moment was, in esoteric parlance, initiatory. Astrologers would fall over themselves for the date.

Through those texts leant to her by her new friends, Theosophy exploded into Alice's life. She devoured the teachings with the appetite of a starved animal, yet she was her grandfather's granddaughter, dutiful, responsible, strict with her time. In the spirit of those childhood years at Moor Park, she carried on with all of her daily duties in a highly regimented routine: up at four to do the chores, off to work to pack sardines, back at home to feed and entertain the girls and then, after the children were asleep and the clothes soaking and the bread left to rise, off to bed to devour every word she read. She would read 'steadily until midnight', allowing her just four hours of sleep, which was fortunately all she needed. She learned to read while ironing, read while peeling potatoes, read while she shelled peas and strung beans. She even read while she sewed. She also read 'with great rapidity, grasping whole paragraphs and pages as quickly as other people read a sentence'.[5]

Although, when she opened *The Secret Doctrine*, she found the subject matter jumbled, the text meandering. She discovered much later from Blavatsky's secretary Claude Falls Wright that when Blavatsky wrote the tome, she would produce page upon unnumbered page, tossing them on the floor beside her. It fell to Mr Wright and her other helpers to collate those pages into a semblance of order.[6]

Alice struggled, as many have before and after her, but she persisted, intrigued. Soon she met 'two very old ladies who lived side-by-side in two cottages—indispensable to each other and quarrelling all the time'.[7] Both had been personal pupils of Blavatsky and discovering Alice's difficulties with *The Secret Doctrine*, they willingly took her in hand.

For Theosophists, and indeed esotericists in general, these relationships are significant. While studying an esoteric text is all well and good, receiving the teachings via an older, wiser disciple or master is preferred. A core feature of all forms of esotericism is master-to-disciple transmission. Further, through these ladies, a direct line of descent from Blavatsky to Alice Bailey is established, bestowing much-needed credibility and authenticity. Alice Bailey mentions this in her autobiography for this very reason.

Alice's need for understanding proved so great, she moved house to be closer to those ladies. While her children played in the garden, she would sit on the porch at one or other of their abodes and listen and absorb.

She was no remedial student. In 1916 she joined the Theosophical Lodge in Pacific Grove and in no time at all she was teaching and holding classes, keeping 'six pages ahead' of her students, as many a teacher is wont to do. 'They never discovered how little I knew. I know that no matter what the class learned I learned a great deal.'[8]

She soon adopted the Theosophical evolutionary scheme, with its emanationist cosmology and concomitant notions of karma and reincarnation. She had no difficulty with the idea of a grand design or pattern to all existence, which she thought of as 'a great and divine Plan'.

The idea of a grand design is not unique to Theosophy. It forms the basis of the teleological argument for the existence of God, known as Paley's Watch. The idea being that since the world is at least as intricate and complex in design as a watch, and the watch was made by a human, then the world must have also been made, and that maker or creator must be God. In Theosophy, this design or Plan is not an abstract concept belonging to some ineffable God transcendent; it is an actual plan or guiding principle for which a small group of spiritually advanced beings are responsible. These beings are the Spiritual Hierarchy or the Masters of the Wisdom. As noted above, it is not possible to adopt a Theosophical worldview without an acceptance of the existence of the Hierarchy, although it is possible to suspend judgement or phenomenologically bracket the Hierarchy in order to engage with and benefit from the teachings.[9] Alice Bailey had no need of such brackets:

 I found that the Head of this Hierarchy of spiritual Leaders was the Christ and when this dawned on me, I felt that He had been given back to me in a nearer and more intimate way. I found that He was "the Master of all the Masters and Teacher alike of angels and men.'"[10]

THEOSOPHISTS ADOPT A POSITIVE, esoteric view of Christ. By the time Alice Bailey found Theosophy, then president of the Theosophical Society Annie Besant had already published *Initiation: The Perfecting of Man*, a collection of lectures released in 1912.[11] The work depicts the life of Christ as Head of the Hierarchy and talks of the second 'Coming of the World Teacher' or World Saviour. The rest of the Hierarchy comprises other Masters and their disciples. Reading such works, Alice would have been reminded of the strange waking dream she had at Castramont when she was about fifteen, of a ceremony being held in a valley surrounded by high mountains. Just as in that vision, Alice found in Theosophy an esoteric presentation of truth that 'in no way belittled Christ'.[12]

The Masters might be considered a spiritual thoughtform as far as average human consciousness is concerned. The Ageless Wisdom teaches, through language, ideas that point towards higher levels of consciousness beyond our comprehension. The Masters can be thought of as a hint, a taste, a subtle flavour encouraging those ready and predisposed to strive to advance beyond human limitations.

The reader should take Alice Bailey at her word when she stresses that every reader must make up their own mind regarding the truth of any presentation and not accept it simply because it comes from some authority. She felt the individual should adapt to an emerging divinity within and not be held back by any dogma, something that is essential in understanding her own body of work.

It must be noted that metaphysics is the study of reality, not truth. Theosophy is an esoteric depiction of reality in symbolic and abstract language which portrays the evolution of

consciousness and is concerned with the inner planes of existence and how they relate to extramental reality, that of the
world in which we live and move. Theosophy is less a body of
knowledge, although it is often treated as such, and more a way
of knowing. Theosophy, like all esotericism, concerns the ineffable, the unknowable. It is only ever a theory or worldview, and a
lived reality in the mind of the believer. To evaluate any metaphysical scheme, including Theosophy, we must assess its
explanatory power, its value or the contributions it makes to the
world and the consequences of holding such a worldview for the
adherent in terms of a life lived. For the non-esotericist, Theosophical teachings can be viewed as provisional knowledge
which may or may not be an accurate depiction of reality. For the
esotericist, Theosophy can be viewed as both provisional knowledge and a way of knowing holding insightful explanatory
power and a complex set of guiding principles. The Spiritual
Hierarchy in this sense is a guiding principle.

Alice Bailey was a believer and an avid one at that. During
those first months of exposure to Theosophy, she started to
realise she could co-operate with the Plan and work with the
Spiritual Hierarchy, although she had no idea what form that
would take. It was all there before her in the realm of possibility,
making complete sense of the strange visitation she had when
she was fifteen and again when she heard her Master's voice in
India.

Her entry into Theosophy was timely. She discovered the
belief system at a point in history when interest in Theosophy
and Spiritualism were undergoing a revival. The First World War
was in full swing, claiming the lives of millions of soldiers. On 6
April 1917, America joined the war, and more than two million
American soldiers joined the battlefields in France. The separa-
tions and the losses triggered a spiritual crisis as many searched
for answers, for meaning, for communication across the divide
of death.[13]

Alice's personal life at that time, one of immense hardship at the cannery in Pacific Grove, along with all that she had endured in her life before, were explained back to her in a remarkable way by the Theosophical texts she read. She came to understand, slowly at first, that she was a disciple on the spiritual path and had already passed through several initiations.

Initiation is one of the core motifs of Western Esotericism. In esoteric sects, this can mean a ritual or ceremony enacted to initiate a member into previously hidden mysteries or secrets. In Theosophy, initiations are points of entry into increasingly more advanced stages of spiritual development. Theosophist and founder of Anthropomorphism Rudolph Steiner (1861-1925) wrote extensively on the processes of initiation.[14] The various stages were also set out in Annie Besant's *Initiation: The Perfecting of Man*, and they are of central importance in Alice Bailey's books.

About half of the teachings Alice Bailey would soon come to write focus on esoteric psychology and concern the nature of the human personality and the soul. Every aspect of the human constitution, along with the journey the aspirant must make along the spiritual path, are given in rich and intricate detail. The notion of initiation is scattered throughout her writings, some works focusing exclusively on the initiatory path itself, with its various stages, hurdles and seminal moments.

Back in Pacific Grove, out of the knowledge Alice was swiftly acquiring, she developed a new esoteric vocabulary. Human beings were 'atoms' in the 'body' of the 'planetary Logos', itself one of seven 'Centres' in the body of the 'Solar Logos'. Humanity as a whole was centred in a solar systemic evolutionary journey of immeasurable proportions. Theosophy places humanity at the fulcrum of the entire scheme. We are urged to take responsibility for our own individual evolution, the evolution of our consciousness, in order to progress the evolutionary journey of the whole. A key stage of this evolutionary process is when the personality registers the existence of, and is influenced by, the soul.[15]

Just as all world religions charge us with self-examination and purification, so too does Theosophy. The teachings are fundamentally soul-centred. Alice Bailey argues that it is only when you remove the soul from the practice of esotericism that it becomes 'black magic', or the left-hand path.

In spiritual stage models, the hallmark of human experience is growth. We journey from childhood, through the tough years of adolescence and those of early adulthood, towards the acquired wisdom of old age. To be conscious is to be awake and aware. To experience consciousness is to be awake to that awareness. A turn of the head and through the eye will appear an altered perspective. A shift of inner focus, and another matter comes under consideration. Wherever our inner attention is drawn, change can occur. In *Varieties of Religious Experience*, William James spoke of it this way:

 All we know is that there are dead feelings, dead ideas and cold beliefs, and there are hot and alive ones; and when one grows hot and alive within us, everything has to re-crystallise about it.[16]

A NEW LOVER, a long journey, a change of career, the birth of a child, the death of a loved one, the entire panoply of life experience offers the potential for transformation. In Alice Bailey's model, the journey towards soul consciousness involves a particular kind of transformation, that of initiatory expansion.[17]

Expansions of consciousness require some sort of trigger, in the form of an existential crisis. Suddenly, everything that was true and believed and could be relied upon becomes inadequate in the face of some new understanding. New answers and explanations must be found, a new perspective adopted, new values incorporated, new attitudes to knowledge and knowing instilled.

This crisis becomes spiritual when suddenly the knower is known, when consciousness becomes aware of itself as the divine intelligent observer, the soul. The key to initiation lies in recognising this is happening.

As soon as the soul is registered, the individual is pulled in two directions, the personality yanking the individual in the direction of the three worlds of living on the physical, emotional and mental planes, the soul in the direction of spirit on its own plane. It's this process of pulling and stretching that expands awareness.

Initiations are key moments in the life of the spiritual seeker marked by sudden and dramatic leaps to another level of awareness. It's a larger self bursting through old skin, an entry into a new life, a deeply felt sense of purpose and direction, an intense and personal experience the result of months and years of hard work. Initiation:

 is first of all the entering into a new and wider dimensional world by the expansion of a man's consciousness so that he can include and encompass that which he now excludes, and from which he normally separates himself in his thinking and acts. It is, secondly, the entering into man of those energies which are distinctive of the soul and of the soul alone – the forces of intelligent love and spiritual will.[18]

INITIATIONS ONLY OCCUR in the lives of those who are subjectively oriented, who seek knowledge from within, and who think reflectively. These individuals enter into stages of intuitive and holistic awareness, the hallmark of spiritual consciousness. The experience occurs in full waking consciousness and is recognised and acknowledged. 'An initiation is a blaze of illumination thrown upon the river of existence, and it is in the nature of a whole experience. There is not indefiniteness in it, and the initiate is never quite the same again in his consciousness.'[19]

During an initiation, the disciple reaches a point of tension involving great stress and strain. Every initiation is preceded by a journey and at each 'a Sign is given' and 'a Voice is heard'. Before the initiate is a crossroads. A choice must be made to relinquish the old and move towards a life of expanded service. Such phases are marked by an intense preoccupation with the world of significances. Eventually the initiate emerges into a new field of experience.[20]

Alice Bailey describes the process of initiation from a variety of perspectives. She advises her students continuously and at great length to prepare for the one ahead. The physical, emotional and mental bodies need to be purified so that the inflowing spiritual energy can flow through unimpeded. When the energy doesn't flow smoothly it is dissipated, scattered about. The result is confusion. The physical body needs a good diet and exercise. The emotional body must be held steady and kept from reacting, and the mental body is trained through meditation to focus and sustain concentration. The student must become aware of their stage of attainment and understand which initiation lies ahead. Only then will they know what steps to take next.

To illustrate the initiatory path, Alice Bailey draws on the life of Christ. She isn't alone in viewing Christ in this fashion. Jung sees in Christ's life a primordial, archetypal hero's journey from birth to adulthood to death, from unconsciousness to consciousness.[21] Whereas Jung takes a mythic perspective, understanding the Gospel story as metaphor, Alice Bailey believes Christ's life was an enactment of the initiatory stages of the spiritual path from the Birth, Baptism and Transfiguration, through to the Crucifixion and Resurrection. His life serves as a template, a pattern for others to follow. To support her view, in *From Beth-*

lehem to Calvary, a book penned in her own name, she relies on Annie Besant's *Esoteric Christianity*, a slim volume that traces the history of the mystery traditions of the early church.[22] Alice Bailey goes further. She offers a re-presentation of the key ideas, reformulated in instructional and explanatory language, narrowing the scope to that of the initiations themselves. *From Bethlehem to Calvary* was written in the 1930s during the build-up to the Second World War and carries a powerful sense of urgency:

 The hearts of men have never been more open to spiritual impression than they are at this time, and the door into the very centre of reality stands wide open. Paralleling, however, this significant development is a trend in the counter direction, and materialistic philosophies and doctrines of negation are becoming increasingly prevalent.[23]

ALICE BAILEY INVITES the reader to map her own personal life to this initiatory model, yet uppermost in the work is a belief in a collective initiation, as by then Alice Bailey believed large numbers of individuals, the 'World Disciple', had attained the same evolutionary stage and were ready to be born into the spiritual life. The Age of Aquarius represents for her a great hope and glory as humanity is poised on the verge of this new revelation.

Just as Alice Bailey construes the life of Christ in terms of the initiatory path, so her autobiography is also a story of discipleship and initiation. She doesn't make any claims or attribute specific details to one or other of the initiations, but it is possible to discern the first and second initiations, and perhaps even the third initiation in her life story. From the moment of her 'spiritual birth' when the turbaned man in the European suit entered her aunt's drawing room Alice was on the spiritual path.

In Alice Bailey's world, the first initiation occurs in the dim, when the first flickers of the inner light of the soul are recognised, and the individual begins to know themselves as a spiritual aspirant. It occurs when the personality has become a self-directed entity. 'This type of individual may be extremely versatile, charming and attractive,' which Alice undoubtedly was. She says the process building up to any initiation is not one of privilege but of 'the utmost difficulty and hardness', which for Alice was surely the case.[24]

The second initiation deals with the emotional body, purged to allow for the inflow of love. The aspirant must demonstrate control of her emotional reactions and selfish desires, her longings and wishes. 'The initiatory process between the first and the second initiations is for many the worst time of distress, difficulty, realization of problems and the constant effort to 'clear himself'".[25] Temptations must be resisted. The initiate must do battle with life experience, with the fogs and the steam created by feelings of anger, despair and desire:

> This initiation will produce in the initiate a growing sense of relationships, of a basic unity with all that breathes, and a recognition of the One Life which will lead eventually to that state of expressed brotherhood which it is the goal of the Aquarian Age to bring into being.[26]

SHE EFFECTIVELY PROVIDES a symbolic summation of her time in India, culminating in her complete breakdown. There was no ceremonial immersion in purifying waters. Just an intense inner struggle on every level of her being, and a light, entering her room one evening, a guiding light that cut through her multiple crises, a light that marked a turning point.

The inflow of love Alice experienced at her symbolic baptism, she directed at Walter Evans. She then entered a period of intense struggle and hardship in her marriage. When at last she had purged her emotional body, she was ready to begin preparations for the third initiation.

Alice Bailey states that it is not always the case that the aspirant is aware they have passed through the first two initiations, but the third always occurs in full waking consciousness:

 Up to the third initiation, man has been occupied with the process of fusing soul and body into one unity. After the third…man is oriented towards, and becomes preoccupied with, a further fusion in consciousness, that of spirit-soul-body. I speak of a fusion in consciousness. The unity is ever there, and man in evolution is really becoming aware of that which already exists.[27]

AN INNER ALIGNMENT TAKES PLACE, the concrete and abstract minds align, and a direct channel to the eye of the soul, or the third eye, is created. The moment it occurs, the initiate experiences a sudden inflow of spiritual energy, a blast of brilliant, illuminating light.[28] It's a feeling of ecstasy like no other. Alice Bailey makes no claim to having experienced the event, but from the point of view of her life story and the teachings contained in her body of work, she must have. She certainly doesn't speak of the sudden inpouring of light. If she had, it would have been claim making, in esoteric circles a matter thought to be proof the event hasn't in fact occurred. Yet the sudden and dramatic manner in which she found Theosophy, the two old ladies that were ready to guide her, the entire devouring of the new knowledge and the emerging sense of important work ahead, her mission, all have the flavour of the third initiation.

Her life, as portrayed by her, fits her own model. She wittingly or unwittingly construes her story in this way, high lighting this over that, shaping her experiences to suit. Yet there is no denying the phases and stages she went through, the suffering she endured.

The hallmarks of character after the third initiation has passed are humility, detachment, endurance and power. The initiate carries an understanding that there is new work to be completed, work she never knew was there and suddenly, her whole life revolves around that work. She becomes dedicated to it as a slave to a master, the soul's purpose. Before the initiate is a life of World Service. A single life activity emerges. The initiate will often work behind the scenes, initiating activities without any need of personal reward. This encapsulates perfectly how Alice Bailey's life would unfold.

It isn't the case that initiation means the individual has left the old self outside the gate and marched through, a new woman. Neither does it mean she has divested herself of her foibles or that somehow, miraculously, she is perfect. More that she is ready; she is good enough, just. The path isn't linear either, one stage leading on to another. It is akin to a spiral, with much overlapping. And it's gruelling. Old issues and themes are revisited as the initiate learns to handle the inflow of new spiritual energies, which can cause inner chaos and throw emotions and thoughts into turmoil. The disciple is both onlooker and dramatic participant in their life. The personality still presents its problems; if anything they are exacerbated by the stimulation of spiritual energy. The nervous system is sensitised. Hypersensitivity to the environment and surroundings may result. The disciple's life becomes more intense, lived faster. The changes may create psychological problems too, as the need to find a new rhythm and a new equilibrium is ever present. 'Ambition is, par excellence, the problem of the developed aspirant and the disciple—personal ambition, love of popularity, worldly ambition, intellectual ambition, and the dictatorship of power over others.'[29] Alice Bailey argues over and again that the way to counter the intensifying effects of the inpouring spiritual energy is to direct it in service to others.

For Alice Bailey, initiation is a universal experience, available to all. Through this assertion, she attempted to wrest the various stages of the spiritual path from the exclusivity of esoteric orders or sects. As she divested the initiations from exclusivity through using the life of Christ as exemplar, she created another difficulty, upsetting orthodox Christians who found her version of their divine being abhorrent. Alice Bailey's strongly held Christian outlook never left her. Instead, she transmuted her belief in Christ as God immanent and made that her own.

MOVING TO KROTONA

*I*n the latter half of 1917, life for Alice became much easier. Walter had secured work with the Young Men's Christian Association in France, and Bishop Sanford arranged for a portion of his salary to be paid to Alice. With her own small income from the family estate, this allowed her to leave the sardine cannery. To further her spiritual interests, with the support of her friend and Theosophist Dot Weatherhead, Alice moved to Hollywood, the original site of the Theosophical Society headquarters at Krotona, nestled in the hills of Beachwood Canyon.[1]

The Krotona Institute was the brainchild of attorney Albert Powell Warrington from Norfolk, Virginia, who joined the Theosophical Society in 1896 at the age of thirty and quickly became a devotee and active member. Warrington was the American Section's President from 1912-20 and personal representative to Annie Besant in America between 1907-1928.[2] By the time Alice was on the scene, Besant had been president of the Theosophical Society for a decade, ever since founding member and president Colonel Olcott passed away in 1907.

A leading second-generation Theosophist, Annie Besant was based at Adyar, India, one of the many lodges she established in her lifetime. She was a powerful figure. Born in London to middle-class parents of Irish extraction, she began her adult life as a clergyman's wife, but soon discovered that marriage before her was unsatisfactory. Like Alice Bailey, she was too strong-willed, too intelligent, too passionate for a crusty vicar. Unlike Alice Bailey, she went on to become an activist and socialist, fighting for women's and workers' rights. A prolific writer and orator, Besant encountered Theosophy in 1889, when she was asked to write a piece on *The Secret Doctrine*. She moved to India four years later in 1893. Under her leadership, esoteric Christianity and the teachings of her 'Avataras' took up a central place in Theosophical teachings.[3] Without her influence, Alice Bailey, with her dyed in the wool faith in Christ, would most likely not have been drawn to Theosophy at all.

It was with Besant's approval that Warrington's plans for the Krotona Institute proceeded. With some generous assistance in the form of private loans, he purchased ten acres of the former Charles Hastings Ranch, Pasadena, and established an oasis in homage to the Crotona community established by Pythagoras in Italy in 518 BC.[4]

Krotona had a dreamlike quality; a community of about three to five hundred devotees residing in a collection of stunning, architect designed buildings, many Moorish in style. These grand buildings were set in peaceful, elegantly gardened grounds, replete with a lotus pond, citrus and olive trees, eucalypts and date palms, an outdoor theatre and spaces for worship.[5] Krotona exemplified the aspirations and elite backgrounds of many of those freethinkers drawn to Theosophy and the mystical traditions of the East. Back then, as now, freethinking was a luxury the working classes could ill-afford.

Many wealthy Theosophists had donated money to Krotona's establishment, and the result was splendid in its conception, secluded and serene. At the institute's heart was Krotona Inn, designed in 1912 by the highly influential firm of architects, Mead and Requa. 'Centered around a lush courtyard, the elegant, stucco complex included guest rooms, a dining room and kitchen, offices for the sect's magazine staff and Krotona officials, a lecture room for many public classes, and a "magnetically charged" esoteric meditation room.'[6] The accommodation quarters were just as impressive, many of the homes fantastical, some of them mansions. Theosophical luminaries included: New Yorker Grace Shaw Duff, daughter of humourist Henry Wheeler Shaw (Josh Billings); heiress of the Pittsburg Paint Company Mrs Christine Stevenson; and opera singer Marie Russak Hotchener. Her mansion, Moorcrest, was the residence at different times of film stars Charlie Chaplin and Mary Astor.[7] Krotona provided adult education classes open to the wider public and put on lavish theatrical productions. For Alice, there could have been no greater contrast between this paradisiacal environment and the sardine cannery at Pacific Grove.

When she arrived, Hollywood was still a gentle place and relatively unspoiled. This soon changed and by 1924, the Theosophists felt crowded out by the burgeoning film industry and relocated to Ojai, California, where Krotona has been ever since.

Alice didn't move into the community itself but rented a cottage nearby, on North Beachwood Drive. With her daughters at school and kindergarten, she was free to attend classes and lectures.[8] She made many friends at Krotona and before long she was asked to run the cafeteria. It was strictly vegetarian. She had already adopted the diet when she became a Theosophist, and she learned to be a good vegetarian cook. The work provided her with an additional income and, no doubt, a sense of belonging, albeit a humble one, for Alice knew she was capable of much more and had a definite hunger not for food but for spiritual knowledge. She was, at this time, something of a waif, worn out and run ragged from factory work and the domestic duties of motherhood. Perhaps it was due to patrons' reactions to her appearance in the café that led her to note an interesting correspondence between the various approaches to diet and spiritual attitude; it seemed to her the stricter and more rigid the former, the more superior and critical the latter.[9] She, in turn, reacted negatively to what she observed. 'Better to eat beefsteak and have a kind tongue' she decided, finding she had no patience for spiritual elitism.

In fact, she had no real idea of the extent of the elitist reality she had walked into. For her, she was at last amongst like-minded people, all of them apparently authentic seekers treading the spiritual path. Unlike the factory floor at the cannery, the Krotona milieu was privileged, comprising a progressive portion of the educated upper classes. The occult attracts the avant garde and suddenly, thanks to Blavatsky and a cohort of second-generation Theosophists, such seekers could commune together in quasi-monastic isolation. It was an idyll, but one not without its shadow.

Within months of her arrival, having served the mandatory two years as a Theosophical Society member, Alice was admitted into the Esoteric Section, the inner sanctum of the Theosophical Society. Meetings were held in the meditation room, or Shrine Room. Hanging on the walls of this room were portraits of the Masters. The first time Alice entered the room, she observed those paintings and there, to her astonishment, was a portrait of the man who had visited her that Sunday when she was alone in her Aunt Margaret Maxwell's house at Castramont. With his suit and his turban, he was unmistakable. She was so taken by surprise she rushed to one of the senior members of the Esoteric Section and asked for the Master's name. She was told he was Koot Hoomi. At this point Alice would have been well advised to keep silent. Instead, she said, '"Oh then, He must be my Master, for I've talked with Him and been under His guidance ever since."'[10]

At which the senior member looked at her and replied with a withering tone, '"Am I to understand that you believe yourself to be a disciple?"'

Alice had collided head on with the competitiveness and

superiority evident among some spiritual seekers. It is a form of spiritual materialism, a term coined by Tibetan meditation master Chögyam Trungpa to refer to a tendency whereby the personality latches on to the idea of spiritual progress and becomes inflated in proportion to felt advancement.[11] Further, only those advanced members of the Esoteric Section could conceive of being in any sort of communication with the Masters. It was every Theosophical seeker's grail and required the seal of approval from Annie Besant. Alice had inadvertently claimed discipleship status for which she was not entitled. It was a *faux pas* purist Theosophists would never find it in themselves to forgive.

FOSTER BAILEY ARRIVES

$\mathcal{R}$unning the cafeteria was not Alice's only role at Krotona. Along with her training in the Esoteric Section, she also gave weekly public lectures. At the end of one of those lectures, her friend Dot Weatherhead introduced her to a good-looking young man named Foster.[1] It was to prove a defining moment in Alice's life.

Lawyer and Freemason, Lieutenant Foster Bailey (1888-1977) was born in Fitchburg, Massachusetts, to civil engineer William Kimball Bailey (1853-1927) and his wife Cora Isabel Wheeler (1859-1945). Foster was a middle child. He had one sister, Lucy Goldsmith Bailey, and a brother, Carroll Capen Bailey. Unlike Walter Evans, Foster hailed from distinguished American stock. On his father's side, his grandmother Dorothy S. Kimball was a life member of the Massachusetts Home Missionary Society and a descendant of founding father of Fitchburg, landowner and proprietor of Cavendish Amos Kimball (1717-1774). Foster's grandfather on his father's side was prominent Calvinist Ebenezer Foster Bailey (1820-1907) who wrote works on church history. Foster's great-uncle was attorney, publisher and politician Goldsmith Fox Bailey (1823-61) who died of tuberculosis shortly after becoming a US

Congressman on the Republican ticket. Foster's uncle and Harvard law school graduate Harrison Bailey (1849-) was also an attorney, admitted to the bar at Fitchburg, Worcester County.[2]

There is no telling why Foster chose to forgo the privileges of his standing and a career in his uncle's law firm, but when he met Mrs Alice Evans, he was living at Krotona in a tent.

By then, Foster had been a member of the Theosophical Society for about a year, having joined on 27 October 1917. [3] He had enlisted in the army branch of the US Army on 18 September 1917.[4] He was released from service just five months later on 28 March 1918.[5] Alice Bailey states he had crashed a plane while training army observers.[6] He was in intensive care for a long period, during which time his hair turned white.[7] He most likely arrived at Krotona sometime after March in 1918, finding in his newly found Theosophy something of a haven due to the Theosophical Society's committed support for servicemen during the war, including fundraising and the establishment of recreational halls for returned servicemen, mostly in the southern states.[8]

In her autobiography, Alice Bailey states Foster was demobilized from the United States Air Force after the November 2018 Armistice, to cohere with her claim that the couple met in January 1919, commenting that he had been on sick leave for months prior to that time.[9] Giving the month as well as the year suggests she was being precise and wanted the reader to believe her testimony.[10] This matter is taken up in the following chapter.

In meeting Foster, Alice would have been reminded of all the soldiers she had tended, the beds she had sat beside in hospitals in India. Their affection for each other was strong and immediate, although perhaps not ardent. He was eight years her junior and upon first encounter, he found her 'in very poor health...and well nigh crushed'.[11] Yet still she impressed him. 'She was an unusually clear thinker. In the early days when I first knew her, her great driving urge was to know, to understand the ancient wisdom, to pierce through and catch more of the vision, to know more clearly what the Masters wanted.'[12]

Alice Bailey never wrote of her impressions of Foster, except to commend him as an outstanding father to her daughters and for sacrificing a promising career in his family's law firm to work alongside her. In Foster, Alice had found her greatest ally. They had a rapport that would endure for a lifetime, and it appears they were united from the first.

Alice had already instituted divorce proceedings, and once the divorce was granted, the couple were engaged. It was at this point that Alice's sister Lydia refused to have anything more to do with Alice and cut her off completely.

Alice had lost the last remaining member of her family of origin. Lydia was an orthodox Christian who regarded 'anyone who has had the misfortune to get a divorce as quite without the pale'.[13] Alice Bailey makes no criticism of her sister, rather she is at pains to praise Lydia's achievements. Yet the rejection must have been deeply felt, for in dismissing Alice in this fashion, Lydia also dismissed her sister's entire life at the very juncture when her astonishing contribution to humanity was about to unfold. Very telling that in her autobiography, there is no mention of Lydia by name.

Foster was an intriguing figure in Alice Bailey's life. Why did he stand by her side? A man eight years her junior, no doubt traumatised by his experiences in the army during the First World War, including and uppermost the plane crash, a man of genial appearance, of a privileged background, yet maverick enough to choose to live, long-term, in a tent, when all around him was opulence. That, of itself, strikes at the heart of the man. He was a champion of a cause and, intentionally or not, his tent-dwelling life was a symbolic form of protest against the wealth evident at Krotona which, to a large degree, was a life of privilege at the expense of the broader American Section membership.

What drew the couple together? A unified if inchoate vision?

They were both outsiders, Alice in her humble role running the cafeteria and renting a house on Beachwood Drive, and Foster in his tent. These circumstances alone would have shaped their perspective of the highly privileged Krotona community, despite the fact they both hailed from the same milieu. Alice's frustrations with the exclusivity of the Esoteric Section and the somewhat dictatorial manner in which the TS was run remotely by Annie Besant, were also shared by Foster. Together, they went on to become comrades-in-arms.

As the months slipped by, Alice attended Esoteric Section meditations and received the teachings. Foster was precluded from doing the same since he had joined the TS on 27 October 1917 and would need to serve his two years.[14] Alice continued to give talks and lectures, and run the cafeteria, and at home she attended to her motherly duties. In Foster, she had a new life partner in the making. He visited her at home and formed a strong bond with her daughters. Alice Bailey talks fondly of their initial meetings, of how Dorothy literally fell into his arms from her perch on the bough of a tree, and of how he helped care for Mildred who was ill with measles.[15] With all that Foster meant to her, in the introduction to her autobiography Alice Bailey states:

 My husband Foster Bailey has for over twenty-five years made all my work possible. Without him I feel I could have accomplished very little. Where there is deep and abiding love and understanding, respect and unbroken comradeship, one is rich indeed. He has been a tower of strength and "the shadow of a great rock in a thirsty land". There are things which are damaged by expression in words and sound meaningless and futile when written down. Our relationship is one of them. For many lives we must have lived and worked together and we both look forward to many more. I have no more to say on this subject.[16]

WHAT MOTIVE ALICE BAILEY had for limiting what she would divulge about their relationship is unknown. What is clear is Foster was her mainstay, there beside her through the decades, foregoing his own career in law to dedicate his life in the service of a shared vision. Alice was frail and thin when they met. Perhaps she regained some of her strength, but her health was never good. Foster supported her when her health declined dramatically through her fifties and sixties. In all, Foster Bailey was a remarkable man, humble enough to take on a carer role more typically adopted by a woman.

THE TIBETAN

One October day, after sending the children off to school, Alice went for a walk on the hill near her house. She sat down, lost in her thoughts. Suddenly she heard a 'clear note of music which sounded from the sky, through the hill and in me'. She describes herself as 'startled and attentive'. Then she heard a voice telling her, '"There are some books which it is desired should be written for the public. You can write them. Will you do so?"' She says at first she refused, saying out loud, 'Certainly not. I'm not a darned psychic and I don't want to be drawn into anything like that.'[1]

According to her own account, the voice – that of the Tibetan or Djwhal Khul (DK) – told her not to make a snap judgment, that she had a peculiar gift and that it was in no way associated with the lower psychism of mediums and séances, or the automatic writing and channelling she abhorred. Again, she expressed her refusal. She wasn't interested. Find someone else. The voice said he would return again in three weeks to see if she would change her mind. Alice shook herself as though awakening from a dream and went home. She promptly tried to forget about the incident, not mentioning it to anyone, not even Foster.

Following the sequence of events, Alice and Foster scarcely

knew each other at the time of this seminal event in Alice's spiritual life, and they were certainly not at the stage of an established couple betrothed to be wed. Alice Bailey's statement that she withheld from Foster the strange contact on her walk is a matter not in doubt, for it represents the moral truth of the autobiography. Where Alice Bailey's own account is unreliable, concerns when.

The timing of this first contact is crucial. Alice Bailey claims her first encounter with the Tibetan took place on 19 November 1919. The letter with the earliest date appearing in the 1993 edition of *Letters on Occult Meditation* is dated 25 September 1919.[2] The letter begins, 'Today I seek to speak to you on the powers of the Dark Brotherhood', and continues with 'As before I have told you the danger is as yet...'[3] It is clear from this letter that there exist other letters carrying earlier dates. In the original 1922 edition, the earliest letter is dated 16 September 1919 and states 'I seek to give you today, in closing this series, something of general use'.[4] Clearly, there were a number of letters preceding this one.

The existence of other letters meant for inclusion in the same book – letters which didn't make the cut and remain unpublished – has come to light. These letters carry a 1918 date, around or at least one year earlier than Alice Bailey claims.[5]

Why Alice Bailey should make the claim that she began writing for the Tibetan on 19 November 1919 when that is plainly untrue is something of a puzzle. Alice Bailey wrote her autobiography in the last few months of her life, at a time when she was gravely ill, which might have caused her to confuse some dates. She might have unwittingly given the wrong date for when she met Foster, that of January 1919, as discussed in the previous chapter, or simply given that date for the sake of coherence.

However, in *The Externalisation of the Hierarchy*, in a pamphlet dated April 1948, eighteen months before Alice died, the Tibetan states 'On November 19th, 1919, I made first contact with

A.A.B.'[6] This is therefore the date the Bailey community adheres to, despite contrary historical evidence.[7] It might also be why Alice Bailey gave the date in her autobiography.

From the perspective of a writer, 1918 offers a more realistic timeframe. During the Christmas period of 1919, Alice went on to hand the editor of *The Theosophist* Bahman Pestonji Wadia three chapters from *Initiation, Human and Solar* amounting to around twenty-five pages of fully edited text, along with thirty-two pages which later appeared in *A Treatise on Cosmic Fire*.[8] It is unlikely that she produced all of that material, fully edited, in just one month as the official date of 19 November 1919 would have it. And it is already clear that she was writing for the Tibetan well before September 1919.

The timing of this seminal moment of first contact is important for another reason. In Alice Bailey's account, she and Foster were already holding key roles in the Theosophical Society administration when she was first contacted by the Tibetan, and embroiled in an organisational row, the subject of the following chapter. Whereas the real sequence is one that places her personal connection with the Hierarchy as one of the prime movers in all that followed, a connection she had formed independent of anyone, including Foster.

Alice Bailey describes how three weeks after that first contact, while she was seated in her sitting room after the girls had gone to bed, she heard the voice again. Once more the request was made and once more, she refused. Only this time the speaker begged her to reconsider. They agreed on a trial period of a few weeks.

In Theosophy, Djwhal Khul is a Master of the Wisdom, an initiate of a high degree within Koot Hoomi's Ashram, and named the 'messenger of the masters', passing on spiritual truths and instructions to disciples to guide humanity. Alice Bailey asserts him as the key author of Helena Blavatsky's *The Secret Doctrine*, published in 1888.

Djwhal Khul is thought to have been an abbot of a Tibetan

monastery near the India-Tibet border not far from Darjeeling. The mountainous terrain is exceptionally rugged, with Mt Everest reasonably close by. Helena Blavatsky identifies Shigatse, Tibet, as the residence of the Masters Morya, Koot Hoomi and Djwhal Khul. The location is known as a hotspot of spiritual tradition and exceptional spiritual and psychic abilities the result of enduring sacred practice.[9]

In her autobiography, in an effort to quell doubters, Alice Bailey goes on to describe how she even received a gift from the Tibetan via her dear friend and ally Mr Henry Carpenter, a personal friend of Lord Reading, once Viceroy to India. Mr Carpenter went off to the Himalayas three times to try to reach the Tibetan at Shigatse. He got as far as the border, but the Dalai Lama refused him entry into Tibet. While he was making these attempts, an abbot of a monastery from across the Tibetan frontier arrived on a donkey carrying two packages of incense, a gift for Alice Bailey. The abbot, known to be a 'very great and holy man', even inquired after Alice Bailey and her Arcane School. Three lamas on donkeys were in attendance, and there was much reverent bowing from locals.[10]

Speculation exists within the Bailey community as to the true identity of the Tibetan. Some are convinced Djwhal Khul is the ninth Panchen Lama Thubten Choekyi Nyima (1883-1937) of the Tashi Lhunpo Monastery, Tibet. However, the ninth Panchen Lama died in 1937, twelve years before the Bailey writings were completed, and there is no mention of such a death anywhere in the corpus, something students feel would have been noted. The dates mentioned of key events in the Tibetan's existence also do not tally with the life of the ninth Panchen Lama; the most salient is the Tibetan stating he is an initiate of the Fifth Degree, having taken that initiation in 1875, eight years before the ninth Panchen Lama was born. The Tibetan goes on to state he still occupies the body in which he took that initiation.[11]

Adding weight to speculations that the Tibetan is the Lama, a framed portrait of the ninth Panchen Lama hangs behind a

Christmas tree in a photo taken in the Baileys' apartment in New York sometime in the 1940s. Alice Bailey's grandson, Gordon Pugh, also understood the portrait to be that of the Tibetan.[12] The matter remains a mystery.

In portraying this early contact, Alice Bailey is at pains to distinguish herself from the average medium, insisting that what took place between her and the Tibetan was co-conscious. She did not enter a trance state and lose her own awareness and become his instrument, undergoing a lower psychic trance state typical of the average medium. Alice Bailey was an active participant. In those early weeks after initial contact, she became a special amanuensis, copying the words dictated to her while remaining in full control of all her faculties. She assumed 'an attitude of intense, positive attention'. She took down in shorthand, word for word, what was given, occasionally smoothing out the language. 'I have never changed anything that the Tibetan has ever given me...I want to make that entirely clear. I do not always understand what is given. I do not always agree.'[13] She began with a clairaudient technique but over time she found she was able to attune to the Tibetan's thoughts as they appeared in her mind.[14]

It is impossible to ascertain if the words written are always from the Tibetan's mind alone and not influenced by Alice Bailey. Sceptics would argue such telepathic rapport is impossible and explain away the occurrence by pointing out that Alice Bailey was by then three years into Theosophy and a natural when it came to studying theology. Therefore, she could easily have formulated her own version of theosophical thought. She was an evangelist at her core, used to espousing. It would have come naturally to her to do the same in textual form. Yet there is a distinct tone to the writings she took down on behalf of the Tibetan, not only a different voice, but an energy, a charge, an atmosphere, a kind of magnetism that strikes the receptive reader from the first paragraph. Unless the critic adopts a hard, sceptical stance, the relationship Alice Bailey and DK had is not easily refuted on the grounds that telepathy does not exist. Evidence supporting the existence of telepathic abilities can be found in numerous studies.[15] Alice Bailey was one of a cohort of those born with this unique ability, and she came to deploy it not in locating missing objects in obscure places, but in world service oriented to human and planetary betterment. This distinction renders hers a higher telepathy.

Alice was far from content to find herself with such a talent. After taking down those early communications, she grew apprehensive, concerned she might go crazy. She couldn't afford to lose her mind. She had three daughters to care for. When she told the Tibetan, he suggested she discuss the matter with her own master Koot Hoomi. She did, and he informed her that she was in no danger, physically or mentally, and that the work would be of great value.[16] He added he was the one who had suggested the arrangement. Persuaded, Alice agreed to continue.

In the months that followed, she took down the early chapters of *Initiation, Human and Solar*, which comprise a chapter of introductory remarks on Theosophical metaphysics; a detailed definition of Initiation; and an outline of the work of the Hierarchy. She also took down at least one section in *A Treatise on Cosmic Fire*.[17]

From the outset, this fresh outpouring of the Ageless Wisdom carries an authoritative tone. The writing is instructional, explicit and matter-of-fact, with diagrams, charts, and step-by-step explanations. The works read more like a student's textbook. There is not one ounce of poetic or flowery language. Although the early writing taken down and then typed up by Alice Bailey was Edwardian in style. An original manuscript of *Letters on Occult Meditation* that has recently come to light reveals a marked difference to the final version later published, demonstrating extensive editing and revising. The original version also includes personal notes to Alice Bailey herself which were redacted prior to publication.[18]

In the nineteen chapters of *Initiation, Human and Solar*, in telepathic rapport with Alice Bailey, the Tibetan went on to lay down the foundations of his teachings, developed and extrapolated in future works, including a depiction of disciples on the probationary path, rules along the way, and the initiations that would put them in closer contact with the Hierarchy:

 A disciple is one who above all else is pledged to do three things:-
To serve humanity.
To co-operate with the plan of the Great Ones as he sees it and as best he may.
To develop the powers of the Ego [soul], to expand his consciousness until he can function on the three planes in the three worlds...[19]

FOUR CHAPTERS OF INITIATION, *Human and Solar* are devoted to the Spiritual Hierarchy, presented as personifications of spiritual energies in the form of abstracted beings, similar to the way the Greek Gods have been aligned in astrology with the planets, yet without their foibles and the associated myths. There's the Master Jupiter, Regent of India, residing in the Nilgherry Hills in Southern India; Master Morya, an Eastern adept and Rajput Prince holding an authoritative position in Indian affairs; Koot Hoomi, of Kashmiri origins with a sound British university education who resides with Morya at Shigatse in the Himalayas; the Master Jesus, currently living in a Syrian body; Djwhal Khul, the Tibetan, the 'Messenger of the Masters'; Rakoczi the Hungarian who at one time or other was the Comte de St Germain, Roger Bacon and Francis Bacon; and the Master Hilarion who was one time Paul of Tarsus.[20]
Each of the Masters works with humanity to help foster the evolution of consciousness.

Alice Bailey invites the reader to only adopt that which invokes inner resonance and not to regard the teachings as dogma, yet the existence of the Spiritual Hierarchy is the one aspect of her opus that she, just like most if not all Theosophists, regards as unequivocal truth, and she is emphatic about it. The Spiritual Hierarchy is foundational for Theosophists. Without at least a provisional acceptance of this group of advanced beings, even if only metaphorically, the entire esoteric current is devoid of meaning and purpose.

Perhaps there is little if anything in this first volume produced by Alice Bailey that is entirely new to Theosophy. The work is set out as though introducing students to esotericism for the first time. The instructional tone alone is a claim to higher authority. Wherever the words came from, Alice Bailey resonated strongly with them. In discussing with her Arcane School students in 1944 the process she underwent each day, she says, 'After his mind and mine got into close rapport, I knew what he was thinking. I wonder if you have any idea what tension it is to take two hours dictation without losing the thread. I can't let myself relax for a minute.'[21]

Much controversy surrounds those of Alice Bailey's works composed in this fashion. She is accused of having a fabulous 'get out' clause, of infusing the Tibetan's thoughts with her own, muddying the purity, of being a complete fraud, of claim making to enhance her own spiritual status. Eminent psychiatrist Carl Jung, who never met Alice Bailey, believed the Tibetan to be a manifestation of her higher self.[22] Alice Bailey refutes the 'higher self' idea emphatically, citing the gift of incense as concrete proof of her special relationship with the Tibetan. In his assessment, Carl Jung also inadvertently credits Alice Bailey with exceptional wisdom.

A TEAPOT TEMPEST

*I*t was the summer of 1919. The Treaty of Versailles had been signed on June 28 in the aftermath of the 'Great War'. The film industry in Hollywood was burgeoning after Charlie Chaplin joined forces with Mary Pickford, Douglas Fairbanks and D. W. Griffith to create the United Artists Corporation. A new era of optimism, hope and booming wealth was in the making. Science and technology were advancing at a rapid rate and there was a prevailing sense of transition from the old to the new in the zeitgeist. Against this backdrop of optimism in Hollywood, Krotona was in considerable difficulty.

A shadow of debt had been hanging over the institute for some years prior to Alice's arrival. By 1917, the balance of debt was $25,000, the equivalent of about $600,000 today. That same year, an additional mortgage of $17,000 was incurred through the donation of an adjoining property, increasing the total debt in today's money to a figure approaching a million dollars.[1] The debt, and the challenges of finding and agreeing on a solution, had reached crisis proportions in 1919, when Foster Bailey and Alice Evans took up key organizational roles.

It is only possible to speculate as to how or why both Foster and Alice were appointed these roles. From the time Alice met

Foster and began writing for the Tibetan, there is no record of the thoughts the pair held concerning the running of the Theosophical Society, or their interactions with various key figures who enjoyed positions of organisational power. A whole six months at least of talking and imagining a vision for organisational change had taken place between the couple and their allies, as they grew closer to positions of influence.

An indication of Alice's involvement at Krotona, and an insight into the path she was poised to take in Theosophy, can be found in a well-attended public class she gave each week in that summer of 1919 on Bible study from an occult standpoint. The class was held in the Temple at Krotona. Alice held a second class of some fifteen attendees at her home to discuss the esoteric side of Christianity. 'The Christian field is still virgin soil for Theosophy, and many are asking for "meat" instead of "milk".'[2] The article in *The Messenger* announcing these classes, also refers to the recent formation of a Christian Lodge by Annie Besant in England.[3] Alice Evans had been appointed as a divisional lecturer sometime before October 1918.[4] She was also a member of the Order of Field Servers, launched 10 March 1919 as a training school offering correspondence courses and awarding diplomas. She delivered two courses: Reincarnation, and Homiletics, or the art of writing and preaching.[5]

There is no mention of Foster Bailey in any edition of the sectional magazine from June 1918 onwards until April 1919, when both Alice Evans and Lieutenant Foster Bailey were appointed as tellers by Albert Warrington to oversee the count of the TS presidential vote. Warrington was re-appointed.[6] It could be surmised that it was through Alice Evans' standing at Krotona that Foster was able to ascend so rapidly as to be considered acceptable for a core administrative position. Given she had been writing for the Tibetan for many months and had in her possession a fresh outpouring of the Ageless Wisdom, it would not be beyond the bounds of reason to suggest she harboured ambitious plans, and Foster was something of an instrument.

On 14 July 1919, Foster was employed as national secretary upon the resignation of Craig P. Garman in June.[7] On 28 August 1919, a meeting of the Board of Trustees temporarily appointed Mrs Alice Evans as editor of the *Messenger* due to May S. Rogers' absence while she was on extended travels in Australia. For these duties, both Foster and Alice earned ten dollars a week.[8] At the same meeting, their ally Dr Woodruff Sheppard was appointed as publicity director.[9] In a Board of Trustees meeting held on 6 September 1919, the appointment of Louis W. Rogers as vice-president was confirmed.

Between them, Foster, Alice and Woodruff were in charge of much of the running of the administration. They were also close friends with Krotona founder Albert Warrington, placing them, or so they thought, in the perfect position to affect organisational change to deal with the debt problem and limit the power of the Esoteric Section in one fell swoop.

An interesting confluence can be found in the discord brewing at that time and an aforementioned letter published in *Letters on Occult Meditation*. On the 25 September 1919, Alice took down a letter dictated by the Tibetan, appearing in a chapter titled 'Dangers to be avoided in Meditation'.[10] The letter concerns the powers and methods of the Dark Brotherhood, those who persistently exalt the concrete mind and refuse entry of the higher. The result is over-development in one direction, and gulfs and gaps where virtues should be. The Dark Brotherhood:

 recognises no unity with his species, only seeing in them people to be exploited for the furtherance of his own ends...They respect no person, they regard all men as fair prey, they use everyone to get their own way enforced, and by fair means or foul they seek to break down all opposition and for the personal self acquire that which they desire.[11]

THE DARK BROTHERHOOD will masquerade as agents of the light, and they will retard the progress of humanity. The letter goes on to explain that the way to avoid the destructive power of the Dark Brotherhood is to deal with one's weak spots, remain pure and clean on physical, emotional and mental levels, lead a balanced life with relaxation and play, get plenty of sleep and exercise, and tackle personal fear because fear opens the door to evil.[12]

It all seems like sound common sense, but the comment on fear appears more pointed. It is as though this part of the communication was directed straight at Alice herself who, ever since that awful day in Quetta, had suffered from gripping fear, fear compounded by the violence she suffered at the hands of Walter Evans. An occultist and a mystic, Alice Bailey was especially sensitive to the need to ward off the Dark Brotherhood which, if taken subtly, can be seen in various ways to have thwarted her throughout her life, a 'Brotherhood' which would go on to thwart the progress of her teachings.

First impressions of the TS administration from a perhaps naïve and inexperienced if scheming Alice were positive, and she says she found much cooperation among the office staff, but the harmony soon proved superficial. When it comes to organisations run by a small committee, new members would be well advised not to rock the boat no matter how obvious, to them, an improvement appears to be. The Theosophical Society was not immune to the indomitable resistance to change of longstanding committee members, many of whom held high positions in the Esoteric Section, and when it came to organisational management, restraint does not appear to be evident in Foster's then youthful personality. Within a few months of taking office, and possibly before, he had a plan for how the Theosophical Society in America should be run, and it wasn't in accordance with the 'reactionary' status quo. It was a plan shared by Alice. The difficulty for them from the outset, was the appointment of Louis Rogers as vice-president.

In Foster and Alice's view, the debt crisis would be solved through a fundamental change in organisational structure that would restrict the power the Esoteric Section had over the society. Theosophical lodges were meant to have local autonomy, but through the placement of key members in the Esoteric Section, Annie Besant and the leaders at Adyar had full organisational control. The Theosophical Society had been founded on the notion of universal brotherhood, but what both Alice and Foster saw instead was an organisation fixated on founding lodges and increasing membership, a strategy they argued should be stopped. Others, Louis Rogers among them, didn't share their view. Not least because an increase in membership would go some way towards resolving Krotona's enormous mortgage debt.

For Alice, the trajectory of sectarianism evident in the Esoteric Section's control of the administration and the TS membership was anathema to all she stood for. After her experiences of common humanity in soldiers' homes and at the sardine cannery, along with all of the support she had received from neighbours and strangers alike during her Walter Evans' years, she saw the Theosophical principle of universal brotherhood as paramount. She also wished to curb the power and authority of Annie Besant in Adyar, India, which she plainly took issue with after her humiliation in the Shrine room. Her motives remain hidden, but at the time Alice Bailey became editor of *The Messenger*, she had been writing for the Tibetan for at least ten months. She knew she was a disciple and the scribe of the second outpouring of the Ageless Wisdom, and by then, she would have been thinking hard about ways to make this known and implemented in some form. A takeover of the Theosophical Society may well have been more than a passing thought.

Realising they faced considerable opposition, Alice and Foster and their allies banded together. Alice remarks that she became caught up in a conflict of interest between her own sense of loyalty and affiliation to her personal friends in the Esoteric Section who were determined to retain the status quo, and her firm adherence to her democratic vision for change, a view Foster shared.[13]

It soon became clear that a schism was fomenting, and the Theosophical Society had already had its share. In 1884, the Theosophical Lodge in London split into two branches, one led by Alfred Sinnett, who was loyal to Blavatsky, the other by Anna Kingsford, who went on to found the Hermetic Society. About the same time, conflict arose between founders, Blavatsky and Olcott, which was only resolved upon Blavatsky's death. Ten years later, in 1894, Annie Besant and Henry Steel Olcott accused co-founder William Quan Judge of forging a letter he claimed to have received from a Master. His accusers decided he had forged 'the Mahatma letter' in a 'successful bid to compete with Annie Besant for leadership of the Esoteric Section', a matter later highlighted by feminist commentators on trends in the TS.[14] A large number of the American section took Judge's side and seceded to form 'The Theosophical Society in America'. Judge died in 1896, and leadership went initially to journalist and writer Ernest Temple Hargrove. He was promptly ousted by Spiritualist and sharp-minded visionary Katherine Augusta Westcott Tingley who then renamed the society the Universal Brotherhood and Theosophical Society. In 1898, Hargrove went to New York to form The Theosophical Society in America. In 1900 Tingley moved the society headquarters to Point Loma, near San Diego, where she established a utopian community. Meanwhile, Warrington, with the approval of Besant, relocated the Besant line of the Theosophical Society's headquarters from Chicago to Pasadena in

1912, with a view to creating a utopian society based on a vision of her associate Charles Webster Leadbeater. Another schism occurred when head of the German headquarters, Rudolph Steiner, broke away in 1912-13, taking his own interpretations of Theosophy with him in the form of Anthropomorphism.[15] Disputes over procedures, and power struggles beset many organisations, and although the Theosophical Society was riven with them for several decades, they were an indication of the intensity of feeling of many a member and of a strong attachment to Theosophy, borne out in the numerous lodges founded and splinter groups formed, many of which thrived and continue to exist to this day.[16]

Back at Krotona, Alice could not have anticipated the scale of the confrontation that was fomenting. What is made apparent by the tone of her own words on the matter in her autobiography, is how upsetting she found the fracas. In her own account, she displays unwavering and uncritical support of Foster, who led the call for change. Had he, had they both not agitated in this fashion, the course of Alice's future life might have been very different.

The resistance to change proved fierce and unyielding. In the face of what she perceived was a form of absolute rule by a bunch of self-inflated initiates, Alice decided she had 'wandered into another sect', seeing in the organization of the Theosophical Society reflections of orthodox Christianity. She was profoundly disappointed.[17]

Through letters and opinion pieces, the battle for organisational control found its way into the sectional magazine, there for the whole membership to see. Members began resigning. The split became so serious, Foster Bailey cabled Annie Besant to inform her that if the Esoteric Section didn't stop dominating the administration, the ES 'would soon be under very serious attack'.[18] What he meant by that remark is unclear.

In response, Annie Besant sent in Bahman Pestonji Wadia, who was at the time in America as Indian delegate to the

International Industrial Conference and also on a tour of the Theosophical Society lodges.

Bahman Pestonji Wadia (1881-1958) was an influential co-worker and editor of the society's international magazine *The Theosophist*. He hailed from a family of wealthy shipbuilders from Surat, north of Mumbai. As a young man, he was sent by his father to Britain to work in a large textile firm. The experience was short-lived. Soon after his return to India, his father died, and Wadia found himself in charge of the family's textile business. He was nineteen. In Bombay, he had met Blavatsky, and he joined the Bombay Lodge in 1903 when he was twenty-two. A year later, he sold the family business and used the proceeds to devote his life to Theosophy. He was quickly appointed key roles in the organisation, first as sub-editor of periodicals, then as personal assistant to Theosophical Society founder Colonel Olcott. Upon Olcott's death, he became personal assistant to Annie Besant, who took over as president in 1907. Wadia moved from Bombay to Adyar, and there became manager of the Theosophical Society's publishing house and assistant editor of *The Theosophist*. He also joined Besant in India's home rule movement and became involved in workers' rights.[19]

Wadia was charged with assessing the situation at Krotona and intervening. He arrived around Christmas 1919. Official meetings were held. On the administrative side were Foster, Alice, Woodruff Shepherd and their supporters, and on the side of the Esoteric Section were prominent Theosophist Marie Poutz, Albert Warrington, and theirs. The meetings descended into full-blown rows. Wadia had been brought in to find a resolution, but rather than mediate between the progressives at the headquarters and the reactionary members of the Esoteric Section, he set about 'stirring up trouble'.[20] At first, Alice and Foster found Wadia sincere, and they collaborated with him believing they had a new ally. They did so in the hope that the society would swing back to its principle of universal brotherhood. He, however, appeared to have his own agenda, one later revealed to them in 1921, when he made his own bid for leadership.

At Krotona, the factional politics continued to worsen. Foster and Dr Shepherd formed the Towards Democracy League, the TDL, hoping to gain membership support. The League produced pamphlets to circulate their beliefs. They did so with the whole-hearted support of Wadia, who at that time also advocated greater freedom for members.

It was at this juncture, amidst all of the fury and upset, that Alice made a defining decision. In the light of the reaction she had received from a key member of the Esoteric Section when she revealed she had been in communication with one of the Masters, she might have withheld her early writings and consid-ered her options. Instead, during that Christmas of 1919, she handed Wadia a manuscript she had written on behalf of the Tibetan.

Was it blind enthusiasm or an eagerness for recognition that caused Alice to hand a copy of her writings to Wadia? Or was she throwing down the gauntlet, testing a reactionary Theo-sophical Society with this new outpouring of the wisdom? Whatever the motive, the act would have major consequences. When she showed him what she had written, he 'became very excited', telling her he would 'publish anything that "came from that source"'.[21] He kept his word. In the February 1921 edition of *The Theosophist* the first two chapters of *Initiation, Human and Solar* appeared, and in March of that year, chapter eight appeared.[22] In the September 1921 and November 1921 issues, a piece titled, 'Cosmic and Systemic Law' was also published in two parts. These thirty-two pages later appeared in her seminal text *A Treatise on Cosmic Fire*, first published in 1925.[23] Alice Bailey makes no mention of handing or sending Wadia a later manuscript and implies in her autobiography not to have done so. It appears likely she gave him this additional material that Christmas 1919.

The pieces were not well received. As Alice Bailey puts it,

'then the usual theosophical jealousy and reactionary attitude appeared and no more was printed'.[24]

From that moment, Alice found she had a key competitor, one she didn't in the least care for: Charles Webster Leadbeater.

Formerly a Church of England priest, Leadbeater (1854-1934) is a controversial figure in Theosophical Society history. Born in Stockport, Cheshire, to a railway contractor's clerk, Leadbeater was ordained in 1879 and soon developed an interest in Spiritualism. He joined the Theosophical Society in 1883 and arrived in Adyar a year later. He claimed clairvoyant abilities and became one of the society's prominent lecturers, touring Europe, America and Australia. He was a close associate of Annie Besant, and for many years, he was the Theosophical Society's second in command.

Two decades on from his arrival in India, a shadow hung over the prominent figure. Allegations of the sexual abuse of boys in his care were brought before a London court it 1906. A further scandal broke in 1909 when Leadbeater homed in on another Indian boy in the grounds of Adyar and, using his clairvoyant abilities, pronounced him the New World Teacher, the second coming of the Christ.

Leadbeater and Annie Besant named the boy Jiddu Krishnamurti (1895-1986) and proceeded to prepare him for his future as the World Teacher, overshadowed by the Christ. In preparation, the Order of the Star in the East was formed in 1911 with the young Krishnamurti as the head, an organisation that attracted a membership of around 100,000 before it was dissolved in 1929.[25] The activities of Besant and Leadbeater regarding Krishnamurti resulted in widespread condemnation and ridicule within the society.

In 1912, Krishnamurti's father brought a custody case against Leadbeater alleging sexual abuse, which was later dropped. Leadbeater then moved to Sydney, Australia, where he remained a leading figure in the Theosophical Society. He also joined forces with James Ingall Wedgwood in forming the Liberal

Catholic Church. He then fell under further police investigations in 1917 and again in 1922 based on the suspicions and observations of inappropriate sexual behaviour involving boys, voiced by Honorary General Secretary of the Theosophical Society of Australia Mr T H Martyn and his wife, in whose house Leadbeater had been residing. The matter came to a head in 1921, when Mr Martyn wrote a private letter to Annie Besant, which was later made public, questioning whether Leadbeater should be deemed an Initiate in the light of his 'sexual irregularity'.[26]

These scandals must have greatly affected Alice. Perhaps they were one source of motivation regarding her wish to democratise the administration, and wrest power from Annie Besant as the Outer Head of the American Section, and place organisational control in the hands of the rank and file.

Leadbeater was a prolific writer whom Alice Bailey held in low regard. His *Man, Whence, How and Whither*, published in 1913, proved to her 'the basic untrustworthiness of what he wrote':

 It is a book that outlines the future and the work of the Hierarchy of the future, and the curious and arresting thing to me was that the majority of the people slated to hold high office in the Hierarchy and in the future coming civilisation were all Mr Leadbeater's personal friends. I knew some of these people – worthy, kind, and mediocre, none of them intellectual giants and most of them completely unimportant.[27]

ALICE BAILEY HAD good reason not to like her rival. In his biography of Alice Bailey, *The Bailey Inheritance*, loyal admirer and follower of her teachings Sir John Rollo Norman Blair Sinclair

(1928-1990), 9th Baronet of Caithness, tells the story of how Lead-beater plagiarised Alice Bailey's first book. Leadbeater's *The Masters and the Path* (1925) was published four years after those first chapters appeared in *The Theosophist* and three years after *Initiation, Human and Solar* was published in 1922, and appears to derive its inspiration from Alice Bailey's book. When her chapters were published in *The Theosophist*, this may well have provided Leadbeater, who was by then living in Sydney, Australia, with an opportunity to plagiarise the work. While Theosophical purists would later denounce Alice Bailey and refuse to read her writing, officially criticizing her for falsely claiming to be in communication with the Tibetan, Leadbeater was known to be quietly purchasing his copy of Alice Bailey's writings the moment they were published. He made enthusiastic comments about them in private, although he never publicly commended her work.[28]

Sinclair's suggestion that Leadbeater had taken Alice Bailey's ideas and re-worked them to form the basis of his own book remains open to speculation. Perhaps neither party plagiarised the other. The version of the matter that persists, even among academics, is that it was Alice Bailey who plagiarised Lead-beater. Scholar of Western Esotericism Olav Hammer's *Claiming Knowledge*, an epistemological study of Theosophy published in 2001, adopts this view.[29]

An alternative way to view the controversy is to acknowl-edge that all ideas are in some fashion shared or derivative, that esoteric knowledge involves the re-working and re-presentation of an Ageless Wisdom to suit a different audience, and that from wherever Alice Bailey drew her ideas, her real contribution was in making them available to all and not a select few, and in a fashion that was astonishingly detailed and exhaustive, as noted by author and Theosophist Kurt Leland.[30]

Some Theosophists claim Alice Bailey plagiarised material only available to those Theosophists in the Esoteric Section. The argument follows that since the material in question has not been made public, allegations of plagiarism have been impossible to assess. Even a cursory reading of the Strictly Private *Esoteric School of Theosophy Instructions* by Helena Blavatsky soon dispels the accusations. Without giving out any secret occult knowledge, this volume contains numerous diagrams and tables of correspondences drawing heavily on Eastern mysticism, tables pertaining to the planets, metals, days of the week, parts of the body, colours, forces, planes and principles, all in series of seven. The work includes a discussion of astrology, theurgy, raja yoga and Neoplatonism. Each of the three longer instructions are prefaced by discursive preambles on the nature of occult knowledge. There is an interesting presentation of the pineal and pituitary glands and how they relate to Manas and Buddhi and the Chakras in general, and another on the Antahkarana, the imaginary bridge between the human ego (soul) and the divine. The work concludes with three further sets of instructions amounting to a lengthy list of paragraph-long definitions of key terms, such as various types of consciousness.

Reading this volume alongside Alice Bailey's *Initiation, Human and Solar*, it is abundantly clear they are entirely different books. Alice Bailey's theme is initiation. She initially presents a diagram labelled the 'Constitution of Man' which is a re-presentation of core Theosophical ideas, and then follows on with a detailed account of the Hierarchy, the nature of discipleship and the path of initiation. Absent is the Vedic language, the historical detail, the justifications and the somewhat meandering discussions evident in Blavatsky's book. Instead, the writing is taut, on point and directive. Should there be any particular points of similarity, it would be little wonder since both books arise out of the same current of esoteric thought.

On the second page of the first chapter of *Initiation, Human and Solar*, and given to Wadia to include in *The Theosophist*, Alice Bailey writes:

In these days of the shattering of the old form and the building of the new, adaptability is needed. We must avert the danger of crystallisation through pliability and expansion. The "old order changeth", but primarily it is a change of dimension and of aspect, and not of material or of foundation. The fundamentals have always been true. To each generation is given the part of conserving the essential features of the old and beloved form, but also of wisely expanding and enriching it. Each cycle must add the gain of further research and scientific endeavour, and subtract that which is worn out and of no value. Each age must build in the product and triumphs of its period, and abstract the accretions of the past that would dim and blur the outline. Above all, to each generation is given the joy of demonstrating the strength of the old foundations, and the opportunity to build upon these foundations a structure that will meet the needs of the inner evolving life.[31]

IN THE LIGHT of this scarcely veiled statement of intention, Alice had given Wadia to publish in the Theosophical Society's key magazine an announcement that there was a new outpouring of Theosophy on its way, and she was the person who would scribe it. It was an act of defiance, one in the eye of the Esoteric Section, submitted at a critical juncture when she might have thought the campaign to democratise the TS would win favour.

The negative reactions she received were hardly surprising and should also be understood in the light of the regular content in *The Theosophist*. Besant wrote polemics on themes such as racism and slavery, and Wadia composed articles concerning organisational matters and the aims and objectives of the society.

Other contributors provided pieces on comparative religion and philosophy, world politics, psychology and second-hand discussions and summaries of Blavatsky's teachings. Alice Evan's pieces leap out at the reader. They are authoritative and clearly designed to represent a new outpouring of the Ageless Wisdom with or without the statement of intention. For orthodox members, this new material would have caused immediate offence. For them, the new teaching was composed by an upstart newcomer and troublemaker who clearly didn't know her place within the Theosophical Society hierarchy and couldn't possibly have been in telepathic rapport with the Tibetan because Besant and Leadbeater had not affirmed it to be true.

When Alice handed Wadia those chapters, she must have known the impact they would have. But she was not to know what lay ahead.

In February 1920, in her role as editor of *The Messenger*, Alice Evan's wrote 'A Vision of Krotona's Future', in which she explained to the membership in a measured and balanced fashion her vision for a more unified leadership, one centred at Krotona. To solve the financial issue and to streamline the organisation, she attempted to persuade the membership to vote in changes so that the Headquarters of the American Section could join forces with the Esoteric Section to form one overarching governing body. The Krotona headquarters would then maintain control of the American Section. The article was written to invite free and open discussion amongst members. Instead, it provoked a storm of vitriol.[32]

In a timely move, Albert Warrington resigned as president on 18 March 1920, a position he had held for eight years, stating he intended to join Annie Besant in India. He was replaced by Louis Rogers, who had served as vice president for the previous seven months.

Louis William Rogers (1859-1953) is a notable figure in the Theosophical movement. He started out as a teacher before becoming a public lecturer and then a prominent and strident railroad unionist and activist in the labour movement, becoming editor of a number of labour movement newspapers. He was active in the American Railway Union, rising to the organisation's executive board before he was sentenced to three months in jail for his involvement in the 1894 Pullman Strike.[33] He joined the TS in 1903 and quickly rose to eminence as a speaker and lecturer.[34]

The change of leadership did not bode well. Rogers made a formidable foe, and he was 'bitterly opposed' to Foster Bailey and the Towards Democracy League and had no qualms at all making his feelings known. Rogers was not alone in his view. In the April and May issues of *The Messenger,* a number of letters were published attacking the TDL. One, composed by lawyer and priest in the Liberal Catholic Church Robert Kelsey Walton, was especially cutting, accusing the League organisers of spreading misinformation and making a mockery of the very democracy they purportedly wished to institute.[35]

Attempts were made by various League members to defend themselves, but the tirade against them was unrelenting and little short of nasty, especially from the new president.

Foster Bailey was no match for Louis Rogers, a man well-versed in organisational battles. Shortly after his appointment, executing his new presidential powers, Rogers promptly threw Foster and Alice out of their roles. By June1920, Alice was no longer editor of *The Messenger,* Rogers announcing in that month's edition her replacement, long-term Krotona resident Mrs Grace Boughton; and Foster was replaced as national secretary by Betsey Jewett in the same month. Woodruff Sheppard was also dismissed.

Without an official post and the income to go with it, Foster continued with his campaign. Meanwhile, Rogers was filling *The Messenger* with venom. In the same issue of *The Messenger,* he states, 'The League seems to be one of the best jokes of the season. In one of the bulletins I am informed that at the bottom of my policies is the "separative instinct". Coming from the

League, that strikes me as being high-class wit. Nobody is so truly amusing as the unconscious humorist.'[36]

His sarcastic tone is indicative of the style of his relentless condemnations. 'It is a bit trying to remain silent under attack when the Section is being flooded with circulars of outrageous misrepresentation by would-be martyrs who have a grievance against the administration...'[37] Louis Rogers dominates the July issue of *The Messenger* in the build-up to the annual convention and launches a pre-convention attack on the League:

> There is no fairer way to judge a person or a league than by contrasting what is promised with what is afterward done. It is not strange that letters from T. S. members are reaching this office showing that they joined the T. D. League under the impression that it was something quite different from what it has proved to be. Nobody can lie blamed for joining it after reading the announcement it put out, but, in the light of what the League has since done, that announcement now sounds like some sinister joke. Probably never in the history of Theosophy in all countries has anybody or any organization been responsible for so much discord, in harmony and general destructiveness in so short a time as the League has accomplished. Lest we forget the fair promise with which it was launched, and which naturally led many earnest theosophists into it, let us read again its original declaration to the world. After referring to the importance of carrying out the ideas of the founders of the T. S., it says: "To this end, a band of harmonious and constructively inclined P. T. S. at Krotona are endeavouring to promote that brotherly tolerance which expresses itself through a spiritually democratic form of

government, and for this purpose have founded a
League, particulars of which are appended." Now
what has the League actually done? It has given out
a mass of absolute misinformation. It has attacked
the present administration without the slightest
effort to first ascertain the facts. It became the
champion of three dismissed officials, accepted
their tale of personal grievance and published their
version without making a single inquiry of any
member of the administration, or attempting to
verify anything told them by the offended trio. It
has published no corrections or apologies, and it
therefore stands today as the champion of
insurrectionists who defy constitutional methods,
for the procedure of the Board of Trustees was
strictly according to the laws of the Section. They
are charged in the By-laws with the duty of
appointing and removing the officials in question.
Had they been elective officers the case would be
wholly different. Their removal then, had it been
possible by some technicality, would have been an
abuse of power indeed. But as it is, the Trustees
merely discharged a duty imposed upon them by
law.[38]

By now Krotona's financial struggle was so severe it could
scarcely manage its debts. A move was afoot, instigated by
Rogers, to have the administrative headquarters moved to
Chicago and sell off Krotona. In the same issue of *The Messenger*,
Rogers sets forward his argument. The idea was pragmatic and
gained popular support.

Rather than concede defeat, Foster, a righteous thirty-two-
year old, took the TDL to the Chicago convention in July1920. He

grossly underestimated his opponent, pitting his wits against stalwart Rogers, a man of some sixty years who stood proud in his own power. In her autobiography, Alice Bailey is vague about the humiliation that ensued and states only that Mr Warrington and the Esoteric Section asserted control and were 'aggressively triumphant'. Accounts in the following months' issues of *The Messenger* tell a different story. When Foster took the stage and gave his presentation in support of the TDL's arguments and vision, he was publicly condemned. Alice and Foster returned to Krotona defeated. Rogers persisted with his antagonism, resorting to ridicule in the September issue of *The Messenger* and calling the dispute a 'teapot tempest'.[39]

The tribulations didn't end there. Rogers tried to have Foster, who still lived in a tent, evicted from Krotona grounds. Foster cabled Annie Besant who stopped the eviction. Meanwhile Foster attempted to have a copy of the conference proceedings sent to Annie Besant so that she could see for herself what had taken place, but Louis Rogers blocked the move claiming it would be too expensive as there were around eight hundred pages of transcripts. Rogers then swiftly moved the administration from Krotona to Chicago in that same month.[40]

Most of the fallout from the failed TDL bid fell on Foster, but unfortunately for Alice Bailey, she had garnered a formidable enemy and her reputation within the Theosophical Society suffered.

During the course of the summer of 1920, throughout the build-up and in the aftermath of the saga, Alice composed the rest of the letters in *Letters on Occult Meditation*, and as the drama peaked, she was scribing the rest of the chapter on the dangers of meditation. The advice she received during this period would have been sorely needed. With Rogers firmly in the seat of power, the situation for Alice was proving an enormous strain. On 18 June 1920, jobless and home alone, she received a direct message from the Tibetan:

And, may I suggest to you one thing? All care and anxiety is based primarily on selfish motive. You fear further pain, you shrink from further sad experience. It is not thus that the goal is reached; it is reached by the path of renunciation...Should lying tongues take action, fear not, but forge ahead...I say no more. I but desire that you do not dissipate needless force in vain imaginings, feverish speculations and troubled expectations.[41]

THOSE WORDS MUST HAVE BEEN of great comfort. It is not clear if Alice had also been ousted from her lecturer and teacher positions, or when she stopped running the Krotona café, but at this juncture, Foster and Alice had no income, and she had three daughters to care for. Alice Bailey states on the day they appraised their situation, their joint finances amounted to $1.85, or $24 in today's money. There were bills and rent to pay. At that time, Alice received nothing from Britain.[42]

The future was uncertain, their prospects not good, but in the days that followed an anonymous donor left some cash in an envelope on her doorstep, and Foster was offered a position as secretary at the Theosophical Association of New York, an unofficial, independent organization that separated from the Theosophical Society in 1899 around the time of Katherine Tingley's succession. He accepted the post, and within days they prepared to move across America.[43]

BREAKING AWAY

*T*he word 'respectable' best describes Alice Bailey's moral outlook. After the Leadbeater scandals, which must have impacted her sensibilities, she was enormously concerned that occultism should not be brought into disrepute by the behaviour of its proponents. Which was why, through all the tribulations back at Krotona, Foster Bailey had remained living in his tent. To avert 'dirty gossip', Alice had living with her an elderly and loyal friend, Augusta Craig, affectionately called Craigie, a woman 'rippling with wit and mentality'.[1] So loyal was she that, despite the attentions of many an admirer, Craigie went on to stay with Alice's family until she grew too old to do so.

A devoted stepfather from the first, Foster regularly visited the house in Beachwood Drive and formed close bonds with little Dorothy, Mildred and Ellison. The girls adored him. To them, he was everything Walter wasn't, and he brought them up as his own. Dorothy was nine when they met and Ellison just five. Until he came on the scene, the girls had known only hardship and poverty. 'I lived once for three weeks on tea (without milk or sugar) and dry bread so that my three children could have what was essential to eat.'[2] The girls must have all carried somewhere deep down unhappy memories of the violence their mother endured. Foster might have felt to them a liberation. Through his new appointment in New York, the lives of those three little girls and their mother were about to undergo a fresh and exciting transformation.

In late 1920, leaving Alice and the girls behind, Foster went to New York and took up lodgings near the Theosophical Society of New York's offices on Broadway.

The association was founded in 1899 by Dr J. H. Salisbury, Donald Nicholson, and philosopher and writer Harold Waldwin Percival. The men were supporters of the late William Quan Judge, and they established the association in reaction against Katherine Tingley when she took over from Ernest Hargrove as president of the Theosophical Society in America.[3] Born in Barbados to a plantation owner, Percival discovered Theosophy in 1892. After Judge's death, Percival also went on to found the Theosophical Publishing Company of New York and through it, he became a major writer and publisher of theosophical literature. The association launched its own journal, *The Word*, in 1904. This was edited by Percival to its last issue in September 1917.[4]

In 1920, the president of the association was financier Mr Ernest Salisbury Suffern (1880-1975), son of Edward Lee Suffern (1845-1925) and Alice de Reimer Adams (1848-1923) of Boston, Massachusetts.[5] Ernest Suffern was a descendant of Rockland County Judge John Suffern, in whose name the village of Suffern, New York, was founded in 1796.[6] A man of considerable wealth, Ernest Suffern not only secured Foster his job as secretary with a salary of three hundred dollars a month, a figure far in excess of the ten dollars a month Foster and Alice had each received at Krotona, but he also purchased a house for the couple in Ridgefield Park, a small town of leafy streets and large suburban houses, across the Hudson River in New Jersey.[7]

As president of the association, Mr Suffern would have known the troubles Alice and Foster had been having at Krotona. He would have been a recipient of *The Messenger*.

Perhaps he had attended the Chicago conference and witnessed for himself the public humiliation. He would have known of Foster's skills in the capacity of secretary and of his belief in the principles of democracy when it came to organisational management. It appears Mr Suffern had his own agenda in appointing Foster. Concerned for the reputation of the Theosophical Society, Suffern later tried to persuade Mrs Besant to act to preserve the organisation's name, and in a letter to her dated 25 April 1922, he expresses his disappointment that she had recommended he end his association with the Esoteric Section.[8] This rejection would have been in part because in 1921 Suffern complained openly that longer notice had not been given to society members to allow time to nominate independent candidates in the forthcoming presidential election. He also sent out a lengthy appeal to the members of the American section of the Theosophical Society, calling for administrative reform. TS president Louis Rogers responded to the appeal in a letter published in the April edition of *The Messenger*, quashing the matter.[9] Given his own desire for reform, and as president of a breakaway group, Suffern would have seen in Foster an opportunity. He clearly believed in the protagonists, pitied them and threw his own cap into the ring. Whatever Mr Suffern's motives, Foster and Alice had a new ally.

At the end of 1920, once he was settled in his work, Foster sent for Alice. Leaving her children in the care of Craigie, she made the long journey by train across America and stayed in an apartment in Yonkers, not far from Foster's lodgings. On 14 March 1921, the couple went to City Hall and procured a marriage license. They married at once and returned to the office to work that afternoon. There was not an iota of romance in the act. One commentator notes their marriage was rumoured to be unconsummated, a 'marriage blanc' based not on passion but companionship. Whether true or not cannot be known.[10] They might each have had their various reasons to form a marriage based on a shared vision rather than romantic love. Foster had piloted an airplane that crashed, and he had also suffered from exposure to mustard gas.[11] Rather than return to his former law career, he chose to forge a life in theosophy. Alice had been subject to years of emotional, mental and physical violence, had endured traumatic childbirth, and her health had never been good. Romance was probably the last thing on her mind. What is clear is they remained married for nearly thirty years and on the face of it were steadfastly loyal to one another in every respect.

Consummation or not, in the initial excitement of married life, the newly wedded couple were busy creating a new home for themselves and the children, setting about furnishing the premises in Ridgefield Park. While his new wife was occupied making curtains and stocking the house with necessities – most of which Ernest Suffern provided – Foster headed west to collect the children. When he returned, exhausted after the long train journey there and back, the Bailey family began their new lives.

The 1920s was an exciting time to be in New York, a city of manufacturing, commerce and culture, with a large migrant population. The American economy was booming. It was a decade marked by consumption. Cars replaced horses and buggies on the streets. Women were increasingly employed in white-collar jobs and the 19th Amendment to the constitution had given them the vote. The drudgery of housework was easing with inventions such as the washing machine. In fashion, the conservative Edwardian-style of dress, with its high collars, tight bodices, mutton sleeves and long flowing skirts, was fast replaced with apparel that hung loose from the shoulders and dropped at the waist, reaching down only as far as the mid-calf, if that. It was the age of the cloche hat and flapper dress. Hair was no longer kept long and tied high in a bun. It was typically cut short and cropped at the neck in an angular bob. Suddenly, women's bodies were liberated from corsetry. They began to wear trousers. These changes in fashion reflected shifting atti-tudes to women in society. Women smoked, drank and danced. Jazz clubs opened and, along with dance halls and speakeasies, provided an outlet for rebellion. The 1920s in America was an era marked by Prohibition on the one hand, and the liberation of inhibition on the other.

Alice watched on with concern. She knew the Victorian era with its restrictive attitudes to sex had been repressive, but she thought the scales were tipping too far the other way. She took a high moral stance on personal conduct, one in concordance with her own strict and pious upbringing. Her daughters attended the local public school, which was co-educational, something else she was forced to come to terms with.

Meanwhile, the campaign to reform the Theosophical Society continued. In an attempt to persuade the membership, Foster organised the Committee of 1400, which 'pledged to endeavour to swing the Theosophical Society to its original principles', and remove what amounted to a theocracy based in India. As far as Alice Bailey was concerned:

 It was a fight between a selective, isolationist, superior group who regarded themselves as wiser and more spiritual than the rest of the membership, and those who loved their fellow-men, who believed in progress and the universality of truth.'[12]

ALICE TOOK ON A SUPPORTIVE ROLE. Foster was at the helm. His frustration was keenly felt and while many others shared his desire for change, including Ernest Suffern, through his previous role at Krotona, Foster positioned himself at the vanguard of the campaign for change.

At home behind the scenes, ensconced in her domestic life, Alice remained part of the campaign. She backed Foster's efforts, if not in some fashion helping to drive them. For her, the soul of the Theosophical Society's organisation needed saving from the foibles of its personality. It was a belief that attracted and continues to attract the wrath of many an orthodox Theosophist.

Wadia continued to be supportive, but it was then that Alice and Foster discovered he had a private agenda. It became apparent that he was using the Committee of 1400 to oust Rogers and take over the presidency for himself. 'Foster, however, had not organised in order to put into power a man who would represent the committee. The committee was organised to present the issue involved and the principles at stake to the membership of the T. S.'[13] When Wadia discovered Foster's position, he threatened to throw his weight behind a rival sectarian group, one that held to the belief that the last word on Theosophy was spoken by Blavatsky. It was a threat he soon fulfilled when he joined forces with the United Lodge of Theosophists.[14] This would have felt like a slap at Alice Bailey, who had previously been led to believe Wadia would publish anything she wrote. Those pieces which appeared in *The Theosophist* in 1921, would be it. Alice Bailey did not bear Wadia a grudge. In a November 1944 talk, she describes him as a 'very great disciple', but 'ambition got to him'.[15]

Evidence of Alice Bailey's desire to forge ahead with her own vision can be found in a lecture she gave to the members of the New York Theosophical Association on White Lotus Day in May 1921, and appearing in the March 1922 issue of *The Theosophist*, in which she presents the Theosophical movement from Blavatsky's era through to the then present, ending with:

 We have got the revelation that H.P.B. brought to us; we have got the explanations and interpretations that Mrs Besant has given us; and, with all that to aid us, surely you and I have got the intelligence and the willingness to go on with the work. We have to give out these truths, not only to a few intellectuals and to the Theosophical

students, but to the general public. The masses of
the people everywhere are crying out for what we
have to give, and now is our day and
opportunity.[16]

ABSENT FROM HER lecture was any mention of the Committee of
1400. 'Now is our day and opportunity' is a call to action,
implying that already, she was keen to advance with her own
projects and had no qualms announcing that desire.

By then, the campaign was over. In March 1921, Foster Bailey
was nominated for National President. He received six votes,
Ernest Suffern received sixty-two, and Mr Rogers enjoyed a large
majority, topping Suffern's with an additional two-thousand, a
clear indication the Committee of 1400 would never gain the
popular vote.[17]

Yet the need for reform was widely recognised, and Rogers
knew it. While he continued to discredit and dismiss Foster
Bailey's efforts, in his president's report in the April 1921 issue of
The Messenger, he went on to argue the case for reform following
the society's British system. In 1924, Krotona was sold and the
Esoteric Section moved to Ojai, California, where it remains to
this day. At Rogers' directive, the Theosophical headquarters
had relocated to Chicago, before then moving to Wheaton, Illinois in 1926, when a ten-acre plot of land was purchased. Under
Rogers, a publicity department and National Library were established, and membership increased from 3,500 – where it had
stood in 1913 after Warrington's first year in office – to an
impressive 8,700. In the light of all of these achievements, it
appears Rogers' animosity towards the Baileys was founded not
on petty mindedness, but on a powerful drive to improve the
conditions of the society, something he clearly achieved.[18]

These organisational changes were occurring at a time of
tremendous spiritual and psychic inquiry as the thinking public

searched for a new modern spirituality both in response to the devastation of the First World War and to a newly emerging optimism for the future, brought about in part by the deals brokered by the League of Nations. In the zeitgeist, there was a deeply held wish to break with the past in all its aspects. The Arts burgeoned. A new wave of authors including Aldous Huxley, Ernest Hemingway, Scott F. Fitzgerald, D. H. Lawrence, Edith Wharton and H. G. Wells, were composing and publishing their influential works.

In the Academy, influential mathematician turned meta-physician Alfred North Whitehead was poised to move to Harvard in 1924 after the success of his book, *The Concept of Nature*. A decade earlier in 1909, psychologist and philosopher William James had presented a series of Hibbert Lectures, published as *A Pluralistic Universe*, in which he discusses the interconnectedness of all existence, drawing on the philosophy of Gustav Fechner. Writer Evelyn Underhill released her seminal work on mystical experiences, *Mysticism: A Study of the Nature and Development of Man's Spiritual Consciousness* in 1911. These thinkers represented an emerging interest and scholarly inquiry into the subjective world of spiritual experience and metaphys-ical explanations of the universe. Professor of Philosophy at the University of Tubingen Dr Konstantin Oesterreich, a scholar influential in the field of psychical research, had even come out in 1921 with the claim that telekinesis and materialisations were facts.

On the popular front, the 1920s witnessed the publication of a plethora of books of varying quality on the topics of psychism, spirituality and the occult. The New Thought movement published the prolific output of inspirational self-help books by author Orison Swett Marden. In 1926, Arthur Conan Doyle released *The History of Spiritualism*. Christian mystic Edgar Cayce was arousing much popular and critical interest in his trance readings. Interest in Spiritualism was proliferating, and Harry

Houdini was kept busy attempting to disprove all claims of the existence of the paranormal.

There was a thirst for something fresh, convincing, all-encompassing, able to explain metaphysical realities, the meaning of life, the origins of the universe, the entire panoply of mystical and paranormal experiences. Sitting quietly at home in Ridgefield Park, Alice Bailey was fulfilling that need. The question would become how to present the fresh outpouring to the world in a way that avoided the difficulties she had found in the Theosophical Society, with all of its organisational infighting, elitism and exclusivity.

A TREATISE ON COSMIC FIRE

*W*ith all of the letters contained in *Letters on Occult Meditation* written—the last published letter was taken down on 7 November 1920—and the contents of *Initiation, Human and Solar* complete, Alice Bailey continued to tackle esoteric cosmology as the Tibetan turned his attention to the material that would become *A Treatise on Cosmic Fire*.

This work serves as the psychological key to Blavatsky's *The Secret Doctrine* and comprises 1,282 pages of pure esoteric thought. The work fulfils a prophecy made by Helena Blavatsky that 'in the 20th century a disciple would come who would give information concerning the three fires with which *The Secret Doctrine* deals: electric fire, solar fire and fire by friction'.[1] It is widely regarded as Alice Bailey's most impenetrable book. All of the DK teachings in the Bailey opus are underpinned by the Theosophical worldview this book contains, and it is impossible to grasp the full meaning and significance of the rest without venturing in. The table of contents alone is likely to puzzle, with chapters on different kinds of fire and motion, on various laws governing the universe, on 'manas' or mind, and the thought elementals. There are rules for magic, along with instructions on how to create 'thoughtforms'.

For those unfamiliar with the terrain, what is portrayed in all these pages constitutes a metaphysical theory of everything, one that sets out to explain the origins and purpose of the universe in a single unified whole. Reading *A Treatise on Cosmic Fire* generates a feeling of wonderment that soon gives way to mental strain as the intricacies of the cosmic scheme engage the reader in an astonishing process of intense visualisation.

From the perspective of the outsider, the cosmology contained within the treatise concerns the evolution of consciousness depicted using a range of metaphors. Each metaphor is itself a vast complex system. Whether wholly believing or not, the reader must expand their mind to embrace it. There is no requirement that the reader views these metaphors as truth. Metaphysics is always concerned with representations of reality. An inner reality that fosters a particular kind of awareness. For the agnostic, a suspension of disbelief, coupled with a willingness to engage the imagination and strive to comprehend may be enough to stimulate significant growth in consciousness.

The treatise is founded on the notion of correspondence, or the principle of relationships of similarity existing in various levels or parts of the universe: the macrocosm and the microcosm, the natural world and the inner spiritual world. Correspondence is a way of understanding through analogy, recognising similarities in structure in outwardly dissimilar groups of things.[2]

The cosmology in *A Treatise on Cosmic Fire* begins at the macrocosmic level with a controlling principle in the universe, a divine Builder or Creative Mind. 'The objective universe is but the product of some subjective mind.'[3] In Theosophical parlance, the treatise describes this mind as the solar Logos. The solar Logos is not to be confused with absolute reality, which is so far out of reach in this scheme it can scarcely be conceived.

The solar Logos is one of numerous evolving logoi in a vast cosmic hierarchy of being. It is the idea behind our solar system's sun. For this idea to find expression, it must blend with pre-existing intelligent substance. This blending of pure spirit and intelligent matter creates light, or objectivity, and so a sun is born, a physical sun, one that is also a symbol of consciousness.

Just as Christianity portrays God, the ultimate creator, his Son and the Holy Spirit as a divine trinity, the solar Logos is one of three aspects or features of manifestation. In other words, our solar Logos is but one aspect or face of a triune Logos. Following a re-working of Neoplatonic metaphysics, this triune Logos comprises will, wisdom and activity.[4]

Adopting a macrocosmic evolutionary point of view, before our solar Logos outpoured its energy (referred to in Theosophy as involution), the third aspect, that of activity, had a turn, and the only evolution which took place back then concerned matter itself.[5] In that manifestation of the third aspect of the Logos, matter was intelligent and evolving. In our current solar system, in this second round of evolution, our solar Logos has outpoured the second aspect, the energy of love-wisdom, our solar Logos representing the sum total of all states of consciousness within it.

If this were all there were to the treatise' overarching cosmo-logical framework, anyone with a measure of religious or spiri-tual understanding would find nothing befuddling. From here, things become complex.

In this esoteric presentation, human individuals are termed atoms, a somewhat fitting appellation when considered from the perspective of the cosmology:

 The goal for the evolution of the atom is self-consciousness as exemplified in the human kingdom. The goal for the evolution of man is group consciousness, as exemplified by a planetary Logos. The goal for the planetary Logos is God consciousness, as exemplified by the solar Logos.[6]

IN THE INTERDEPENDENT, interrelated scheme, the solar Logos cannot achieve its evolutionary goal except through humanity. It is up to each individual human atom to develop control of her thoughts, emotions and physical habits and appetites. A great weight of responsibility is suddenly imposed on all of us. We're charged with refining ourselves for the good of the whole, in the same way that Christianity invites us to follow in the footsteps of Jesus, or Buddhism invites us to follow the eight-fold path, or Islam the five pillars, all paths of purification and service to others.

An ordered or non-chaotic universe with a single evolutionary purpose must have some governing principles or laws that explain and direct the entire enfolding of consciousness back to its source. The supreme rule under the second solar Logos is the Law of Attraction and Repulsion and its keynote is love wisely.[7] Under this law, we exist as aspects of the subjective life of the solar Logos. The Logos thought, therefore *we* are. It is the law that governs our soul. The most obvious manifestation of this law in the animal kingdom is sex and sexual attraction. It concerns the way we are drawn towards or repulsed by each other. Love binds us together, hate pushes others away. In the one direction, it is a dynamic that creates opposition, in the other, unity.

Humanity exists within the energies of another evolving entity, the planetary Logos. Imagine the energy exhaled by our solar Logos swirling around its body, our solar system, and then settling into a complex system comprising seven vortices or whirlpools of energy. Each of these seven concentrations or centres of whirling energy is called a planetary scheme.

The evolutionary goal is simple, the attainment of a perfect harmony of unimpeded energy flow into and through the energy centres. The obstacles are many: us.

To complicate matters still further, our solar system is electrified by energy emanating from the cosmic mental plane.

While the energy centres, or chakras, depict foci of energy, the planes portray both levels of manifestation and stages of evolutionary progress. The planes are integral to Theosophical thinking. They are planes of achieved awareness, and there are seven in all. The first is a universal field of potential, waiting to take form. Each descending plane becomes denser, moving through gas and liquid, and arriving at the seventh, the physical plane of matter. Moving up the planes, the liquid plane is the plane of emotions, and the gaseous the mental.

The planes can also be thought of as vast rotating spheres.

Just as there exist chakras within chakras, so each plane comprises seven sub planes. All that exists within our solar system is located on the various sub planes of the cosmic physical plane. Rocks and trees, for example, are located on our physical plane, which is the seventh solar systemic sub-plane, the lowest sub-plane of the solar system's physical plane, itself the lowest sub-plane of the cosmic physical plane. And so, it goes on. Confusing by any measure and probably best thought of as a sort of cosmic babushka doll. Our planet is the smallest doll and we are just flecks of paint on its skin.

The planes afford a pathway for the evolution of consciousness. The idea is that as we gain control of our various bodies which have their manifestation on the lower planes, we are able to ascend and gain access to the higher planes of awareness. Although that access is by no means a given and is by no means simple.

While the spheroidal planes of the solar system rotate latitudinally as energy centres or chakras, they are affected by a vast downpouring of energies rotating longitudinally. These energies are the Seven Rays, spheroidal bands of colour that form a vast interlacing network.[8] Our solar system is suddenly an iridescent dance of colour and light:

 The Three major rays of aspect (emanations of divine essence)

Ray IWill or Power
Ray IILove-Wisdom
Ray IIIActive Intelligence
The four minor rays of attribute
Ray IVHarmony through conflict
Ray VConcrete knowledge or science
Ray VIDevotion or abstract idealism
Ray VIICeremonial magic or order.

'The whole system of ray influence, or radiatory warmth...is one of an intricate circulation and interaction.'[9]

THE SOLAR SYSTEM has become kaleidoscopic, evolution the adjustment of energies into alignment to form beautiful patterns. If he'd been teaching today, the Tibetan might have drawn on complexity thinking and referred to fractals, ever repeating patterns at infinite degrees of scale.

The non-esoteric reader might already be reeling in incomprehension, and there's much more to follow in this treatise. What is the point to such a convoluted system? For the non-practitioner, it may all appear irrelevant or worse, gobbledygook.

The treatise' elaborate conceptualisation has a dual function. It carries a powerful message and has a profound effect on the mind. The presentation leaves most of us on page one, unable to cross the threshold into this strange universe of subjective meaning, relying, if interested at all, on others to interpret and re-language the ideas in a simpler streamlined fashion, as Robert Ellwood achieved with his book, *Theosophy: A Modern Expression of the Wisdom of the Ages*.[10]

In summation, from a metaphoric perspective, *A Treatise on Cosmic Fire* amounts to a way of knowing that involves the ability to be able to imagine reality from multiple points of view, and to visualise the interconnectedness between these points of view through an understanding of the esoteric principle of correspondence. The higher or abstract mind is heavily stimulated, as is the intuition, or the grasping of wholes. The treatise invites the reader to embrace the universe in all of its vast proportions and understand that we as human units locked inside our own awareness and filled with our own self-importance are in fact miniscule. Writing this work at home in the small hours in Krotona and Ridgefield Park, Alice Bailey must have enjoyed an extraordinarily otherworldly and immersive experience.

A SECRET DOCTRINE CLASS

*A*fter the failure of the Committee of 1400, the Baileys quickly lost interest in Theosophical Society politics. It was the summer of 1921, and Alice Bailey was by then renting a room on Madison Avenue where she held a Secret Doctrine class and saw people by appointment in the capacity of spiritual advisor. The classes were well attended by students of Theosophy and the occult. Richard Prater, a former pupil of Blavatsky and close associate of William Quan Judge, handed over his own Secret Doctrine class to Alice Bailey after attending just one session.[1] The act made her class an instant success. Prater knew that she had received a comprehensive and intensive instruction in Theosophy by former personal pupils of Blavatsky back in Pacific Grove, and he was deeply impressed by the results. He saw in Alice a special student and went on to gift her his copy of the Esoteric Section instructions that Blavatsky herself had written, telling her that she could use the material as she liked. Later, upon his death, she would receive Prater's entire Theosophical library.[2]

Support came from many quarters. Another old pupil of Blavatsky and Olcott was Miss Sarah Jacobs who gifted Alice the photographic plates of the Masters' pictures.[3]

Bolstered by this much-needed endorsement, Alice began mailing out lesson outlines of her classes to study groups that were forming all over the country. Unfortunately, the classes were proving so successful they quickly aroused the antagonism of Theosophists and her associate Dr Jacob Bonggren warned Alice that her classes were under attack. From where and in what manner is unclear, but it didn't matter. A new organisation was starting to take shape. It would be one based on the principle of universal brotherhood, open to all; the gates of secrecy that had kept esoteric knowledge from the masses would, for better or worse, be thrown open. Alice Bailey was poised to germinate the foundational seeds that would eventually give rise to the New Age movement. No other occultist or mystic would contribute so comprehensively to its genesis.

In 1921, Alice formed a small, private meditation group with seven members. The group met every Tuesday after work, 'to discuss the Plan of the Masters of the Wisdom and to meditate awhile on our part in it'.[4] As a result of those meetings the Baileys founded the Lucis Trust, incorporated on 5 April 1922, 'as a vehicle to foster recognition of the universal spiritual principles at the heart of all work to build right relations'.[5]

A month later, they established the Lucifer Publishing Company, wisely changing the name to the Lucis Publishing Company in 1924 when Alice grew concerned about misinterpretations of the word 'Lucifer', especially amongst orthodox Christians. The change came too late. Evangelical Christians in the 1980s used the original name of the publishing company to shore up their argument that Alice Bailey was possessed by the antichrist. One leading critic was Christian activist Constance Cumbey (1944-). 'Lucifer' might mean light bearer, but to Cumbey the word denotes pure evil.[6]

Everything that Alice Bailey wrote was seen by Cumbey through the lens of Lucifer. The Plan of the Spiritual Masters that she and her co-workers spent years meditating on, is for Constance Cumbey, a lot more than simply an unorthodox formulation. 'They intend to utterly root out people who believe in the Bible and worship God and to completely stamp out Christianity.'[7] Consequently, even the notion of 'holding the mind steady in the light' is seen as an act of pure evil.

Cumbey's work continues to circulate, aided by Cumbey herself, who maintains an online presence. There are scores and possibly hundreds of conspiracy theory websites and blogs dedicated to attacking Alice Bailey, propped up in part by Cumbey's book *The Hidden Dangers of the Rainbow*.[8]

Back in Manhattan, *Initiation, Human and Solar* and *Letters on Occult Meditation* were the first texts to be published by the Lucis Trust.

Another work, *The Consciousness of the Atom*, also came out in 1922. It comprises a series of seven lectures Alice Bailey gave in New York in the winter of 1921, about nine months after the Baileys were married and settled in Ridgefield Park, and well into the time she was composing *A Treatise on Cosmic Fire*. The lectures concern the evolution of matter and consciousness from a Theosophical perspective and were intended to serve as a basic introduction to occultism. The lectures journey from a simple presentation of an esoteric view of evolution in nature, through to the idea of the evolution of consciousness, its goals, and cosmic evolution.

Alice was coming into her own. Those early days espousing the Gospel in soldiers' homes in India were paying dividends. She would go on to give about six to eight public lectures a year, something she thoroughly enjoyed.

She was lecturing at a time well before radio and then television captured the attention of society, a time when people of all classes participated in life outside the home. Entertainment was sought wherever it could be found. The public lecture was the 1920s version of a documentary. So great was the public's hunger for new presentations of spirituality, metaphysics and psychology that 'every kind of psychologist was lecturing up and down the land'.[9]

Alice Bailey's lectures were well attended. Initially she charged no admission and drew audiences of over a thousand, but she soon realised that many of those seated were 'floaters' attending any free lecture on offer. Once a small fee of twenty-five cents was imposed, attendance halved to around five hundred, all of them interested to hear what she had to say.

As those first works were published, the Baileys established their organisational magazine *The Beacon* which was also launched in April 1922. A magazine of esoteric philosophy, *The Beacon* – still in print today – provided and provides a space for students to present their views. Topics include the nature of man, God and the universe, the emergence of the new age, world events and the problems facing humanity. Twelve issues were released each year. Today, the magazine is issued quarterly and mailed to subscribers the world over.[10] In February 1934, the prestigious *Occult Review*, then carrying the title *The London Forum*, welcomed *The Beacon* as an 'intellectual periodical' and went on to quote Alice Bailey on the 'present need for optimism'. The June1934 edition describes the April issue of *The Beacon* as 'an excellent occult magazine' that 'continues to maintain its usual high standard'.[11] High praise from a journal that is generally quite reserved.

The first issues of *The Beacon* contained re-printed pieces by Olcott and Blavatsky, and a series by Alice Bailey called 'Outline Lessons on the Bhagavad Gita'. Other contributors included: Bengali attorney and author Mohini M Chatterji (1858-1936) with 'The Crest Jewel of Wisdom'; and Orientalist Sir John Woodroffe (1865-1936), aka Arthur Avalon, with 'Sensation and the Senses'.[12] Later contributors would include renowned psychiatrist and close associate Roberto Assagioli, and notable author, composer and astrologer Dane Rudhyar, who met Alice Bailey in 1920 at Krotona and held her early works in high regard.[13] Others featured include author, inventor and systems theorist Buckminster Fuller; Secretary-General of the United Nations (1961-71) U Thant; Assistant Secretary-General of the United

Nations for forty years Robert Muller; and economist E F Schumacher, author of *Small is Beautiful*, who contributed two pieces to the magazine.[14]

Back in 1922, typifying those gravitating to Alice Bailey's fledgling organisation was Swedish writer and publisher Dr Jacob Bonggren (1854-1940), who was to prove a loyal supporter. A long-standing Theosophist, Bonggren was a close personal friend of William Quan Judge, taking Ernest Hargrove's side in the Katherine Tingley takeover and leaving the society. When Besant became President, she invited Bonggren back, and he rejoined the Esoteric Section. Between 1886 and 1927 Bonggren had many articles published in *The Theosophist*. He went on to be a regular contributor to *The Beacon*. His piece on occult chromotherapy, appearing in the October 1923 issue, was later translated into Spanish and appeared in book form in 1934.[15]

In December 1923, Bonggren came out in defence of Alice Bailey in a letter published in *The Theosophist*: 'As we have in the past served our great and wonderful HPB, so we will in the present and the future serve her faithful pupil and successor as Light-bringer, our incomparable leader, AB...'[16]

It is interesting to note both Jacob Bonggren and the founders of the Theosophical Association of New York had stood firmly on the side of William Quan Judge. By association, Alice Bailey also found herself amongst those who had sided with the Theosophical Society co-founder and Irish-American lawyer, who had contributed enormously to the spread of Theosophy in the United States of America and was then slated for forgery.

Despite her own critics and perhaps in large part due to the actions of those who stood by her, Alice Bailey was beginning to establish a good reputation. In December 1922, *The Occult Review* included a review of her *Letters on Occult Meditation*:

 The volume is essentially one for the serious inquirer into the subject, and scattered through its pages will be found much valuable teaching…it is long since we have come across a work of such considerable interest to students of occultism, especially along Theosophical lines.[17]

THIS, at a time when numerous books were being published on psychism, clairvoyance, telepathy, astrology, secret societies, Spiritualism, Eastern mysticism and Theosophy. Rudolph Steiner's *Christianity as Mystical Fact*, originally published in 1914 and reprinted that year, received a glowing review in the same edition.

THE ARCANE SCHOOL

*A*s book sales grew, so did the correspondence. Letters came in from far and wide asking for instructions on meditation. Others sought advice on the Masters of the Wisdom or information on the Secret Doctrine classes. To answer this groundswell of need, in April 1923 Alice Bailey established an esoteric school. It was to form the heart of her vision, a training school for disciples on the spiritual path. It would become a core aspect of the work she would commit to for the rest of her life, and if she is worthy of being called the 'Mother of the New Age', the appellation has as much if not more to do with her school and the students it attracted, as it does the body of work she wrote on behalf of the Tibetan.

Founding a school of any sort is an ambitious undertaking, involving hours of planning, from the original aims and objectives through to the creation of a curriculum and course material, and then its delivery. Alice Bailey had already gained valuable experience as part of Krotona's Order of Field Servers, and she was well practiced in preparing lecture notes and teaching materials. The school emerged out of two years of running Secret Doctrine classes and meditation groups, and the great many inquiries she received about them. In her heyday, she would dictate ten thousand letters a year and it would take her forty-eight minutes just to slit the envelopes of the letters she received in a single day.[1] It is no exaggeration to say, in the early 1920s the felt need for an advanced esoteric training school of some kind was great.

Her principle aim for the school was little short of revolutionary. In existence at the time were numerous occult schools associated with various orders, including the Esoteric Section of the Theosophical Society. They were generally run along exclusive lines and typically involved pledges of allegiance or devotion to a higher figure in the organisation. The Order of Field Servers delivered courses on a range of esoteric topics, but in no way constituted an esoteric training school. Alice Bailey conceived of something different. Essentially, she combined the style of delivery of a correspondence school with the principles of an occult school. For her, *learning about* a topic was nowhere near as important as putting into practice various techniques and *learning from* any knowledge taught through the student's own inner experiences.[2]

Naming the school was easy. In the Theosophical material Richard Prater gave to Alice Bailey was a paper in which Blavatsky expressed her wish that the Esoteric Section be called the Arcane School. 'It never was and I made up my mind that the old lady should have her wish.'[3]

The word 'arcane' means secret, hidden, esoteric, occult, and comprehensible only to a few. A fitting term for a school intended to prepare students for the path of discipleship and put them through serious spiritual training. Alice Bailey wanted to mould students into disciples equipped for world service. As far as she was aware, no esoteric school formed along these lines had previously existed. The ones that did exist were only preparatory.[4]

Other objectives of the school are contained in the vague-sounding but significant statement that the training would concern *'the revelation of divinity in man and in the universe...'*

[italics hers][5] The school would be non-sectarian, non-political and international in scope. Training would be expressly for adults and not for spiritual devotees. Attendance would be free of charge. The Arcane School would demand no obedience or exclusive allegiance. No Master would run it, and no theology would be taught. Students would not be required to accept any of the teachings as true, including the existence of the Spiritual Hierarchy – even though the school recognises the Spiritual Hierarchy as fact – and a rejection of any aspect of the teachings would not affect that student's standing in the school.

The Arcane School was Alice Bailey's own project. Although the original idea came from the Tibetan, for Alice Bailey, the school was her opportunity to address what she perceived as the misplaced devotion of TS members to various Esoteric Section personalities in the Theosophical Society, and the resistant behaviours of some of those personalities to relinquish power. She strove to form her school along lines that would obviate any form of personality worship.

She made it a condition that the Tibetan would have no control over the policies and curriculum. Of the teachings written on behalf of the Tibetan, only some aspects of *Glamour: A World Problem* and, by popular demand, a course of study based on *A Treatise on White Magic* were used. All other course material was created by Alice Bailey.[6] 'The basic training given in the Arcane School is that which has been given down the ages to disciples...It is intended to be a school for those who can be trained to act directly and consciously under the Masters of the Wisdom.'[7] This training would be comprehensive, including techniques of meditation, recognition of soul impression, the laws of the spiritual world and the nature of energies and forces within it and, especially, esoteric psychology. The aims of the school would be training students to control their inner nature and foster soul contact, eventually establishing permanent contact with their inner spiritual being. The school would teach the Ageless Wisdom and meditation, emphasising 'the necessity *to live* the spiritual life and reject all claims to spiritual status.'[8]

Alice Bailey intentionally created a school with limited appeal. 'No teaching is given at any time in the development of the psychic powers; people are not taught to be clairvoyant or clairaudient; no training is given in magic or in the use of magical rituals, and nothing is taught at any stage on sex magic.'[9]

Then, as now, the usual glamours of esotericism tend to lure and side track would-be disciples, veering towards the formation of cults centred around self-appointed, charismatic guru figures. Alice Bailey was never going to fall into that trap, and she was wise to avoid it.

As noted above, it was not necessary to believe in the existence of the Masters to join the school. Rather, Alice Bailey wanted her students to reach a stage when they simply knew. 'In the Arcane School we are not after belief; we are after knowledge.'[10] Alice Bailey means the kind of knowledge that comes from direct experience.

She wanted the school to be of a very high standard, since its intention was to foster world disciples, those who would go off and be of significant service in the world, either on their own, or through joining in the activities of other former students. Their mission was to found a new and spiritual world order.

Some of those graduating from the school would remain working within Alice Bailey's various organisations. Others would prove to be highly influential in their fields of endeavour, as later chapters in this biography will show. It was in this fashion that Alice Bailey created the conditions for the emergence of the New Age, in part by spiritually birthing legions of dedicated spiritual 'activists', and also by providing an early model of adult education that may well have gone on to inspire her students, many of whom were psychologists and educators.

Her efforts are commendable. As her husband Foster later says:

She worked self-sacrificingly, often with the hardship of great fatigue, for long, heart-breaking hours, perfecting school courses of study, writing accompanying papers, producing more teaching as the years went by, and so changing and modifying these courses and studies.[11]

FOSTER STRESSES that Alice never went about promoting the Arcane School. She never mentioned the school in her public lectures or advertised its existence. This was at a time when *The Occult Review* carried numerous advertisements from a raft of occult and spiritual groups, publishers and individuals, including various Theosophical societies, offering diverse pursuits including tarot and astrology readings, 'How to Read Tea Cups', spiritual healing, and invitations to study.

Alice Bailey did promote her books. In April 1923, the month the Arcane School came into being, *The Occult Review* featured a half page advert from The Lucifer Publishing Company, promoting Alice Bailey's first three titles.[12] It was through her books, which established her as an authority, along with word of mouth, that readers would become students of the Arcane School.

She envisioned a student body small in number. At first, she accepted all applicants, later imposing a method of selection as it became clear many were unsuitable. She favoured no one and would drop students even if they were big donors. She never tried to retain students.[13] Despite these strictures, the Arcane School attracted thirty thousand students from around the world between 1923 and 1945 – a high number considering how specialised the school is – and enjoyed a good retention rate.[14] The school was and still is known and recognised worldwide. By

1947, the school had a headquarters in New York, England, Holland, Italy and Switzerland. Despite the disruption of the Second World War, the Arcane School at that time comprised one hundred and forty school secretaries, or senior students, overseeing the progress of beginners.[15]

It would take many years for the outcomes of the school to manifest in the world.

Naturally, the school's very existence inflamed those Theosophists who believed that their Esoteric Section, with its exclusive practices and requirements of allegiance, offered the right approach to walking the spiritual path. They saw the Arcane School in opposition to their own. As Alice Bailey required no such pledge of loyalty, anyone in the Esoteric Section was welcome to join the Arcane School. In this fashion, unlike the ES, her school was not exclusive. Although, paradoxically, the Arcane School could not help but manifest its own form of exclusivity, the course content and tone designed to put off the average seeker. Training was 'hard and stiff and difficult' to eliminate the 'non-intelligent'.[16] In short, it was a school for the well-educated with a penchant for the esoteric.

A helpful way to view the difference between the Arcane School and the Esoteric Section is provided by scholars Dick Anthony and Bruce Ecker who devised a framework for assessing spiritual and consciousness groups and called it 'The Anthony Typology'. The Arcane School falls into the technical style of practice, one in which training 'guides from the side'. The Theosophical Society falls into the charismatic style, one that relies on the 'transformative potency' of a personal relationship with a Master.[17] Alice Bailey recognised the distinction and decided, correctly or not, that her school offered training of a more advanced kind to that of the ES, which in her view catered for probationers and not disciples. In the 1930s, while staying in Paris, she made the mistake of explaining this, without tact, to then head of the Theosophical Society in France, Mr Marcault. He 'was neither impressed nor pleased' by what he heard.[18]

With hindsight it might be easy to think she would have done better to keep her own counsel, but Alice Bailey could be impulsively honest at times, and it wasn't until after she had spoken that she saw her mistake. To her credit, she was humble and brave enough to share such an embarrassing moment in her autobiography and in this limited fashion shoulder some of the blame for the ongoing tensions with the TS. She never considered herself perfect.

Those antagonisms would continue to this day. Another crisis lay ahead. But for what remained of the 1920s, Alice Bailey settled into a rhythm, devoting all her available time, freely and willingly, to the development of her various organisational activities, writing for the Tibetan, giving lectures, fulfilling her endless appointments, and attending to the mountain of correspondence. She had gathered around her a small group of loyal co-workers to share the load, and of course, Foster.[19] In those early years, the team worked out of an office situated at 140 Cedar Street, Manhattan, New York.[20] They would soon need a much larger office.

SOME INFLUENTIAL FRIENDS

*I*n New York, Alice Bailey's social standing was restored. She moved in similar privileged circles to those she grew up with as a La Trobe-Bateman. She was a member of New York society. She was on the ascendency when it came to her reputation as an occultist, and for Alice Bailey, reputation was everything.

In1925 she published her seminal work *A Treatise on Cosmic Fire*, a work of over one thousand two hundred pages. Two years after that, she released *The Light of the Soul: The Yoga Sutras of Patanjali*, another hefty read of some four hundred pages, offering her own interpretations of the ancient sutras which form the basis of Raja yoga.

In her version of the sutras, Alice Bailey relies on nine other translations and commentaries, including one composed by William Quan Judge and another by Swami Vivekananda, disciple of Indian mystic Ramakrishna and one of the key figures involved in introducing Eastern philosophies to the Western world. A publication of Vivekananda's version received glowing praise in the November 1922 edition of *The Occult Review*.[1] It was released at a time when there was a burgeoning interest in yoga. It might be said that for Alice Bailey to establish herself as a serious contender in a competitive market, something she was certainly aiming to achieve, she needed to produce her version of ancient sutras.

Indian sage Patanjali compiled the series of 196 yoga sutras, or aphorisms, in the period $2^{nd} - 5^{th}$ century BCE, the compilation serving as one of the most important texts of Hindu philosophy and originally translated into scores of Indian languages before drifting into obscurity. It was Vivekananda who first presented the sutras to the West. For Alice Bailey, the significance of the sutras lay in their capacity to train the mind to become an instrument of the soul. Her book, which comprises a detailed explanation of each sutra, enabled her not only to establish herself as an authority on meditation in her own right, but it also provided a means through which to tie her esoteric worldview to its Eastern mystical roots.

It should be noted that of the twenty-four volumes known as the Blue Books, six were composed by Alice Bailey herself, four of those prior to 1932 during the initial phase of rapid organisational expansion. She also penned *The Labours of Hercules: An Astrological Interpretation*.

While Alice was kept busy with her school and her work for the Tibetan, Foster Bailey attended to the numerous administrative tasks with the assistance of a small team. There is no indication in Alice Bailey's autobiography regarding what Foster's family of origin thought of his decision to forego his law career in favour of matters Theosophical – although it is doubtful they offered any financial assistance to the fledgling Lucis Trust – or whether they approved, accepted, supported or condemned him, or if his wife and stepdaughters were welcomed into the fold of his family not too far away in Fitchburg, Massachusetts. With Alice Bailey's aunts now deceased and her estrangement from her only sister permanent, Foster's people were all her daughters had by way of family. Dorothy, Mildred and Ellison did have a relationship with Foster's family, although the only evidence is a trip Dorothy made to Hawaii in 1928 when she was eighteen, with Foster's brother Harry and his wife Kathleen and their children Margaret and Joseph, ages one and three.[2] Dorothy is listed as living in Ridgefield Park, New Jersey. Harry Bailey's family lived about twenty miles away in Maplewood, New Jersey.

In 1928, the Baileys moved from Ridgefield Park to a much larger house in Stamford, Connecticut, made available to them for a few years. The house, or rather, mansion, belonged to their friend, American aristocrat, political activist and philanthropist James Graham Phelps-Stokes (1872-1960). Phelps-Stokes was a millionaire socialist, son of prominent banker Anson Phelps-Stokes and his wife Helen Louisa Phelps. Graham Phelps-Stokes graduated as a medical doctor in 1896 but forewent medical practice to devote his time to a wide range of organisations helping the poor and disadvantaged, including Legal Aid, the Prison Association, and the Institution for the Instruction of the Deaf and Dumb.[3]

The house Phelps-Stokes gifted the Baileys the use of, which came with its own little beach, is situated on Greenaway Island, Long Island Sound. The island is a private idyll of some two acres also known as Caritas Island, which the millionaire had inherited. Before the Baileys took possession, the residence had been the site of a well-known intellectual salon, artists' colony and retreat, which Phelps-Stokes established with his then wife, activist, feminist and ardent communist Rose Harriet Pastor Stokes (1879-1933).[4]

They made a curious couple. Pastor Stokes was born in Russia to Orthodox Jews Jacob and Hindl Wieslander and came to America as a poor Jewish migrant. She spent over a decade working in a cigar factory in Ohio, and it was there that she began agitating for workers' rights in letters submitted to the *Jewish Daily News*. By 1903 she was employed as a columnist. Within months she was assigned to interview Phelps-Stokes. They were married two years later in 1905. The couple remained active in the labour movement, but Pastor Stokes's activism was considerably more intense. She helped to lead workers strikes and was an advocate of birth control. Through the war years, she campaigned across the country denouncing the war effort, and was sentenced to ten years in prison for criticising America's involvement in the war, until the sentence was overturned on appeal. By 1919, Pastor Stokes had developed strong associations with the Communist Party and in the end, she proved too radical for her more conservative, Episcopalian husband. After some years, he found the salon and artists' colony at Caritas Island overwhelming, not least over the flirtations of Pastor Stokes's numerous admirers, for she was beautiful and charismatic. In 1925 in a letter to his wife, he accused her of bringing 'nothing but shame' to him through her use of the cottage.[5] Eager to put his past behind him, he invited the Baileys to live in the house after the marriage ended.

Alice Bailey and Rose Pastor Stokes could not have been more distinct. Alice Bailey was a demure, private woman who, while definitely a social being, was not given to the risqué manner of a socialite. Her version of activism was spiritual, not political, and she gathered around her those whose desire to change the world came from an esoteric space and took place inwardly, on the inner planes through focused advanced meditation, through exerting influence behind the scenes, or through incorporating the teachings into one's thinking, outlook and daily work without any mention of the source. Alice Bailey attracted folk whose desire to do good works arose out of a detached notion of human betterment, not from a strident passion for a single cause. In this, she also differed from Annie Besant.

How Phelps-Stokes met Alice Bailey is not known. They may have encountered each other in any number of ways. Although not known to be an occultist himself, another of his friends, author Upton Sinclair, had an interest in the field. Sinclair experimented with telepathy and the topic of his book *Mental Radio* went on to inspire the development of inquiry into parapsychology at Duke University. Maybe it was through Sinclair that the friendship was born. Upton Sinclair attended founder of Biosophy Dr Kettner's Spinoza group, which, in its early days, held some of its public lectures at the Arcane School.[6] The Spinoza Institute, founded in 1928, established its headquarters in 1929 at the Roerich Museum, upon the invitation of Nicholas Roerich.[7]

Whatever the circumstances, through the patronage of friends such as Phelps-Stokes, Alice Bailey had firmly re-asserted herself in the aristocratic milieu she had been born into. She adored the house on Caritas Island – and little wonder. A fourteen thousand square foot stone mansion filled with impressive features including Herringbone oak floors, wood panelling and chandeliers, and twelve bedrooms.[8] Alice Bailey describes one wing of the house which consisted of a large room with windows in three of the walls. The maid's quarters were below. There, in quietude, with sweeping views of the sound, she lived and worked. For her, they were wonderful years. The domestic luxury even inspired her to host her own gatherings. 'Every Sunday, practically, we were at home to friends and guests and frequently had 20 or 30 people at the house.'[9] She writes fondly of her dog, her cat, the car they were gifted – in which they drove to New York and beyond – and of her daughters entering their teens.

At first, the girls attended the local state school, but Alice became concerned about the boys they were mixing with. 'The three girls never gave me any real anxiety and never gave me cause to distrust them,' she says, yet she couldn't help listening and watching for a car to make its way down the little causeway and pull up in the drive if one of them happened to be out with a boy. Alice always knew her daughters were 'downright decent', but still she fretted as any mother would. At eighteen, Dorothy would have been the biggest worry.

Relief came when her closest friend, poet, author and philanthropist Alice Eugenie du Pont Ortiz (1876-1940), paid for the girls' tuition at Low Hayward School.

A major donor of the Arcane School, Alice du Pont was the daughter of Alexis Irénée du Pont and Elizabeth Canby (Bradford) du Pont, and the wife of Julien Leon DeVilliers Ortiz (1868-1955), whom she married in 1906.[10] Descended from French Huguenot Pierre Samuel du Pont de Nemours (1739-1817), the du Ponts made their wealth from explosives and supplies to the United States military, quickly establishing themselves as a wealthy aristocratic family of Wilmington, Delaware. In 1913, Alice du Pont and her husband Julien Ortiz founded a Theosophical Lodge in Wilmington and were original members of the local Theosophical library. Alice du Pont wrote two collections of poetry, *The Witch of Endor*, published in 1937, and *The Scene Shifter*, in 1939. She collaborated with her daughter, Marguerite de Pont DeVillers Boden, on *A Tradition Concerning Mary Dyer 'the Quaker Martyr"*, published in 1938. She also contributed four pieces to *The Beacon*.

Alice Bailey's affection for Alice Ortiz was deep. She meant more to her than anyone other than Foster. 'This friend was simplicity and sweetness and selflessness combined, and she brought a richness and a beauty into my life of which I had never dreamed.'[11] Ortiz 'had a deep and profound knowledge of the Ageless Wisdom' but this knowledge distanced her somewhat from family and friends. Alice Bailey says Ortiz was too afraid of being misunderstood. They remained close friends for seventeen years. 'To understand her, to stand by her, to let her talk to me freely and to feel safe in so doing was the only compensation I could make to her for her endless goodness to me.'[12] Ortiz gifted Alice clothes and jewellery, paid for return passages to Europe and Britain. She even gave large sums of money if the need arose. 'I remember once being ill in England some years ago and within a few hours she cabled me £500.'[13]

At home in the Phelps-Stokes' mansion, in her room overlooking the sound, Alice would have found the perfect environment for further works. The only sad event she mentions during this period was when someone broke into the house and stole two items: a broken rocking chair and a Bible that she had held dear since it was gifted her by her friend Catherine Rowan-Hamilton, whom she met while working for Elise Sandes in Ireland. Alice Bailey speaks fondly of that Bible, with its wide margins filled with annotations describing her spiritual journey spanning almost twenty years.[14]

Operations continued to expand. In 1928, the Baileys took offices on the top floor of Salmon Tower soon after it was built in West 42nd Street, directly opposite the New York Public Library. Co-workers Victor Fox and Regina Keller assisted with the mounting administrative tasks, along with some volunteers. Serving as Alice Bailey's secretary, Victor Fox (1893-) would remain a loyal co-worker until at least 1948.[15] Regina Keller (circa 1883-1966) was a Hungarian-American lawyer who went on to work closely with Alice Bailey for decades, helping with editorial work and tutoring advanced students in the Arcane School.

As the Arcane School, the Lucis Trust and *The Beacon* began to mature and garner a global reputation, an important figure entered Alice Bailey's life, Grand Duke Alexander of Russia (1866-1933), brother-in-law of Tsar Nicholas II. The Grand Duke had come to New York in 1929 on a promotional tour after the publication of his book *The Religion of Love*. He was a mystical Freemason and Rosicrucian, and he was giving a lecture at the Nobility Club in New York. The club was established to enable Russian nobility to mingle with 'serious-minded and cultured' Americans.[16] A friend and unnamed Baroness had invited Alice along. As the Duke gave his talk, which concerned the subject of the soul, she remarked to her friend that it would be nice if she could introduce the Duke to some likeminded people she knew. The Baroness arranged a meeting the following day.

The Grand Duke and Alice Bailey enjoyed an immediate rapport, and in the months that followed, he would spend week-ends with the Baileys at Valmy, the du Pont mansion in

Greenville, Delaware, where they would hold 'little séances in Alice's huge living-room'.[17]

One evening, the Baileys were asked by his secretary to take the Grand Duke to two of his speaking engagements, and it was on the way home that he informed Alice that he also knew the Tibetan. It was the last time she saw him. His piece 'The Nature of the Soul' was published in *The Beacon* in February 1930.[18] In 1933, upon the hour of his death, Alice Bailey recalls she was sitting up in bed reading, when the Grand Duke walked in wearing his dark blue pyjamas. He smiled, waved and disappeared. She went and told Foster the Grand Duke had died. His passing was listed in the following day's obituary column.

An autobiography is only ever the edited highlights of a life. Alice Bailey does not mention her association at this time with prominent Canadian Theosophical lecturer Charles Lazenby, author of *The Work of the Masters*.[19] A psychology and philosophy graduate who went on to study Jungian psycho-analysis in Zurich, Charles Lazenby is best known today for his interest in sexological theories and reincarnation. He counted among his close associates Havelock Ellis and Edward Carpenter – whom Alice Bailey quotes in *From Bethlehem to Calvary*[20] – and his views are cited by scholars in the field of Gender Studies due to his exploration of the blurred boundary between physical sex and sexual identity, whereby a reincarnated soul making the switch from male to female may find themselves in a female physical body but with a male mental and emotional (desire) body.[21] This exploration into reincarnation and gender rendered him a colourful figure in his day. During his lifetime, he was also known for his superb public speaking prowess, a rival to Besant herself.

Charles Lazenby (1878-1928) was born in Brussels, south-western Ontario, Canada, to Methodist parents, both of whom were ministers. His father died before he was born trying to rescue a child from a river.[22] Lazenby married Scottish-born Margaret Clark in 1912, and together the couple travelled Europe and America on his lecture tours. In 1913, they settled in Detroit and pursued their Theosophical activities, particularly in Wilmington, Delaware, in the Lodge co-founded by Alice Ortiz du Pont.[23]

From July 1910, Lazenby published the independent journal *The Path*.[24] In 1925, the journal re-published Alice Bailey's article 'Chelaship', originally published in *The Beacon*.[25] A clue to their friendship can be found in Charles Lazenby's enduring passion for freedom of thought and speech within the Theosophical Society. It is likely he was a loyal if hidden figure during the acrimony at Krotona, perhaps later becoming acquainted with Alice Bailey through her close friendship with Alice du Pont. The wealth of appreciation Alice had for Charles is evident in the Lucis Trust's release of a memorial edition of Lazenby's *The Servant*. The book was first released in 1920, and after his death in 1928, his wife Margaret Lazenby held copyright.[26] The Lucis Trust was not and has never been in the habit of publishing anything other than the Bailey books, rendering this memorial edition significant.

A SPIRITUAL SUMMER SCHOOL

*A*nother important figure entered Alice Bailey's life towards the end of the 1920s, one who would lead her into a period of difficulty. The association goes some way towards explaining the derision with which a certain section of the intellectual elite views Alice Bailey and her corpus. Dutch spiritualist, seeker and artist Olga Fröbe Kapteyn (1881-1962) had recently inherited Casa Gabriella, a property on the shores of Lake Maggiore in Ascona, southern Switzerland. There she wanted to create a spiritual centre to serve as a meeting place between Eastern and Western philosophies, and she enlisted Alice Bailey's help.

Olga Fröbe was born in London to inventor and engineer Albertus Kapteyn, general manager of the British Westinghouse Brake and Signal Company, and his wife Truus Muysken, an intellectual anarchist who was friends with playwright George Bernard Shaw and Russian philosopher, activist and anarchist Prince Kropotkin. While at school in London, Olga was a childhood friend of paleobotanist Mary Stopes. The family moved to Zurich in 1900 when Olga was nineteen, and there she studied art and art history. In 1909, she married flautist and flyer Iwan Fröbe, who died in a plane crash six years later, just prior to the birth of their twin girls, Ingeborg and Bettina, leaving Olga Fröbe apparently penniless. Fröbe returned to Zurich and applied her artistic skills to jewellery and embroidery. A champion skier with a daredevil spirit, she was headstrong and formidable. During this period, she established a salon and surrounded herself with the region's intellectual and artistic haut monde, including professor of German literature Robert Faesi and singer, dancer and esoterically minded illustrator Alastair and his patron André Germain, whose father founded the French bank Crédit Lyonnais. In 1926, Fröbe's father purchased Casa Gabriella, former home of André Germain, where Fröbe resided with her girls. Upon her father's death, she inherited the property.[1]

Fröbe was a freethinker 'searching for something to believe in'.[2] She had an enduring interest in comparative religion, mythology, spirituality and Steiner's anthroposophy. In her desire to found something more than an intellectual salon, she was responding to the 'general intellectual climate of the 1920s' that was particularly strong in post-war Germany, one that was 'open towards oriental and esoteric modes of thought'.[3] Such modes included Hinduism, Buddhism and Taoism.

Fröbe was also looking for 'someone around whom to focus her quest'.[4] She had been influenced by prominent philosopher Martin Buber, whom she had met at Monte Verità in 1924 and with whom she corresponded.[5] She moved on to become a devotee of poet and eccentric Ludwig Derleth (1870-1948) who upheld a strict Christian belief in a return to a medieval, male-only hierarchy of leaders, which he thought should replace democracy, a system for which he held nothing but contempt. No one could be further from everything that Alice Bailey stood for, than him.

André Germain and Ludwig Derleth were among a large number of alternative thinkers associated with Monte Verità, a hill on the edge of Ascona where a utopian community had, since 1900, attracted numerous freethinkers from throughout

Europe and beyond, including 'artists, writers, dancers, political radicals, utopians, gurus', all of whom found their way to Monte Verità. 'The list included Lenin, Trotsky, Bakunin, Kropotkin, Hesse, Stefan George, Rudolph Steiner, Mary Wigman, Isadora Duncan, Hans Arp, Paul Klee, Emil Jannings, Emil Ludwig and Erich-Maria Remarque.'[6]

Despite apparently having no time for the Bohemian crowd the community attracted, Fröbe hung around others at Monte Verità, which was established originally as a health institute and comprised numerous small huts. The main building was purchased in 1926 and run as a hotel by former banker to the German Kaiser Baron Eduard von der Heydt (1882-1964). The baron was a renowned transvestite and *saloniste*, who would 'flutter about' in flamboyant style amongst his guests, including King Leopold of Belgium and Thomas Mann. Fröbe watched on, seeing in the effete Heydt, a rival and competitor.[7]

In 1928, Fröbe came up with a scheme to outdo Heydt. Apparently without knowing its specific purpose, she had built beside her house a lecture hall. It was constructed of stone and cut into the steep hillside, with large windows opening out onto verandas on the north and east sides, overlooking the lake. Inside, rows of rush-seated chairs faced a small lectern. All she needed to do next was fill the space.

Fröbe already had a collaborator in mind, and it wasn't to be anyone associated with Heydt and the milieu at Monte Verità, about whom she seemed to have little but contempt.[8] She already knew of Alice Bailey and her teachings and might well have been a student of her Arcane School. For how long is unclear, but in a letter addressed to Alice Bailey dated March 1933, Fröbe states, 'I have for many years worked along your lines.'[9] This sentence implies that Fröbe had much more than a passing familiarity with Alice Bailey's work, one that had endured longer than the three short years of their collaboration at Ascona.

Fröbe had a brother living on Long Island. She made contact, probably in late1928, with a view to collaborating with Alice in establishing a 'School of Spiritual Research' at Casa Gabriella, tapping into the European appetite for exploring East meets West, as exemplified by Hermann Keyserling's School of Wisdom. There was an exchange of letters. In May 1929, *The Beacon*, a magazine generally not given to publishing works by those not closely associated with the Arcane School unless they are composed by notable figures, published a short piece composed by Fröbe titled 'Know Thy Self'.[10]

Late one evening in the autumn of 1929 – Alice Bailey gives the year as 1930 but she is mistaken – Fröbe arrived at the Stamford house and put her vision before the Baileys. She told them she had a beautiful house in a lovely setting, and she explained her plans. The spiritual centre was to be 'undenominational, non-sectarian, and open to esoteric thinkers and occult students of all groups in Europe and elsewhere'.[11] Fröbe's contribution was to provide the venue, and Alice Bailey would initiate the project, lecture and teach.

The project was timely. Alice Bailey was as keen as ever to establish herself as a serious occultist and not a run-of-the-mill medium or worse, a charlatan. *The Light of the Soul: The Yoga Sutras of Patanjali* was published in 1927. The next work in line, one she penned herself, and one that would prove highly influential in the New Age movement, was *The Soul and its Mechanism*, published in 1930 and composed when she was residing in Phelps-Stokes mansion in Long Island Sound. It was written under her own name and dedicated to her dear friend Alice Ortiz. The work concerns the relationship between the physical body and its etheric, or energetic counterpart, with particular attention paid to the endocrine system and the chakras. A glance at her footnote references and bibliography provides a quick indication of how widely Alice Bailey had read Eastern philosophy in relation to contemporary psychology. Another is the foreword composed by bestselling author and psychologist Harry Allen Overstreet (1875-1970). Chair of the

Department of Philosophy and Psychology at City College, New York, Overstreet's *The Mature Mind* (1949) sold half a million copies. In his foreword to Alice Bailey's book, he remarks that her study of the endocrine glands 'opens up fascinating possibilities for further research' and is 'singularly illuminating'.[12] This work exemplifies her contribution to esoteric healing in the New Age.

A second volume, *From Intellect to Intuition*, again penned by Alice Bailey, published in 1932 and probably written after the first summer school took place, might almost be considered tailored for Fröbe's school. In this volume on the various aspects of meditation, there is much mention of East and West, and a great deal of reference to eminent scholars in the field, including Carl Jung. Alice Bailey was eager to impress not so much her general readers, but the intellectual milieu and in particular, those eminent European scholars of the day in the fields of Psychology, Philosophy and the History of Religion.[13]

Back in Stamford in 1929, in the face of the proposal, Alice Bailey was receptive but reticent. She wanted time to think. Fröbe was persuasive and determined to have her way. 'She offered us full hospitality and was willing to have the three girls accompany us if we went to Ascona, offering board and lodging to us all.'[14]

It is unlikely she would have proceeded had Fröbe not been a student of her work. She already had her own organisations – at the time, the Arcane School had members in America, Britain, the Netherlands, Italy, Switzerland, South America, Turkey and West Africa – but Fröbe's proposal was a novel way to consolidate her efforts in Europe. No doubt she was tempted if perhaps ambivalent; there were the logistics to consider and the travel expenses to meet.

Around that time, and without knowing what Fröbe was offering, Alice Ortiz, who had been paying for Alice's daughters' education, asked if she would prefer her to pay for the girls to go to college or travel abroad. By then, Dorothy was twenty,

Mildred approaching eighteen and Ellison sixteen. Having benefited from the insights into other societies and cultures that
travel affords, and not having a college degree herself, Alice
chose travel.

In the early summer of 1930, after a flurry of planning and
the purchasing of suitcases and clothes, the family set off from
New York to Antwerp.

The girls were 'exceedingly excited'. None had travelled
overseas except Dorothy. They were 'full of life and energy' and
Alice Bailey says, 'keeping track of them was no joke'.[15] By then
Alice had reached fifty years of age, and she had never enjoyed
good health. Even so, she made ball gowns for each of her girls,
in which they would dance with officers, and most patriotic
looking they were too, with dark blue skirts and bodices of
white, trimmed with red stars.

Committed as ever to elevating common humanity over
knowledge and history, in Antwerp, rather than visit the
tourist sites, she encouraged the family to spend a few days
seated in cafes and 'drifting about the streets' absorbing the
atmosphere. Instead of staring at artefacts in museums, they
would 'take a walk to the suburbs'. By the end of their stay,
Alice Bailey says the girls were imbued with a good knowledge of the town and surrounds.[16] From Antwerp, the family
took a circuitous route by train to enjoy the vertiginous trip
through the Simplon Pass, and arrived at Locarno, Switzerland, from where Fröbe drove them to Casa Gabriella, some
five kilometres further south. It would have been an exceptionally pretty drive.

Situated at the head of Lake Maggiore, Ascona is a village of
cobbled streets lined with tall, four-storey buildings with colourful, rendered facades and low-pitched roofs. The village overlooks the lake and the surrounding mountains. Ribbons of
narrow lanes thread their way through the steep-sided, wooded
slopes, reaching down to the main road cut into the mountain-
side beside the lake. To access her property, Fröbe would have

driven right past Monte Verità, located on the edge of Ascona some two kilometres from Casa Gabriella.

Alice Bailey found the setting exquisite. 'The lake is so blue, the little villages are so picturesque, perched as they are on the sides of the hills reaching down into the water.'[17] Yet behind all the beauty, she knew there to be 'corruption and very ancient evil'. She believed the area was at one time the centre of the Black Mass in Central Europe.[18]

It is unclear to what she was referring but the area did have strong Theosophical associations. In 1889, German doctor, astrologer, geomancer and Theosophist Franz Hartmann (1838-1912) established a Theosophical lay-monastery in Ascona, along with philosopher and moral force behind Monte Verità Alfredo Pioda, and a close friend of Blavatsky's, Countess Constance Wachmeister. Hartmann's periodical, *Lotusblüthen* was the first publication in Germany to feature the Theosophical swastika on its cover.[19] Hartmann also supported controversial Austrian occultist Guido von List – founder of Wotanism, a philosophy advocating the revival of the ancient German race – whose ideas influenced or helped justify the views of the Nazi party.

Whatever Alice Bailey thought she knew, she found evidence of it along the country roads. What she saw she doesn't mention, but at that time the community at Monte Verità practiced nudity and homosexuality. Through her Edwardian eyes, such free living would have been abominable and anathema to her austere spiritual principles. As soon as she had the opportunity, she sat her daughters down and warned them in clear and certain terms to keep their guard and their distance from the 'degeneracy' and 'homosexuality' she saw.[20]

Casa Gabriella is tucked down a steep embankment right beside the lake. There, in great contrast to whatever she had just seen, Alice took in the house, the lecture hall, the beautiful grounds, and saw 'promise of wide future opportunities for expansion'.[21]

The Baileys were installed in the house. On 3 August 1930,

the summer school commenced. It was to last for three weeks, with an additional week made available for private interviews with leaders. Every day except Sunday, three lectures were given, two in the morning and one in the afternoon. There were eighty seats in the lecture hall and over fifteen nationalities represented. Fröbe gave the opening address:

> Our purpose is to create a meeting point where those of every group and faith may gather for discussion and synthetic work along spiritual lines…We are profoundly conscious that the source and the goal of humanity are one and the same for every unit, and that here lies the fundamental truth of Brotherhood.[22]

HER LANGUAGE IS CLEARLY INFLUENCED by the DK teachings. She refers to people as 'units' and speaks of 'synthetic work along spiritual lines', language straight out of a Bailey text.

The morning lectures were mostly conducted by Alice Bailey. Her topics included "The Occult Significance of Speech", "The Stages in Meditation" and "The Religion of the New Age". Other lecturers included Foster Bailey; Professor Kettner, who spoke on "Spirituality and Divinity"; Shri Vishwanath Keskar from India; Roberto Assagioli, who gave four lectures, including one titled "Rays, Planets and Astrological Signs"; his associate, Professor Vittorino Vezzani, who spoke on Yoga; Grand Duke Alexander, who gave two talks, one on "Spiritual Education" and another on "Spiritual Nature of the Human Being"; Irish poet and Theosophist James Henry Cousins (1873-1956), who spoke on aesthetic topics including "Poetry as Scripture"; and Scottish author and Spiritualist Violet Tweedale, who spoke about "The Cosmic Christ". A joint lecture was given by Alice Bailey and

Olga Fröbe on symbolism, and featured eighty occult symbols, geometric in form, which Fröbe had painted on large posters.[23]

For Alice Bailey, the talks by Roberto Assagioli, who had by then been a secretary of the Arcane School for a number of years, was one of the highlights. 'The talks by Dr Assagioli were outstanding features of the Ascona conferences. He would lecture in French, Italian and English and the spiritual power which poured through him was the means of stimulating many into renewed consecration in life.'[24] Until that first session at Ascona, they hadn't met.

Neither had Alice met Violet Tweedale (1862-1936), who immediately became a close personal friend. Tweedale was by then almost seventy and well established in her literary career, having published numerous novels and short stories as well as around thirty works of spiritual non-fiction. She was a close associate of Blavatsky, a member of the occult Order of the Golden Dawn and counted among her friends poet Robert Browning. 'I can see her now coming down the hillside with her husband, and, immediately through the power of her spiritual personality, dominating the whole centre. She was so beautiful, so gracious and so stately.'[25] From then on, until Tweedale's death in December 1936, when they visited Britain, the Baileys would stay in her 'beautiful home' in Torquay, South Devon.

The second summer school session in 1931 comprised a similar line up of lecturers, with the addition, among others, of Bahai teacher Mizra Ahmad Sohrad, and director of the American Conservatory at Fontainbleau, Gerald Reynolds. Others invited either declined or were unavailable. Things seemed to be going well and may have continued, were it not for the fact that Fröbe now had eminent psychologist Carl Gustav Jung in her sights.

Alice Bailey, too, would have welcomed the opportunity to meet her rival. Seekers following Alice Bailey were also drawn to Jung. His influence was present at that second session. Two students in attendance, travelling as followers of Alice Bailey, were Americans Nancy Wilson Ross and Ann Moyer. Ross was later to become a close friend of Mary Mellon, founder of the Bollingen Foundation, formed in homage to Jung. Ann Moyer met her future husband Erlo Van Waveren, a young Dutchman and loyal student of the Arcane School, who helped organise lecture tours in Europe. After the couple married, they switched their allegiance to Jung.[26] From then, the Dutch and Belgian section of the Lucis Trust was headed up by Gerhard Jansen.[27]

This apparent mood of defection was to manifest most strongly in Fröbe.

Alice Bailey avoids mentioning the demise of the collaboration, except to say that in the session of the third year, 'the place was overrun by German professors and the whole tone and quality of the place altered…the teaching shifted from a relatively high spiritual plane to that of academic philosophy and spurious esotericism'.[28]

Fröbe had invited Jung to attend the 1932 summer school, but he declined. She would have been much more than disappointed. Ever since she met Jung at Keyserling's School of Wisdom 'sometime around 1930' – either before or after the first summer school but certainly after she had committed herself to her collaboration with Alice Bailey – Fröbe considered him to be 'an important influence on her life'.[29]

In all likelihood, her desire to have Jung at her sessions was a little more complex. It wasn't until he accepted her invitation the following year, that she had at last bested her competition up at Monte Verità, the flamboyant Heydt, and founded her own centre for intellectual discussion, which she named 'Eranos'. The name was suggested to Fröbe in November 1932 by scholar of religion Rudolf Otto, whom she had visited 'in order to discuss her intention of organizing a less esoteric and more academic type of summer school'.[30] All that remained was to find a way to end the collaboration with Alice Bailey.

Fröbe instigated her plans for Eranos six months before she

confronted Alice Bailey with the news. The final parting of the two women was not pleasant. Foster had already met with Fröbe's disapproval for bathing in the nude on a raft on the lake. But in truth, his behaviour was a side issue. Sometime earlier, Fröbe had suggested to Alice Bailey that German writer Eugen Georg attend the next session. Alice Bailey found the suggestion repellent and dismissed the idea on the basis that his views, delineated in his *Adventures of Mankind*, were sexually perverse. In a letter to Fröbe, she wrote, 'It will not be possible to get anyone of the calibre of Paul Claudel unless the whole standard of our speakers is raised.'[31]

Olga did not take kindly to the tone. In an angry letter from Fröbe to Alice Bailey dated 22 March 1933, many months after the 1932 summer school, she disinvites the Baileys to the next. Fröbe refers to claims that Dorothy, Mildred and Ellison had behaved flirtatiously and inappropriately while at the previous summer school. Fröbe alleges they had formed an association with Baron von der Heydt, and they had gone 'on an escapade to France, driven by Mario Nigra, the taxi driver who chauffeured Olga in later years'.[32]

Alice Bailey's daughters denied any impropriety.

Clearly an exchange of letters had taken place, for in the March letter, Fröbe accuses Alice Bailey of hypocrisy and double standards, of taking a high moral stance when it suited her and not when it came to her own daughters. Fröbe was probably referring to Alice Bailey's reaction to Eugen Georg, more than her distaste for the lifestyles practiced at Monte Verità. In the letter, Fröbe took the opportunity to cut off all ties with Alice Bailey from that point forward. Tellingly, that letter had been composed on paper already carrying the Eranos letterhead, written in German.[33]

Reading between the lines of her autobiography, in which Alice Bailey is at pains on numerous occasions to explain her mothering style, her high moral standards and her belief in the calibre of her daughters, Fröbe's letter upset her greatly.[34]

For all their apparent licentiousness, all of the girls were married soon after.

Sometime prior to 1931, the Baileys had moved from Phelps-Stokes mansion on Caritas Island into a more modest house on Soundview Avenue in Stamford. Alice was eager for all of her daughters to find suitable matches and intimates some concern in her autobiography that perhaps Stamford was not the ideal locale. She did not have long to wait. Dorothy married Colonel Terence Morton in September 1934 in Faversham, Kent.[35] Ellison married his fellow officer Arthur Gordon Poyntor Leahy in 1936 in Tonbridge, Kent.[36] The couple had three children. Elizabeth A. Leahy was born in Tonbridge in 1938.[37] And Arthur Ronald W. Leahy in Quetta in 1944.[38] In a letter from Alice Bailey to Mildred in April 1949, she mentions Ellison's third child, but no record has yet been found.[39] Mildred married Meredith Pugh in America in 1935. The marriage was short-lived. She had one son, Gordon, born in Tonbridge in 1936.[40]

Alice would have been relieved by her daughter's marriages and somewhat vindicated after the hurtful allegations. From March 1933, she would have been able to erase Fröbe from her mind and put the collaboration behind her. But Fröbe was a powerful, influential and ambitious woman who admits 'she could not work with committees, boards or even individuals'.[41] She was also scheming. She had set in train the formation of Eranos in the weeks after the third session. The rest, the accusations and the apparent hurts, were excuses to justify the split. It appears Alice Bailey had served her purpose in running those first summer schools. From 1930, Fröbe knew that Jung would be her drawcard, attracting to Eranos many eminent intellectuals of the day.

In the summer of 1933, at the inaugural session of Eranos, Jung was in attendance, and any hopes Alice Bailey may have held of gaining his favour were dashed. In independent scholar Thomas Hakl's account in his book *Eranos*, Fröbe told philosopher of religion Alfons Rosenberg that Jung had told her to 'turn away from the group surrounding Alice Bailey'.[42] Although the remark, made by a man who held Eranos and its founder in high esteem, amounts to gossip and cannot be relied upon, especially since Fröbe was running her own agenda and would say anything to condemn her foe. If Fröbe's remark is to be trusted, then it may well have been the core reason why she turned against her former associate and teacher. Rosenberg reinforced his own account by citing Fröbe's claim that when she showed Jung one of the large meditation tableaux of geometrical forms she created following Alice Bailey's instructions, he reacted dismissively, telling her it 'radiated a horrifyingly cold atmosphere' and 'one could see that she "was dealing with the devil"'.[43] Again, Jung may not have said any of this. If he did, why the vitriol? Or was it an off-the-cuff comment said to appease his friend. What is known from biographer Diedre Bair's account, is that Jung remained in loyal admiration of Frau Fröbe.[44]

Others, including philosopher of religion Friedrich Heiler, did not share Jung's apparent condemnation of Fröbe's artworks. Indeed, Heiler found the tableaux 'most valuable'.[45] What does seem clear is that Fröbe was intent on breaking away from Alice Bailey with her own reputation undamaged.

Whether Alice Bailey knew of the scorn Jung poured on the tableaux is unknown. Interestingly, she remarked to a group of her Arcane Students in a talk given in 1944 that Jung's representative in Amsterdam 'had a great portfolio of drawings by her patients depicting their psychological concepts. She was trying to work from the bottom up, following Jung's methods. I was never so shocked in my life. I think a great number of them were efforts on the part of the patients to satisfy the doctor, so to speak, and a great number of them were the result of a prurient imagination. Most unwholesome.'[46]

In 1933, Alice could certainly have done without the drama. She had far more important matters to attend to both at home, with the weddings of all her daughters, and with all of her organisational activities.

The acrimonious 'parting of the ways' of these prominent women – both in the prime of their lives and driven to succeed in the fulfilment of their visions – wouldn't matter, were it not for the consequences regarding how Alice Bailey would be viewed by certain scholars.

Eranos soon attracted a number of renowned European academics including: philosopher and student of Jung, Erich Neumann; zoologist Adolf Portmann; psychologist, philosopher, theologian and Professor of Islamic Studies at the Sorbonne Henry Corbin; and historian of religion, Professor Mircea Eliade. All of these men admired, almost revered Fröbe as the founder of Eranos, with the exception of Italian philosopher and esotericist Julius Evola, who is known to have described her as 'fanatical' with 'highly spiritual' pretentions, a woman he 'wholeheartedly' detested.[47] This condemnation mirrors the caustic view of Alice Bailey held by Mircea Eliade, who considered her work 'unreadable and absolutely worthless'.[48] It is not possible to take seriously Eliade's view of Alice Bailey, since he was known to be Fröbe's confidant and no doubt biased. It is also curious to wonder how he could know that Alice Bailey's writing was 'absolutely worthless' if he was not able to read it.

All of these remarks are opinionated and patronising. It is unfortunate that most of the disdain fell on Alice Bailey. All hopes of gaining favour amongst that crowd were dashed.

It appears the prejudices of these scholars fed the next generation of academics, shaping their view of Alice Bailey. Prominent French scholar of Western Esotericism Antoine Faivre (1934-) was a close associate of Corbin and delivered lectures at Eranos. Professor Emeritus of Religious Studies at the École Pratique des Hautes Études and Chair of the History of Esoteric Currents in Modern and Contemporary Europe at the Sorbonne, Faivre defined the field of Western Esotericism as an academic discipline. Yet he fails to acknowledge Alice Bailey in his *Theosophy,*

Imagination and Tradition: Studies in Western Esotericism. Rudolph Steiner gets a mention. Not, on any of the pages, does Alice Bailey. Faivre's associate and co-editor of the prestigious esoteric journal *ARIES*, Professor of History of Hermetic Philosophy Wouter Hanegraaff (1961-), similarly passes over Alice Bailey. Founded in 1985, *ARIES* originally had on its board Mircea Eliade and other Eranos participants.[49] Swedish professor in the field of the history of religion Olav Hammer, another leader in the field, accepts the purist Theosophical view of Alice Bailey and her work, and scarcely grants her more than a passing mention, although there are signs that attitudes are changing.[50]

In the Theosophical Society, Alice Bailey's work threatened the orthodoxy. Fröbe's troublemaking fed the scorn of an academic elite. More generally, Alice Bailey's teachings were anathema to the fiercely guarded desire of many traditional esotericists and their academic counterparts to ensure esoteric knowledge remained reserved for themselves. It is secret knowledge and must stay that way.

Even today, the problem for Alice Bailey is these powerful forces of orthodoxy are apt to combine to form a confluence of negativity, one projected at a body of work and a set of organisations that warrant genuine open scrutiny and consideration.

THE PERENNIALISTS

Another attack, expressed through purism and intellectualism and targeted at Theosophy itself, has also affected Alice Bailey's reputation. Prominent French metaphysician and esotericist René Guénon (1886-1951) began exploring Eastern religions in his twenties. He discovered Hinduism but converted instead to Sufism, the esoteric heart of Islam. Of interest to him was exploring the idea of a transcendent unity of all religions, an inner metaphysical basis that could be found in both the East and the West. It is an area of interest pursued by, among others, Aldous Huxley in his book *The Perennial Philosophy*.

Guénon became a vocal critic of Blavatsky and Theosophy, particularly in his *Introduction to the Study of the Hindu Doctrines.* Although he shared with Theosophy an understanding of the universality of ideas about God, he was adamant that such unity should exist on its own plane. In other words, each variant religion and sect should be left as it is, separate from others, for, in his view, it isn't possible to unify faiths in their outward expressions of religious scriptures and practices. Theosophy sought to make this inner unity universal in the exoteric world, blending faiths into a single whole. Guénon found this a travesty.

One leading proponent of Guénon is publisher Sophia Perennis, self-proclaimed proponents of the perennial wisdom tradition. It appears Sophia Perennis opposes, in principle and in practice, anything Blavatsky, Bailey and others like them, stand for. Consequently, this publisher stands against the development of what they call an über religion with its implications of global governance. For them, any form of Ecumenism is much more than a corruption of faith.[51] Which perhaps explains why Sophia Perennis published a work by Christian fundamentalist author Lee Penn. His book, *False Dawn: The United Religions Initiative, Globalism and the Quest for a One-World Religion,* is a comprehensive analysis of the roots of a global ecumenical movement seated at the United Nations, including a chapter devoted to Alice Bailey's teachings. In a tone inflamed with his own apprehensions, Penn begins his book with, 'I am writing to warn the public worldwide against the activities of the United Religions Initiative, against its support in the New Age movement, and against the URI's globalist, utopian allies within the State of the World Forum, the World Economic Forum and the Earth Charter movement'.[52]

In the preface to Penn's *False Dawn,* editor and prominent figure in the esoteric establishment Charles Upton is concerned 'that the pseudo-esoteric underworld of Guénon's time has mushroomed, and is now poised to make itself of great and terrible use to the global power elite'.[53] For Upton, Theosophy is an anti-religion preparing the way for an Antichrist regime. He shares with Penn a fundamentalist purism, arguing that faiths are distinct outpourings from God transcendent and cannot be blended by man, and that esotericism cannot ever be a religion in itself.

Upton's reaction is perhaps best described in terms of the ongoing esoteric culture wars that have had Alice Bailey in their sights ever since she inadvertently upset the Theosophical orthodoxy who ousted her from Krotona, and then a decade later Fröbe who ousted her from their collaborative project at Ascona. It is one that Upton and Penn have drizzled with conspiracy thinking, furthering that fiercely anti-Bailey discourse, a discourse which seeks to oust Alice Bailey from the pages of history altogether.[54]

THE NEW GROUP OF WORLD
SERVERS

*O*lga Fröbe may have had another reason to harbour resentment towards Alice Bailey. In 1931, during the second session at Ascona, Alice received a message from the Tibetan. He wanted to form a new group, the New Group of World Servers (NGWS), who would be charged with acting to change the world for the better. There would be an esoteric and an exoteric dimension to the NGWS, and it meant an organisational reorientation of the Lucis Trust.

Until this point in time, the teachings she had taken down for DK and the works she had composed herself concerned pure esotericism including: cosmology, teachings on white magic, meditation, the soul and consciousness. Attention was on the subjective life of the individual, on consciousness and how to expand it, how to connect with the soul. Now the focus was on groups.

Daunting as another project might have appeared to the already overworked and tired Alice Bailey, the NGWS would have appealed to the missionary side of her nature; she would not only create a new, more open version of the old inward-looking esoteric schools, but she would also attempt to influence the whole of humanity through specialised training and outreach work, putting the teachings into practice in exciting new ways.

Her old evangelical self was elevated to new heights, but she was also responding to the turbulent times of the early 1930s. The single initial aim of the whole project was to avert a second world war. The world was in the grip of the Great Depression after the Wall Street stock market crash of 1929. In America, banks were failing, and unemployment was fast approaching fifteen million. In Germany, things were especially grim. The country was still suffering the economic consequences of the reparations imposed by the Treaty of Versailles. In 1932, unemployment there had reached six million. The Weimar political parties were perceived by many as weak and ineffectual. The Nazi party was on the rise. Hitler was hard at work campaigning throughout the nation, and SA storm troopers were parading the streets. The Tibetan's request carried with it a sense of emergency. The NGWS would need to roll up their sleeves and tackle the problems of the times through spiritually focused effort.

Spiritual values were also needed to offset the fast-paced growth of the 1930s, which, despite the poverty and unemployment, witnessed a proliferation of consumerism and a rise of popular culture, including mass marketing of books, magazines and newspapers. In Britain, the decade witnessed a rapid, widespread construction of new buildings and homes, and the expansion of the electricity grid meant ordinary families had domestic appliances and radios, as well as telephones. Humanity was at the dawn of a new era, one that, disturbingly for Alice Bailey, carried with it the stamp of materialism.

The NGWS had two divisions. The first were to have a close relationship with the Spiritual Hierarchy and would work in an international capacity towards 'world salvage'. These world servers would be 'pledged to work without cessation for the promotion of international understanding, economic sharing and religious unity'.[1] They would be trained to serve humanity. They would display 'a spirit of inclusiveness, a potent desire selflessly to serve one's fellowmen plus a definite sense of spiritual guidance, emanating from the inner side of life'.[2] Selected disciples would be guided in recognising spiritual energies that take the form of ideas revealed to them, and out of those ideas, create thought-forms to send out into the world. They would be involved in a process of revelation and transmission of seed thoughts.

Ten groups of nine disciples were to be created, comprising ninety participants in total. Known as the 'groups of nine', they were charged with collectively helping to save humanity from disaster and seed the New Age. It was to be an experiment. The first group would be telepathic communicators, selected for their receptivity to impression from a Master and each other. They were the custodians of the whole project. The second group would be trained observers, able to see clearly into and through all events. The third were magnetic healers, the fourth educators of the New Age, the fifth political organisers, the sixth would work in the field of religion, the seventh as scientific servers, the eighth psychologists, the ninth financiers and economists, and the tenth would be creative workers.[3]

It was Alice Bailey's initial task to find appropriate members. She turned to her pool of Arcane School students for likely participants. Olga Fröbe was invited to join in a letter sent from New York by Alice Bailey in January 1932. Only she had not been selected for the first group of nine disciples, those telepathic communicators who were central to the whole experiment. Included in that first group were the Baileys, Alice Ortiz and Assagioli. Fröbe was invited to join the second group of trained observers.[4] This group was charged with dispelling glamour and illusion, including propaganda, misinformation and lies, and illuminating or pouring light and love into the emotional plane to dispel the mists created by fear, anger, selfishness and hatred. It was important work, considering the times. Fröbe declined to participate.

Out of all those invited, only forty-five agreed to sign up to the experiment and four full groups were formed, along with a partial fifth.[5] Members of the experiment received personal communications from the Tibetan via Alice Bailey, including advice on meditation, initiation and the stages of discipleship, and the development of group consciousness. With their permission, the advice and instructions were published in *Discipleship in the New Age (Volumes I and II)* and *Glamour: A World Problem*, amounting to 1,800 pages of text.

Alice Bailey received the first letters to disciples in November 1931, a few months after the second Ascona summer school. Each participant was allotted three keywords that summed up their life intention. Alice Bailey is DRS: detachment, rest, skill-in-action.[6] Those letters are not included. The first letter to Foster, J.W.K-P. – Joy, Wisdom, Knowledge of the Plan – opens with:

 I would conjure you to face the future with joy and optimism. Courage you always have but joy you lack. With you, as with F.D.C., much of the physical plane activity is hampered by etheric devitalisation, though the causes producing the existing condition differ. During the past years, I have many times conveyed to you a message the summation of which lies in the emphasis I lay on the steadfastness in meditation. Etheric vitalisation lies in meditation where you are concerned and the bringing in of energy to your physical body through its instrumentality.[7]

THE QUOTATION SHOWS a level of scrutiny which is deep and sharply observed. All of the participants, some known to Alice Bailey personally and others not, received letters carrying an identical tone and containing the same pointed insights. Even an outsider unfamiliar with the participants would be confronted by the intimacy.

The experiment was never completed, and the groups of nine disbanded in 1939, the Tibetan forming out of his promising disciples a New Seed Group comprising twenty-four members in an experiment in group initiation. Together these experiments endured for eighteen years. Alice Bailey took down the last of the letters to disciples in the weeks before her death in December 1949.

The letters to the groups of nine and the new seed group, filled with personal observations and advice, were upsetting for some participants. A number of participants left the experiments as a result. Alice Bailey was accused of taking down DK's words incorrectly and of simply writing them herself.[8]

The resultant publication of these letters and instructions is intended to help influence the way later students think about discipleship and World Service. Although the instructions are personal, the reader inescapably becomes involved in the strengths and weaknesses and struggles and challenges that befall each participant.

The second division of the NGWS comprises women and men of goodwill. 'These are not strictly speaking spiritual aspirants…They do, however, want to see right relations established among men. They want to see justice and kindness prevail on earth.'[9] To foster the expansion of the NGWS, the Tibetan 'advocated the building up of mailing lists…He suggested our organising what He called Units of Service in as many countries as possible. He outlined for us the nature of the teaching which they should receive and these suggestions and injunctions we immediately proceeded to carry out.'[10]

Between 1933 and 1939, the Baileys organised Units of Service in nineteen countries. The idea is goodwill comes before peace, that there will never be peace on earth while gross inequalities exist, while people starve, while others are underpaid, while child labour persists. The Tibetan went on to issue to this second exoteric division of Units of Service a series of pamphlets which were later published as *The Externalisation of the Hierarchy*.

Goodwill is much more than simply doing a neighbour a good turn, although such acts are certainly an expression of it. Goodwill refers to eunoia, a form of altruistic or selfless love. 'Good' denotes ultimate worth or value. In a sense, goodwill is willing the good, willing into being things of ultimate value, and willing love. Goodwill is an expression of love-wisdom combined with spiritual will. It is love in action, and its ultimate expression is service.

Service involves 'much sacrifice of time and of interest and of one's own ideas; it requires exceedingly hard work, because it necessitates deliberate effort, conscious wisdom, and the ability to work without attachment'.[11] The personality becomes subsumed under the will of the soul. A life of service is a soul-centred life, one based on the urge for group good, not one based on ambition or desire for wealth, power, control or fame.

While the notion of goodwill forms part of Alice Bailey's Christology, a life of goodwill expressed in service fosters right relations, or a 'proper sense of spiritual values' as depicted in the Buddhist eight-fold path: Right values, right speech, right mode of living, right thinking, right aspiration, right conduct, right effort, and right rapture or true happiness.[12]

Alice Bailey and the Tibetan wrote extensively on goodwill and service across the entire body of work. Together, the words function as a fulcrum, a pivot, an axis around which the world-view turns. Through it, together with the concept of right relations, Alice Bailey and DK not only blend the ethical essence of Christianity and Buddhism, they wrest esotericism from the clutches of the superior and the exclusive, and empower, as they call to all with ears to hear to work towards authentic spiritual living. No other concepts better illustrate the transformation of Alice Bailey's evangelical nature from a Bible-clutching fundamentalist into a Theosophical firebrand.

It is this very combination that makes Alice Bailey the Mother of the New Age. Through it, she outed esotericism, forced it from the closet of obscurity and tried to turn esoteric dabblers into seekers and seekers into spiritual warriors.

To enable the NGWS, Alice Bailey founded Men of Goodwill in 1932, which became World Goodwill in the 1950s and is today listed as a non-government organisation with the United Nations. That communication Alice Bailey had received at Ascona in 1931 added to, and to some extent re-oriented all of her efforts. Suddenly, the Arcane School, *The Beacon*, and the Lucis Trust were no longer simply providing students with a fresh approach to esoteric training and knowledge. A new and ground-breaking project was afoot, one that would go on to shape the direction of her life's work and perhaps ought to have helped to establish her place in history.

With the groups of nine and the New Seed Group, both Alice Bailey and the Tibetan wanted students and co-workers to rise above spiritual seeking for its own sake, with all of the trappings of the personality that entails, and do something on the inner planes to make a difference. Yet this central aspect of the teachings, constituting the very heart of what the Tibetan was hoping to achieve, has not been acted upon in a significant way, or at least not enough to make its presence felt in the world as widely as they had hoped, although there are some who have been inspired to follow through on this intention.[13] For some reason, students of the Ageless Wisdom have shied away from pursuing and developing advanced esoteric group work. The second arm of the NGWS, the Units of Service, has been much more successful. The outer work continues apace, demonstrated in the World Goodwill program of the Lucis Trust today, with Units of Service hosting meditations, especially Full Moon meditations, along with hosting talks and disseminating goodwill in numerous cities and countries around the world.[14]

Overall, Alice Bailey's efforts along the lines of the NGWS were not in vain and they were far from impotent. Just as the more widely known Rudolph Steiner has significantly influenced the education of children, and methods in agriculture such as biodynamics, Alice Bailey's vision continues to influence and be implemented. Paradoxically, a key locus of her influence is international and known to all, yet to a large degree invisible; for many decades her co-workers at the Lucis Trust have dedicated their NGWS efforts within and alongside the United Nations, explored in a later chapter.

UPSETS WITH HELENA ROERICH

*A*s Alice Bailey forged ahead with her vision through the difficult decade of the 1930s, she had to shrug off yet more antagonisms, this time from Agni Yoga founder Helena Roerich who accused her of perpetuating the very darkness she strove so hard to avert.

Russian Theosophist Helena Ivanovna Roerich (1879-1955) was born into a wealthy and cultured family. She was the daughter of well-known architect Ivan Ivanovich Shaposhnikov and Ekaterina Vassilievna Shaposhnikova, who belonged to an ancient Golenischev-Kutuzov family. An accomplished young woman, Helena married renowned painter Nicholas Konstanti-novich Roerich in 1901. They had two sons, scientist George and painter Svetoslav. Nicholas was also a writer, archaeologist, Theosophist and public figure, and the family travelled widely, settling in London in 1919 and a year later in New York, where Helena and Nicholas founded Agni Yoga. From 1928, after moving to the Western Himalayas, Helena devoted her life to scribing the teachings of the Master Morya.

Agni Yoga, or Living Ethics, is another example of the vast Theosophical outpouring of wisdom that occurred during the late 1800s and early 1900s. At its heart lay core elements of East and West, Eastern mystical traditions blending with Western science. The writings differ enormously from Alice Bailey's instructional volumes, and might be viewed as more along the lines of inspirational texts, albeit of the highest calibre. The early writings were composed in telepathic rapport by Nicholas Roerich, then Helena continued the work.

Once the Roerichs moved to New York, Helena had issues with Alice Bailey. An early reference can be found in disciple Sina Fosdick's *My Teachers: Meetings with the Roerichs*. In an entry dated 3 March 1923, Fosdick states Helena purchased a copy of *Initiation, Human and Solar*, 'because it talked about the Masters', and then details Helena's negative reaction in response to the text:

 That one Master studied at an English university and another one knows more than the others about the planets. E.I [Helena] was, of course, indignant about that, and M.[Morya] told them, "It is not given to anyone to learn about the White Brotherhood".[1]

DISMISSIVE COMMENTS and from the very first, Helena was ill-disposed towards her rival, a rival making authoritative statements on the Spiritual Hierarchy.

Five years passed. On 21 September 1928, there is mention in Fosdick's memoir of a letter being sent to Alice Bailey, the day after the Roerichs returned from a trip to Darjeeling, perhaps in response to one from her.[2] Alice Bailey would no doubt have taken an interest in the Roerichs' visit to the general vicinity of the Tibetan and the other Masters. The Baileys and the Roerichs were well acquainted. By then Nicholas Roerich and Alice Bailey were on the advisory board of Svetoslav Roerich's planned

Museum of Religion and Philosophy, a project which did not come to fruition. Also on the board were Sina Fosdick and Nicholas Roerich's close friend and financial supporter Louis Horch.[3]

Alice Bailey and Helena Roerich met, presumably not for the first time, during the period when Olga persuaded Alice to collaborate on plans for the Spiritual Summer School. Alice would have had in the back of her mind the need to find suitable lecturers for the event. She was also keen on finding possible ways to collaborate with the Roerichs. On 25 November 1929, Fosdick notes, 'Alice Bailey visited N. K.; she talked about cooperation and how all great people should be meeting in our house.'[4] A flattering remark, and it is clear Alice preferred collaboration over competition. It is also clear that the Baileys and the Roerichs moved in the same circles. Nicholas Roerich had breakfast with Alice's close friend Grand Duke Alexander of Russia the very next day.

The first known private letter to Agni Yoga's New York group in which Helena Roerich wrote criticisms and rejections of Alice Bailey and her work is dated 9 February 1931.[5] What had turned her so firmly against Alice Bailey? Could it have had something to do with the Ascona project? Were the Roerichs invited to speak? Did Helena Roerich feel in some way threatened or snubbed?

There is no known further mention of Alice Bailey until 17 February 1934, when Helena Roerich writes, 'There is the Arcane School in the United States, which has special classes for studying books on Agni Yoga'. An emotionless acknowledgement and it seems fair to deduce at this point there existed no tremendous animosity between the two women. Rather, in a shrewd move, through these classes, Alice Bailey appears to have gone to some lengths to foster collaboration.

Her efforts were to no avail. In the same letter, Roerich identifies a continuity of descent in which after Blavatsky's death, the teachings came through Theosophist Francia la Due, 'through whom the Master Hilarion gave his teaching'.[6]

Francia la Due and Dr William H Dower founded the Temple of the People, established first in Syracuse in 1898 and then relocated to Halcyon, California, in 1903 where it exists as a centre for meditation and courses today.[7] Francia la Due's most important work is *Theogenesis*, a third section of the Stanzas of Dzyan, which form the basis of *The Secret Doctrine*. When Francia died in 1923, the teaching, according to Helena Roerich, then came through herself. For her, Alice Bailey did not enter the frame.

Roerich seems keen to position herself above Alice Bailey, which perhaps explains why she reacted so strongly when *A Treatise on White Magic* came out in 1934, a reaction she never managed to transcend. About two thirds of the volume was composed in the period prior to 1931, that moment when the New Group of World Servers came into being, and from page 398, the latter half of the text is sprinkled with references to the project. Contained in the volume is one single statement which compounded all that Alice Bailey, or rather the Tibetan had written about Agni, Lord of Fire, in *A Treatise on Cosmic Fire*:

 In the book Agni Yoga, some of the teaching to be given has filtered through but only from the angle of the will aspect. No book has as yet made its appearance which gives in any form whatsoever the "yoga of synthesis".[8]

IF ROERICH HAD READ that statement – and presumably if she hadn't, one of her close associates would have pointed it out to her as it even appears in the index – it would have been the final straw. In her eyes, Alice Bailey had diminished Agni Yoga. Roerich would have been incensed in the reading. Her response was emphatic and scathing. Quoted here is an extract from a letter dated 23 August 1934, [published in Letters of Helena Roerich Vol I, but without the fragment included here], in which Roerich implies Alice Bailey is evil:

 Many naïve people think that the dark forces work only through evil, moral corruption, and crime. How they are mistaken. Only coarse and lower-degree forces work in that way. Much more dangerous are those who come in the guise of the Teaching of Light. You already know of one such example. In America there is a very large Society, and its head receives teaching from a teacher who does not reveal his name, calling himself the Tibetan Brother. We know who is hiding behind this pseudonym. His force is great. And the aim of this teacher, personifying a teacher of the White Brotherhood, is to lure into his ranks as many good and useful people as possible, people who could otherwise have actively assisted in the Great Plan of the Lords, the plan of the salvation of the planet. And those unfortunate ones, who do not possess the true discrimination of the fires of the heart, flutter like little butterflies towards the black fire that will turn them into ashes. Ignorance, the absence of feeling knowledge, draws them into the embrace of darkness and deprives them for a long time, if not for ever, of the beneficent action and attraction of the Rays of the Great Fortress of Light.

I have some books by this Tibetan teacher, they are extremely dry. One book is called White Magic. I have been told that the best pages are borrowed from the Teaching of the White Brotherhood. It is interesting to note that the head of this Society, for her greater prestige and to entice adherents of our books, recommends them to her members and has founded classes for the study of the books of Agni Yoga. In this manner darkness is intertwined with Light on Earth. The network of darkness is being woven by skilful hands.[9]

ROERICH'S RAGE BROILED. Alice Bailey must have known full well Roerich's foibles, although not back in the 1920s when they had initial dealings with each other and *A Treatise on Cosmic Fire* came out, a work that makes numerous references to Agni, Lord of Fire, the Vedic fire god central to Roerich's writing. Up until that one statement in 'White Magic', Alice Bailey had been able to maintain cordial if strained relations. Why in 1934, did Alice Bailey let that single sentence be printed when she must have known the furore it would cause? The Tibetan may have wanted it said, but she had editorial control. Making matters worse, Roerich's son, Svetoslav, was a student of Alice Bailey, a situation that must have been a thorn in his mother's side, perhaps helping to perpetuate the animosity.

Compounding the situation, in that same year of 1934, Nicholas Roerich was sponsored by the United States Department of Agriculture to travel to Manchuria to collect plant seeds to help deal with the severe dust storms that were sweeping through the prairies during the 1930s. Known as the Dust Bowl, these storms, the result of poor agricultural practices, were an ecological disaster. Helena accompanied him and while they were there, suspicions arose over his Bolshevik ties and:

 the Roerichs became persona non grata in America. Helena Roerich who had corresponded with Roosevelt, was forbidden to continue doing so.

Louis Horch...to whom operation of the Master School of United Arts had been entrusted, also turned against the Roerichs, accusing Nicholas of being "an imposter and a cheat," and "a dangerous person who mixed "politics with art and would be a troublemaker wherever he went". Horch even managed to oust Nicholas Roerich as a trustee of the School—the very institution that Nicholas had conceived of and founded. Priceless works of art and Helena's private diaries were seized.[10]

IN A LETTER from Nicholas Roerich to Alice Bailey in 1938, he expressed his chagrin over the matter with 'you can imagine what a breach of trust has taken place'.[11] His letter is in reply to one from her requesting more copies of the Agni Yoga books. He ends the letter with:

 We constantly are reading your books and have much occasion to speak about your blessed work in most cordial terms. We shall be glad to hear of your further plans and Mme Roerich and we all are sending to you and your husband our sincerest wishes.[12]

HIS REMARKS SUGGEST he did not share his wife's jaundiced view of Alice Bailey. Further, it appears Helena Roerich was two-faced in her dealings with Alice Bailey, cordial in public and indirectly in correspondence via her husband and, on occasion, dismissive and derogatory in the private sphere of her own group.

Nicholas Roerich passed away on 13 December 1947.

Bereaved, Helena continued with her scathing remarks of Alice Bailey. In 1951, she wrote, 'Do not have connections with Bailey's school, for they have proved to be hidden enemies'.[13] She accused Alice Bailey of being a medium, her 'compilation works' 'very harmful and her treatise on White Magic intertwined with the most definite Black Magic'. Alice Bailey herself, 'was definitely a collaborator with the dark forces'. She continued to denounce her rival in this fashion until her death in 1955.[14]

In the light of the devastating events that befell the Roerichs after 1934, deep down, was Alice Bailey nothing more than an easy target for Helena's distress? Was Helena seeking to ruin the reputation of a woman she saw as nicely placed at the heart of power, mingling with the very cohort who had turned against her husband? Or were her cutting words simply raw jealousy holding sway over an otherwise impressive individual who made a significant contribution to Theosophy?

The tensions between the two women were never resolved. The only evidence of Alice Bailey's view can be found in a private talk she gave to a select group of Arcane School students in May 1943:

> I am not sure how accurate the Roerich books are. They are like the Mahatma Letters. It is claimed that they were dictated by the Master M.' [group member] Joseph Lovejoy responded with, 'Roerich makes a differentiation between inner consciousness and the subtle worlds.' To which Alice replied, 'The Roerich books are very badly translated. If you read them in the French you get the real thing.'[15]

SHE DID NOT VIEW Nicholas Roerich's *Hierarchy* in the same fashion, affirming its value a year later as giving 'a complete picture of the chain of Hierarchy from the atom of substance up to the highest'.[16]

On the face of it, Helena's remarks can be construed and perhaps dismissed as nothing more than an enduring rivalry, or understood in the context of a turf war between two remarkable women, both in communication with a Master, both writing books that would go on to form a core part of the Theosophical canon. The matter is also heavily one-sided since whatever Alice Bailey privately thought of Helena Roerich is not known, although she clearly had little to no regard for Agni Yoga. The rift has been damaging for students of both streams, those drawn to Agni Yoga especially challenged to take seriously the works coming from Alice Bailey's pen with many in the Agni Yoga milieu strongly opposed to her. Coming as it were from the pulpit and not the choir or the congregation, these vitriolic condemnations from Helena Roerich filtering into the public domain have impacted and continue to impact Alice Bailey's reputation through those who prefer fragmentation over unity, and discord over harmony. Perhaps this is why Helena Roerich herself wisely chose to edit out the most damning of her remarks from the first two volumes of letters prior to publication.[17]

HEADQUARTERS AT TUNBRIDGE WELLS

$\mathcal{I}$n the 1930s, a new way of life opened up for Alice Bailey as operations expanded into Europe. After twenty years of not visiting Britain, she began to divide her time between the two continents, spending about seven months of each year in New York, and the remainder in Britain and Europe, giving lectures in Holland, Belgium, France, Italy and Switzerland. Ospringe Place, today a Grade II heritage-listed building near Faversham, Kent, was made available to the Baileys for several years during this period.

A large country house built in 1799 of white stone replete with Doric columns and balustrade parapets, Ospringe Place was then owned by Benjamin Henry Percy-Griffiths and his wife Hilda Louise (George). The Percy-Griffiths were part of the thriving Theosophical milieu of Faversham. Both Blavatsky and Besant are also known to have stayed at the house on other occasions.[1] It was in this milieu that Dorothy and Ellison met their future husbands and married nearby. Those local Theosophical contacts also provided for the much-needed development of a new Lucis Trust headquarters.

Alice was now approaching her mid-fifties. She no longer had the burden or the worry of bringing up her daughters, but her health was deteriorating. She suffered from pernicious anaemia, a vitamin B 12 deficiency leading to a lack of red blood cells, an autoimmune disease most commonly caused by a lack of 'intrinsic factor', a protein created by stomach cells. The loss of these cells may be the result of the body's own immune system. Alice Bailey's vegetarian diet would not have helped, and at some stage she began consuming meat under the advice of doctors.[2] A debilitating illness even when treated, pernicious anaemia comes with an array of incapacitating symptoms including weakness, extreme fatigue, numbness and tingling in the hands and feet, mouth ulcers and a swollen or cracked tongue, confusion and memory loss and dementia, shortness of breath, slow reflexes, fibromyalgia, dizziness and vertigo, tinnitus, and unsteady walking and spasticity. Pernicious anaemia can damage the heart, as was the case with Alice Bailey. Symptoms develop over many years and the longer the condition is left untreated, the more likely those symptoms will become permanent.

Clearly, Alice needed much support. More and more Foster was Alice's mainstay as she became increasingly disabled. He travelled everywhere with her, driving her to where she needed to be and attending to her needs.

Not one to cave in to her frailties, she forged ahead with all her projects. This was a prolific period in her life. She commenced writing another of her own volumes, *From Bethlehem to Calvary*, detailing the initiations of Christ. She was at work with the Tibetan on a new treatise. There were the New Group of World Servers projects to further with pamphlets to take down, along with instructions and letters to the disciples in the groups of nine, which given the content, was not always a pleasant task.

Around the middle of the 1930s, the Baileys moved from Ospringe Place and established another headquarters of the Lucis Trust in nearby Royal Tunbridge Wells, acquiring a house at No. 38 Broadwater Down, one of a number of mansions in a quiet street lined with leafy trees.[3] How the property was acquired is not known. Alice, Foster and Mildred were residing at the Broadwater Down house on 29 September 1939, the night the Pre-war Register was taken. There is no mention of Mildred's son, Gordon, the result of her short-lived marriage to Meredith Pugh. That September, Gordon would have been about three years old. Present were a number of Arcane School students and *The Beacon* contributors including Alan Murray (1897-), accompanied by his wife Marjorie, and Dean W. Rockwell (1871-) with his wife Fannie.[4] As ever, Alice and Foster were surrounded by co-workers in what was, when the administrative workload was set aside, a tightknit coterie of likeminded souls.

The Broadwater Down house was commandeered in 1940 by the British Army for the duration of the war. The 12th Corps of the British Army, led by General Montgomery, acquired a handful of residences on Broadwater Down during the war. In the vicinity, Montgomery established top-secret tunnels leading to an underground war bunker nearby, and only discovered in 1969.[5] All Alice Bailey would have known was that she could not return there until after the end of the war.

Sometime during the war, Ellison moved with her husband and their young daughter, Elizabeth, to Quetta where Ellison gave birth to their son, Arthur, and another child.[6] Dorothy and Terence Morton also went to Quetta, the location of a military staff training college. The area had been devastated by an earthquake in 1935. The college escaped damage and became a locus of the relief and rebuilding efforts that followed.[7] For Alice, her daughters' relocation would have brought back memories of her former life at Quetta in the soldiers' home. There, she had given her failed lecture on hell. As her daughters enjoyed the high altitude, the world languished in its own hell.

Once the Broadwater Down house had been acquired by the British Army, Mildred and her son resided with her parents in New York. By the time the war was over and the house returned to the Baileys and the Lucis Trust, Alice was an invalid based for the most part in their New York apartment overlooking the Hudson River.

THE SEVEN RAYS

In Tunbridge Wells and New York, the Baileys continued to expand and work tirelessly. Back in 1936, Alice Bailey published *Esoteric Psychology: Volume I*, the first of five volumes in *A Treatise on the Seven Rays*. The treatise serves as a comprehensive extrapolation of DK's initial presentation of the rays in *A Treatise on Cosmic Fire*.

In that earlier work, the Tibetan portrays the rays as waxing and waning in great cycles. Each form or body will absorb the various ray energies, or transmit them elsewhere. In *A Treatise on the Seven Rays*, DK applies this energetic formulation to human psychology, providing a matrix of energies in the form of personality profiles. In this aspect of Alice Bailey's canon, the Tibetan took a few hints on the rays found in Blavatsky's work, and turned them into many thousands of pages of text.

Esoteric Psychology: Volume I, written in an introductory fashion for those who might not have read the other teachings, sets forth a new psychology, introducing the reader to the nature of the soul and its plan and purpose, and delineating the rays: The Three Rays of Aspect and the Four Rays of Attribute.

Theosophy is a hylozoistic theory, positing that all matter has life:

 Life is the synthesis of all activity – an activity which is a blend of many energies, for life is the sum total of the energies of the seven solar systems, of which our solar system is but one. These, in their totality, are the expression of the activity of that Being Who is designated in our hierarchical archives as the "One About Whom Naught May Be

Said." This seven-fold cosmic energy, the fused and blended energies of seven solar systems, including ours, sweeps automatically through each of the seven, carrying the qualities of
Impulse towards activity.
Active impulse towards organisation.
Active organised impulse towards a definite purpose.
This triple energetic impulse, borne on the impetus of the seven great breaths or rays, started the world process of Becoming, and manifested as the urge towards evolution, – towards an evolution which is active, organised, and which works undeviatingly and unerringly towards a specific goal.[8]

FROM THERE, this abstract and cosmological text goes on to explore the rays in the various Kingdoms in Nature, and discusses the various rays in manifestation. The second volume, published in 1942, focuses on the rays manifesting through the human personality and soul, and it is this text that has gone on to inspire others to explore and develop esoteric psychology. It is not surprising that many co-workers have dedicated themselves to advancing this aspect of the teachings. The completion of the treatise, including *Esoteric Astrology*, *Esoteric Healing* and *The Rays and The Initiations* would take Alice Bailey the rest of her life. The titles were published posthumously.

ANCIENT UNIVERSAL MYSTERIES

The 1930s saw Alice Bailey involved in numerous projects. At some point in the late 1920s, DK had begun issuing her with bi-annual instructions to set about transforming Freemasonry in line with the teachings.[9]

Freemasonry has its origins in fourteenth century Europe and Britain, when stonemasons formed fraternities to protect their interests. Originally there were three degrees: apprentice, fellow-craftsman, and master mason. In the early 18th century, some of these fraternities adopted an esoteric worldview, largely through the adoption of higher degrees, granted in ceremonial rites involving the use of esoteric symbolism. Freemasonry began to absorb esoteric currents, including Rosicrucianism and Hermeticism. Widely criticised for its pledges of secrecy and obedience, Freemasonry has long been viewed as a sort of exclusive 'old-boys' network, giving advantage to members in the realms of business and politics.

The Theosophical Society has a long association with Freemasonry. All the international presidents of the TS were Freemasons, and all except Henry Steel Olcott were Co-Masons.

Co-Freemasonry began in 1882, when author, lecturer and humanitarian Maria Deraismes was initiated into a freethinking lodge in Paris. She spent ten years trying to open Freemasonry to women before founding her own lodge in 1893. Numerous distinguished Theosophists joined the new movement. Annie Besant was ruler of the first English Co-Masonic Lodge, consecrated in 1902.[10]

DK's version of Freemasonry, the Ancient Universal Mysteries, or AUM, was a project entirely separate from the Lucis Trust and the Arcane School, involving a complete re-working of the 'entire Masonic edifice'. Freemasonry was fashioned to include the new outpouring of the Ageless Wisdom, including the solar Logos, the Seven Rays and various cosmic Laws, along with the Plan for universal brotherhood. He required changes in masonic rituals in accordance with the new esoteric overlay. Above all, Freemasons were charged with serving others in the spirit of Love and Goodwill.

By the1930s, a small working group was established to

develop the AUM, including Alice and Foster Bailey, Regina Keller, Betty Harris and Marian Walter. Mildred Bailey and Svetoslav Roerich also participated.[11] Ancient Universal Mysteries was incorporated as an entity in its own right in 1935, 'to foster the study and understanding of the mystery teachings of the ages' and signatories included Regina Keller and Alice Bailey, along with Anna B. Schutz, Brahna Welsh, Lilian G. Peper and Leo Rohe Walter, husband of Marian Walter.[12]

Svetoslav wished to include an Ancient Universal Masonic Reading Room in his Museum of Religion and Philosophy project, of which Theosophist and Jungian Leslie Grant Scott was to be director.[13] Leslie was the wife of Major RTM "Rex" Scott, a British thriller writer and Chairman of the New York Section of the American Society of Psychical Research.[14] The Scotts were part of New York's literati scene at the time.

Alice Bailey apparently disbanded the AUM group in the early 1940s, not comfortable with the way things were unfolding.[15]

SOME COMPETITION

*T*hrough the 1930s Alice Bailey was far from alone in wanting betterment for the world. Hopes for a new utopian age were prevalent in Europe, Britain and America. Within the spiritual milieu, while dedicated seekers were committing to particular esoteric currents, dabblers continued to try out various strands, everything from the ideas of Mary Swainson, through Gurdjieff, Ouspensky, Meher Baba, Sufism, Rosicrucianism, Swami Vivekananda and Jung, along with the Theosophists. Alice Bailey was a prominent figure in the scene. She lectured far and wide. *The Beacon* was acknowledged to be a high-quality occult periodical, and as mentioned above, book reviews and her letters appeared in the *Occult Review*.[1] But with so much competition, how were her organisations to rise above the rest. How could the Lucis Trust and the Arcane School, which had set themselves apart, make it known that through the NGWS they offered a solution to the ongoing global malaise. How, when others seemed to be offering a similar package.

One competitor was author Dion Fortune, who advanced an almost identical ambition. Born Violet May Firth (1890-1946) into wealthy Christian Scientist parents in North Wales, Dion Fortune joined the Theosophical Society for a brief period in 1906. She went on to join an occult lodge led by occultist and Freemason Theodore Moriarty, joining the Hermetic Order of the Golden Dawn at the same time. It was in this period that she developed mediumistic abilities. In the early 1920s, she started to believe she had a close personal connection with the Masters of the Wisdom, claiming she was in contact with the Master Jesus, her spiritual guide. The resultant communications formed the basis of *The Cosmic Doctrine*. In the late 1920s, Fortune broke away from the TS after publicly criticising Charles Leadbeater and the Liberal Catholic Church, going on to form her own organisation, the Community of the Inner Light. She gathered around her a group of students, gave lectures, founded a magazine, and published numerous articles, non-fiction works and occult novels. During the Second World War, Fortune organised meditations and visualisations to protect Britain, and started to plan for the post-war dawning of the Age of Aquarius.[2] The similarities with Alice Bailey are striking. Fortune died of leukaemia in 1946. Her extraordinary occult life and her spiritual activism, which have been documented in several biographies, demonstrate the groundswell of interest in matters spiritual and occult, and a concomitant response to the call to action of the times. Whatever Alice Bailey may have thought of Dion Fortune, she was no threat to the Lucis Trust.

Some problematic competition arose in the 1930s in the form of the I AM movement, founded by mining engineer and Theosophist Guy Ballard (1878-1939). Ballard claimed to be in communication with – among others of the Great White Brotherhood – the Master St Germain. I AM refers to the Sanskrit mantra, 'I Am That I Am'. Ballard's *Unveiled Mysteries* was published under the pseudonym Godfré Ray King in 1934, and following his death in 1939, his wife and accomplished harpist Edna Anne Wheeler Ballard (1886-1971) led the organisation.[3] Before his death, the couple held training sessions and conclaves around the United States and gathered a large following, purportedly around a million followers by 1938.

Guy Ballard was a spiritualistic medium who would, according to his son, spontaneously channel El Morya or Koot Hoomi and proceed to speak on family matters at the dinner table.[4] It was in this fashion that Ballard displayed the lower psychism Alice Bailey shunned, a form of psychism which from her Theosophical perspective can only ever access the astral plane and never the plane of intuition. For Alice Bailey, the I AM movement represented everything she abhorred in a spiritual organisation. She is not alone. Much has been written to discredit the I AM movement and particularly the authenticity of its founder, including allegations of plagiarism and the 'borrowing' of ideas from a range of sources.[5]

In offering a watered-down and more accessible if distorted version of Theosophical teachings, the Ballards appeal to devotional types of seekers, those after an easy pathway to spiritual growth involving an assortment of affirmations, gratitude and devotional practices, and prayers and mantras designed to lead to positive change. In Alice Bailey's view, or indeed that of numerous spiritual and religious leaders, no such easy pathway exists.

I AM was a charismatic movement, and its popularity posed a difficulty for Alice Bailey. The movement pivoted on Ballard's portrayal of the Masters of the Wisdom, or rather his misleading misrepresentation. Naming members of the Great White Brotherhood 'Ascended Masters', a term connoting disincarnated beings past the sixth initiation, and having one of them supposedly possess Ballard at his own dinner table, is not only ridiculous from a traditional Theosophical perspective, it brings the entire notion of a Spiritual Hierarchy into disrepute. Worse, the Ballards promised their followers that for them, too, ascension was possible by, of course, following the will of the Ballards. The word 'ascended' has jarred with serious students of the Ageless Wisdom ever since.

In *The Rays and The Initiations*, DK is scathing of the I AM movement in this regard. In discussing the evolution of the Hierarchy and the Law of Ascension whereby senior disciples, the initiates in the various Masters ashrams, are raised to more important work, and their work in turn is taken on by disciples and probationers, DK remarks:

 It is this truth, misinterpreted and shockingly travestied, which lies behind the teaching anent the so-called Ascended Masters, put out by the leaders of the "I AM" movement, thus prostituting and bringing down almost into the realm of cheap comedy one of the most notable happenings which has ever taken place on our planet.[6]

CHEAP COMEDY PERHAPS, but Alice Bailey could do nothing about the output of other leaders and those who chose to follow them. Neither did she demand any allegiance to her own teachings. The DK instructions form part of a large and diverse array of spiritual and occult texts that proliferated and still proliferate, filling bookshelves in New Age stores. Seekers will always be at various stages, willing to adopt whichever version they prefer.

What mattered to Alice Bailey was a strongly felt wish to be regarded of the highest calibre in every respect. To that end, she wanted Theosophy to be regarded of the highest calibre as a source of knowledge. Unlike Ballard, she was not setting about to influence her flock through her own charisma, instead she and DK were endeavouring to change the whole of humanity through training disciples to be fitted for World Service, in a most serious and disciplined fashion. It was only in this way, her way, that the New Age as she, as DK conceived it, would flourish.

The Ballards went on to inspire similar approaches emerging in the latter half of the twentieth century and explored in a later chapter, the I AM movement influencing a significant portion of the New Age movement and serving to, at least in part, define the terrain. This New Age was nothing like what Alice Bailey had in mind, and to some degree has brought discredit and ridicule to the doorstep of Theosophy and trivialised the Spiritual Hierarchy in the eyes of believers and the wider public. Indeed, it is the notion of the Great White Lodge of wise Masters that serves to define Theosophy, distinguishing the esoteric current from other forms of esotericism, and this very defining aspect has resulted in the inclusion of the I AM movement in the Theosophical pigeon hole. With all the talk of 'Ascended Masters', Alice Bailey would not have cared for the enduring association.

THE REAPPEARANCE OF THE CHRIST

*A*lice Bailey's original acceptance of Theosophy was in large part due to the Christology developed by Annie Besant, culminating in a conviction, shared by Besant and Steiner, that Christ would make a reappearance on earth in the not too distant future. With the Second World War fast approaching, the Baileys concentrated their efforts to help harness or draw down spiritual energies and prepare the way. In 1937, Alice Bailey founded Triangles, a meditation network organised in groups of three individuals who commit to reciting a special prayer called The Great Invocation:

> *From the point of Light within the Mind of God*
> *Let light stream forth into the minds of men.*
> *Let Light descend on Earth.*

> *From the point of Love within the Heart of God*
> *Let love stream forth into the hearts of men.*
> *May Christ* return to Earth.*

> *From the centre where the Will of God is known*

> *Let purpose guide the little wills of men –*
> *The purpose which the Masters know and serve.*
>
> *From the centre which we call the race of men*
> *Let the Plan of Love and Light work out*
> *And may it seal the door where evil dwells.*
>
> *Let Light and Love and Power restore the Plan on Earth.*

1

* IT SHOULD BE NOTED that 'May Christ return to earth' does not necessarily refer to a Second Coming, but rather to the externalisation of the Hierarchy, its exoteric or 'real to us' appearance on earth.[2]

THE GREAT INVOCATION was given out in a series of stanzas between 1936-45 and serves as a universal mantra or world prayer. The stanzas are based on ancient wordforms. The 1945 version is entirely different in composition from its predecessors but carries broadly the same intent.[3] So important is this single prayer, it appears on Lucis Trust bookmarks, fliers, postcards and posters.

No caveat on the phrase could make an iota of difference for certain outspoken Christians. In 1987, evangelical Australian writer Morag Zwartz wrote *The New Age Gospel: Christ or Counterfeit* – a work that furthers Constance Cumbey's mission – stating that Alice Bailey's call for the return of the Christ is 'in fact an invocation of the antichrist'.[4] For Zwartz, Alice Bailey's teachings represent a 'false religion' filled with an 'idolatrous belief in the spiritual powers of mankind'.[5]

An open-minded reading of the prayer leaves little doubt Alice Bailey and the Tibetan stood unwaveringly on the side of love and light. The Great Invocation is an example of the practice of thoughtform making, which is central to the teachings. It was this practice that the discipleship groups in the New Group of World Servers were charged with actualising, and it is this aspect of esotericism that Alice Bailey believed would inaugurate the new age:

 A man sees a vision and a possibility. He broods over it and it enters then into the realm of mental invention. A thoughtform is then organized, whether it is the thoughtform of a sewing machine, of a political party, of an economic idea...Much reflection and brooding will eventually produce a magnetic field which will become so potent that desire will enter in; then the dream or vision enters into a new stage of visualization...[and] when the processes of desire have adequately developed, the vision will precipitate upon the physical plane.[6]

In DK's language, thoughtforms, or incarnated ideas, are imbued with vitality and purpose and sent out into the world to complete a specific mission.[7] They are the hallmark of the initiate, whose role is to 'correctly apprehend the precipitating truth, information or revelation, and then to give it an equally correct *format* so that it can meet the immediate human need'.[8] Such thoughtforms are to carry wisdom to help deal with world affairs. Wisdom 'is revealed through ideas, against which (very frequently) much mundane knowledge powerfully militates. The concrete mind often inhibits...the free flow of ideas intuitively impulsed; it is with this free flow of the new ideas...their right application and interpretation, which determine the future of humanity and of the planetary life.'[9]

The Tibetan isn't referring to the term 'idea' as a plan, aim, or project, for that would be reducing the notion to the plane of thought. Ideas emanate from the intuitional plane as abstractions sensed by the mind as impressions. The higher mind strives to attach to the felt impression, concepts that will give it meaning. In other words, wrap the idea in a set of clothes. It's a delicate task. The potential for error is great, and all thoughtforms have consequences on the three planes of human endeavour.

In Alice Bailey's scheme, for humanity the Spiritual Hierarchy is the source of guiding ideas of human and planetary betterment. This hierarchy functions as an intermediary body between humanity and the macrocosm. As previously noted, the Hierarchy is a group of enlightened beings working behind the scenes. It is a form of inner government, or benign theocracy, operating subjectively.

Alice Bailey devoted thirty years of her life to laying the foundations for the externalisation on the outer planes of this inner government. She saw it as a major opportunity for the spiritual advancement of humanity, ushering in a new age of light and love and peace. She claims that since 1925, in a phase of divine intervention, the Hierarchy has been pouring out the energy of spiritual love and trying to instil right relations in an effort to stimulate humanity to make the next evolutionary leap into the kingdom of God. Only, there are other forces at play, deliberately impeding the evolutionary flow, forces attracted to matter and the preservation of form, an ancient vortex of hatred and vengeance that is highly resistant to change, whipping up further hatred, cruelty and fear. These are the materialistic or 'involving' forces which, in humanity, have become laden with negative psychological qualities. Writing through the build-up and enactment of the Second World War, Alice Bailey saw through the lens of her esoteric worldview, the need for a tremendous redirection of human will in order to overcome these forces. She suffered greatly through the war period, acutely sensitive as she was to the horrors of that war.

She was convinced that the inpouring of spiritual energies stimulating humanity were in preparation for the reappearance of the Christ, and she penned a work with that title. *The Reappearance of the Christ* was written in telepathic rapport with the Tibetan, yet unlike his esoteric texts, the book reads a little like evangelical exposition laced with Christian millennialism. Alice Bailey, or rather the Tibetan, is quick to counter the view. 'I write here in no fanatical or adventist spirit; I speak not as a speculative theologian or an exponent of one phase of religious, wishful thinking. I speak because many know that the time is ripe and that the appeal of simple, faithful hearts has penetrated to the highest spiritual sphere and set in motion energies and forces which cannot now be stopped.'[10] As head of the Spiritual Hierarchy, Christ, along with the Masters of the Wisdom and their disciples, will usher in the Plan of Love and Light. The door into the place where evil dwells will be sealed.

In this work, the Tibetan writes of the emergence of a new world religion, 'a universal faith which will have its roots in the past, but which will make clear the new dawning beauty and the coming vital revelation'.[11] The new world religion will be based on: the fact of God, both transcendent and immanent; the fact of immortality and eternal persistence; and the continuity of revelation and divine approaches.[12] The new faith will blend Christianity and Buddhism, or West and East, in part by honouring the festivals of Easter and Wesak, along with a new festival of Goodwill to be held on the full moon of June.[13] It will be a synthesis of faiths, one that will 'emphasise the unity and the fellowship of the spirit'.[14] A new world religion which for all its acknowledgement of Eastern ideas is at root Christian in emphasis.

The Reappearance of the Christ might be viewed as a culmination of all that Alice Bailey believed in as a once devout Christian who had never relinquished her faith. Composed in the few years between 1945 and her death in 1949, during a period of her life in which she was seriously ill, the work represents a confluence of her vast store of Theosophical knowledge and her deeply felt faith in Christ. It may be the case that as such, with the imminent externalisation of the Hierarchy, Alice Bailey was the perfect recipient of this outpouring of higher wisdom, able to receive the revelation and transmit it to others. It may also simply be that in this example at least, she poured forth the workings of her own extraordinary mind. Some would go so far as to argue that all of the Christian phrasings in the Bailey teachings are her own style and not that of the Tibetan.

DYSTOPIA

Throughout Alice Bailey's body of work is a powerful undercurrent, a conviction that humanity is fast approaching an eschatological precipice and may either fall into darkness and death or enter the kingdom of God. The sense of urgency, ever present in the tone, the imperatives, the insistent manner, is borne of the context of the age in which she wrote and yet points to a larger context in evidence today.

Alice Bailey strove to point humanity in the direction of its soul. It's worth appreciating what she meant by soul consciousness, involving the fundamental principles of love and wisdom, an awareness of the interconnectedness of all, and an evolutionary pull back to the Divine. It is also worth considering what has manifested since her death: the new world order of free market capitalism manifesting in extreme inequality and a ravaged planet, all in the name of selfishness and greed. Through the lens of Alice Bailey, the dark forces of materialism are running rampant on our earth.

A large section of the discipleship instructions Alice Bailey received from the Tibetan for the New Seed Group were extracted and collated to form *Glamour: A World Problem* and speak directly to one of the most powerful tools used to manipulate the way humanity thinks and feels.

'Glamour' is a keynote of the occult. The magician casts a

spell, or swings a watch on a chain back and forth before the eyes, and the recipient's mind is fogged. She enters a trance. She is no longer in control of her thoughts or her emotions. She is under the magician's command like an automaton. In the occult, the power of mind over matter is paramount. When Spiritualism and Theosophy were enjoying a resurgence in the first decades of the 1900s, this was part of the fascination. Jung and his followers picked up on it, as did the transpersonal psychologists; suddenly they had access to pathways into the mind formerly not realised. Through this ability to send a patient into trance, access to the unconscious opened, parts of the mind that spoke in symbols, and archetypes became recognised and used in therapy.

While the psychologists were busy exploring this uncharted territory, Alice Bailey had other concerns. Uppermost in her mind was the need to offset evil. She knew that esoteric practice would be used as much for selfish as altruistic purposes. She saw that the same processes at work in the magician's chamber, were manifesting on the world stage in the realm of ideas.

In Alice Bailey's view, all ideas emanate from a higher plane. They are abstract, free floating, owned by no one, and exist in communion with each other, all serving a current purpose in the evolution of consciousness. The human thinker takes an idea and dresses it up in language. When the thinker regards the idea separately from all others, the idea becomes an ideal, or an ideology. That single ideal then takes up a dominant position in the mind, and all other ideals are shunned. The individual becomes attached to her one ideal and all others are made wrong.[15] It is in this way that humanity becomes imprisoned in mental illusions. Collective attachment to any ideal is a kind of mass trance. Humanity is enslaved, chained in Plato's cave, unable to see reality. The consequences can be disastrous.[16]

Alice Bailey was far from alone in sensing an emerging dystopia. While George Orwell was writing *1984*, and Franz

206 | ALICE A. BAILEY

Kafka composed *The Trial* and *The Castle*, Alice Bailey wrote her entire body of work in an attempt to offset a new dark age.

Meanwhile, other thinkers alive at that time were developing ideas that would come together to form what many would argue is a new world order, one that emerged in the aftermath of the Second World War and has been moving steadily towards corporate-led globalisation ever since. Its materialistic form is exactly what Alice Bailey was trying to avert, and despite her best efforts she was powerless to stop it. Economics has become cultish and esoteric, concentrating wealth and power in too few hands. This new world order is anathema to the one Alice Bailey envisaged. What has emerged through decades of free-market economics is a form of totalitarian rule by an elite cluster of self-serving corporations with more power than many individual nation states.[17]

Alice Bailey's organisations were designed to produce a cohort of thinkers who would influence world affairs at a high, international level. DK's first division of the New Group of World Servers were charged with creating thoughtforms in the fields of politics and economics that would make the world a fairer, more loving place. The second division of the NGWS, the women and men of goodwill, disseminated pamphlets in the hope of achieving just that, world salvage.

Unfortunately, while the discipleship groups were apparently busy trying to co-think into being thoughts that would help humanity, countermoves were at work implementing a parallel strategy that would prove astonishingly effective in swaying mass opinion. Propaganda was developed in the 1920s by, among others, public relations pioneer Edward Bernays (1891-1995), after many were impressed by the success of wartime propaganda efforts deployed as a recruitment and galvanising tool. Bernays saw that the approach could be used in peacetime too.

Propagandists deploy various techniques to create or transform public opinion. In *Glamour*, DK identifies the ease with which the masses are manipulated through glamour, a term used to describe illusion infused with emotion, the illusion becoming 'smothering, vague, and enveloping'. Illusion creates confusion, glamour creates a 'sea of fog'.[18]

In the decades after the Second World War, methods of propaganda, and of thought manipulation more generally, have become increasingly sophisticated. For the propagandist, any idea or concept that threatens their status quo must be diffused through condemnation and attack, or through appropriation. In other words, propagandists latch on to concepts that might threaten their aims and objectives and bend them to suit themselves. Alice Bailey's volume on glamour provides a useful lens through which to view propagandists as magicians and understand the illusions they create.If she and the Tibetan were writing today, they would be training their co-workers in white-magic methods of dispelling illusions.

Alice Bailey saw the dark path humanity was on. She set about creating an alternative that would rise above it, rather than go into battle with it on its own terms. Back in the 1930s and 40s, she placed the weight of responsibility for the evolution of the entire planetary scheme on her disciples who were charged with practicing goodwill and fostering loving understanding in themselves and others. The true goal of all spiritual endeavour 'is this arousing of public opinion to world rights, to inclusive human interests and to international cooperation'.[19]

Alice Bailey was adamant that her readers and followers refrain from focusing on their own spiritual development and orient themselves to service. In a pamphlet composed for the NGWS on 30 June 1940, as the Second World War was in its first year, DK wrote: 'Who will arrest the progress of aggressive self-ishness if the men and women of goodwill rest back upon their idealism and do naught that is practical to justify their hope or aid in the materialisation of the desired idea?'[20]

HEALTH IN DECLINE

*I*n 1940, Alice was in her sixtieth year and her health was failing her. It was a year marked by the death of her dearest friend and patron Alice Ortiz, who was four years Alice's senior. She would have felt the passing as she might her own sister, for Alice Ortiz must surely have fulfilled this role in her life after Lydia chose to have nothing to do with her. Ortiz had supported the Baileys for almost twenty years, was a key benefactor and member of the first group of nine in the DINA project.

By now, Alice and Foster, along with Mildred and her son, had left Stamford in favour of a New York apartment over-looking the Hudson River. It was there that Alice is known to have hosted tea gatherings for New York City socialites, by invitation only. The gatherings were conducted along the lines of a salon, current events discussed and ideas for solutions generated.[1] Alice Bailey held a position of eminence among the New York who's who, enjoying the same sort of respect as that afforded her grandfather John Frederic La Trobe-Bateman, albeit in an entirely different field. She also penned numerous letters to influential figures in which she discussed the problems humanity faced and the role the United States might play, addressing those holding positions of power, including Eleanor Roosevelt, with whom Alice had a reasonably close association. On one occasion, Eleanor Roosevelt is said to have invited Alice Bailey to the Rose Garden at the White House.[2]

After the Japanese attack on Pearl Harbour triggered America's entry into the war, New York became a main port for troop embarkation and the dispatching of supplies. New York also received the inflow of war refugees, and the city took on a military feel, the streets filled with servicemen as workers were mobilised, and military training camps spread throughout the city. With the onset of America's war involvement, residents learned to cope with rationing.

In the midst of all the disruption, the Baileys and their co-workers carried on in their organisational roles. Between 1939-45 *The Beacon* issued its regular number of editions. The magazine continued with its usual format, containing a mix of esoteric pieces with commentaries on the problems of humanity. Extracts from Agni Yoga made a regular appearance. Among a wide range of contributors were author, composer and astrologer Dane Rudhyar; muralist, painter and author Auriel Bessemer (1909-86); and pianist Evelyn Benham Bull (1897-1983), author of *The Creative Activity: Introspective Experiments in Musical Composition* (1929). Reading through the list of contents feels like stepping into another world, one in which the war was not taking place. Lacking overall, was the urgent tone of the pamphlets and instructions given to the New Group of World Servers. *The Beacon* provided a business-as-usual normalcy to an otherwise ragged set of war-time conditions.

Alice Bailey was determined not to let the dire circumstances undermine her mission, although the war affected her greatly, sensitively attuned as she was. Fortitude is scarcely an adequate word to describe the resilience and determination she displayed during this period. Her efforts to reach and sustain the NGWS – who were themselves demoralised – proved onerous. The work took its toll. With the death of her chief benefactor, the trust began to suffer financially. Funds to continue the work were scarce. At the war's end, the matter had become so serious that in a pamphlet issued for distribution to her women and men of goodwill in June 1947, Bailey wrote a lengthy plea in an effort to solicit funds from supporters, asking them to 'make sacrifices… to the limit of their capacity'.[3]

She refused to be defeated. She worked and worked hard, just as she had done her whole life, getting up early, scribing for the Tibetan, then putting in a full day at the office. She felt she had no choice. Her pernicious anaemia had by now weakened her heart, yet she was more driven than ever. Her attitude is revealed in the following statement, given in September 1943:

 Don't tell me, as one student did, "I am well over 50 and can't have any fire." I have lots and I am 63. You can have fire if you want it, but you only get it when your sense of values is properly adjusted and nothing matters to you but what you can do under the inspiration of your Soul to give your full quota of help, even if it kills you. It does not matter one bit if you die. What does matter is that we go all out to meet the need.[4]

SHE WAS SURELY GIVING her full quota. Realising her life was coming to an end, she needed to press on with taking down all the Tibetan wanted her to write and overseeing the progress of all aspects of the work. There were books and *The Beacon* to publish, the Triangles network to promote, the Arcane School teaching sets to compose and the DINA letters to disciples to take down. There were lectures to give and private interviews too.

Her friends and family marshalled their efforts to support

her. Ernest Suffern was working as treasurer. Regina Keller held her key editorial role on the publishing side and worked closely with the advanced students in the Arcane School. Foster was in charge of the New Group of World Servers among other roles. By now, her daughter Mildred, who was approaching thirty years of age, was assisting, taking on the role of preparing the reading sets for Men of Goodwill.[5]

Mildred, affectionately known as Billy, would go on to become director of Men of Goodwill for several years. Demonstrating that the goodwill movement was more than just words, she also actively participated in the rehabilitation of child refugees at the end of the war.[6]

By this time the Lucis Trust occupied the top two floors of Salmon Tower, with the Arcane School offices and meditation room on the top floor and the other offices including Men of Goodwill and the library beneath.[7]

As if she didn't have enough to do, in New York from 1943-46, in a bid to successfully hand over the Arcane School after her death, Alice Bailey gave Friday evening talks to selected advanced Arcane School students who were all either members of the Headquarters Group, worked 'in connection with the four meditation groups', led one of the groups, were responsible for the papers to go out, or handled groups of students.[8] All of the thirty participants had a role to play in the leadership of the school. Alice stressed that such leadership emanated from the group and not its individual members. 'The School will measure up to its destiny if this group stands as a unit together in all the work it has undertaken...'[9] Present among others, were Foster Bailey, Regina Keller, Florence Garrigue, Ernest Suffern and Marian Walter. Alice Bailey's remark, carrying the subtext of its opposite, a situation in which group disunity prevails, was prescient.

There were two further aims behind the talks. Firstly, Alice Bailey wanted to advance the work of the New Group of World Servers by forming a true esoteric group and secondly, she

wanted to explore ways to further the teachings of the Arcane
School itself. 'I want this group to be an outpost of the Hierarchy.
I want it to be our imaginative replica of a Master's ashram…
The Masters are not interested in individual disciples; they are
only interested in groups, and then from these groups, they
gather people who will be in their ashram.'[10]

The idea was to develop the spirit of the group. Each talk
involved Alice Bailey presenting material for discussion, much
of it later published in *The Rays and The Initiations*, the final
volume of *A Treatise on the Seven Rays*. Despite wishing for a
group that would require no leader, the transcripts of the talks
indicate that group members looked to her for confirmation of
their ideas, and she was very much at the centre of things.

Concerns for the Arcane School and how it would progress
into the future after her death, remained uppermost in Alice
Bailey's mind. In 1944, she remarks: 'The reason I talk about the
School is because the School should be an expression of what
happens in this meeting, because this is the most important
group in the School – from the spiritual angle, I mean.'[11] She
goes on to voice concerns over the calibre of the secretaries, or
commentators on students' papers, and their ability to respond
spiritually and not exoterically. Based on this concern, she had
Alan Murray, a co-worker based at the Tunbridge Wells headquarters, send out 'to all the secretaries in the Arcane School in
Great Britain a statement about what he regarded as their weaknesses and their strengths'.[12] She noted the difference between
disciples Roberto Assagioli and Eugene Cosgrove, who had both
entered the school having already established their own spiritual
groups, as compared to those who were taking their first steps.[13]

Alice Bailey wanted to form a secretarial group with an overseer role to supervise the one hundred secretaries of the school
worldwide. 'My nightmare is that we would have a static group
of secretaries and settle down into a crystallized group. We will
if we don't keep fluid and become esotericists ourselves. How

can we pretend that it is an esoteric school if we ourselves are not esotericists?'[14]

She harboured misgivings over the progress of students, and voiced the need to move beyond meditation into states of contemplation in which self-consciousness and preoccupations with the self are lost.[15] That somehow, the school had advanced students so far, but not far enough. 'I just don't know how long I have. Who among all the people that we have been training in the School is an esotericist who can carry on? Who is a real esotericist? How are you going to gauge an esotericist? How do we know what constitutes an esotericist?'[16] In the same comment she states she had asked the same of co-worker Alan Murray, who she had singled out as a potential candidate to run the school. She did not provide his response.

She was acutely aware that the Arcane School taught occult information and gave advice on how to meditate to develop soul awareness and was indeed a highly spiritual metaphysical school, but there was something missing. It was not, yet, an esoteric school. 'I imagine if we heard a real declaration as to the nature of an esoteric school we would feel that we knew nothing; we would be amazed at our lack of perception.'[17] She was pushing the group beyond soul awareness towards that further achievement of spirit-soul connection, one receptive to spiritual will and purpose. It is also worth noting Alice Bailey employs inclusive language throughout the talks, referring to 'we' and 'us', veiling her own esoteric abilities which may or may not be reflected in her comments.

Despite her best efforts, the matter of who would run the Arcane School and how, refused to resolve.

By the mid-1940s, Alice's health was in rapid decline. She received monthly blood transfusions administered by Foster under her doctor's supervision.[18] At the beginning of her 5 November 1943 talk, she mentions she had heart failure in the preceding week.[19] In May 1945, Foster led the weekly talk, stating that Alice had had a mild heart attack and was receiving blood transfusions to raise her blood count.[20]

In a talk Alice Bailey gave in April 1945, Florence Garrigue asks: 'What form of simplification will this group take as it gets more unified?' Someone responds with, 'More work and less talk.' Alice then somewhat ironically says, 'As far as I can see, it is mostly talk and no work.'[21] The weekly talks appear to be a disappointment, and sometime in 1946 Alice Bailey either lost interest or became too ill to continue. Besides, another avenue to advance the teachings had caught her attention.

That April, the Tibetan gave out the final stanza of the Great Invocation and called upon his disciples to use it daily, as many times as they could.[22] Franklin Roosevelt had passed away in the same month. By June, the San Francisco Conference was in full swing, and the United Nations Charter was signed by fifty nations on 26 June, with Poland signing two months later. The talks Alice gave to her headquarters group around that time, contain much discussion regarding the end of the war and hopes for the future, and much sadness over Franklin Roosevelt's passing.

By the end of the Second World War, Alice Bailey, like many others of her time, yearned for better global governance. She was distressed by the war, deeply affected by the suffering she saw, and appalled by the aggressor nations, which she often described as 'agents of the Black Lodge'.[23] In response, she argues the need for a new world order, one that would meet:

 the immediate need and not be an attempt to satisfy some distant, idealistic vision...[one] appropriate to a world which has passed through a destructive crisis and to a humanity which is badly shattered by experience...[one] founded on the recognition that all men are equal in origin and goal but that all are at differing stages of evolutionary development;

that personal integrity, intelligence, vision and experience, plus a marked goodwill, should indicate leadership.[24]

ALICE BAILEY and the Tibetan advocated equality of opportunity for all, individual freedom and autonomy, the eradication of poverty, the sovereign rights of all nations, a universal education, shared resources, distributed fairly, and disarmament.[25] They both sat firmly on the side of social democracy on a global scale. Writing in the late 1940s, the Tibetan states:

 Socialism can degenerate into another form of totalitarianism, or it can be more democratic than the present expressions of democracy. These issues will emerge clearly in Great Britain, where the socialist point of view is gaining ground among the masses, but which at present is a mixture of nationalisation of the public utilities and free enterprise - a combination which may have true value, if preserved.[26]

THERE EXISTED no outward anchor for these reflections until the founding of the United Nations on 24 October 1945 in San Francisco, when its charter was ratified. The imminent formation of the international organisation provided a fresh focus. From then on, in the last four years of her life, Alice Bailey directed her students and co-workers towards it.

Alice Bailey had held no equivalent aspirations regarding the League of Nations. In *Telepathy and the Etheric Vehicle*, the Tibetan states that the former league was the result of an idea of 'world unity in the realm of politics' had by Master Serapis, who passed it on to Master Jesus, who presented it to his group of disciples, the idea eventually registering in the brain of Colonel House who then passed it on to Woodrow Wilson.[27] In 1945, he describes the League of Nations as 'an abortive effort – well-intentioned but relatively useless'.[28] By implication, the idea for the United Nations came from the Hierarchy.

That Alice Bailey endorsed the United Nations is understandable. The organisation had the potential of cohering with her spiritual ethos, while offering a means of preventing another world war. International laws would force nation states to conform to higher standards and human rights would be of paramount importance.

The Universal Declaration of Human Rights was proclaimed by the United Nations General Assembly on 10 December 1948. The driving force behind the declaration was Eleanor Roosevelt, then chair of the United Nations Human Rights Commission. It is fair to suggest that behind Eleanor, issuing thoughts of encouragement in correspondence and meditations, would most certainly have been Alice Bailey.[29]

There was, at last, hope of a world founded on unity, goodwill and right relations:

 The United Nations, with all their faults, limitations, weaknesses and nationalisms, are focussing the conflict between the Dweller and the Angel, and…gradually and decisively throwing the weight of their effort and aspiration on to the side of the Angel…This they are doing by the increased clear thinking of the general public of all the nations, bound together to conquer the three Axis Powers, by their growing ability to conceive ideas in terms of the whole, in terms of a desirable world order or federation, and their capacity to discriminate between the Forces of Light and the potency of evil or materialism.[30]

In 1947, Alice Bailey wrote *Problems of Humanity*, a slim volume she composed herself, containing seven pamphlets composed between October 1944 to December 1946 in which she offers solutions to world problems. In the final pamphlet, she discusses world unity 'which is based on simple goodwill and on cooperative interdependence', noting that since there exists no 'counsel of perfection to give the world or any solution which will carry immediate relief', the United Nations '*must* be supported; there is as yet no other organization to which man can hopefully look.'[31]

The Destiny of the Nations contains a delineation of the problems facing the United Nations from an esoteric perspective. The Tibetan asserts the 'true problem of the United Nations is a twofold one: it involves the right distribution of the world's resources so that there may be freedom from want, and it involves also the bringing about of a true equality of opportunity and of education for all men everywhere.'[32]

For Alice Bailey, the United Nations was a vehicle for goodwill. She called on those women and men of goodwill in her NGWS, encouraging them to help 'restore world confidence', and 'to educate the masses in the principles and the practice of goodwill'.[33]

A shadow loomed despite the good intentions of the United Nations. Back in April 1942, Alice Bailey acknowledged the difficulties facing the United Nations as nations followed their individual desires rather than follow 'an organised spiritual will'.[34] Interestingly, the United Nations was named, three years prior to its existence.

In the later sections of *The Rays and The Initiations*, the Tibetan voices concerns with the Zionist movement and the formation of

Israel.[35] 'Zionism today stands for aggression and for the use of force, and the keynote is permission to take what you want irrespective of other people or their inalienable rights. These points of view are against the position of the spiritual leaders of humanity.'[36] The Tibetan continues in the same anti-Zionist vein with:

 The leaders of the Zionist movement of aggression constitute a real danger to world peace and human development and their activities have been endorsed by the expediency policy of the U.S.A. and, in a secondary degree, by Great Britain, under the influence of the U.S.A. It is the Zionists who have defied the United Nations, lowered its prestige and made its position both negative and negligible to the world.[37]

CONTENTIOUS REMARKS that have inflamed allegations of anti-semitism. In the same passages, DK is critical of Russia's communist orientation, dooming the freedoms of individuals under, not an authentic communistic form of brotherhood as portrayed in the writings of Lenin and Marx and with which he had no issue, but a group of ambitious and evil men. An April 1948 pamphlet comments on the difficulties emerging after the United Nations 'compromised its principles and admitted Russia' before the other nations had had a chance to unite on economic reforms, national reorganisation and of regional groups'.[38] For DK, both the Russian form of communism and Zionism were manifestations of the forces of evil.

In June 1947, in a pamphlet titled 'Preparation for the Reappearance of the Christ', frustrations with the progress of the

United Nations are clear. After presenting the many hindrances to Christ's reappearance, the Tibetan states:

 The United Nations is occupied with rapacious demands from all sides, with the angling of the nations for place and power, and for the possession of the natural resources of the Earth – coal, oil, etc. – and also with the underground activities of the great Powers and of the capitalists which they all create.[39]

DESPITE THE OBVIOUS problems emerging shortly after its genesis, if a new world religion founded on esoteric principles was to emerge, and the Hierarchy to externalise, then the singular hope for humanity was to be found in the UN, an organisation capable of manifesting humanity's highest aspirations. The little said in the Bailey corpus was sufficient to direct students, co-workers and followers from then on into its arena.

At the end of the war Alice had become gravely ill. In the final three years of her life, her 'heart and blood condition' had deteriorated dramatically and she was, for the most part, bed ridden.[40] Still, she persisted. In the aftermath of the war, she set to task re-establishing her global networks. When the house at Broadwater Down was returned in 1947, Alice and Foster Bailey made the journey across the Atlantic for the annual Arcane School conference. They would make the journey twice more, including in 1949, the year of Alice Bailey's death.

In 1947, insurance broker and co-worker Frank Hilton, a key figure in the aftermath of Alice's passing, arrived at the New York headquarters where he was employed as an educationalist. He would go on to become vice-president of the Lucis Trust from 1952-1956.[41]

In July of 1949, Alice Bailey wrote a letter to all on her mailing list. She was by then spending much of her time in Roosevelt Hospital where she received numerous blood transfusions, and in between them, she carried on writing for the Tibetan, taking down the ideas in shorthand and then writing them up in full, a task that fell to her, she says, due to her self-confessed illegible shorthand. Above all, she writes of the rapid post-war expansion of the work:

 We found when the war was over that our work had grown numerically in Holland, Belgium, Italy, in German Switzerland and in Great Britain, which latter country we were fortunately able to service during the war from New York. We found also that the few students in France, Poland and Romania were still holding on; they got in touch with us within a few months of the end of the war.

Since then the growth of interest in every land has increased phenomenally; the workers in Europe scarcely know how to cope with the situation. Students from every country are joining the Arcane School daily. The work in Germany and Austria (which was quite negligible prior to the war) is now so great that the German - speaking section promises to be, relatively, the largest we have... The Belgian Congo is opening up and Liberia also; the work in Egypt and in Greece is growing fast and we are inundated with appeals for the Tibetan's books, for the work of the Arcane School and for the Service Activities.[42]

THIS LETTER IS over five-thousand words long. The Lucis Trust's New York headquarters was facing a severe financial crisis. The training of four hundred fourth degree Arcane School students needed to be met, along with those of the third degree. There was an 'emphatic demand' for books in foreign languages and there was no money to print them. She writes of the heavy work-load, the lack of secretaries and the dire need for funds to service all aspects of the work, including the much-needed funds for postage and printing. She details how hard Foster worked, and her daughter Mildred, whose health was not good and yet, like her mother, she carried on. 'In 1947, [Mildred] was in bed for nearly six months, but worked constantly all the time, sometimes from 5 a.m. on.'

In a letter to Mildred, 'my beloved Billie', written on 20 April 1949, when Alice and Foster were staying at Broadwater Down for the Arcane School conference, Alice talks of eating meat – something she had taken to doing for her health – when she could get it, and of drinking ale. She complains of the house-keeper Miss Burgoyne, 'a strict vegetarian [who] eats lettuce with a superior air', and her decision to fire her and get 'a cook and not a lady help, sitting upon a gilded pedestal'. These remarks, unfiltered, are a rare insight into Alice Bailey's person-ality, remarks echoed in some of the passages in her autobiogra-phy. She never could stomach 'superior airs'.

She writes of Ellison's struggles with her health – she had phlebitis, thyroid and heart problems – and of the rationing and shortages in post-war Britain. In a letter to Mildred from Foster sent a few days later, he mentions 'the jerks', a symptom of pernicious anaemia, and the medication Alice took to help prevent them. Alice had also suffered another heart attack.

All the while, Alice was still taking down DK's letters to disciples that made their way into the second volume of *Disciple-ship in the New Age*. She was at work on *The Labours of Hercules*. The Tibetan wanted her to scribe his translation of the *Bhagavad Gita*, something she 'dearly wanted to do' before she died. She had also just commenced writing her autobiography. Ever self-effacing, she writes, 'I hate autobiographies, but it is inevitable that my biography will be written after my death, and I do not want any eulogistic biography written about me; the value of my life lies in the fact that I have been just an ordinary girl, Church worker, mother and house worker, and I felt that I might encourage others to do what I have tried to do – tried so hard to do.'[43]

Alice Bailey passed away in New York during the afternoon of Thursday 15 December 1949 with her husband Foster Bailey by her bedside. Among her last words spoken to her husband were:

 '"I have much to be thankful for. I have had a rich and full life. so many people all over the world have been so kind to me."'[44]

PHOTOGRAPHS

Castramont House (photo, M J Richardson / Carstramon
and Rusko Castle / CC BY-SA 2.0)

Alice Bailey, c 1908 (photo courtesy Rose Bates)

The Methodist Episcopal Church (1892) and Parsonage built in 1901.

Alice and Walter Evans' residence c. 1912. (photo www.reedley.com)

Alice Bailey, c 1920s (photo courtesy Steven Chernikeeff)

Alice Bailey and Ellison c. 1922 (Photo courtesy of Rose
Bates)

Foster Bailey, c.1917. (photo courtesy Rose Bates)

Alice Bailey with Dorothy, Ellison and Mildred, c. 1920.
(photo courtesy Rose Bates)

B P Wadia, Alice Evans and Foster Bailey, 1 February
1920 (photo courtesy Lucis Trust)

Foster Bailey, 1922 (photo courtesy Lucis Trust)

Alice and Foster Bailey, c. 1932. (photo courtesy Rose Bates)

Casa Shanti, Ascona, c. 1931. (photo courtesy Rose Bates)

Foster Bailey at work in Casa Shanti, c.1932. (photo
courtesy Rose Bates)

Foster Bailey, Olga Frobe, Violet Tweedale and Zorab, c. 1931. (photo courtesy Rose Bates)

Alice Bailey, Mme Lorsa and M. Meyer Willing, Ascona,
c.1931. (photo courtesy Rose Bates)

Alice Bailey, Ellison Bailey, Dr Keskar, Ascona, c. 1931.
(photo courtesy Rose Bates)

Alice Bailey, Ascona, c. 1932. (photo courtesy Rose Bates,
edited by Steven Chernikeeff)

Olga Frobe, Ascona, c 1931. (photo courtesy Rose Bates)

Alice Bailey with grandson Gordon, c. 1936. (photo
courtesy Rose Bates)

Foster, Alice, Gordon and Mildred, 1937. (photo courtesy
Rose Bates)

Gordon and Mildred Pugh, portrait c. 1942 (courtesy
Rose Bates)

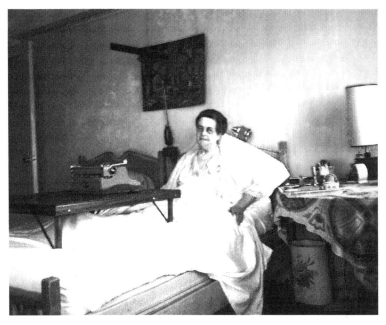

Alice Bailey, 1949, at work shortly before her death.
Before his own death, her grandson Gordon Pugh
wished this photo to be shown as it portrays Alice
Bailey's dedication and sacrifice. (photo courtesy Rose
Bates)

38 Broadwater Down, rear, c 1940s (photo courtesy Lucis
Trust)

Foster and Mary Bailey, c 1960s (photo courtesy Lucis
Trust)

Florence Garrigue, Norma Artus, Clara Weiss, Margaret
Schaeffer, Regina Keller, Ellen Schwarz, Helen
Hillebracht, Frank Hilton and Hilda Hilton, 1957. (Photo
courtesy School for Esoteric Studies)

Frank Hilton 1957. (photo courtesy School for Esoteric
Studies)

Mary Bailey, c 1970/80s (photo courtesy Lucis Trust)

FRAGMENTATION AND HEALING

APPLICANTS AT THE PORTAL

fter Alice's death, the running of the Lucis Trust was thrown into considerable chaos. The cohort of co-workers charged with continuing the work in a united fashion turned in upon itself and the organisation splintered. A lack of necessary group cohesion in the New Seed Group, cohesion that would enable the group to adopt a collective leadership role, proved highly problematic. In January 1949, in one his talks to his disciples, the Tibetan states:

> The past record of this group in effective and steady work would not incite A.A.B. to have much confidence in your leadership. You have shown no organised group ability to take a piece of work embodying some one or other of my suggested spiritual enterprises and effectively work together for its furtherance. What have you done *as a group* to aid the Triangle work or the Goodwill work, or to throw yourselves successfully behind the work of the School? There are many outside the New Seed Group who have done a more consecrated and

selfless task than have you, though there are a few
exceptions. But, my brothers, out of fifty-one, how
few!![1]

IT WAS for this reason that the Tibetan and Alice left Foster in
charge. 'When A.A.B. passes on she will leave the Arcane School
and, with my full approval, all the other activities in the hands of
F.B. She will leave also, in the departments, dedicated men who
will continue to assume, as far as in them lies, the direction of the
work, in consultation with F.B.'[2]

Foster had no choice but to take complete organisational
control. He did not want the added burden of the Arcane School
but felt he had no choice but to take charge of that as well
because as far as he could tell, no one else had been left to run it.
Foster was to oversee all aspects of the trust, including the
publishing of future books, the continuance of a monthly issue of
The Beacon magazine, the Triangles work and Men of Goodwill.
He had to do all that while grieving the loss of his wife and
companion. He was physically, emotionally and mentally
exhausted from the burden of caring for Alice for years in her
invalid state and enabling the work to continue. The carer is
often overlooked in such situations.

In 1950, Foster withdrew to the Tunbridge Wells headquarters to recuperate. He was found by his future wife Mary to be in
a 'seriously depleted physical condition'.[3] He left behind a core
of loyal co-workers who were already in charge of various
aspects of the work. Regina Keller and Frank Hilton were
eminently capable. As was Barbara Amos, head of the British
work. Alice's daughter Mildred continued to play a key role in
the Men of Goodwill work. Foster also left Mildred and her son
Gordon behind in the New York apartment.

Mildred had been devoted to her mother's work from the
outset, running the Men of Goodwill outreach program and

organising European lecture tours and speaking engagements. She was also heavily involved in the post-war rehabilitation of children and veterans in New York, approaching dignitaries and actors, indeed anyone in the society circuit she thought would respond favourably and assist.

In support of Men of Goodwill, Mildred had already produced a number of well-presented study sets of some twelve typed pages each, including: The Challenge and Opportunity of Goodwill, Goodwill as the Science of Relationships, Goodwill Work as Adventure in Leadership and Goodwill as the Dynamic Factor in Human Affairs. The aim was to expand on the good-will thoughtform with ideas and arguments designed to appeal to and convince the public.[4] In a letter to Mildred dated 25 April 1949, Foster Bailey offered his full and wholehearted praise of her Men of Goodwill Study Set II. 'I am more confident and happy and look more eagerly into the future of the Goodwill work under your leadership than I have ever done before.'[5] A strong endorsement with a powerful subtext. At the time of writing, they both knew her mother was dying. And that Mildred had been singled out to take full charge of Men of Goodwill.

She continued to run Men of Goodwill, but it has come to light that some tensions with Foster resulted in her incorporating Men of Goodwill as a separate entity no longer under the auspices of the trust and therefore cut off from any financial assistance. She incorporated Men of Goodwill in January 1951.[6] Any issues arising between Mildred and Foster during this time must be viewed in the light of the enormous strain both were under. Correspondence by letter across the Atlantic would have exacerbated the discord.

Problems arose in the running of Men of Goodwill from then on due to the ongoing and severe lack of funds in that post-war period and, for various reasons, Mildred withdrew.[7] Foster, still based at the Tunbridge Wells headquarters, then went on to continue the goodwill work under the name of World Goodwill. The first reference to World Goodwill appears in the April 1948 pamphlet included in *The Externalisation of the Hierarchy*.[8] Presumably, this accounts for the new name.

The effective if unintended ousting of Mildred would have sent a ripple through the New York headquarters where all were forced to come to terms with the absence of Alice and the presence of Foster, remotely in command. Even though they were all long prepared for her passing, Alice's death left her closest co-workers and family members grieving and bereft of a leader and figurehead. Suddenly, everyone had to defer to Foster, who had a different sort of personality to that of his late wife. Some, like Mildred, found him difficult to work with. Yet, in the words of his future wife Mary Turner, 'All his life he was a rebel, unconventional, a non-conformist, sweetly unreasonable at times but always unutterably sweet, a true disciple in the purest human and hierarchical sense.'[9] These heartfelt terms of endearment, written decades later, were no doubt a defence of her husband.

Continuing to overshadow the trust was a severe lack of funds, which added considerably to the mental and emotional strain of all those working at the headquarters. There was no money to hire secretaries to deal with the mounting workload. Co-workers carried on as best they could but the single outstanding matter that had not been addressed prior to Alice's death, who would run the Arcane School, proved a powder keg.

Included in the August issue of *The Beacon*, is an address Foster gave to the Annual Conference Banquet of the Arcane School, New York, in May 1950, titled "The Arcane School: Its Esoteric Origins and Purposes", an address also published in *The Unfinished Autobiography*. In his address, Foster highlights the importance of the school and Alice Bailey's intentions behind it. Of note, he states, 'Both A.A.B. and the Tibetan have definitely stated that after she died He would not continue to function through any other channel as he did with her, and she is not attempting to control the Arcane School or direct its affairs, nor any of the service activities by means of any messages of any sort or kind.'[10] His remarks seem pointed, a veiled censure perhaps, and they certainly serve as a preface to what followed.

The lack of a successor to the school would go on to cause two schisms and some tensions within the Alice Bailey community, schisms which continue to this day. In January 1949, DK addressed the New Seed Group on the leadership matter, urging participants to cease talk of reorganisation, as it would 'immediately disrupt the present smoothly working organism', and called for the end of 'all talk of executive heads, of assumed responsibility'.[11]

Alice had given her weekly talks for over three years in the hope that some solution to the problem of leadership would emerge. It didn't. In Foster's words:

 Alice made two abortive attempts to find and train her successor to head the Arcane School. The burden therefore fell on me, although it had never been in my schedule. I just had to do the best I could, and we did finally pull through. One headquarters worker was bitterly disappointed. She thought she was entitled to the job, but Alice would not risk it. I had to struggle, but I am glad she made that decision. There is a great difference between a glorified probationary path School with old age overtones, and an esoteric discipleship School with new age overtones.[12]

THE WOMAN FOSTER refers to is Marian Walter. A family friend and senior member of the school, Walter had been helping organise the papers for a fourth-degree training program which Alice Bailey had called the Applicants at the Portal, a group formed to enable disciples to pass through the second and third initiations and prepare for group initiation, a process the Tibetan was keen to make manifest. From the outset, Walter set out to achieve what Alice Bailey had been describing for the Arcane School in her weekly talks, namely to gain group polarisation among students of the fourth degree.

Walter was a participant in the Friday evening talks, although not vocal according to the transcripts, and there is one particular exchange between Alice Bailey and Marian Walter in January 1946 which gives a glimpse of Alice's view that Marian was not quite suited to the task of running her school.

Walter opens the exchange by portraying the group attending the weekly talks as an atom, albeit one that is not fully formed. Alice Bailey takes issue with the notion of the atom, ignoring the second part of Walter's argument. Walter offers a defence. Then Alice Bailey says, 'I don't quite see the analogy because you start with the completed atom. We are balancing and making something.' Walter tries to elucidate, a short exchange occurs, and then Walter is put in her place when Alice says, 'It's a dangerous thing for a group to start with the idea that it is a finished thing.'[13] Walter makes no response.

Such comments from Alice Bailey were not unusual. If she thought another's perception was not quite right she was quick to correct it. Yet embedded in the remark is a seed of doubt. The successor of her school would need to be absolutely precise about such matters as fundamental as the nature of her group.

Walter did not pick up on the implications. She could not detect or she chose to overlook that Alice doubted her capacity. She later chose to sincerely believe Alice Bailey had put her in charge of the Arcane School.

The daughter of an English dry goods merchant, Marian Bath Walter was born in Muncie, Illinois, on 2 November 1898.[14] She was a psychologist with an interest in music, wife to building supplies manager Leo Rohe Walter.[15] On Alice's passing, Walter was fifty-one years old. She was a woman in her prime. She had been placed in DK's third group of nine, the healing group, and after those first groups folded, she was invited into DK's second experiment of group initiation, the New Seed Group. Walter is RSW in the DINA groups: rest, stability, wisdom.

The letters from DK addressed to Walter in both volumes of *Discipleship in the New Age* shed some light on why she felt entitled to run the Arcane School, along with various reasons Alice chose not to give her the role. Back in March 1936, DK describes Walter as a psychologist with a loving heart and an over-active mind.[16] In August of that year DK writes, 'I somewhat fear the academic teaching for you', referring to Walter's emphasis on an intellectual approach to psychology and search for academic knowledge. He was trying to steer her away from the psychology of the then present, and towards esoteric psychology and the study of the seven rays, making soul psychology her life's work.[17]

This matter was taken up again in January 1940 when Walter joined the New Seed Group. In a letter from DK, she is advised to strive to see her soul purpose more clearly by ridding herself of selfishness, cultivating an attitude of unconcern when it comes to the experiences of her own personality and curbing impulsivity.[18] In August 1942, she is advised to reflect on the chain of Hierarchy, looking towards those who are above and beyond her.[19]

Difficulties arose in September 1943. DK writes, 'I have been concerned about you. The strain under which you live and work is not good'.[20] A month later:

 The next statement sought to swing you into the circle of your service in relation to your group brothers and the senior group within the Arcane School. Circumstances, however, moved you from my Headquarters, and this became difficult of fulfilment.[21]

THERE IS a hint that she had been earmarked to take charge.

The statement in the paragraph that follows concerns the need for Walter to study deeply and work completely along occult lines and to engage in mundane tasks in her family to offset the strain of tuning into world distress. 'Your work for another year should be primarily with the senior students, and you should endeavour to have a larger and more organised output of work in that connection; it will serve to focus the consciousness more firmly in the head.'[22] The remark again hints at a mandate for some greater role of responsibility within the school, although DK had no right or authority when it came to who ran the school, which was strictly Alice Bailey's own project. However, Walter may have felt singled out, especially after DK went on to suggest Walter talk to Alice about the difficulties she was having.

In November 1944, there was a definite shift in tone. DK tells Walter she is too zealous, too determined. 'Your fourth ray mind, constantly presenting fields of conflict which you must conquer, deflects energy which, pouring through your soul, could lead to a planned and organised activity on the physical plane.'[23] In short, DK identifies Walter's over-analytical mind. 'You play around with ideas all the time; you experiment all the time, but that should be past history.' DK then calls upon Walter to find her right place in his Ashram and later in the same letter, to ascertain her field of service, which should not be assisting a person here and there in 'flighty service', which he likens to 'spiritual adolescence', but to a whole group.[24] 'Your field of service is clear, could you but see it, but of no use to you unless you enter it voluntarily, freely and with understanding.'[25] It was a moment akin to that which Alice received from Koot Hoomi when she was fifteen years old, to shape up and mend her ways. Many of the DK letters to various disciples express similar sentiments.

In August 1946, DK reinforces for Walter her special role when he explains he is seeking to pass on certain responsibilities to the Arcane School, just as he had lifted some responsibilities in training disciples off the shoulders of the Masters K.H. and Morya:

 In the advanced section of the Arcane School this experiment is going on, though as yet only in an embryonic manner; more difficult and specific training should be given to the few who are reacting correctly to the "Call of the Hierarchy". I have spoken to A.A.B. upon this matter, and along the line pointed out to her I ask your help and your time: I would ask you also to permit A.A.B. to train you more specifically for this work…[26]

THIS IS REINFORCED in November 1948 with, 'In the reorganisation of the Arcane School, I would ask you to take your full share and to concentrate your major effort upon the work of the senior students. Have in mind always that it is *spiritual* esotericism that is required; teaching the students to create a line of light between themselves and all circumstances and problems.'[27]

Given all of these comments, how then was Walter to believe anything other than that the training of the advanced students of the Arcane School should fall to her?

The Applicants at the Portal work had originally been given to Regina Keller, and Alice Bailey had then singled Walter out as she was younger, and placed Keller in an overseer role, hoping Walter would stabilize in some fashion.[28] It would appear that she did not and no other leader was found prior to Alice's death. According to Foster, Walter was one of the two abortive attempts to find someone to head the school. Walter was the co-worker

Alice would not risk. The risk might pertain to Walter's mental polarisation and psychological unpreparedness for the task.

When Walter assumed control of the Applicants at the Portal project and proceeded to produce new study sets, those who had reached that stage of the Arcane School's training included head-quarters' co-workers, among them Frank Hilton. The misgivings Alice Bailey had held found an echo.

In a letter dated November 1950, Hilton responds critically to the first study set created by Walter, voicing concerns over the manner in which she was leading the group, cautioning her against coming across as 'a teacher talking to a class of students' and making unilateral changes to the meditations. Uppermost in his mind is the need to foster a group along Aquarian lines, a group of souls who are 'united in aspiration and objective, and submerge their interests to the soul purpose of the group as a whole'.[29] He suggests Walter draw on a small nucleus of group members who can agree on future changes. From his perspective, Walter's approach was along the lines of the outgoing Piscean groups, gathered around a leader.

Walter did not change her methods. Instead, she announced that the Arcane School 'would be cut off from the benefit of its spiritual relationship to the Tibetan' if H.Q. did not accept her way of running A at P, a matter Foster Bailey describes as 'quite fantastic'.[30] Referring to a letter Walter wrote to Keller in August 1951, Bailey tells Walter, 'Your insistence that R.K. came to you and admit yourself right and herself wrong or you could not let the A.S. have D.K.'s Ashramic force, was the height of spiritual pride, separateness and glamour.'[31]

By 1952, the manner in which Walter continued to run the group became of grave concern. From the outset, she felt she had a mandate to run A at P. In March, she claimed DK had posi-tioned the group:

on the periphery of His ashram, and there to receive His advanced work formerly given to His personal group, – this work to be adapted to the needs of the group and the immediate cycle of the Plan's need, - it is fitting and correct, not only for the needed service, but for the training which was requested, that this group should receive the Tibetan's 1936 esoteric instructions. They will be found elsewhere in this set of papers.[32]

THESE INSTRUCTIONS WERE among unpublished material that made its way into *Discipleship in the New Age Vol I* and *II*.[33]

In April, Hilton brought the matter of Walter's leadership style to the attention of A at P members and some left the group.[34] In October of that year, after a year in which attempts were made 'to reach a constructive and harmonious solution', Frank Hilton, Regina Keller, Florence Garrigue and Joseph Love-joy, together with Olga Bata, Victor Fox, Charles C. Hill and Gerhard Jansen, ended their association with Applicants at the Portal. The resignation letter was approved by Foster Bailey. The letter goes on to explain to Arcane School and A at P members that it was not advisable to remain in both groups as it would 'only lead to confusion' regarding the meditations and they should make a choice. The tone of the letter is not acrimonious, but rather wishes Marian Walter well in her initiative.

In a letter to 'Priscilla' (Frank Hilton's wife) dated a month later, Keller points out that the Arcane School planned to continue with the advanced training for those taking and moving beyond the fourth-degree course of study and that all the material Walter had, the Arcane School also had and more besides. 'The Tibetan's Teachings are <u>all</u> in the possession of the Headquarters here; Marian is using the text of what I am no in process of getting out as Volume II of Discipleship in the New

Age. But I have here much more which she does not have. Some of it I let her borrow last year when I had high hopes that she will recover from the glamour of authority and will take her place to supplement the group, same as the rest of us do; but her idea was not to supplement but to supplant. And when I showed her an excerpt from the Tibetan's statement, written in November 1944, to the effect that when AAB passes over and is no longer with us here, that the Arcane School must be guided by a group, Marian said to me: "Don't show this to the others." I did show it nevertheless and why not?'[35]

In the same letter, Keller states 'I could not possibly stand by and see AAB's project jeopardized and maybe wrecked by Marian's megalomania.' Keller also mentions that Walter had wrecked four other projects and quotes Alice Bailey saying, 'What can we do with the little fool, except to love her?'[36] There is no indication regarding the nature of these projects.

In June 1953, Foster Bailey wrote a letter to Walter, standing fast beside Keller and Hilton's decision to resign from the group. He sums up the situation with:

 I do not want the Arcane School members whom you are continuing to drain off, to enter the new cycle unduly influenced by glamorous attraction to offered special spiritual status, claimed superiorities under the influence of the proclaimed authority of a Master of the Wisdom.

Let it be clearly understood that during her lifetime A.A.B. never gave me any knowledge or indication that it was her plan that you should take the position you are now taking....I deeply regret that you are continuing to use the prestige of A.A.B. to attract people to your group and that you are now basing your position on your claim making and authoritarian basis of discipleship work in the world....Your assertion that the difficulties between the A.S. and the A. at P. resulted from their inferior understanding is a completely unjustifiable transferring of blame onto them. The situation after Alice's death was, in fact, the result of your attitude and conduct and your belittlement and criticism of H.Q. group and how they were doing things.[37]

HE GOES on to voice his despair over Walter's announcement in 1950 that she planned to use A at P to re-create the Tibetan's groups of nine and New Seed Group experiments and that he believed her to be in spiritual danger. Foster Bailey ends the letter by stating he could no longer cooperate with Walter as things stood.[38]

Ostracised and hurt, Walter went on a campaign to invite Arcane School students to join A at P.[39] She had her supporters. She took with her four participants in DK's DINA groups and others. There were twenty-seven members of Marian's group including: Alice Bailey's personal assistant Louise Benesch (wife of Bernard Morrow); opera singer Ann Dixon, Homer Carnegie (brother of writer and lecturer Dale Carnegie), and Lillian Morris, all members of the original DINA groups; benefactress and patron of the arts Grace Rainey – who had dropped out from participating in the DINA groups of nine in 1939[40]; musician, composer and prolific Theosophical author in the Ageless Wisdom tradition Rev. Torkom Saraydarian, who was very young at the time; and astrologer Marcia Moore.[41]

With the Applicants at the Portal group now firmly in her control, in a letter dated October 1953, Walter states:

 The reason it took over three years to bring this group into cohesive condition of group intention is that *it is an ashramic group*. Bringing this group into existence inevitably provided a testing in the *wider* area than just within this group itself because the A at P is a unit with the Plan of the Hierarchy (tiny as that unit is) with regard to the particular phase of this Plan concerning the training and service of disciple groups, it was necessarily brought into juxtaposition and consequent inter-relationship with *other* units which serve the Plan on their various levels of awareness which to do so as far as they are able to grasp the Plan.'.[42]

WHICH IS a veiled way of alluding to the acrimonious split. There had been some dissatisfaction in her group, Walter writing partly in response to expressed regret among her members that Alice Bailey had not left instructions for the running of the school. Walter notes that neither DK nor Alice Bailey gave out clear instructions for who would be responsible for the Arcane School and they had done this intentionally, in keeping with the esoteric hierarchical relationship of the ashram – to avert compliance and interfere with freewill – and that gradually, over time, Walter herself was made aware that this was to be her future service. 'Hints are permissible and this is the time-honoured hierarchical method of teaching. In this situation, both A.A.B. and D.K. gave hints – several instances – to individuals and to His group.'[43]

Walter then states that due to the need for compliance with the Laws governing the Hierarchy, a period of testing ensued, which was much larger than just the A at P group. 'We who have the responsibility of guiding the A at P group and who were, because of the nature of things, closely involved at the centre of this crisis, are deeply grateful to all who...stood waiting.[44] It is clear from her letter that she adopted the higher ground and positioned herself above the ructions, and that she felt entirely justified and unrepentant in her decision to break away and form Applicants at the Portal II, regardless of any damage to the wider group this caused. Towards the end of the letter, she expresses her gratitude to her friend Louise Benesch, who offered to mimeograph group papers, study sets and the monthly mediation reports.[45]

When she broke away, Walter took with her copies of material that was meant to stay in the Arcane School. She continued to produce her own study sets, comprising an amalgamation of her own creation and material from Alice Bailey's study sets, along with the Tibetan's Ashramic Series written in the 1940s.[46]

Walter's study sets amount to 519 pages of material. Study Set III provides useful instructions on the building of the second half of the antahkarana – the bridge between the soul and spirit – in preparation for group initiation, which were taken from the Tibetan's original notes and satisfy the core intention of the breakaway group. According to Walter, this material meant for fourth degree students had already been separated from the Arcane School by Alice Bailey.[47] The same instructions for the building of the antahkarana can be found in *The Rays and The Initiations*.[48]

In an effort to explain to her group the purpose of Applicants of the Portal II, which was to form a group of nine, Walter writes:

 We promised to write the group why the "A at P II" was a definite part of the Plan of DK's new ashramic group. The plan was that I start three such group-nucleii, as soon as possible, and later to form, as occasion permitted, other nuclei groups with their corresponding members at a distance. The first three were to be established respectively in New York City, Washington DC and Los Angeles, thus bringing the throat centre, head centre, and the future heart centre of the United States into a subjective yet conscious and cohesive etheric linking pattern – a lighted living etheric triangle with an unimpeded circulatory flow of energies between them. The group will recognise that this particular triangle of relationship is symbolic of the triangle of centres, which is peculiar to disciples in training. The members of these nuclei who live at a distance, geographically speaking, are to be considered radiating points of extension into the wider areas of the body of the New Group of World Servers. Other nuclei of disciple groups were later to be established in Europe, including London and Geneva or their adjacent environs.[49]

AFTER SET III WAS GIVEN, Walter appears to deviate from her initial goal. For reasons that are unclear – evidence, perhaps, of the instability referred to in DK's letters to her, or of mental strain due to the pressure to prove herself to those who had followed after the split – in almost feverish fashion, Walter delivers long tracts comprising her own opinions supported by vast strings of quotations from various Ageless Wisdom sources including DK, to prepare for the Second Coming of the Christ and a new world religion. There is a strong astrological emphasis. A marked deterioration is evident from Set V onwards. In a letter to her group in the fifth set, dated February 1955, Walter admonishes the poor effort of members who failed to complete the tasks allotted them in the previous year.[50] She ends the letter with an affirmation of her own telepathic abilities.[51] The need to prepare for the Second Coming dominates Set VI with talk of the world in crisis reaching a peak.

In the eighty-nine pages of her study Set VII, in her letter to A at P II members dated July 1955, Walter discusses arrangements for the group to meet, as before, at Grace Rainey's New York apartment for the Leo New Moon ritual.[52] From there, she issues pages and pages of commentary supported by many dozens of extracts, largely drawn from *A Treatise on Cosmic Fire*, *Esoteric Astrology* and *The Secret Doctrine*. Evidence of misquoting suggests the set was probably put together in a hurry.[53]

Walter goes on to make a number of claims anent the Masters and their activities, including that our planetary Logos took the second initiation at Wesak in May of that year.[54] She asserts some changes in the organisation of Hierarchy and issues a raft of portents based on the astrological chart of the New Moon in Leo 1955, involving 'a terrific flood of energies'.[55] She then writes:

 One wonders if the Tibetan was speaking with pre-vision when he wrote in His instructions to His former group that this stage of His activities would be finished by 1956. That year is later than the end of the 30-year cycle of writing through AAB, of which he also spoke.[56]

FOR REASONS THAT ARE UNCLEAR, the Applicants at the Portal II project then came to an end. Reflecting back on that time, Foster's future wife Mary Bailey looks at the split this way:

 Group members stand at many different stages on the path, linked together in service by love of the work and the soul's inclination. But sometimes differences can arise at the outer level of the work and its activities and within the personalities of the workers which may supersede the inner strength of commitment and love. When this happens there can be change and movement in personnel.

There is also the fact that not all who try the experiment of group work and group training are necessarily soul-directed. There can be what the Tibetan Master calls "spiritual selfishness" both in motive and in performance...[57]

HER REMARK, written in the late 1980s, surely and at least partially points back to Marian Walter, and indicates the longevity of the hurt and disappointment felt over her decision to break away.

Is Mary Bailey's comment fair? Did Marian Walter go off the rails, the result of her own 'glamour of authority'? Or had she been ostracised by those a generation older, who wished her to toe the party line and defer to her seniors? Was Walter a megalomaniac or was she ousted as a result of her own ingenuity and freedom of expression? Perhaps Walter was simply a free-spirited soul, genuinely under ashramic impression, meant to use the Applicants at the Portal to continue developing the groups of nine, a project that met with derision when she confided her plans to Foster. Whatever the case, Applicants at the Portal II was dropped.

THE SCHOOL FOR ESOTERIC STUDIES

From 1952, the Tunbridge Wells office was the headquarters for World Goodwill and it was there that Foster Bailey continued the New Group of World Servers work which had always been his responsibility. He should be credited with his own achievements during this phase of organisational adjustments in the years after Alice's death. In line with the Tibetan's wishes, most notably, was Foster's founding of World Invocation Day in 1952:

 The year 1952 will be a year of spiritual crisis and a year when it should prove possible to close more tightly the door where evil dwells. The Invocation has been sent out by the combined Ashrams of the Masters and by the entire Hierarchy; it is used by its Members with constancy, exactitude and power. It will serve to integrate the two great centres: the Hierarchy and Humanity, and to relate them both in a new and dynamic manner to the "centre where the Will of God is known."

I ask you, therefore, during the coming years to prepare to use and distribute the Invocation and make it a major endeavour. I would have you call all the people in every country in the world (whom you are in a position to reach) to a united voicing of the Invocation on the same day in every land. I would ask you to collect all that I have said or written anent the Invocation and then prepare a brief manual as to its use and purpose, putting a copy in the hands of all those who are willing to use it. A comprehension of its origin, meaning and potency will render it far more effective. The year 1952 should see a major turning point in the thinking of humanity, in human goals and human affairs. For implementing this I would ask you to work.[1]

FOSTER BAILEY FOUNDED World Invocation Day on 9 June 1952, on the Gemini Full Moon. World Invocation Day observes the Great Invocation, designed to invoke the spiritual energies of love, light and power to foster unity, cooperation and peace. On the Lucis Trust website, Eleanor Roosevelt can be heard reading the prayer in a broadcast inaugurating the special day.[2] According to her, 'someone' gave her the prayer. That someone would most likely have been Foster Bailey.

Early that year, the head of the British work at Tunbridge Wells Barbara Amos became ill with terminal cancer. A replacement was needed. Mary Turner, a part-time worker at the Tunbridge Wells office at the time, stepped into what she thought would be a temporary role. It was to prove permanent.

Mary Turner (1909-2007) was a self-described single mother with a young daughter and had been working as a volunteer in the war effort. She was at that time searching for something more than day-to-day survival and came across the Bailey books. She joined the Arcane School almost straight away and began volunteering at the Tunbridge Wells headquarters in 1949.[3] Once she took on Barbara Amos' role, Mary Turner and Foster formed an alliance.

While Alice Bailey refrained from describing how she felt about her husband, Mary was more forthcoming. She said he worked with total dedication in a manner that was 'non-fanatical, quiet, humorous, but intense'.[4] On occasions he gave the impression of ruthlessness, or of being over-forceful and disregarding of others' feelings. There was a softer side to the man. Mary found him to be 'loving, compassionate, tender and acutely sensitive'.[5]

The Tibetan had other views, suggesting that in some respects, Foster was at times not best suited to the leadership role he had been allotted. He was in the first group of nine as JWK-P: Joy, Wisdom, Knowledge of the Plan. While eminently capable at the level of the work, he struggled to accommodate those around him. Comradeship was not his forte.[6] He had a tendency, the result of a certain forthright approach to 'shatter and hurt'.[7] In a letter from the Tibetan in 1946, Foster is cautioned that 'every time that first ray energy pours through you it leads to a trifling or a true crisis in your relationships with others'.[8] He was told to develop a genuine liking for his fellowmen.[9] 'You are apt to be suspicious of people's motives. Give them due credit for sincerity and for having something yet to learn.'[10]

The advice proved portentous, perhaps in some regard because Foster had found a powerful ally in the very efficient Mary Turner, a woman prepared to back him to the hilt. They joined forces on one side of the Atlantic, with the New York headquarters running the Arcane School on the other. A second schism was fomenting in the months immediately after Marian

Walter broke away, and again the issue driving the split was the Arcane School.

The schism began in 1954, when the New York headquarters led all fourth-degree students worldwide to understand they had had sole charge of the fourth-degree work all along. Foster was incensed. In March 1954, in a letter addressed to the head-quarters groups in New York, Tunbridge Wells and Geneva, he issued a curt response, stating it was not the role of one or two people at the New York office – Frank Hilton was the executive head of the Arcane School in New York, and the other person Foster refers to is Keller – to 'exercise a final decision' regarding what to do with students who had finished the fourth-degree training.[11] Later the same month, the New York headquarters put out a long statement outlining how all the various views put forward by those concerned with the future of the advanced teachings of the Arcane School were complementary. A defensive and appeasing tone is evident.

Foster responded and Keller addressed his response in late April. Clearly upset by his reaction, she states the reason for her delay as 'the points you raised created a crisis affecting the very life of the Arcane School'.[12] She tells Foster he made a number of assumptions with regard to how the school was being run and what lay behind the thinking of those in charge. 'It is my hope that you will see how completely groundless is all the mistrust, suspicion, fear and consequent misunderstanding which you have been projecting upon us, with me as a special target.'[13]

Foster, who never had a large role to play in the esoteric side of the work, felt control of the Arcane School slipping from his grasp, particularly when faced with the following remark from Keller:

 Judging by your letters, it was a grave and serious mistake on my part to take for granted a certain amount of familiarity on your part with the teaching side of the School; and another mistake was my taking for granted that you have as complete confidence in my integrity and the purity of my motive as your fellow server in the One Work, as I have in yours.[14]

IN THIS LETTER she is at pains to explain the various decisions that had been made regarding the training and their justifications.[15]

She may have been reconciliatory but she was not about to acquiesce. In a second letter dated several days later, she accuses Foster of attacking the school. Again, she explains the rationale behind pursuing training for those few who had passed through the fourth-degree.[16]

In response, Foster threw down the gauntlet, putting out a letter to Arcane School members stating his views on the handling of fourth-degree students. Appalled by his intransigence, Keller responded to Foster in June, stating in no uncertain terms that those responsible for that training do not agree with him, either in method or principle.[17]

Alice Bailey would have been dismayed to see her school succumbing to the very organisational power struggles that beset the Theosophical Society, power struggles that created disunity and degeneration. And there was to be no healing or transcending the rift. Around that time, in a move that could only inflame an already tense situation, Foster and Mary visited the New York headquarters and took back with them the work of the British students in the third and fourth degrees.[18]

By January 1955, Mary Turner had stepped into the fray. She wrote a letter to Frank underscoring the apparent fact that Foster had been given full responsibility for the Arcane School, a matter Keller refuted in a memo to Frank in response, providing numerous extracts in the galleys of *Discipleship in the New Age Vol II* as proof.[19] The extent of her chagrin is evident in the number of pages and the volume of material she provided to prove her point.

Keller had been among the most active members of Alice Bailey's Friday talks. It is this close proximity to Alice, evidenced in the Friday talks as a mind attuned and on point, a mind in rapport, participating fully and confidently, that to a large degree explains and justifies Keller's discontent over Mary Bailey's involvement. Mary Bailey, who through Keller's eyes would have appeared a rank outsider, an upstart, the new kid on the block.

Letters back and forth were detailed, long and persuasive, filled with explanations and justifications. Many letters over many months but no solution could be found. Foster, for his part, was intractable. Keller, who held dear the role of advancing the esoteric work, made every effort to persuade him to no avail.

By 1956, the acrimony had spilled into a financial dispute between the New York headquarters, who had control of the American budget, and Foster Bailey. Whether justified or not, his issues concerned a paucity of administrative funds and a lack of adequate remittances being sent to Europe. Frank Hilton and Florence Garrigue were then Trustees. In February, in a letter to the trustees, Foster outlined his concerns point by point, planting the blame firmly on New York's doorstep.[20] Hilton and Garrigue would have been affronted.

The Lucis Trust was cleaving, with the esoteric work in New York at odds with the outer work in Tunbridge Wells. That was the way Foster saw it, and he decided the discord could not be allowed to continue. His solution was to take absolute control, demonstrating, in an ironic twist, similar qualities to those displayed by Louis Rogers back at Krotona. Just as he had been singled out by Rogers, Foster singled out Hilton as the chief instigator. An ousting was inevitable. In a private letter to Assagioli in March, Foster indicated his plan to demote Frank Hilton through an organisational restructure to prevent any unilateral action from being taken in New York.[21] In a letter to trustees two days later, Foster expressed his regret that he had relinquished complete control of the Arcane School and left it in the hands of the New York headquarters, and he apportioned blame at their feet for refusing to bend to his view that there should be no further training offered beyond the fourth degree. He then went on to imply that those delivering the more advanced training were in danger of being superior, controlling and authoritative, and the New York headquarters of becoming 'personality-centred'.[22] Hurtful remarks, intended to sting.

In a further ironic twist, given that Frank had been instrumental in ousting Marian Walter about four years earlier, Foster announced Frank Hilton's dismissal in an April letter addressed simply to friends. He writes, 'Foster Bailey has resumed his duties as chief executive officer of the Lucis Trust and the leadership of the New York headquarters. Frank Hilton is no longer the leader of the headquarters nor of any of the activities in America.'[23]

Whether through remorse, cunning or genuine goodwill, or perhaps a mixture of all three, two months later Foster Bailey held out an olive branch to Keller, asking her to work with him. In the same letter, he singled out Garrigue, who had used the Geneva conference to put forward Hilton's defence. Foster accuses her of being a bad influence on Hilton. In all, a divisive letter designed to separate Keller from her allies.

Of all those involved in the dispute, Foster knew Keller was the most significant and he did not want to lose her. She was an advanced disciple and had been a dedicated co-worker for decades. Keller was in the first DINA group of nine as RSU, Restraint, Strength, Understanding. *Discipleship in the New Age, Vol 1* is dedicated to her, 'a fellow-disciple who for more than twenty years has walked with me upon the way'.

Foster's words did not have the desired effect. In July 1956,

Hilton and Keller, along with Garrigue and Marguerite Schaefer, announced their withdrawal from the Arcane School to pursue the more advanced training Foster and Mary Bailey refused to allow. By then, the Baileys had moved back to New York and were preparing to take over the headquarters. Mary Bailey went on to become director of the Arcane School.

For six years, those in key roles at the New York and Tunbridge Wells headquarters had fought for the soul of the Arcane School. It was a struggle which played out through the various personalities, stakeholders, all who felt they knew what Alice Bailey had wanted and the work the Tibetan had outlined for them. The Friday talks express in essence Alice's nagging anxiety, her deep concerns and her indecision over how the school should be run after her death. The preservation of the intended purpose and stated directions for the school were of paramount importance to all involved. Due to the unfolding tensions among those hampered by loss and grief, fatigue, stress and overwork, and the shadow of severe financial difficulties, together with the distance between the two headquarters making face-to-face dialogue difficult, fragmentation was perhaps inevitable. The testing that had been predicted resulted in two splits, which were not meant to happen. As a result, some crystallisation set in, the organic, fluid whole of the worldwide Bailey community becoming separated at the centre by two walls, walls of righteousness and indignation, disappointment and hurt, along with a shared commitment and dedication to the vision. All of it understandable given the tumultuous emotional reality of the post-Alice context and how much the Arcane School meant to the key players.

To his credit, Foster Bailey expressed some remorse in a letter he sent to Keller in 1962, acknowledging the 'crisis years' and that he had 'made mistakes'. Quoting Franklin Roosevelt's "If I can bat 75 percent I will be lucky" Foster says, 'Neither of us can accurately assess either our own or each other's percentage.

Disciples do not assess blame on each other.'[24] He also made an allusion to her failing health.

In 1956, driven to pursue their vision, Hilton and Keller wasted no time founding the School for Esoteric Studies with Garrigue, Helen Hillebrecht and Margaret Schaefer, renting offices not far from the Lucis Trust headquarters. There, they put together the materials for new lessons.

The name 'School for Esoteric Studies' was chosen as it was felt the name reflected the depth and integrity of the teachings pursued. Hilton became the SES' first chair. He helped develop the school's Approach to Group Initiation, 'serving as a foundation for the development of additional advanced courses'.[25]

Keller worked to her strengths, tutoring senior students, handling the correspondence, and establishing collaborative relationships with individuals and other groups.[26]

In 1957, Assagioli, with whom Foster Bailey had been corresponding concerning the matter of the split, joined the SES and became an active member and advisor. He collaborated with Hilton in the formulation of an SES course which still forms part of the more advanced Arc of Training at the School.[27]

The co-founders did not restrict themselves to the school. As is ever the case with co-workers active in service work, new collaborations and projects were formed, and new alliances made. Hilton went on to co-direct the Psychosynthesis Research Foundation, which he co-founded with Assagioli. Keller, who worked in the field of social work in orphanages, helped launch Meditation Mount, which was co-founded by Assagioli and Garrigue at Ojai, California. Meditation Mount is a centre for meditation groups focused on world betterment, completed in 1971.[28] At one time, the centre served around 5000 correspondents and organised meditation programs based on themes extracted from the Tibetan's teachings.[29]

Regina Keller passed away in 1966 at the age of about eighty-three. Hilton and Foster Bailey managed to heal the disagreement that had led to the split. In the last year of Bailey's life, he corresponded with Hilton, expressing his appreciation for all the work that he was doing and inviting him to visit.[30] Just three weeks before he passed away, Bailey praised Hilton's address at a Wesak event saying, 'I agree with it 100 per cent from beginning to end.'[31]

In 1996, the office headquarters of the School for Esoteric Studies relocated to Asheville, North Carolina, in the heart of the Blue Ridge Mountains.

Academic recognition was something Alice Bailey was keen to see established in some fashion in her own lifetime. Realising scholarly output and rigour would be of enormous benefit to the Bailey community, in 2004 the School for Esoteric Studies sponsored the creation of *The Esoteric Quarterly*, a peer-reviewed journal of scholarly calibre. Former director of the school John Nash was the journal's founding editor.[32] The journal has helped raise the esteem and credibility of the teachings in the hope of arousing broader interest and advancing the ideas.

In 2012, the School widened its outreach to include website materials in French, Greek and Portuguese and discipleship training in English, Italian and Spanish:

 The School continues to bring the Ageless Wisdom teachings to a wider public via their website and to mentor students on the spiritual path worldwide. Ongoing esoteric research is at the heart of the School's mission, including updating, translating, and developing both original and new course materials, based on the Ageless Wisdom and contributions from the fields of psychology, science and the humanities.[33]

THE SCHOOL IS CURRENTLY LOOKING at expanding training on the service aspect of the work. With inclusivity at its heart, the school actively pursues intergroup collaborations in addition to providing discipleship training from introductory to advanced levels. The school has co-sponsored radio programs with other groups and given talks at other groups meetings. Establishing closer relations with the Lucis Trust has been slow, but progress has been made, particularly since 2014.[34]

ROBERTO ASSAGIOLI

*W*hile the storm brewed in the New York headquarters, ensconced in the tranquil setting of Broadwater Down, Tunbridge Wells, five important figures were poised to embark on ground-breaking new initiatives furthering and developing the Ageless Wisdom through the field of Transpersonal Psychology: Roberto Assagioli, Nancy Magor and Michal J Eastcott; and Ian Gordon-Brown and Barbara Somers.

Alice Bailey held Assagioli in the highest regard. In one of her weekly talks she says, 'I have never seen in Roberto the faintest trace of separateness with any human being. I never knew of anybody who was his enemy.'[1] In commenting on loving understanding she states, 'Roberto doesn't know how to handle it yet, and he is just as attentive to the idiotic people who don't repay his effort as to a person who warrants his attention.'[2]

Born in Italy to Jewish parents, esteemed psychologist Roberto Assagioli (1888-1974) gained a medical degree in neurology and psychiatry from the University of Florence before turning his attention to psychology. His interest lay not in the psychology of mental problems and illness, but in the psychology of wholeness. He is the founder of Psychosynthesis, which incorporates transpersonal aspects of human experience into psychotherapeutic practice through meditation and inner dialogue. In 1926, Assagioli founded the Institute of Psychosynthesis and oversaw the development of his ideas into a branch of psychology that would go on to become his life's work. He went on to co-found the Psychosynthesis Trust in London in 1965, the largest psychosynthesis institute in Europe outside Italy.[3]

Born into a Theosophical family, Assagioli came across Alice Bailey and gravitated towards the teachings sometime in the 1920s, which became for him a key source of esoteric wisdom. He joined the Arcane School and worked his way up to the grade of secretary before giving a lecture at the inaugural Spiritual Summer School at Ascona in 1930, where he met Alice for the first time. They became firm friends. He went on to write the foreword to the Italian edition of *The Light of the Soul*, Alice Bailey's commentary to Patanjali's Yoga Sutras.[4]

Assagioli remained largely private about his Theosophical views and his association with Alice Bailey and her school, choosing to keep them separate from his academic life.[5] A prudent decision, in the light of the negative and derisory attitude towards esotericism at the time within academic circles. Assagioli knew if he had been open, his own ground-breaking ideas would have come under ruthless attack. Evidence of the derision to which he would have succumbed is evident in the low regard for Alice Bailey held by the European scholars and peers with whom Assagioli was seeking to gain acceptance of his ideas.

Whether the knowledge aspect of the Bailey teachings had an influence on the development of Assagioli's academic thinking is doubtful and is perhaps of lesser importance than the esoteric training of the Arcane School itself, with its fostering of soul-connectedness and the overarching esoteric way of knowing, which Assagioli carried within. He was no dabbler. He was in the first of the DINA groups of nine, the telepathic communicators, and he participated in the New Seed Group in the 1940s. He was FCD: Freedom from ties, Chelaship, Detachment. The groups and organisations which Assagioli went on to establish on the spiritual side were to some degree based on instructions he received in letters from DK that can be found in the DINA books.[6] The letters also reveal the loneliness and isolation Assagioli endured in the 1930s and something of his personal struggles.

In August 1940, while Mussolini had joined forces with Hitler, Assagioli was under enormous strain. Acknowledging this, the Tibetan writes, 'The past few months have been extremely difficult for you, have they not', going on to note Assagioli's 'extreme fatigue and tension'.[7] Above all, the letters speak of the task or tasks assigned to him, which 'will be work of the profoundest difficulty. You will meet with rebuff from those you seek to help and...find very little understanding; you will meet with encouragement and assistance from the enlightened among the New Group of World Servers, and this will make your work possible but it will also greatly handicap you...'[8]

A deeply spiritual man keen to actualise projects in line with these tasks, in the aftermath of Alice Bailey's death, Assagioli was forced to bide his time. He knew what was happening through the correspondence he received both as a member of the Arcane School and as a close associate of Foster Bailey. The Applicants at the Portal difficulties would have perhaps been of lesser concern than the argument between Bailey and Keller, who were two of his closest allies in the school. Years went by, years of acrimony, years in which he could do nothing other than quietly observe those 'enlightened' in the NGWS struggle through the crisis.

In 1957, having observed the unfolding drama of the split and waited long enough for emotions to settle, Assagioli joined the School for Esoteric Studies and became an active member and advisor. He maintained a close association with the school, contributing to their efforts. His collaboration with Frank Hilton resulted in the creation of the Will Course which forms part of the advanced training arc at the school, comprising eighteen lessons on how to contact and use Shamballa energy in service.

Assagioli also enjoyed a long association with Meditation Mount in Ojai. His vision helped establish the 'foundations for global esoteric education', drawing on his contacts with the global network of Bailey students. It was one of his groups that settled in Ojai and formed Meditation Mount, which was created in an administrative sense by Florence Garrigue.[9]

Assagioli is known to have kept all of his various projects separate from each other, something he achieved through strict discipline.[10] Which was why he was also able to draw on his alliance with Foster Bailey. After Alice's passing, he worked closely with Foster on the formation of a new project, a group dedicated to meditation. Assagioli needed some collaborators and thought to source them from the Arcane School. Initially, Foster asked selected co-workers but none took an interest except Nancy Magor and Michal Eastcott who had both been co-workers at the Tunbridge Wells headquarters since the late 1940s.[11]

Together, Assagioli, Eastcott and Magor, along with a growing team, co-founded the Group for Creative Meditation based at Sundial House in Nevil Court, Tunbridge Wells, in close proximity to Broadwater Down.

Both heiress Nancy Magor and author Michal Eastcott were women of means. They financed the project and went on to pay for a secretary and translator for Assagioli who travelled with him back and forth from Italy. The trio worked closely on the development of the project. Michal performed a secretarial role, tape recording discussions and making notes of conversations about the meditations. Michal took on the role of scribe and Nancy that of editor.

In July 1956, Assagioli wrote to Foster asking him to distribute to Arcane School members an introductory paper on his creative meditation project and gather interest. From there, the project grew and flourished. Today, the Group for Creative

Meditation distributes Assagioli's study booklets to over 7,500 workers in 85 countries.[12] The worldwide Group for Creative Meditation offers study and meditation training by correspondence, and hosts retreats around the world as well as providing daily meditation.[13]

Through his detachment and commitment to world service, Assagioli transcended the conflicts over the teaching of advanced students in the Arcane School. By choosing to maintain good relations with both the School for Esoteric Studies and the Lucis Trust, he instigated projects aligned to each 'side' both geographically and through shared affiliations of members, and became a healing force, indirectly and symbolically most certainly, and also as a perfect example for others to follow. Perhaps the work of world salvage envisaged for Assagioli was thwarted nevertheless, by the ongoing lack of unified relations.

Assagioli actioned many projects and had many allies. Among them was industrial psychologist Ian Gordon-Brown (1925-1996), who worked for the Lucis Trust for fourteen years, becoming director and executive director of World Goodwill (1959-69).[14] Gordon-Brown was a regular contributor to *The Beacon* and had worked together with Assagioli in the United States. In 1971, he went on to meet literary editor and Jungian-oriented psychological counsellor Barbara Somers. They shared a profound interest in methods of expanding consciousness.[15] By 1973, they had founded the Centre for Transpersonal Psychology in London and offered weekly workshops and training programmes. Over five hundred people graduated from the training.[16] Assagioli would have been pleased. He passed away a year later.

In 1994, Gordon-Brown established the Centre for Transpersonal Perspectives, and together, Somers and Gordon-Brown offered highly successful lectures and workshops for counsellors and psychotherapists in ways to journey to find the inner spiritual self or soul within. They produced a small number of books on the subject, including *The Raincloud of Knowable Things: A*

Practical Guide to Transpersonal Psychology. Their co-authored book, *Journey in Depth: A Transpersonal Perspective* is described as a classic in its field.

It is through Gordon-Brown and Somers and many others besides, that Assagioli's significant contribution to advances in psychology has been furthered. His legacy, through his tightly held esoteric way of knowing, his training in the Arcane School, his friends and allies within the Bailey milieu, not least Alice Bailey herself, is unequivocally coloured and inspired by the Ageless Wisdom.

THE LEGACY

THE UNITED NATIONS

*U*nder the steady leadership of Foster Bailey and Mary Turner, the Lucis Trust weathered the upheavals of those early years. In 1955, a third headquarters was opened in Geneva, Switzerland, to serve six European languages. In 1960, the British headquarters was relocated to Whitehall Court, London, where it exists today. In 1965, the New York offices moved to a location close to the United Nations, considered to be the right environment for world service. Much of Alice Bailey's material that had yet to be published, was edited and went to print.[1]

The couple worked together closely, finally marrying in 1962. By then Foster was seventy-four and his health was deteriorating. Mary Bailey began to work alone, travelling the world on public speaking engagements and meeting students. For the last ten or twelve years of his life, Foster was a semi-invalid, confined to their Manhattan apartment. He died on 3 June 1977 at the age of eighty-nine.[2]

Mary Bailey took on the role of head of the Arcane School, and continued in that capacity for about two decades.

Of paramount importance to the Baileys and their successors

was (and is) the purity of the organisation and its vision, which has been tightly held ever since.

Towards the end of her life, the UN had gifted Alice Bailey a point of focus, and if her following of high achievers working within its auspices is anything to go by, her Arcane School yielded some impressive results. A cohort of her co-workers took her at her word and forged links with the organisation, not only through World Goodwill, but also via a raft of other initiatives including hosting seminars, conferences, meditation days, founding magazines, and other organisations. One co-worker and past director of World Goodwill, holistic spiritual counsellor and prominent speaker Ida Urso, went on to found The Aquarian Age Community, an organisation that has as one of its goals the promotion of the United Nations.[3]

However, the influence of the Bailey teachings within the auspices of the United Nations is not as significant as Christian evangelical conspiracy theorists believe, the ideas of Sri Chimnoy and Teilhard de Chardin having a far greater impact. It is one thing to hold an organisation as a point of focus, and another to gain any sort of foothold of influence within that organisation.

An example of the influence of spiritual teachings on individuals holding key positions within the UN can be found in Robert Muller (1923-2010), a serious student of Teilhard de Chardin.[4] *The Beacon* published five of his articles and invited him to address Arcane School conferences, but according to those closest to him, he was not overly familiar with the Bailey books. In 1948, when he was twenty-five years old, Muller won an internship at the United Nations for his essay on how to govern the world. From that moment, he dedicated his life to developing the vision of the organisation. He played a vital role in the conception and creation of numerous UN programmes including: the UN Development Programme, the World Food Programme, the UN Population Fund and the World Youth Assembly.[5]

An important book in Alice Bailey's oeuvre is *Education in the New Age*, a slim volume of 153 pages. Like Steiner and Krishnamurti, both founders of systems of schooling, Alice Bailey saw the importance of education. Unlike her contemporaries, who emphasised the education of children, the Tibetan focuses on the education of the whole of humanity. Written at a time of re-evaluation of educational theory and practice, the work contains an eight-page preface composed in 1953 by eminent professor of philosophy Oliver L Reiser (1895-1974), a personal friend of Albert Einstein. In his preface, he draws parallels between Bailey's thinking and that of John Dewey whose educational philosophy is seminal.

Of concern at the time of writing – in the 1940s – was the need to educate the masses to realign values from material to spiritual; to find educational methods to synthesise discrete areas of academic thought to offset polarisation; and to find a unity of principles. In other words, to universalise education. Cross-curricula and interdisciplinary studies is evidence of this. In the face of nationalist and selfish values, and accompanying racial hatred that led to the death camps of the Second World War, Alice Bailey, like many others at the time, saw a great need to address the nature of humanity. Reiser concurs with, 'There is a remedy for "the sickness of modern man' and many of its constituents are found in this book.'[6]

Education in the New Age covers theory, methods and goals, a discussion on the mental development of humanity, and the need for personality control. The premise of the book is simple. Humanity too easily slips into selfishness and greed, and the entire educational curriculum worldwide needs to change. 'The purpose of the coming educational systems will be to preserve individual integrity, promote the sense of individual responsibility, encourage a developing group consciousness of basic individual, national and world relationships, meanwhile extroverting and organising capacity, interest and ability.'[7]

Despite the confluence of ideas in this volume, it is not known if Muller drew inspiration from it, or indeed had even come across it when he created the World Core Curriculum, for which he has been described as the father of global education, receiving the UNESCO Peace Education Prize in 1989.[8] However, in the context of education, a connection to the Bailey teachings exists through his close association with Bailey co-worker Gloria Crook, founder of the School of Ageless Wisdom.[9] In 1979, Muller and Crook founded the first Robert Muller School in Arlington, Texas, which now serves as a model for schools established worldwide, and for those wishing to implement the curriculum.[10]

Muller is an important figure in the United Nations community. He worked as assistant Secretary-General at the UN, serving under three Secretary Generals. In 1982, he released his book, *New Genesis: Shaping a Global Spirituality*, a work that discusses the difficulties and the spiritual aspirations of the United Nations.[11] While it is not possible to demonstrate Muller was influenced by the Bailey teachings, through his association with Gloria Crook, it is clear then, as now, that those with a profound spiritual orientation commingle and draw inspiration from a variety of sources.

One well-known Bailey co-worker who worked within the UN is Donald Keys, author, founder and president of Planetary Citizens, and speechwriter for third UN Secretary General U Thant. Keys dedicated his book *Earth At Omega: Passage to Plane-tization* to Alice Bailey, for which political journalist Norman Cousins (1915-1990) wrote the introduction. The work serves as an accessible, potted version of DK and Alice Bailey's thinking, and covers the New Age movement, from transpersonal psychology to Findhorn and the role of the United Nations. 'The struggle at the UN is, in the last analysis, a struggle between separatism and human unity; between selfishness and the community good; and States, similar to people, are at various stages of development in expressing higher qualities.'[12] The first endorsers, advisory council and board of directors of Donald Keys' Planetary Citizens founded in the 1970s makes for an impressive read.[13]

In a speech he composed in the 1970s and published on the Aquarian Age Community's website, Keys writes, 'In one of Alice A. Bailey's books, written in the 1930s, there is a statement that a leading Swedish disciple would soon be working in the world. A high Swedish initiate who was a friend of mine was once asked if the foretold one were he. His answer was "no, it is Dag Hammarskjöld."'[14] The second UN Secretary-General, Hammarskjöld (1905-1961) was instrumental in creating the United Nations' new meditation room, planning and super-vising every detail.[15] His tenure was cut short by two years when he lost his life in a plane that was shot down over Northern Rhodesia (Zambia).

Between 1966 and 1972, Alice Bailey's *The Beacon* magazine published seven articles composed by U Thant, who succeeded Hammarskjöld as UN Secretary General, serving between 1961-71: 'The Making and Building of Peace', 'What Could we Build if we Worked Together', 'The United Nations and Human Rights', 'Trade, Aid and People', 'Message for Youth', 'The United Nations: Crisis of Authority' and 'The United Nations and the Human Environment.'[16] This is not to suggest that U Thant was a Bailey follower or sympathiser, rather, these articles reveal the value *The Beacon* editor placed on the ideas of the most powerful members of the UN, and their suitability for publication in the Lucis Trust's magazine.

In a chapter in their book *Spiritual Politics: Changing the World From Inside Out*, a work that carries forward the Ageless Wisdom, authors and co-workers Corinne McLaughlin and Gordon Davidson believe 'The Soul of the United Nations is the Soul of a Nascent One Humanity'.[17] For these writers, the UN is a 'living thought-form' and an 'evolving entity', birthing a new ethics and a new synthesis. 'The UN is a multifaceted organization with many functions, including synthesizing information about humanity and the planet as a whole.'[18]

It could be argued that through the influence of her students over many decades of dedicated hard work, Alice Bailey has shaped the spiritual ethics of the United Nations. A cohort of followers seeking to carry forward that vision can be found on the council of the Spiritual Caucus on the United Nations, which originated in 2000 and meets twice a month to meditate and 'explore ways to use this inner group focus to serve the highest potential of the UN'.[19] It should be noted that the caucus is comprised of representatives of organisations. The meetings are open to all who seek a similar goal.

Given the number of members in this group of eleven who follow or are in varying degrees influenced by the Ageless Wisdom, the Spiritual Caucus might almost be considered an embodiment of one of the groups of nine. Members include co-worker Nancy Roof, founder of *Kosmos,* an award-winning journal for world citizens and planetary civilisation. Nancy Roof is also a UN lobbyist and founding member of the Global Commons Initiative, the World Wisdom Council, the Creating the New Civilization Initiative, the 2020 Climate Leadership Campaign, and World Shift 2012.[20] In her spiritual autobiography posted on P2P Foundation's Wiki page, Nancy Roof states that she came across esotericism in the 1960s. It was the esotericism of Alice Bailey.

Nancy Roof's husband, author and graduate of the Arcane School Simons Lucas Roof (1920-2008), co-founded with her the Mountain School for Esoteric Studies. Simons Roof's first wife was astrologer Marcia S. Roof (1928-1979) née Moore, daughter of founder of the Sheraton Hotel chain Robert Lowell Moore and artist and book illustrator Eleanor Turner Moore. All three followed Alice Bailey, Robert and Eleanor Moore helping establish Meditation Mount at Ojai, California.[21] Both Simons Roof and Marcia Moore had articles published in *The Beacon.*[22]

Another spiritual caucus member, New Zealander Steve

Nation, along with his then wife Janet Nation, co-founded the Triangles Centre in 1975, in Wellington, New Zealand. Steve Nation went on to join the Lucis Trust headquarters in London in 1978.[23] He has worked closely with the organisation ever since and is currently Director of Lucis Trust's New York office. In 1999, he co-founded Intuition-in Service, an organisation that includes in its aims the promotion of United Nations' Days. Steve Nation is also a writer and speaker on global issues and meditation.[24]

Also a caucus member is Steve Nation's second wife Barbara L Valocore who has been associated with the Lucis Trust for many years. She is the co-founder and president of the Lifebridge Foundation (1992), an organisation with associative status with the United Nations' Department of Public Information.[25]

Co-founder of the Hill Center for Psychosynthesis Tara Stuart, another caucus member, is also on the board of directors of the aforementioned *Kosmos* magazine. Stuart has also participated in Sundial House Summer Conferences since the 1960s.[26]

Caucus member Michal Johnson is the Pathways to Peace representative to the United Nations. Pathways to Peace contains a sizeable number of co-workers, including Avon Mattison, founder of the United Nations International Day of Peace and close colleague of Robert Muller.[27] Also involved in Pathways to Peace are Steve Nation, Barbara Marx Hubbard, David Spangler, Gordon Davidson and Corrine McLaughlin.

Other caucus members who appear to have an indirect association with the Bailey teachings through the Findhorn Foundation are Frances Edwards and John Clausen. Another caucus member, Diane Williams, is founder and president of the Source of Synergy Foundation, an organisation *en rapport* with the Bailey ethos and worldview, although Williams has no strong association with the Bailey teachings.[28]

With so many co-workers dominating the spiritual caucus at the United Nations, it might appear surprising that Alice Bailey isn't a household name beyond the conspiracy theory milieu, whether people agree with her worldview or not. However, the caucus is comparatively tiny and perhaps insignificant, and when considered alongside other NGO caucuses the Spiritual Caucus has limited and insignificant influence within the United Nations.

THE NEW AGE MOVEMENT

*O*utside of her own esoteric milieu, most who know of and respect Alice Bailey can be found in the New Age movement, yet few may realise just how influential her work has been in the movement's foundation.

Narrowly circumscribed, the New Age refers to an astrological moment when our sun moves into the zodiacal sign of Aquarius. It's referred to as the precession of equinoxes, in which our entire solar system spends around two and a half thousand years in each sign. We're leaving the Age of Pisces behind, with its glyph of two fish swimming in opposite directions, an age of world religion co-ruled by Jupiter and Neptune – planets of expansion and optimism, and illusion, delusion and mysticism. The hallmark of the old age is the rise of global religions, along with religious fervour and dogmatic righteousness, an age that unfolded as much through war and persecution – the Crusades, the Inquisition – as it did religious devotion and pilgrimage.

Will the new age be any better? Aquarius is ruled by Saturn and Uranus, and in Greek mythology both were tyrannical rulers. Yet it is the sign of the water bearer, of humanitarianism, brotherhood and innovation. There is no fixed date of ingress and astrologers state that the phasing out and in of each new age is slow. What the hallmark of the New Age will be is yet to manifest, although already emerging are the forms of tyranny associated with those old Greek gods, along with myriad technological advances that are rapidly and radically transforming the human world, along with humanitarian consciousness.

Setting aside the astrological backdrop, numerous scholars have offered descriptions of the New Age movement that emerged in America in the early 1960s and spread through the Western world.[1] Here, the 'New Age' refers to a cohort of spiritual seekers searching for ways to contact an inner spiritual self. It marks a move away from organised religion and represents the flowering of an array of beliefs and practices, many derived from Eastern mysticism, traditional cultures including Native American, and Western esotericism.[2]

THE ROOTS OF THE NEW AGE

The New Age began as a utopian counterculture, which rejected mainstream beliefs and values and searched for alternatives. Writing in 1980 from a perspective infused with Alice Bailey's ideas and language, New Age advocate Marilyn Ferguson views the New Age as a benign conspiracy of love and light, an intimate joining and breathing together. 'It is a conspiracy without a political doctrine. Without a manifesto. With conspirators who seek power only to disperse it.'[3] She even named her book *The Aquarian Conspiracy*. It was an unfortunate choice. Whatever playful or purposeful intent Ferguson had in mind, she played into the hands of Bailey's enemies who latched on to that word 'conspiracy' like limpets on a passing ship.

The New Age represents for Marilyn Ferguson a paradigm shift, one of 'continuous transformation and transcendence', a new perspective that 'respects the ecology of everything'. One marked by deep inner shifts of awareness.[4]

The roots of the New Age can be traced back at least to the

1800s when interest in spirituality as an alternative to main-stream religion and dull intellectualism burgeoned, culminating, in esoteric circles, in the founding of the Theosophical Society in 1885. Alice Bailey, along with Rudolph Steiner and Jiddhu Krish-namurti, brought Theosophical teachings to their own audiences, helping to perpetuate continuing interest in the Ageless Wisdom.

Another influence emerged even earlier, in the 1830s, when the transcendentalists, including Ralph Waldo Emerson, Henry Thoreau, Bronson Alcott and Margaret Fuller turned to 'experi-ence, intuition, the Quaker ideas of the Inner Light, the *Bhagavad Gita'* and especially to spiritual philosopher Emanuel Sweden-borg (1688-1772) for inspiration. The transcendentalists, along with German physician and founder of hypnosis Franz Mesmer (1734-1815) and founder of Christian Science Mary Baker Eddy (1821-1910), influenced New Thought, a healing movement of late-nineteenth century New England led by Emma Curtis Hopkins, Horatio Dresser and Charles Brodie Patterson. New Thought believes in a continuous evolution of thought; that truth can be found across a range of doctrines; and healing can occur through the realigning of thought, mind over matter style. In the early 1900s, the New Thought movement continued to flourish, spawning numerous institutes and schools.[5]

Another notable influence on the New Age was French idealist philosopher and Jesuit priest Pierre Teilhard de Chardin (1881-1955), whose posthumously published work *The Phenomenon of Man* set forth a radical new view of evolution and the interconnectedness of all creation, including a mystical Christ viewed as the organising principle of the universe. He conceived of the idea of an Omega Point towards which all evolution was heading, a notion later picked up by Donald Keys.

Alice Bailey differs from her contemporaries in the style of presentation. DK's instructions are given in plain language in a straightforward style. The structure of the teachings emulated the Modernist architecture of the age, all ordered clean lines, arranged in neat blocks, with nothing fancy to distract the eye.

The atmosphere is business-like and evokes ideas of quiet leadership and executive management. Out of the general pool of seekers, Alice Bailey continues to draw towards both the teachings and the Arcane School those who are as serious, focused, and committed as she.

There is a distinction to be made between the emergence of a new spiritual movement growing out of existing pursuits in a kind of natural evolution of ideas and awareness, and the cementing of the concept of the New Age. Alice Bailey played a significant part in the formation of the New Age, influencing many of the early and later influencers who went on to develop their own particular strand or brand. Above all the title is hers conceptually.[6]

Concepts not only carry explanatory power, they focus the will, direct energy, shape our worldview and our values. The Tibetan's concept of the New Age was clearly defined. The entire body of work can be described a New Age thoughtform. Alice Bailey and DK sought to establish a paradigm, not a movement of spiritual seekers. All the personal growth training contained in the New Age movement was in Alice Bailey's worldview, meant to be preparation for world service, not self-aggrandisement. Healing of various emotional and mental wounds is a side issue, something that may occur solely to divest the personality of its own obstacles.

Not only did the Bailey oeuvre contain three titles carrying the term 'New Age' – *Discipleship in the New Age Vol I and II,* and *Education in the New Age* – in her Master Index, there are over 250 direct references to the New Age, including characteristics and methods, along with many more references to the Age of Aquarius. Most of the references appear in her later works, composed in the 1930s and 1940s, including the aforementioned texts along with *Esoteric Psychology Vol I and II, The Externalisation of the Hierarchy* and *A Treatise on White Magic.*

One of her earliest references to the New Age can be found in *From Intellect to Intuition,* a work written in her own pen and devoted to 'the nature and true significance of meditation'. She writes, 'They [that bridging body of men] will act as the pioneers of the New Age, when men will be practical men of affairs with their feet firmly planted on the earth and yet, at the same time, be mystics and seers, living also in the world of spirit and carrying inspiration and illumination with them into the life of the everyday.'[7]

Two years later, *A Treatise on White Magic: or The Way of the Disciple* was published, a work prized as a training manual for spiritual discipleship, containing fifteen 'rules' of the path, in essence a guide on how to avoid the dark path of black magic and become equipped for world service. The first reference to the New Age states: 'Another object is the preparing of an instrument of service in the inauguration of the New Age during the next two hundred years...According to the response of disciples, of mystics and knowers everywhere, so will be the rapid coming in of the New Age.'[8] These 'instruments of service' are disciples who are charged with developing the intuition and a right sense of values, and turning 'the inner ear to those voices on the subtler plane' in order to inaugurate the New Age, for it is the disciples' responsibility and theirs alone. Should disciples fail in their responsibilities, then the Masters will withdraw, change their plans, and find some other way to proceed. Bailey's entire canon pivots on this one single charge. An opportunity exists for a new orientation, for humanity to pass through the portal of initiation into the kingdom of the soul. This is the New Age, should we want it.

For Alice Bailey, the New Age is the dawning of global consciousness, the manifestation of the World Disciple, one with an expanded awareness of affairs affecting humanity and the planet. The hallmark of such global consciousness is world service, manifesting in those who have relinquished the selfish desires of the personality and act in goodwill to foster right relations for the good of the whole. Through the Arcane School, Alice Bailey didn't only help conceptualise the New Age, she energised the thoughtform with her powerful drive. Her mission, DK's mission, was to foster the birth of the soul on a global scale.

For decades the term 'New Age' has carried derogatory connotations and many seekers and practitioners shun the appellation. New Agers have become the subject of ridicule and controversy, with scandals breaking out over fraudulent claim-making and profiteering. Known for its eclecticism and pick-and-mix style of seeking, the New Age movement has been criti-cised for its relativist and subjectivist philosophy and its hedo-nistic tendencies and consumerism.[9] The seeker constructs her own spiritual reality out of a conglomeration of beliefs and prac-tices. Ancient teachings are stepped-down and often distorted. There is a tendency towards spiritual materialism and ego infla-tion, partly through the glamour or allure of mystique and other-worldly belonging. Navigating this reality with all of its accoutrements can lead to a spiritual awakening, but as Alice Bailey was wont to stress, it's a long process with many rude shocks along the way. In DK's language, the 'dweller on the threshold', that glamour of the personality impeding full soul consciousness, can take on magnificent proportions if not handled correctly. Many remain trapped inside the spell and become self-obsessed. Alice Bailey's focus was the decentralisa-tion of the personality. Many New Age seekers become temporarily full of themselves.

From the opinions expressed in her autobiography, it is clear Alice Bailey would have baulked at the movement carried on in her name. She was dismissive of much of the then contemporary teachings and attitudes:

 I've always been annoyed at the rubbish talked by people about "recovering their past incarnations." I am a profound sceptic where this recovery is concerned. I believe that the various books which have been published giving in detail the past lives of prominent occults are evidences of a vivid imagination and that they are untrue and mislead the public. I have been encouraged in this belief by the fact that in my work dozens of Mary Magdalenes and Julius Caesars, and other important people, have confessed portentously to me who they were; yet in this life they are such very ordinary, uninteresting people.[10]

SHE IS EQUALLY dismissive of the attitudes many seekers have of the masters, who 'never tell a disciple what to do or where to go, or how to handle a situation, in spite of all the bunk talked by nice, well-meaning devotees'.[11]

Alice Bailey had no time for fixating on personal problems. When talking about her own difficulty with fear, she describes how she practiced a form of mindfulness, recognising the fear and moving on. 'I think people have to learn a much more patient acceptance of what is, and not spend so much time wrestling with themselves over their individual problems... Concentration on service can and does lead to self-forgetfulness.'[12]

Initially, the counter-cultural movement of the 1960s did carry a strong ethos of social and political change, manifesting in the civil rights movement and the protests against war in Vietnam. Yet the progressive, humanitarian spirit soon dissipated as attention turned inwards on personal growth and spiritual enlightenment.

VERA STANLEY ALDER AND ESOTERIC HEALING

The filtering of Eastern mysticism into Western consciousness was in large part the result of Theosophists Blavatsky and Olcott, who went to India in 1879 on the search for ancient Hindu teachings. So unexpected was this interest that the pair were welcomed by Hindus and Buddhists alike.[13] Blavatsky opened the door through which their teachings could flow. Later Theosophists, including Besant, Steiner, and Woodroffe (Arthur Avalon), went on to develop an understanding of these Eastern teachings and incorporated them into their own Theosophical interpretations.

Although according to author and Theosophist Kurt Leland, it was Charles Leadbeater and Alice Bailey who, between them, fostered the Western Chakra System.[14] In his book *Rainbow Body: A History of the Western Chakra System from Blavatsky to Brennan*, Leland is at pains to attribute ideas utilised by later chromotherapists and esoteric healers to their rightful sources. He cites as original Alice Bailey's linking of the chakras with the endocrine glands, her use of the colours of the rainbow in describing the seven rays, her coining of the term 'sacral chakra', and her method of linking together the initiations, planes, bodies and chakras into one unified 'roadmap of mastery'.[15]

The path of these ideas can be traced through the works of co-worker Vera Dorothea Stanley Alder (1898-1984), a successful British-Danish portrait painter and mystic who popularised Alice Bailey's teachings, particularly *Initiation: Human and Solar*, and became a spiritual teacher in her own right. Alder was educated at Roedean School in Sussex then attended the Slade School of Art in London. After a successful career as an artist, Alder discovered the Ageless Wisdom and underwent a profound conversion. Alder went on to compose seven books, including her spiritual autobiography *From the Mundane to the Magnificent*. She also founded the World Union Fellowship, which became the World Guardians Fellowship, which published the Journal of World Guardians.[16] Among her own followers was Elvis Presley.[17]

Vera Stanley Alder was a member of the DINA group of nine focusing on education as LDO: Light, Detachment, Organisation.

In a letter to her dated November 1937, the Tibetan tells her, 'You are in a position to aid and help many people. See to it, my brother, that you aid with wisdom, discernment and discretion and that you place your effort where the best results can be achieved.'[18]

Alder's potential for world service along the lines of writing was noted in the following letter of February1938. All of the letters addressed to her point towards her creative work and her contribution and attempt to facilitate that process.

In 1938, Vera Stanley Alder's first book *The Finding of the Third Eye* was published. Here, Alder depicts techniques of working with colour, sounds, numbers, breath, diet and exercise. She goes on to explore astrology and meditation and their purpose. Prior to Alder's works, esoteric healers, including colour therapists, drew inspiration directly from Alice Bailey's *Letters on Occult Meditation*.[19]

With or without Vera Stanley Alder's contribution, recognition of Alice Bailey's contribution to esoteric healing is hard to find. In his informative book, Leland presents Alice Bailey's chakra list as found in *The Soul and its Mechanism*, a list that has appeared in many subsequent Western texts on the chakras, influencing polarity therapy, Reiki and Pranic healing.[20] For Leland, Alice Bailey was as much an innovator as Helena Blavatsky, and because she went to such lengths to explain everything, 'she produced a rich vein of material on the chakras for later writers'.[21] Sadly, many Western writers on the chakras, including controversial guru Osho or Bhagwan Shree Rajneesh; authors on the chakras Jack Schwarz, Christopher Hills, Norah Hills, Alex Jones, David Tansley and Zachary Landsdowne; and popular New Ager Shirley MacLaine, have all chosen to sidestep crediting Alice Bailey, despite drawing on her ideas.[22] So widespread is this lack of acknowledgement, Leland labels it 'source amnesia'.[23] An exception is holistic health trainer Barbara Ann Brennan who, Leland is keen to point out, lists Alice Bailey as one of her sources in *Hands of Light*.[24]

DAVID SPANGLER AND FINDHORN

The alternative community of Findhorn in Scotland's northeast, had its genesis in 1962 when cofounders, spiritual seekers and mystics Peter Caddy – who counted Alice Bailey among his influences – his wife Eileen and Dorothy Maclean moved to a caravan park on the peninsula east of Inverness. In meditations, messages from higher sources were received by the two women who were instructed to create a garden under spiritual guidance. They did, and as the garden flourished, others gathered around the trio and a community formed.

In 1967, Eileen Caddy had a vision in which she was told that a man of twenty-five years would arrive to live and work at Findhorn. Then, in 1970, a young man of twenty-five did arrive: David Spangler.

Born in Columbus, Ohio, in 1945, American spiritual philosopher, practical mystic and prolific author David Spangler was a natural clairvoyant and mystic who gave up a degree in biochemistry in 1965, at the age of twenty, to give lectures to spiritual and metaphysical groups around the United States. He was deeply influenced by the Bailey teachings, having been introduced to them at the age of fourteen, and went on to become a key founding figure of the New Age movement.[25] His books, *Festivals in the New Age* and *Revelation: The birth of a new age* helped foreground the notion of the New Age in the zeitgeist of the times.

The foreword to *Revelation* was written by another prominent figure in New Age history Sir George Trevelyan who was predominantly a student of Rudolph Steiner as well as favouring Alice Bailey and, at that time, involved in establishing Findhorn.

David Spangler had arrived at Findhorn at a time of rapid community expansion. As Peter Caddy retreated from his leadership roles, Spangler quickly took on co-directorship of the community and became co-director of Education. He remained at the community for three years before departing with Dorothy

Maclean and several other members to found the Lorian Association in Seattle.[26]

In 1974, Spangler helped found the Lindisfarne Association, a group of intellectuals that included eminent anthropologist and ecologist Gregory Bateson, renowned economist E F Schumacher, and scientist and environmentalist James Lovelock, author of *The Gaia Hypothesis*. This group drew much inspiration from the works of Teilhard de Chardin and English mathematician and philosopher Alfred North Whitehead, thinkers who, like Alice Bailey, advanced the interconnectedness of all creation. Co-founder of the Lindisfarne Association, social philosopher William Irwin Thompson (1938-), shared an interest in the general pool of Eastern mystical thought, esoteric Christianity and the evolution of consciousness.

The Bailey teachings do not seem to have played any part in the Lindisfarne Association. Rather, it was through the influence of the vision, values and ethos embedded in the mind of Spangler, all inspired by Alice Bailey, that she played a subtle background role in providing the conditions for and stimulating the emergence of holistic, ecological thought.

Back at Findhorn, the organisation flourished and went on to inspire numerous intentional communities and projects. Today, over thirty organisations form part of the overarching Findhorn Foundation community association.[27] Findhorn hosts a range of workshops, residential courses and conferences throughout the year.[28] Alice Bailey's influence there lives on. All those in high positions are expected to have a solid working knowledge of the Bailey books. To pay homage after the attacks on the World Trade Centre on September 11, 2001, the Great Invocation was used at Findhorn in prayers.[29]

One prominent Findhorn figure is holistic educator and author, William Bloom (1948-), a follower of the Bailey teachings, who spent two decades on the faculty of the Findhorn Foundation. Bloom is a one-stop shop for a raft of mind-body-spirit workshops, articles and books, including *The Power of Modern*

Spirituality and *The Endorphin Effect.* Unlike other New Agers who prefer to keep their Bailey roots hidden, Bloom has no qualms referring to Alice Bailey in his writings.[30]

UTOPIA

Ever since Findhorn, many Alice Bailey followers have chosen to dedicate their lives to creating and nurturing alternative models of living. Such followers take on the essence of her message and commit to it, not least because her complex, intricate, all-encompassing worldview resonates strongly with the sort of ecological thought arising, among other places, from the Lindisfarne group.

One keynote of the Utopian movement is based on the esoteric notion that energy follows thought. Negative thoughts accumulate to form a dark cloud. Keeping hold of positive thoughts makes it easier for them to manifest, mobilising the good and not giving the bad any energy. In Alice Bailey's model, the good can be manifested through inner work, meditation, visualisation, prayer, ritual, ceremony and through sending Light.

Bailey co-workers McLaughlin and Davidson argue entirely from a DK perspective in their book *Spiritual Politics: Changing the World From Inside Out,* and provide the essence of Bailey-inspired utopias, affirming an 'interconnected, whole-systems view based on mutual causality'.[31] The authors met at Findhorn and went on to found the Sirius Ecological Community in Massachussetts. They also founded the Center for Visionary Leadership in Washington DC. In addition, McLaughlin worked on President Clinton's Council on Sustainable Development.

In their book, McLaughlin and Davidson cite the need to shift thinking from separative to community oriented, linear to holistic, polarized to unitive, and from crystallised to expanding. These ideas are prevalent in all the utopian projects Alice Bailey inspired.

For McLaughlin and Davidson, shifting to a new paradigm

requires a move towards transformational politics, one that values non-adversarial ways of knowing and acting, and creates new templates based on notions of interconnectedness, inclusivity, synthesis, empowerment and whole systems. The authors discuss how the new paradigm might look in the spheres of politics and government, welfare, law and order, and economics based on justice and sharing and community. They go on to cite numerous organisations founded on these principles, including: Pathways to Peace, founded by co-workers Avon Mattison and Sheldon Hughes; Multitrack Diplomacy, with its emphasis on mediation; and the Rocky Mountain Institute, along with an array of grassroots groups and communities around the world at local and global levels whose aims are to find better pathways towards better solutions.

Another example which embraces Alice Bailey's thinking is The Global Ecovillage Network, GEN, which was founded in Denmark in 1991 by Ross and Hildur Jackson. GEN villages are designed to carry a small ecological footprint while fostering more sustainable, community-oriented lifestyles. It is a 'deliberate, strategic response to the destructive consequences of the dominant worldview'.[32] Findhorn is seen as an exemplar GEN village. Demonstrating the interconnectedness of the network informed in large part by Alice Bailey's vision, United Nations representative of the GEN, and co-worker Vita de Waal, addressed a World Goodwill seminar in 2016.

Vita de Waal plays a prominent role in The Institute for Planetary Synthesis, which was founded by Rudy Schneider in Geneva in 1981 and enjoys NGO consultative status with the Economic and Social Council of the United Nations, ECOSOC. The Institute 'aims at reawakening an awareness of spiritual values in daily life and promoting planetary awareness, leading to planetary citizenship based on the spiritual values: love of truth, personal responsibility, sense of justice, constructive co-operation and selfless service of the greater whole'.[33] The Institute follows in the footsteps of the original DINA groups of nine, operating in ten fields of service: education, politics, religion, science, psychology, economics (including finance), communication (including telepathy), enlightened observation, healing and creativity. The group hold a triannual General Assembly and are hoping to create a University for Planetary Synthesis based on DK's seed groups, with branches around the world.

Another notable example of the continuance of the Bailey teachings is The Hechal Centre for Universal Spirituality in Jerusalem, founded by student and teacher of the Ageless Wisdom Uta Gabbay in 1997. Originally established as a school for meditation, the Centre is run by a group of co-workers and serves as a 'subjective outpost, holding regular weekly and monthly online meditation as a service to Jerusalem, the Jewish people and the planet'.[34] The Hechal group seek to 'weave lines of relation between Israel/Palestine and the rest of the world', and to foster self-reflection and right relations. They make use of and advance Assagioli's pioneering work on the psychosynthesis of a nation, which he applied to the Jewish people. The Hechal Centre serves to highlight the misplaced accusations of anti-Semitism launched at Alice Bailey.

A key figure in the closely interconnected milieu is groundbreaking visionary economist Ernst Friedrich Schumacher (1911-1977). Whether he knew Alice Bailey personally is unknown. Schumacher was born in Germany to a professor of political economy and became a Rhodes scholar and protégé of economist John Maynard Keynes. The influences on his life and thought were many and varied, not least a spell in Burma in the 1950s, upon which he began to proclaim Buddhist economics. He centred his economic model on the principle of having 'enough', sufficient to requirements rather than surplus. In 1966 he founded Intermediate Technology, which developed basic technologies, such as hand pumps, to enable poor farmers in the Third World to help themselves.

Two years later, the March/April 1968 issue of *The Beacon* published his piece 'The Philosophy of Aid'. His seminal work

Small is Beautiful was published in 1973 and *The Beacon* featured his piece by the same title in May/June of 1974. *The Beacon* bears no resemblance to *Resurgence*, for which Schumacher wrote regularly. It most likely isn't the case that Schumacher submitted these pieces for publication. But rather that the editor of *The Beacon*, or even Mary Bailey herself, sought Schumacher out as a thinker most suited to the content of the magazine. What can be said is that his writing appeared in *The Beacon* on two occasions, with a gap of six years in between. A close associate of Spangler, Schumacher addressed the Findhorn community in 1976, with a talk on the spiritual and economic crises facing humanity. There is no doubt he was part of the Bailey-inspired intellectual and socially prominent milieu. Schumacher was also on the Advisory Council for prominent Alice Bailey figure Donald Key's Planetary Citizens in 1975.[35]

One idea leads to another, and out of Schumacher's vision, not only has emerged the Schumacher Institute and the Schumacher College, but also the space for the emergence of The Venus Project. This contemporary movement aims to achieve a sustainable new world civilisation, made possible by redesigning our culture in keeping with a resource-based economy, a culture envisioned by Futurist inventor Jacque Fresco (1916-). A resource-based economy is founded on a belief in a holistic, global economy which makes use of human and planetary resources in wise ways. The project, based in Venus, Florida, came into being in the 1990s and set out to find better ways to use engineering and technology.

Peter Joseph, founder of the Zeitgeist movement, initially endorsed Fresco's vision, but the two men parted ways over a disagreement. The Zeitgeist movement was founded in 2008, as a sustainability advocacy organisation comprising chapters based in countries worldwide oriented towards community-based activism. The core tenet of Zeitgeist is that all the world's ills are rooted in an outmoded social structure. The movement advocates a Schumacher-inspired, resource-based economy.

Behind the scenes, Alice Bailey's World Goodwill gathers together these initiatives from around the world and provides a locus of intent through its seminars and conferences. World Goodwill, under the auspices of the Lucis Trust does this because these are the initiatives that best reflect Alice Bailey's New Age.

AN ADVERSARY AND AN ENTHUSIAST

The New Age movement is diverse. There are perhaps as many lost personalities, charlatans and self-appointed gurus as there are genuine seekers and practitioners. For Alice Bailey and Theosophy, the popularisation of the Spiritual Hierarchy has proven highly problematic.

Emerging out of the New Age milieu, in the tradition of its precursor the I AM movement, is author and popular quasi-spiritual leader Elizabeth Clare Prophet (1939-2009). Prophet grew up a Christian Scientist. She met her second husband Mark Prophet in 1961 at a talk he was giving on the 'Ascended Masters' under the auspices of his spiritual organisation The Summit Lighthouse, which he founded in 1958. Mark had been inspired by the I AM movement via its offshoot The Bridge to Freedom. During his talk, Elizabeth received a vision. The couple clicked, and Elizabeth soon commenced training to become a messenger or channeller. Before long, she became, she believed, a messenger of the Master Morya. The couple went on to publish numerous volumes based on these channelled communications and spread their message far and wide, with study groups and teaching centres dotted around the world.

A charismatic figure, Elizabeth Prophet, known as 'Mother'

by her followers, taught that through meditation, prayer and visualisation, Christ consciousness could be achieved. She had worked for a time as a secretary for the Christian Science church acquiring organisational skills that enabled her to become the leader of The Summit Lighthouse upon the death of Mark Prophet in 1975. The Summit Lighthouse then came under her Church Universal and Triumphant. The movement combined a potent blend of patriotism, evangelism, and Theosophy, largely inspired by Leadbeater's *The Masters of the Path*.[1]. The keynote of the Church and the Lighthouse is personal spiritual growth following the guidance of the masters through the messages they gave to Prophet, the 'Messenger'. A charismatic group, the locus of influence was fixed on Prophet at the centre, a 'flawed spiritual leader' with an 'indomitable spirit' holding 'manipulative dominion' over her flock.[2]

As with the I AM movement, the notion of ascension, or of having reached heaven without having died, the result of a point of spiritual attainment in which the self is completely purified, is the cornerstone of the Prophets' New Age belief system.[3] They are the Keepers of the Flame. The glorification and erroneous portrayal of the Masters in this fashion has bled into the general seeker's perception not only of the Masters, but of Theosophy in general and Alice Bailey in particular. There is an unfortunate popular and scholarly perception that the I AM movement and the Prophets can be bundled in with Alice Bailey and her Theosophical contemporaries and predecessors to form a single cohesive group all proposing the same or similar esoteric ideas.[4] Any self-respecting Alice Bailey student would be appalled by this. From a Bailey perspective, Elizabeth Prophet and her ilk serve to bring the entire realm of channelling or telepathic rapport into disrepute.

Prophet claimed to have channelled the Masters Koot Hoomi – whom she termed Kuthumi – and Morya. In asserting this spiritual authority, she succumbed to a measure of pride and set about discrediting her predecessors. In an exposé of false teachings published in *Pearls of Wisdom,* Prophet's 'Kuthumi' dismisses both Alice Bailey and Krishnamurti as not being adequate vehicles to do the work of the Masters. If Prophet is to be believed, 'Bailey suffered intellectual pride and a brittleness of the lower mental body…and [was] totally unfit as an instrument of the Tibetan master.'[5]

Such personal attacks are unhelpful to those wishing to understand Alice Bailey and her work. Prophet's damage to Alice Bailey's reputation in this fashion is perhaps limited, coming across as it does as an assertion of superiority more reflective perhaps of the character casting the aspersions, but unfortunately these comments bring the entire terrain into disrepute in the eyes of outsiders, and particularly scholars.

From the perspective of the pure esoteric thought contained in the Bailey books, Prophet's attacks appear keen and meddlesome, and her output in direct competition, stealing the ground of the Spiritual Masters away from the authenticity apparent in traditional Theosophical outpourings. Bailey students would argue Prophet was indeed a false prophet and her teachings of an insufficient standard commensurate with the Masters' teachings. If Alice Bailey had been alive, she would no doubt have dictated a scathing remark of The Summit Lighthouse, similar to the one issued against the I AM movement of the 1930s.

The Prophet legacy lives on. As noted on the distinctly violet website of the Heart Center, even after her death in 2009, through 'David Christopher Lewis, The Heart Center's spiritual director and amanuensis for the Universal Brotherhood, Elizabeth, now Ascended Lady Master Clare de Lis, continues to teach her students.'[6]

The Bailey books help give credence, within New Age circles, to light work, or working with spiritual entities for the purposes of healing. In DK language, for the second ray disciple, the light of the soul bears down on the personality. 'In that light, the man sees Light, and thus becomes eventually a light-bearer'.[7] To achieve this state of consciousness, the disciple must meditate to achieve inclusive reason. 'The creative imagination will be occupied with those measures which will "throw the light" into the dark and unrelieved places in the (as yet) incomplete creative process. The man then works consciously in the light, as a Light bearer.'[8]

The most well-known light worker is clinical and research psychologist Helen Schucman (1909-81), who somewhat reluctantly composed *A Course in Miracles*. A hugely popular work, scribed between 1965-72 and translated into twenty-two languages, and containing the verbal communications of Jesus channelled in full waking consciousness. Schucman was clairaudient. Whether the voice she heard was Jesus is perhaps moot. The course contains a lesson for each day of the year and is meant to recondition the student's mind, from fear to love.[9]

Without wishing to discredit Schucman's work, there is no comparison to be made between *A Course in Miracles* and any of Alice Bailey's books. Leading scholar of Western Esotericism Olav Hammer places the two influential figures side-by-side in *Claiming Knowledge: Strategies of Epistemology from Theosophy to the New Age* when he writes, 'It is something of an oddity that prominent religious innovators such as Alice Bailey or Helen Schucman and their respective doctrines have been slighted by historians of religion.'[10] A serious student of the Ageless Wisdom might be affronted by the remark, since through it, the author positions Bailey and Schucman together as equals.

BENJAMIN CREME

Another light worker who might have inadvertently harmed Alice Bailey's reputation is Scottish author, accomplished artist, writer and esotericist Benjamin Creme (1922-2016). Creme was a student of Blavatsky's work before discovering Alice Bailey. He became a student and was especially inspired by Alice Bailey's Christology, believing wholeheartedly in the second coming of Christ. He too, believed he was contacted by a Master of the

Wisdom, this time a disciple of Maitreya, the Head of the Spiritual Hierarchy, and based on the messages he received, he lectured around the world to millions of listeners.

Creme's sincerity is not in question and unlike Prophet, he cast no aspersions on Alice Bailey. He claimed to have received his first message telepathically back in 1959 and was reluctant to take down what was said. In 1974, he formed a Transmission Meditation group and between the members, they received numerous communications, particularly in the years 1976 and 1977. Creme was then urged, telepathically, to go public with what they had been told. He became a sort of prophet for the reappearance of Maitreya, which had been predicted by Helena Blavatsky herself. At times Creme felt overshadowed by Maitreya, transmitting his messages through mental telepathy while retaining his own awareness.

In 1975, Creme founded Share International, or the Tara Centre, an organisation that continues to host meetings and events around the world, and keeps Creme's works in print. He also co-edited *Share International*, a global magazine read in over seventy countries and concerned with political, economic and social change.[11] Most of the sixteen books composed by Creme are comprised of his lectures.

Creme gained global attention in 1982, when he placed full-page announcements in major newspapers around the world, claiming Christ had returned to earth to solve the world's problems and usher in the New Age of peace:

 Creme explained his announcement at a packed press conference in Los Angeles on 14 May 1982. He said that Maitreya had left his abode in the Himalayas and flown from Pakistan in a Jumbo jet to London, where he had been living among the Asian community since 19 July 1977. Creme further explained that Maitreya is an enlightened world teacher who has come to aid humanity in solving its political, economic and social problems. "He is not a religious leader," according to the ad, "but an educator in the broadest sense of the word – pointing the way out of our present crisis."[12]

DESPITE HIS SINCERITY and popularity and indeed all the good work he set out to achieve, the newspaper announcements harmed Creme's own reputation in the eyes of the broader public and his detractors. Through charismatic figures such as Creme and Prophet, and the Ballards of the I AM movement, theosophy in the scholarly milieu and the wider esoteric community might be all too easily dismissed as fanciful, the stuff of charlatans, and ridiculed as pseudo-philosophy. Not least, because all these movements are grouped together under the one theosophical umbrella. Ignorance of the very existence of the Masters might have been better than a warped perception of them. As a third-generation Theosophist with many other controversies surrounding her, when it comes to reputation, Alice Bailey probably comes off worst, despite the fact that she was anything but a charismatic figure, the teachings she scribed and the organisations she created technical in nature.

CEDERCRANS AND LAURENCY

*W*ithin the Theosophical segment of the esoteric community, there exists considerable debate as to who had the last word when it comes to wisdom pouring forth from the Hierarchy, some arguing it was Blavatsky and others Alice Bailey. Then there are those who argue that occult wisdom will always continue to pour forth, and it is up to each individual to assess the merits of each outpouring and compare and contrast and tackle the contradictions through a combination of hermeneutics and exegesis, just as theologians tackle religious texts. And, of course, on the level of the individual seeker, we each gravitate towards and favour that which resonates, which may lead to the shunning of other wisdom streams and currents. Such debate does not include those writings readily dismissed as markedly inferior or worse, travesties, but rather centres on works of merit scribed by those who sincerely wish to hold to the Ageless Wisdom. The theological pursuit of truth and accuracy of various occult teachings appeals to the intellect eager for reliable knowledge. For some, the quest might constitute a diversion, however intriguing and worthy in and of itself, from the practice of applying an esoteric way of knowing in lived experience both inwardly and outwardly. Scholars will frame this knowledge and knowing distinction by referring to the etic and emic levels of inquiry. There are numerous ways to approach and engage with the Ageless Wisdom at both levels, and it is primarily at the etic level that we evaluate various esoteric bodies of work. In the light of this, a biography of Alice Bailey would not be complete without a short introduction to Lucille Cedercrans.

Esoteric mystic Lois Lucille Stickle Johnson Cedercrans Schaible (1921-84) was born in Bowmanville, Ontario, Canada. The family moved to the USA soon after her birth, where she endured an unhappy childhood reared by feuding parents. She left school with no qualifications, married and bore seven children. With her life filled with humdrum housewifery, she wasn't to know her own esoteric mystic disposition. Then in 1948, when she was twenty-seven years old, she experienced the flooding of her mind with strange ideas. Eventually, she heard a voice communicating that she was about to enter a new phase of her life and become a teacher of the wisdom. An astonishing notion, for a humble woman without a good education.

Lucille Cedercrans went to write for the Master R (Rakoczi) among others, including DK. Her life was transformed. Faced with needing to do something with the wisdom she received, she familiarised herself with Theosophical teachings and set about organising groups around the United States, in which she taught meditation and her 'New Thoughtform Presentation of the Wisdom'. She wrote numerous titles including *The Soul and Its Instrument* and *Ashramic Projections*. After enjoying two decades of success, she was struck down with rheumatoid arthritis in 1972 and was rendered permanently disabled until her death in 1985.[1]

In her biography, *Luminous Sitting, Tortuous Walking*, Cedercrans expresses her dismay over accusations she had plagiarised Alice Bailey's writing, apparently voiced by those close to Alice Bailey in the late 1950s, and a matter Zachary F. Lansdowne tackles in his paper 'Cedercrans' Writings Compared to Bailey's

Technique of Integration for the Seventh Ray'.[2] Lucille claims she wrote all of her seminal work *Nature of the Soul* having never come across the Bailey books and later, once she had, she claims never to have ever fully read any of those texts.[3]

Lansdowne suggests that Cedercrans fulfils one of DK's predictions, namely that certain chosen disciples from five Ashrams had been or would be trained to contact the public. The prediction was made in November 1948.[4] Rather than address claims of plagiarism, he deploys discourse analysis to DK's Technique of Integration for the Seventh Ray found in the Bailey books, in the light of Cedrecrans' statements. He concludes that, 'Cedercrans appears to build upon Bailey's earlier material, in the sense of clarifying some of Bailey's obscure hints and phrases'.[5] Lansdowne goes on to remark, 'Moreover, Bailey's Technique of Integration for the Seventh Ray seems to have anticipated the subsequent publication of Cedercrans' material, because every segment of this abstruse technique appears to be clarified by Cedercrans' corresponding passages.[6] This is reinforced by Cedercrans' claim that the Tibetan was involved in the creation of her material.

Many within the Ageless Wisdom milieu accept the quality of Cedercrans output, regarding it as a stepped-down and extrapolated version, one that, as Lansdowne states, may serve to clarify obscure portions of the Bailey books, but that cannot replace the original, pure form. There is, however, some doubt concerning the source, some arguing that Cedercrans did not enjoy the Ashramic contact from a Master as she claims, but that of an initiate instead.

Another question in the reader's mind might be if Cedercrans's work really did come from one Ashram, what of the other four mentioned in DK's prediction mentioned above?

HENRY T. LAURENCY

Another important figure in the Ageless Wisdom tradition is Henrik Teofron Laurentius von Zeipel (1882-1971), better known under his pen name of Henry T. Laurency. The esoteric philosopher was born in south-east Sweden and studied philosophy at Uppsala University. He dedicated the larger part of his life to the study of the texts of Blavatsky, Leadbeater, Besant and Bailey. Of importance to Laurency became the standing of these teachings within the intellectual and academic community. To address this, he set about presenting Theosophy as a credible worldview to scholars and philosophers, in works including *The Philosopher's Stone* and *The Knowledge of Reality*, and a series titled *Knowledge of Life*, all of which were published in the English language from 1979 and were originally written in Swedish from 1930 to 1971. Those editions were published in Sweden from 1950 to 1998.[7]

As part of his campaign to impress his scholarly peers, Laurency thought to render the Eastern mystical content of Theosophy more palatable to the Western mind using mathematical phraseology, or as he called it, Pythagorean hylozoics. Problematic, perhaps, from the sceptic's standpoint, Laurency then claimed his writing had been dictated to him by Hilarion, an adept in the Hierarchy. Laurency's contact aligns with the following remark in *A Treatise on White Magic*, written with regard to the work of the Master R. and the Master of the English race: 'They are aided by a disciple of rare capacity in Sweden, and by an initiate in the southern part of Russia, who works much on the mental levels.'[8]

A cursory glance at Laurency's work reveals somewhat terse yet lucid writing, exacting and certainly lacking appeal for the average seeker. This is a sharp intellect at work. Clearly an erudite scholar with a keen mind for accuracy, Laurency might lack appeal in other respects as Swedish scholar, Håkan Blomqvist notes:

Students who enter a study of Laurency will immediately notice a few idiosyncrasies in his philosophy. He often has very critical remarks on democracy without presenting a political alternative. This could be taken as an excuse for a fascist view, but this is not a correct interpretation. Laurency is clearly a definite opponent of all forms of totalitarianism. Very peculiar is his total misunderstanding of social democracy, which he equates with communist dictatorship. His views on socialism are definitely not in line with his favourite esotericists Blavatsky and Bailey.[9]

THIS IS unlikely to be a view shared by Swedish author and esotericist Lars Adelskogh, who translated Laurency's volumes into English and currently holds copyright. Former editor-in-chief of the Swedish edition of *Nexus* – an Australian magazine publishing articles on conspiracy theories and alternative medicine – Adelskogh is understood to be a Holocaust revisionist.[10]

Laurency's abhorrence of totalitarianism is certainly an attitude shared by Alice Bailey. However, that might be where the rapport ends, for Laurency is critical of Alice Bailey. In his book *Knowledge of Life Three*, he takes her to task, albeit in sympathetic fashion, over the quality of her writing. In all fairness, he acknowledges her difficult personal life circumstances, lack of academic training and the limitations of the English language, while also noting the infiltration of Christian descriptors into the language, which he believes come not from DK but from her. Laurency argues that Alice Bailey was sent to 'win over the emotionalists to whom feeling is the most important factor'.[11] Since many of those emotionalists had Christian upbringings:

Being an old Christologist, A.A.B. found it easiest (which presumably also was the intention) to use her old Christian outlook when choosing terms for esoteric ideas. Her writings are bristling with words and phrases from the "New Testament", so that the Christians can identify themselves with it and are not at once repelled by a strange terminology.[12]

WHEN LAURENCY CRITICISES Bailey's writing in his essay on *The Reappearance of the Christ*, appearing in his book *Knowledge of Life Five*, it is where there exist discrepancies regarding her choice of language. He blames her abilities and makes much of the hindrance they posed for DK, who he holds in high regard. He is not unduly cruel to Alice Bailey, rather he is somewhat despairing of her capabilities, as if reiterating Elise Sandes' remark in Ireland when, since there was no one suitable available to take on the India work, Alice would simply have to do. Coming from Miss Sandes' observing an innocent twenty-two-year old she was about to send off to run soldiers' homes, such a remark is entirely appropriate. From Laurency, it cannot help but come across as patronising, although, in his comments, he by no means overlooks her achievements in scribing twenty-four often dense and thick volumes, or in running her Arcane School and establishing the Lucis Trust with its subsidiary programs, *The Beacon*, Triangles and World Goodwill. His concern was ever the purity of esoteric writing, the need for clarity and precision to ensure the ideas and the reality were portrayed as adequately as possible. Further light is cast on Laurency's views of Alice Bailey by considering his scathing condemnation of Helena Roerich as an 'imposter' with her 'so-called agni-yoga', precisely because she in turn was scathing of Alice Bailey. He also rendered Roerich's writings as 'emotional mysticism'.[13]

DOCUMENTS

*T*his chapter is based on limited source material and interviews conducted by the author and remains a partial account of a difficult period in the Bailey community history.

WHEN MARIAN WALTER left the New York headquarters of the Lucis Trust to pursue Applicants at the Portal II independently, she took with her Louise Benesch, who was Alice Bailey's personal secretary and a close friend of Walter. Evidence of the formation of an alliance between the two women can be found in a letter dated August 1946, in which DK advises Louise's husband Bernard Morrow – LUT: Love, Understanding, Trans-mutation in the Glamour DINA group of nine and the New Seed Group – that, 'RSW [Marian Walter] helps you not, much as she has attempted to do so. She does not accept or recognise you for what you are – a man whose lower nature dominates most of the time, but whose basic intent is identification with the higher nature; she sees you differently and her surety along this line is no help to you.'[1] The letter was written after Alice Bailey ended her Friday talks, having all but given up on finding a solution to the running of the Arcane School.

When Walter and Benesch left the trust in the early 1950s, they did not go empty-handed. Walter took material for use in her Applicants at the Portal study sets, including copies of the Tibetan's ashramic papers and Arcane School material produced by Alice Bailey, along with copies of papers and essays written by Arcane School students. All of this material in a fashion belonged to Walter in her previous role and since she planned on continuing with the Applicants at the Portal, she believed she needed to take it, whether or not the act met with approval at the time. It is understood that Walter also took the incense gifted to Alice Bailey by the Tibetan via Henry Carpenter, incense of enormous symbolic value, a treasure, and the one single piece of concrete evidence that ties Alice Bailey and DK.[2] Although it is not known if Alice Bailey had already gifted Walter the incense prior to her death. Around this time, Benesch assumed ownership of and took all the documents and associated paraphernalia pertaining to the Ancient Universal Mysteries.[3] Both Marian Walter and Louise Benesch were members of the AUM before the group was disbanded in the 1940s – as mentioned earlier, Marian was the wife of Leo Rohe Walter, one of the original signatories to AUM's 1935 incorporation – and it is claimed that Louise Benesch had been put in charge of the material, and therefore was well within her rights to take the AUM papers from the offices of the Lucis Trust.[4]

More material taken from the trust has come to light. On 15th December 2020, the anniversary of Alice Bailey's passing, and after the first and second editions of this biography were published, a box of manuscripts dating back to 1920 came into the possession of Steven Chernikeeff. Included in the box are manuscripts of *Letters on Occult Meditation* (including the Stanzas of Dyzan which appear in *A Treatise on Cosmic Fire*), *Esoteric Astrology, From Intellect to Intuition, The Light of the Soul* and *The Soul and Its Mechanism*, along with seventeen fragments of Alice Bailey's handwriting and a double page of DK transmission writing. This box was discovered in a closet in an apartment in

Ronkonkoma, Long Island, New York in 1993. According to Chernikeeff, the box has the name 'Walter' written on it three times, and he is convinced the box forms part of the collection of material Marian Walter acquired when she left the trust in the 1950s. The details as to why the box was left in a closet are unknown, but existence of manuscripts that appear to have nothing to do with either AUM or Applicants of the Portal begs the question why Marian Walter would want or have them, if indeed they were in her possession. Of note in this regard and as previously quoted, is the letter from Regina Keller reassuring Priscilla Hilton that whatever was taken, the trust had that and more besides.[5]

A mystique has built up over the AUM papers, pivoting on a claim apparently made by Benesch that she was told by Alice Bailey to store the AUM material until later in the century when someone would come along, someone who was meant to have the documents, someone who could advance the work.[6]

There is no written evidence from that time to demonstrate that this was ever said, let alone how it was said, and therefore if it were misconstrued. As is evident in the Marian Walter chapter above, remarks made in letters from the Tibetan were apt to be misinterpreted. The claim that she was to store the papers and that someone would come along to advance the work remain unsubstantiated beliefs in the mind of Benesch. What is known is that she believed in this wholeheartedly.[7]

In 1977, Benesch was introduced by her son to a young Freemason and Lodge master with whom she had been impressed after reading his papers on Masonry. His name is Keith Bailey. The surname is coincidental.

A drummer by profession, Bailey (1948-) was well-known in the British jazz scene and once had an opportunity to perform with Jimi Hendrix when he was just seventeen years old.[8] Bailey had worked at the Lucis Trust in London in 1974-5 before developing a sudden interest in Freemasonry. To this end, he consulted another co-worker and one-time chairperson for the

Radionic Association Lily Cornford (1906-2003). A leading colour therapist, Cornford founded the Maitreya School of Healing in 1974.[9] She also inspired renowned singer-songwriter and close friend Kate Bush to write a song about her.[10] Cornford arranged for Bailey to join a Co-Masonry lodge in London. He learned fast and before long, he moved to New York and joined and became heavily involved in a lodge there.

Bailey visited Benesch on her request at her home in Washington. There, she quizzed him on what he knew about the Ancient Universal Mysteries. Once satisfied that she had found the person Alice Bailey had indicated would come, she told Keith Bailey he was the one she had been waiting for, and she in due course passed on all the AUM papers and associated paraphernalia.

According to Bailey, the Tibetan had begun giving the AUM instructions on a six-monthly basis from Wesak in 1935, and sometime in the early to mid 1940s Alice Bailey suspended the project due to time commitments and concerns over the direction the project was taking. Bailey states that Alice Bailey had told Benesch to store the AUM paraphernalia in trunks.[11] The mention of 'trunks' went on to compound a mystique over the quantity of material that fell into Keith Bailey's hands. A trunk can be another word for a type of suitcase and they come in various sizes, large and small. Twice-yearly instructions given for at most ten years would amount to about 40,000 words. Presumably the AUM charter group would have gone on to produce associated material. However much there was, it might be reasonably assumed that if Alice Bailey had used the word 'trunk', she was referring not only to volume but to the vessel's capacity to hide and keep safe.

Through Benesch, Bailey was introduced to Walter and the two women explained the Ancient Universal Mysteries and how Alice Bailey had made it very clear she did not want the project associated with the Lucis Trust and the Arcane School. Keith Bailey took that as an imperative, and, as the one chosen by

Benesch, he endeavoured to ring fence AUM, keeping it separate and distinct as he established and developed this version of freemasonry. In following this path, and based on his own testimony, Bailey claims – whether wittingly or otherwise – a sort of spiritual entitlement which some may dispute. This entitlement pertains to the nature of transmission – for example, from master to disciple – and what might be described occult lineage.[12] Such matters are paramount among esotericists, especially in hierarchical schemes as found in theosophy. Which goes some way to explaining the heated nature of the situation explored below.

Keith Bailey honoured his mandate. Today, AUM has a website and eleven lodges established around the world.[13] As mentioned in an earlier chapter, the original AUM was incorporated by Alice Bailey in 1935 as an entity separate from the Lucis Trust and, at a later date, Keith Bailey also incorporated the Grand Lodge AUM organisation.[14] The lodges hold open ceremonies and the AUM masonic symposiums. One prominent master mason is author and public speaker Kevin Townley, who has made significant contributions to contemporary understandings of Tarot and Qabalistic thought.[15]

In the 1990s, Bailey hoped to gain some acceptance of the AUM within the broader community of Co-Freemasonry, a movement with a long association with the Theosophical Society. Unfortunately, it appears his efforts were not well-received, and were apparently thwarted in January 2000, when according to a Circular posted on the Masonic Forum of Light, the Supreme Council of the Co-Freemasons put out the following statement:

 After examination of the Constitution of the Grand Lodge Ancient Universal Mysteries (AUM), the Supreme Council instructs Representatives of the Supreme Council to Federations, Delegates of the Supreme Council to Jurisdictions and RR.WW.MM of Pioneer Lodges to suspend all relations with the Grand Lodge Ancient Universal Mysteries.

Consequently, dual membership cannot be authorised.

The Supreme Council requests strict observance of this circular.[16]

A SUSPENSION of all relations and a denial of dual membership amounts to an outright rejection of the Grand Lodge AUM. The motives behind it are unclear, although the surrounding discussion on the forum indicates that the instruction may have its roots in anti-Alice Bailey sentiment which was very much in evidence on the Masonic Forum of Light and shows the enduring nature of the opposition Alice Bailey faced in her lifetime. It is unfortunate that Keith Bailey, or indeed anyone endeavouring to do good work, should suffer a setback due to the animosity towards Alice Bailey found in some quarters.

BACK IN THE late 1970s or early 1980s, Walter introduced Bailey to renowned teacher of the Ageless Wisdom and psychologist Michael Robbins. Walter took the two men under her wing and guided them for four years. In this time, the men gained an account of what happened after Alice Bailey's death in 1949, from Walter's perspective.

Walter passed away in 1987 and according to Michael Robbins, two days before her death, she inserted a codicil passing on ownership of all her papers to them, including all the papers that were taken from the Lucis Trust headquarters in the early 1950s.[17] Both men have chosen to retain exclusive right to the material, which they are entitled to do, yet it is a decision which has caused a damaging rift in the Alice Bailey community.

Although it should be noted that these papers are separate from the AUM papers which Benesch passed on to Keith Bailey.

Upon Walter's death and in compliance with the codicil, the papers were delivered to the address of Mary Ann Casalino's home in New Jersey, which served as the headquarters of the fledgling Seven Rays Institute, founded by Mary Ann, Dot Maver and Michael Robbins. The papers were stored in eight boxes, each about the size of a twelve-bottle wine case, were sighted by Geoffrey Logie – who had recently travelled from New Zealand – before apparently being divided up between Bailey and Robbins. It is alleged that Bailey, for an unknown reason, took the larger portion. By that time, the material Walter had in her possession would have included all the Applicants at the Portal II sets, associated materials and students' essay papers, along with papers pertaining to her Group of Nine project which she ran in the 1980s, along with anything else she may have initiated in the intervening decades. Logie sighted the essay and study papers belonging to various disciples, some original papers belonging to Alice Bailey and the incense.[18] It is understood that Bailey and Robbins each made a copy of the papers in their portion of the papers for the other to keep, so that they both had a complete set.

About fifteen years passed before matters came to a head. In 2005, esoteric astrologer Stephen Pugh joined The Polaris Project, a Yahoo group convened to evaluate the global Bailey community, articulate the group history and the study of the fundamental aspects of the teachings.[19] The problem for the group was the missing papers. Pugh and others argued that an archive of all of the Bailey material should be created, papers digitised and made available to all via a university library or similar. Championing the cause, he was eager to access the material he felt Bailey and Robbins were hoarding, and strove to persuade Bailey and Robbins to release what they had. The men refused (and still refuse). They also refused to divulge the contents of the Marian Walter codicil papers, which might well amount to little more than the Applicants at the Portal papers and the associated materials of Walter's own projects and little else. Or, the papers might contain at least one or two documents of importance. As for the AUM papers, as custodian via Louise Benesch, Keith Bailey felt entirely within his rights to keep all that material hidden within the auspices of the AUM Grand Lodge.

Pugh acquired all of the Applicants at the Portal II study sets in 1985, from an associate who had discovered them in an attic in Florida, and it is very likely he already has much of the vital material in the Robbins' portion of the codicil papers.[20] But he remains convinced Robbins is sitting on more and persisted for some time trying to persuade Robbins to open up.

It is not an unreasonable quest. Copies of the Zodiacal Meditations were discovered hidden or buried in the School for Esoteric Studies files back in 2000, in poor quality and with areas blank and other patches scarcely decipherable. There were only three meditations. No one knows if the other nine exist, and it is natural to wonder if they might form a part of the papers in Bailey and Robbins' possession. The source of the ZMs is unclear, yet as noted by then SES director John Cobb, the documents carry the phrase "Disciples Degree", in the style of the few other original Arcane School documents, along with Frank Hilton's signature.[21]

Unfortunately, the astonishingly acrimonious exchange that took place on the Polaris forum, in private emails and later on Facebook descended into a dispute over Marian Walter's integrity. Adding to an already fraught situation, a devastating wildfire broke out in 2007 in Rancho Santa Fe, where Keith Bailey was living. Whether there was any damage to his papers is not known, although some suspect that might be the case.

After close scrutiny of the evidence made available to me, it was my earlier contention that there exists little material in the Walter codicil papers beyond the Applicants at the Portal papers, Walter's own papers, and copies of papers held by the School for Esoteric Studies and the headquarters of the Lucis Trust.[22]

However, the unfortunate situation will continue until Bailey and Robbins reveal what they have. Meanwhile, no one knows or is prepared to reveal what happened to all of Alice Bailey's letters and personal papers, or of the many hundreds of thousands of letters she wrote to students, academics, politicians and numerous others in prominent positions.

The matter of these documents feeds an issue of accountability and sources. Robbins is said to have made use of material in Walter's codicil papers without giving the esoteric community access to the documents in question, a matter raised in The Polaris Project. Some of that material pertains to copies of letters from the Tibetan to members of his DINA groups. Portions of these letters were redacted for various editorial reasons by Regina Keller prior to publication. One issue of concern for the Polaris group at the time is an apparent prediction that the Age of Aquarius starts in 2117, which DK purportedly stated in a letter to Roberto Assagioli in 1940: 'I would suggest that another 177 years must go by before we enter into what you have called the last decan of Aquarius but which might, from a certain point of view be the first decan.'[23] Such a prediction means a lot to students of the Ageless Wisdom, many of whom would wish to see the original letter before relying on the claim.[24]

Another matter that has been upsetting for some concerns Robbins' publishing of redacted material in letters from the Tibetan to Roberto Assagioli on the Jews and Zionism, which Robbins then discusses in a post on astrologer Phillip Lindsay's website.[25] Without access to the primary source, readers must take as given the accuracy of the quoted text.

The group was also concerned that a list of fixed stars appearing in Robbins' *The Tapestry of the Gods* is identical to that appearing in Walter's Applicants at the Portal II study sets, a list which Walter then extrapolates by correspondence in the following manner.[26]

```
Star I - - - - -Benetnasch – Head centre (1000 Petalled Lotus) – -Ray 1.
Star II - - - - Mizar - - - - - - Ajna centre - - - - - - - - - - - - - - - - - - -Ray 2.
Star III - - - -Alioth - - - - - - Alta major centre and throat centre - -Ray 3.
Star IV - - - -Megrez - - - - -Heart centre - - - - - - - - - - - - - - - - - - Ray 4.
Star V - - - - Dubhe - - - - - -Solar plexus centre - - - - - - - - - - - - -Ray 5.
Star VI - - - -Merak - - - - - - Sacral centre - - - - - - - - - - - - - - - - - Ray 6.
Star VII - - - Phegda - - - - - Base of spine centre - - - - - - - - - - - -Ray 7.'
            Marian Walter, Applicants at the Portal Study Set VII
```

TO HIS CREDIT ROBBINS' does acknowledge that, 'The Tibetan does not go so far as to assign a particular ray to a particular star, but there is strong reason to think that the seven rays should be associated with the stars in the order given above'.[27] Unfortunately, there is no reference to Marian Walter. To be fair to Robbins, his omission could easily have been an unintentional oversight and certainly not intended to deceive.

These matters raise concerns for those with a scholarly disposition regarding authenticity and the accurate citing of source material which arguably should be in the public domain in some fashion.[28] Others may argue that all these concerns are trivial and it would be better for the Bailey community to focus on cohesion and goodwill, in keeping with the spirit of the teachings. Above all, the entire issue of these documents reveals how passionately all involved feel about the integrity of the Bailey teachings.

ADVANCING THE TEACHINGS

While most Bailey students have either applied the teachings as practitioners in various healing modalities and meditation groups, or quietly lived out their lives in accordance with the Ageless Wisdom, sometimes blending in other sources of wisdom, a small number of followers have sought to advance esoteric or soul psychology by extrapolating and developing the teachings, particularly those contained in *A Treatise on the Seven Rays*.

Among them is Kurt Abraham, a former Arcane School student who studied the Bailey texts for over forty years. Abraham founded the School for the Study of the Seven Rays in the 1990s. Still active today, the school offers a free, home-study course delivered by Abraham based on his collected works, which are published by Lampus Press, his own imprint. For income, the organisation relies on book sales and donations from students. It is impossible to ascertain its reach, but its website claims to have delivered its three-year tuition to students from numerous countries around the world.[1] The Lucis Trust, which rarely endorses the works of those outside its tightknit organisation, lists Abraham's books on its website, serving as endorsement of the quality of his output.

In his texts, Abraham re-languages DK's teachings to render them more accessible to those who are not students of the works. He provides a good example of the style of thinking and writing that has arisen from Bailey's more abstruse esoteric thought, including his thoughtful work, *Threefold Method for Understanding the Seven Rays*, which provides a detailed and accessible case studies of the rays.[2]

Prominent in the non-academic field of esoteric psychology is the aforementioned Michael Robbins, a teacher of the seven rays and esoteric astrology, delivering courses to students internationally. Robbins has written a number of commentaries on Alice Bailey's teachings, and composed fifteen musical, ceremonial ritual dramas designed to invoke and express the energies of the zodiacal signs. Along with his wife Tujia Robbins, he also runs the Northern Light Mystery School in Finland.[3]

In 1985, Michael Robbins co-founded the Seven Ray Institute, and two years later its sister organisation, the University of the Seven Rays, which is registered as a non-profit educational organisation in the United States and provided workshops, seminars and educational programs. Between 1985-1999, the university published the *Journal of Esoteric Psychology*, a bi-annual non-peer-reviewed collection of papers on an array of topics including the seven rays and esoteric astrology. Through the Institute of the Seven Rays annual conference held in Phoenix, Arizona, over a fourteen-day period, many others have gained insights into the field. The international conference is now in its 34th year.

Another organisation associated with Robbins and dedicated to delivering teachings is the Morya Federation.[4] Established in 2008, the federation provides webinars and broadcasts, and promotes several similar organisations that work in cooperation with and form a part of Robbins' network.

In late 2019, the Federation took over the programs previously offered by the University of the Seven Rays and now delivers them online, through webinars, coursework, mentors and advisors. Courses are free, donations encouraged. The Morya Federation offers three main areas of study: Meditation Quest; The Great Quest; and Quest Universal, all involving meditations, study and written reports, touching on an array of topics including *A Treatise on Cosmic Fire*, the Rays, glamour and esoteric astrology. All of the materials distil the Ageless Wisdom.

A fourth website under the Robbins banner is the Makara online portal, which provides access to all of Robbins' writing, a vast storehouse of webinars and commentaries on the Bailey books, along with open access to six volumes of his *The Tapestry of the Gods* series. He has also developed an online self-assessment tool providing personal identity profiles for the various ray combinations.[5]

Through the commendable efforts of Robbins and faculty members delivering courses in the various educational programmes offered, the USR has been influential in the promulgation of esoteric psychology, or rayology as it is sometimes called, providing an alternative to the Arcane School and the School for Esoteric Studies. Students have gone on to establish websites, organisations or have incorporated their understanding of the rays into their own practice.

Michael Robbins and his organisations are all-encompassing when it comes to teaching, learning and experience, and have become something of a one-stop shop.

The symbolic degrees gained at the University of the Seven Rays lack formal academic accreditation, Robbins' own teachings have not been published widely outside of his own milieu, and it appears little if any progress in bringing this new specialism to the attention of his academic peers has been made through Robbins – who holds a PhD in Psychology along with a PhDE in Esoteric Philosophy from his own organisation – yet in founding his organisations, Robbins has made a substantial contribution in advancing the teachings, drawing to the Ageless Wisdom those New Age seekers who may otherwise not have taken a deep interest, and invigorating the teachings with fresh energy and insight. The aforementioned *The Tapestry of the Gods*, which 'elucidates the Science of the Seven Rays and the new and developing Science of Esoteric Psychology' and 'provides deep insight into the manifestation of the Rays in the human energetic system by explaining how they variously combine, fuse and blend,' and 'a meticulous analysis of the evolutionary, psycho-spiritual applications of the Ray energies to the evolving human energy system', is undoubtedly his greatest contribution to the nascent field.[6] At the time of writing, only one of the ten volumes in *The Tapestry of the Gods* is available for purchase in online bookstores.

As with all institutions centred around a charismatic figurehead, there arise dangers of devotion, obedience and the fostering of an in-crowd mentality, something to which the New Age movement has been especially prone. This tendency undermines the very essence of the Ageless Wisdom tradition, which is oriented not towards any form of idolatry, but towards world service, a matter of paramount importance to the Hierarchy and forming a cornerstone of the Bailey books. No spiritual group, no matter how rarefied, is immune. Which is perhaps why, despite his obvious popularity, Robbins has chosen a more distant and impersonal style of delivery through his webinars and his federation.

A project emerging out of the USR milieu was founded in New Zealand when esoteric wisdom teacher and author Bruce Lyon, architect Lynda Vugler and Vicktorya Stone established a school at the exquisite Highden Manor on North Island in 2000. Finn Anderson from the Hummelgarten Healing Centre, Denmark, was an initial financier of the property, along with Lynda, Vicktorya, Bruce, and two USR students Daniel Krummenacher and Dany Vecchio. Initially, the School at Highden offered a DK-inspired five-year curriculum for adults living and working on site. In the second year, courses covered other sources of the Ageless Wisdom, including Cedercrans. The school ran for three years, during which time Highden attracted visits from luminaries in the Bailey community, including

Michael Robbins, Phillip Lindsay and Stephen Pugh, enjoying a brief yet colourful history, descending from its initial high ideals into various personality conflicts. Due to financial pressures in Denmark, Finn Anderson sold his share to Santa Barbara headmaster Kent Ferguson. Highden Manor was eventually sold and, after passing ownership several times, was eventually repurchased by Bruce Lyon who renamed Highden Manor as Highden Temple, which served as the base for his Shamballa School.[7]

Between 2001-2003, Lyon claimed he was in telepathic rapport with Djwhal Khul, or at least with a member of his Ashram, and he wrote down the communications he received. The result can be found in his book *The Mercury Transmissions.* According to his own website, Lyon blends the Ageless Wisdom with the shamanic and mystery school traditions.[8] Under the auspices of his school, Lyon hosts events around the world, varying in length from a few days to six weeks. His approach exemplifies the merging of various traditions, drawing on handpicked elements from each, found in the New Age movement. Some might accuse Lyon of watering down the DK teachings. Others might point out that he brings the Ageless Wisdom tradition to a fresh audience.

Diverse approaches to the Ageless Wisdom abound. Of note is artist Duane Carpenter who produces dynamic esoteric symbols to convey the deeper meanings of the Bailey teachings and evoke responses in the beholder. A teacher with the University of the Seven Rays, his primary aim is to help prepare humanity for the reappearance of the Christ via the 2025 Conclave of the Spiritual Hierarchy. Carpenter enjoys a high profile in numerous DK-oriented Facebook groups.[9]

Beyond the USR milieu, another notable contributor to the promulgation of esoteric psychology is British astrologer and medical doctor Douglas M. Baker (1922-2011). He was a prolific author of some one hundred books, including volumes on esoteric astrology, healing and psychology. Baker delivered thou-

sands of lectures, helped develop the trend in alternative medicine and made a significant contribution to esoteric astrology.
His *Esoteric Psychology: The Seven Rays* and *The Seven Rays: Keys
to the Mysteries* re-languages the Ageless Wisdom, rendering it
somewhat more accessible to the interested reader.[10] Whatever is
thought of the quality of his writing or the various directions he
took – towards the end of his life, he became especially interested in Dark Energy and Dark Matter – Douglas Baker deserves
to be commended for his dedication.

Non-esotericists who seek wisdom and insight must settle for
indirect approaches to the advancement of the psychology of the
seven rays, as found in the work of Assagioli's student, author,
psychotherapist and philosopher Pierro Ferruci, whose *Inevitable
Grace* contains seven chapters on seven pathways, each corresponding in a veiled manner to one of the seven rays. The book
constitutes a valuable contribution to the field. It will be through
works such as provided by Ferruci that the advancement of
esoteric psychology will filter into the mainstream.[11]

What is lacking with regard to esoteric psychology, or indeed
with respect to Bailey's entire body of work, is the advancement
of the teachings in the academic sphere. In part, this can be
attributed to the lack of respect for Alice Bailey held by key
scholars in the field of Western Esotericism. Yet, as scholar David
C. Borsos notes, 'Bailey's corpus constitutes a specific, modern,
comprehensive, and coherent model that can make powerful
contributions to many areas of academic thinking.'[12] Borsos is
one of a small cohort of Bailey students who recognise a missed
opportunity. 'In order for the Tibetan's teachings to reach the
wider public, the intelligentsia, and academics, it is important
for Bailey students to address, critique and incorporate ideas
that are circulating today in the public sphere rather than
focusing exclusively on dated esoteric writings.'[13] What is
required and what was hoped for in the teachings, is sustained,
concentrated effort by illumed higher minds to promulgate the
teachings in order that they exert influence in various fields.

Instead, as Borsos notes, the Bailey community falls down when it comes to reaching out to the wider community, preferring to turn inwards, subjectively, fixed in rituals of meditation and little else.

THE LUCIS TRUST

The Lucis Trust is the most influential of all Bailey-inspired organisations, standing as the editorial authority of the Bailey books, administering World Goodwill, the Arcane School, The Beacon and Triangles and presenting Alice Bailey to the world. The trust is depicted by scholar Steven Sutcliffe, who visited the London headquarters in 1996, as operating 'more like a government department or a firm of stockbrokers' than a religious organisation. 'The atmosphere was calm, sober and somewhat bureaucratic: the general impression was of a small business or family firm.'[14] Sutcliffe found the Trust austere. Perhaps this austerity can be attributed to the Trust's commitment to retaining the integrity of the structure and mandate of the original organisation.

Each of the three offices of the Trust is run by a small group of paid staff, with the Geneva office relying on volunteers to assist with the different language sections in the activities. The board comprises trained disciples committed to fostering the unity of purpose of the Trust and serving accordingly. No one outside of the board of directors has any influence on the decisions and operations of the Trust. Positions on the board of seven trustees are tightly held – there are no member votes – and the Trust is financed by donations large and small. Mary Turner (Bailey) was elected as president in 1957 and held that position until 1984, a term of close to thirty years. The presidency was then shared between Perry Coles in New York and Winifred H. (Jane) Brewin who held the London chair. A year later, Jan Nation replaced Brewin. Coles retired in 1989 and was replaced by Sarah McKechnie, and together, McKechnie and Nation retained

ADVANCING THE TEACHINGS | 337

their roles as co-directors for about a decade until 1997 when Nation resigned. From then, McKechnie acted as president of all the branches of the trust in New York, London and Geneva. When McKechnie resigned in 2012 after holding her position for twenty-three years, Christine Morgan took on the role, which she holds to date.[15]

The Lucis Trust is not a membership organisation; there are no fees or dues. The Trust is comprised of three separate legal entities, each financed by donations, legacies and special gifts. Funds are shared between the three entities if and when a need arises. The same board of trustees is responsible for the three legal entities. In 2018, expenditure in the New York office exceeded income by almost $500,000 due to fewer gifts and the purchase of a condominium overlooking the United Nations for the New York headquarters. The Trust's website operates in seven languages and makes all the Bailey books available online for free. The Arcane School has its own interactive website for ease of administration. The Trust produces polished and professional promotional videos for some of their events.

The Lucis Publishing Company book sales (in the Americas only and not including English titles sold in the Commonwealth) in 2018 'showed significant improvements over the previous year (shown in parentheses): 3,676 (2,675) publications; 69 (55) CD-ROMs; 384 (421) audio books; and 1,849 (1,303) e-books. The three best sellers, across all platforms, were *A Treatise on White Magic, Esoteric Healing* and *Esoteric Psychology, Vol I*.'[16] Global paperback sales across the twenty-four Bailey books and other volumes in various languages, amounting to around a hundred sales per book if broken out evenly, appear poor. E-book sales of only fifty copies per book even worse. It is hard to imagine students using the free online versions as study texts, and the books are not something to be borrowed, passed around and shared. The only conclusion that can be drawn is that fresh interest in Alice Bailey and her teachings has declined despite the vast improvement in sales compared to the previous year. Yet any diminishing numbers of book sales is not reflected in the ongoing interest and support of co-workers and supporters.

The Beacon continues to maintain a high standard, with the October-December 2019 and January-March 2020 editions containing a number of Bailey inspired, insightful and relevant pieces reflective of contemporary global issues, including 'Africa and the Planetary Picture', by Bette Stockbauer, 'The Paradoxical Utopia of Piet Mondrian' by Anne Woodward, and 'Pluto and Global Economics' by Christine Aagaard.[17]

An outstanding achievement of the Trust is the building of an interconnected web of global discipleship, fostered in part through global Full Moon monthly meditations and the concomitant festivals which attract large numbers of participants via the Units of Service dotted around the world, including Sydney Goodwill.[18] Special campaigns include the Easter and Wesak festivals, World Invocation Day, the World Goodwill Seminar and the Arcane School Conference.

An interlinked event across London, New York and Geneva, The World Goodwill Seminar 'In Resonance with the Living Earth' in 2018 featured talks from mathematician and physicist Jeremy Dunning-Davies, executive-director of the Psychosynthesis Trust Jen Morgan, and high-profile management consultant Giles Hutchins.[19]

The Arcane School conference also comprises a series of interlinked events across New York, London and Geneva, held over three weekends and commencing on the weekend closest to Wesak, the Full Moon of May. All the events include private meditation sessions for Arcane School students and open sessions for the public. The primary aim of the conference is to build 'a focused point of tension in the group mind' around a particular keynote, the 2019 conference focusing on group consciousness and group initiation.[20] This subjective aim of fostering spiritual tension in service of humanity and the Plan distinguishes Arcane School conferences from regular academic-style events.

The conference features speakers of similar calibre. Psychotherapist Dina Glouberman, Tanzanian green energy company CEO John Tate and Associate Professor of computer science Norun Sanderson spoke at the conference in 2019, along with distinguished former Prima Ballerina with the New York City Ballet Maria Calegari, psychotherapist Catherine Crews, and Associate Professor of Sociology and Anthropology at Illinois State University Dr Thomas Burr. In Geneva, leading pioneer in the field of Music Therapy with the NHS in UK Mario Eugster spoke, together with a number of other Arcane School students from the different language sections. [21] All of these speakers explore the Bailey teachings in some fashion, and all address an audience of Bailey sympathisers. As such, the conferences do little to address the issue of inward turning raised by Borsos above. Although, given the abstruse nature of the esoteric genre, it is difficult to conceive of how to retain subjective purity, focused, through a keynote, on a spiritual point of tension, and reach a wider audience not conversant with the teachings.

The seven-yearly New Group of World Servers Festival held in December, the last in 2019, again provides a wealth of speakers. This festival is held to help energise all those participating in elevating humanity. 'The Alice Bailey writings state that every seven years the energies of Capricorn are augmented by the forces from a much greater constellation which is, to our zodiac, what the zodiac is to the earth. This gives tremendous impetus to the work of the New Group of World Servers.'[22]

There can be no doubt that the Lucis Trust works hard to maintain the integrity of the Bailey teachings and strives to embody and carry forward the core ideas and values upon which Alice Bailey formed her organisation. The board of directors must be commended for their efforts. However, they are not without their critics.

Having complete control of the Bailey teachings, in the eyes of some the Lucis Trust has become something of a fortress, albeit one with many Units of Service outposts, leaving the

wider Bailey community out of key decisions such as the decision to re-language aspects of the teachings to, it would appear,
appease contemporary politically correct views. One example is
the Mantram of Unification.

ORIGINAL
The sons of men are one and I am one with them.
I seek to love, not hate;
I seek to serve and not exact due service;
I seek to heal, not hurt.
Let pain bring due reward of light and love.
Let the soul control the outer form, and life and all
   events
And bring to light the love that underlies the
   happenings of the time.
Let vision come and insight.
Let the future stand revealed.
Let inner union demonstrate and outer cleavages be
   gone.
Let love prevail.
Let all men love.[23]

IN THE LUCIS TRUST'S adapted version which they present alongside the original, the first and last lines have been changed to:
The souls of all are one and I am one with them; and Let all
people love.[24]

These changes are problematic. 'Sons of men' has a specific
Judeo-Christian meaning. 'Son' is the love-wisdom aspect of
God, the soul, and 'man' sits in an implied juxtaposition with
'God', in acknowledgement of man's foibles and weaknesses.
Jesus humbly called himself a 'son of man' to emphasise his own
humanity. 'The sons of men are one' is a recognition that the

souls of all humanity are a unity and the readers of the mantram humbly position themselves as part of that unity. 'The souls of all are one' carries the same basic meaning, yet devoid of the Judeo-Christian underpinning with its implied humility, and the concomitant power inherent in the phrase. The last line 'Let all people love' has been changed to cohere with the first, in accordance with contemporary sensitivities of gender bias in language. The matter of revisions to appease political correctness when it comes to ancient language is difficult terrain and a thorough analysis is beyond the scope of this biography. The matter has been presented to demonstrate the sensitivity of the Trust, and its openness to modifying certain aspects of the teachings to make them cohere with contemporary trends, to some degree bending to presentism in the hope of fending off complaints and attacks. What has been sacrificed here, however, is a deeper truth inherent in words of power, a matter of much importance to those valuing the purity of the original. Should the Bailey teachings be stripped of their Christian emphasis in an effort to render them universal and contemporary?

The decision of the Trust in this matter is indicative of the pressure they are under to balance the diverse wishes of the Bailey community, including those who seek to retain the original language, and external pressures emanating from criticisms among the politically correct Left, vicious attacks from various offended interest groups, the relentless crusade of the conspiracy theorists and fundamentalist Christians, and derision and condemnation from those adherents in other esoteric groups, including some in the Theosophical Society itself. The Trust must balance all of that while seeking to be relevant, contemporary and attractive to new seekers, and at the same time preserving the integrity of the teachings, as they were originally given. Any alterations to the Mantram of Unification ought to be considered in the light of the Bailey opus in its entirety, the language of which continues to be published by the trust in its original form.

This decision to modify the language of the Mantram legitimises further changes from others. The following version was recently shared in the Reappearance of the Christ Facebook Group – the Alice Bailey community is very active on Facebook. It is not known who wrote this version. The first line in the Mantram has now become 'Humanity is One, And We are One with All', a phrase that bears little resemblance to the original.[25]

The matter of the purity of the teachings versus adapting them to suit the times, using them as a springboard to convey other and diverse spiritual meanings, or customising them for differing purposes, appears a universal dilemma among all esoteric and spiritual traditions.

ESOTERIC ASTROLOGY

$\mathcal{I}$t is difficult to conceive of astrology as forming part of the New Age movement. The esoteric system of thought and divination has existed for millennia. Alice Bailey incorporated astrological thought into her canon through two works, *The Labours of Hercules*, in which the Greek myth is aligned with the twelve signs of the zodiac, and the third volume in DK's treatise on the seven rays, *Esoteric Astrology*. In this latter work, a revolutionary new astrological model is proposed, one that sits on top of pre-existing understandings. It is the astrology of the soul and its relationship with both the personality and the spiritual self.

In astrological circles oriented to soul astrology, Alice Bailey is held in high regard. DK's contribution to the vast storehouse of astrological knowledge accumulated over thousands of years, lies in the development of humanistic and soul-centred astrology. In *Esoteric Astrology*, a hefty text of almost seven hundred pages, astrology is turned on its head. The planetary rulers are assigned to different signs of the zodiac, their esoteric and hierarchical rulerships. The fixed star of Sirius takes on a new and important stature. The cosmic energies of the twelve constellations enter the solar system through the seven centres or chakras of the planetary bodies. The three modalities of cardinal, fixed and mutable, become the three crosses, that of the hidden Christ, the Crucified Christ and the Risen Christ. A large section of the work is given over to the science of triangles.[1]

A precursor to *Esoteric Astrology* which helps situate the work within the Ageless Wisdom tradition can be found in the writing of British Theosophist and astrologer Alan Leo (William Frederick Allen, 1860-1917), who wrote and published his own volume titled *Esoteric Astrology* in 1913.

Leo was introduced to Theosophy by astrologer Sepharial or Walter Richard Old, whom he met in 1889, and quickly became a devotee.[2] Both astrologers are referred to on a number of occasions in Bailey's *Esoteric Astrology*, serving as acknowledgement, particularly for a learned Theosophical readership much-versed in the output of her predecessors.

There are many points of similarity between Alan Leo's volume and Alice Bailey's much more complete esoteric astrology presentation, and also significant points of difference. In a paper discussing the role Leo played in the development of the field, astrologer M. Temple Richmond notes, 'This historical context arises from the sequential nature with which the Ageless Wisdom is in the process of being revealed.'[3] And does not suggest a 'shameless borrowing on the part of Alice Bailey, but rather an inspiration common to both'.[4]

Almost two decades before *Esoteric Astrology* was published, eminent astrologer and Theosophist, musician and composer Dane Rudhyar (1895-1985) (aka Daniel Chenneviere), met Alice Bailey at Krotona in 1919 and drew inspiration from her early teachings. It was around that time that he became interested in astrology. They remained close friends and in the early 1930s, upon reading a collection of articles on astrology composed by Rudhyar, Alice Bailey urged him to expand his writings into a treatise which she offered to publish. The result is *The Astrology of Personality: A Re-formulation of Astrological Concepts and Ideals, in Terms of Contemporary Psychology and Philosophy*, a book he dedicated to her, and in a signed copy to her he wrote 'this book is sent in deep friendship, and in the hope that it will fill the Purpose which called it forth into being', 3 Dec 1936, New York.[5] Rudhyar's next book, *New Mansions for New Man*, was also published by the Lucis Publishing Company in 1938.[6]

Rudhyar was never a member of the Arcane School, and it cannot be said that he was an exclusive devotee, for he was eclectic in his interests, drawing on Blavatsky, Jung, and especially astrologer Marc Edmund Jones (1888-1980). But Rudhyar makes reference to the Bailey teachings. He held Alice Bailey in high esteem, and his respect for her sanctioned her canon in astrological circles. An eminent astrologer, his *The Astrology of Personality* is considered a classic of twentieth century astrology.

DK's *Esoteric Astrology* and the Bailey books in general filtered into the thinking of myriad astrologers. Two of her followers Frances Sakoian and Louis Acker, composed a popular trilogy of astrological reference books in the 1970s, *The Astrologer's Handbook*, *Predictive Astrology* and *Ladder of the Planets*. Sakoian and Acker's works offer practitioners the nuts and bolts of the terrain and are infused with DK's ideas, emphasising the evolutionary journey of consciousness. Their aim was to spiritualise exoteric astrology. Their books were written when the humanistic psychology of the New Age was filtering into and continuing to transform astrology. Through their efforts, the occult science, formerly concerning itself with events and predictions, became a powerful tool for personal insight and growth.

After the influences of Rudhyar, and Sakoian and Acker, the next generation of astrologers adopted an evolutionary model of consciousness. Astrology took on a distinct psychological feel and became infused with the notion of understanding and transcending limitations, drawing on the various energies at play within the personality to fulfil potential and become a fully actualised individual.

Pure esoteric astrology has been much slower to catch on. Very little of the seven rays and the various other elements of

DK's treatise has filtered into understanding and practice, leaving those who have attained self-actualisation and are living life as a fully rounded out personality without the further guidance for spiritual development along Ageless Wisdom lines. Kurt Abraham's *The Moon Veils Vulcan and the Sun Veils Neptune*, a short book approved by the Lucis Trust and released in 1989, serves to develop one crucial aspect of esoteric astrology, the notion of esoteric veiling, but the author does not offer any guidance for application.

In 1990, astrologer Alan Oken published *Soul-Centred Astrology*, which adapts DK's teachings and places astrology firmly in the realm of the soul. In his preface, he acknowledges the assistance and support of a raft of fellow co-workers, including those at Meditation Mount at Okai, California, Sir John Rollo Sinclair and Michael Robbins. The work comprehensively steps down DK's abstruse text and makes it accessible to the average practitioner. Consequently, a smattering of soul-centred astrology websites have come into being drawing in Oken's work.[7]

Stepping beyond the confines of the esoteric astrology given by DK, Vietnam veteran and prominent astrologer Jeff Green, or Jeffrey Wolf Green, explores soul-centred astrology in depth through focussing on Uranus and Pluto, which despite being demoted to dwarf planet status in 2006, retains its status in astrological circles. *Pluto: The Evolutionary Journey of the Soul* was released in 1992. Alan Oken composed the foreword it contains in 1985, around the time he was composing his own work. Green's book is seminal and has inspired countless astrologers outside the Ageless Wisdom milieu.[8] Green has steered the course of soul-astrology in a different direction, and many astrologers have been caught up with the significance of the horoscope placements of these two outer planets, and especially Pluto ever since. For purist DK students, Green's work might be considered a deviation and a distraction from the core teachings in *Esoteric Astrology*.

Helping to advance the specialism provided by DK is renowned esoteric astrologer and historian Phillip Lindsay, who has made a significant contribution in furthering an awareness and understanding of the terrain among the Bailey community and beyond, in large part through capturing the rich history of the Ageless Wisdom tradition, and composing numerous volumes including *The Shamballa Impacts: Their Esoteric Astrology in World History* and his series *Soul Cycles of the Seven Rays*. Lindsay produces webinars and a regular newsletter, and he continuously lectures around the world. He has also produced countless insightful astrological biographies, including one of Krishnamurti. His popular website provides a feast of knowledge for his sizeable following.[9] Demonstrating a widespread interest in esoteric history, his in-depth documentary 'The Hidden History of Humanity', a companion to *Unveiling Genesis,* has received over seven million views on YouTube.[10] In a newsletter to honour the New Group of World Servers' Festival Week 2019, raising awareness to the urgency felt by many as the 2025 Conclave of the Spiritual Hierarchy approaches, and giving voice to concerns for humanity and our planet strongly felt by the Bailey community, he writes:

 It will be a potent opportunity for the New Group of World Servers to give their all, to transform the mental and psychic atmosphere of our struggling planet, so that Humanity may be positively influenced, empowered and encouraged to effect all the urgent changes that are needed; to push back at the opportunistic and ruthless materialistic forces that work through the global culture; to make a stand and bear our burdens and hold fast.[11]

ALSO COMING from within the Ageless Wisdom tradition is prominent astrologer M. Temple Richmond, an internationally recognized authority on esoteric astrology. A prolific writer on esoteric studies, she recently founded the StarLight Ashram, an online discussion group dedicated to the study of esoteric astrology, and she issues a weekly newsletter. She is the author of the milestone book *Sirius*, which takes a comprehensive look at the Dog Star, a book which serves well as a companion to *A Treatise on Cosmic Fire*. M. Temple Richmond contributes frequently to the peer-reviewed journal *The Esoteric Quarterly*, helping to advance the field. Her 'Light on Esoteric Astrology', an unpublished work of thirty-two chapters, offers an interpretation of the field in terms loyal and close to the original teachings, and forms a bridging work, sections of which have found their way to publication in *The Esoteric Quarterly*.

Out of the vast pool of esoteric astrologers practising today is established and well-regarded astrologer Lynn Koiner, whose other astrological interest is medical astrology. Lynn Koiner dedicates much space on her website to the esoteric astrology of Alice Bailey. Adopting a simplified view indicative of the light-touch manner in which many astrologers currently approach the DK teachings, Koiner focusses on the triangle formed by the Rising sign, its planetary ruler, and the ruler of the sign where the Rising sign ruler is found.[12] This contribution provides a taste that does little more than whet the appetite, yet it is through the efforts of practising astrologers such as Koiner that esoteric astrology is at least brought to the attention of the wider public. A point of entry through which the curious may find their way in.

Another astrologer focussing on medical astrology is Leoni Hodgson, author of several esoteric astrology books including *Medical Astrology: Discovering the Psychology of Disease using Triangles*. Also of note are Donna Mitchell-Moniak and Sara Traub who co-authored *Astrology Illumed: Revealing soul through astrology*, and Peter Kubaska who developed heliocentric astrology drawing on Alice Bailey, his articles available via his Seven Suns website. Other esoteric astrologers following the Ageless Wisdom include counsellor and teacher Tara Douglas, ordained minister and intuitive consultant Al Florey and author, teacher and counsellor William Meader.

One outstanding technical astrologer advancing the field is Stephen Pugh. Raised in the Bailey tradition since adolescence, Pugh [no relation to Mildred] is a pioneer in the field of esoteric astrology and astro-rayological thought. For many years, he has focused particular attention on developing a comprehensive and consistent paradigm for the theoretical exposition and practical application of esoteric astrology. For decades, he has taught and utilised the esoteric process of Monad, Soul and Personality horoscope superimposition, along with charts of the crosses, all based on the instructions of the Tibetan. One of Pugh's main contributions to the field is his Triple Sun Chart, a whole sign method which might best be roughly described by imagining a natal chart and standing at three different locations, then swinging the houses around to where you are standing: the Sun sign representing the personality; the rising sign representing the Soul; and the Sun's opposite sign representing the Monad or spiritual aspect. Pugh then uses the Triple Sun Chart as a tool through which to deploy his expansion and development of the Tibetan's Zodiacal Meditations.[13] He hosts an esoteric astrology group on Facebook in which he shares his insights.

Pugh is one of a small group of astrologers who assert Alice Bailey's Ascendant or Rising Sign to be Pisces rather than the traditionally held Leo.[14] In her autobiography, Alice Bailey clearly states her belief that she had Pisces rising.[15] Pisces is the sign of the medium or mediator and a Pisces emphasis is often found amongst leaders of large organisations. A Pisces first house rules Alice Bailey's early childhood influences and both her father and grandfather were water engineers, installing whole systems in cities around the world, another Piscean-type activity.

Pisces is also the sign of the world saviour. Pugh understands Alice Bailey to be a senior disciple in the Tibetan's Ashram, like her Master K.H. who also had a Gemini Sun sign with Pisces rising. In his Zodiacal Meditation papers, of which only three were given, DK shared the combination of Pisces rising with a Gemini Sun sign.

Of interest to any astrologers wishing to consider this proposal, Pisces rising puts Alice Bailey's Sun in the 4th House, corresponding to Cancer, the Mother principle, and Alice Bailey, who resonated strongly with Cancer, is the mother of the New Age. As Pugh rightfully affirms, '[Alice Bailey] triumphantly opened herself to receive the impact of many types of destructive forces during the world turmoil and how amazingly she transmuted them, thus safeguarding the way for the younger disciples and struggling aspirants who came to her through the years and for generations to come.'[16]

WHITE MAGIC

$\mathcal{T}$he Tibetan's teachings have ever had a specialised form of group work at their core. 'Meditation groups will change from their present status, which is that of bands of earnest aspirants seeking illumination, to bands of workers constructively and intelligently working together for certain ends.'[1] For eighteen of the thirty years DK issued his instructions with Alice Bailey, he was primarily concerned with one overarching aspect of the teachings: manifesting in the New Group of World Servers. Initially, for his new seed groups, he chose the number nine, comprising in essence three triangles, and then he proceeded with a larger group of twenty-four, in an experiment in group initiation. The number of participants is significant. Considering the esoteric progression from the core group of three, the triangle, it is possible DK had in mind with his group of twenty-four, two groups of twelve.

Students in the Bailey tradition follow the path of esoteric group practice set out by DK. The most well-known is Triangles, a form of white magic using the Great Invocation, that aims to pour the energy of Goodwill into the planet's etheric body. Along with Assagioli's Group for Creative Meditation discussed in a previous chapter, there are other groups practising forms of group meditation, groups that draw on the Triangles work and the principles given by DK in the DINA groups of nine teachings, unknown groups large and small working quietly behind the scenes, preferring to remain hidden. However, one known group of this kind is Italian-based The Planetary System, which describes itself as 'an idea and project of coordinated cooperation between all who care about the planetary development', engages in advanced meditation in groups of seven.[2]

In his book *The Other Universe*, released in 1973, co-worker Sir John Rollo Sinclair argues the case for groups of nine, which he terms organons. This nine formation acts as an energy channel. Sinclair provides a template for others to use, stating, 'The operational structure offered by such groups of nine can be adapted by anyone wishing to experiment with group work.'[3] He mentions the Human Development Trust in this regard. Nothing more is known about the Trust but presumably his organon structure was tried out.

In 1984, Marian Walter established a meditation group called the Group of Nine – three sets of Triangles – dedicated to the 'Healing of the Nations (via the General Assembly of the United Nations)'.[4] Along with John Sinclair, members included Marion Crusselle, Hilda Dean Going and Vera Stanley Alder.[5] How the group came about is not known. According to Walter, the group had been accepted into DK's ashram and would be given training in the continuity of consciousness – an ability she claimed she had – to receive further training from the ashram while asleep.[6]

This Group of Nine was formed by Walter in recognition that the Avatar of Synthesis overshadowing the Christ 'can only work with very large groups':

 He needs the Service such as our "Little Group". We do so by realisation of His service as is possible – via our "group mind", our desire to serve

Mankind, and to our Soul's Enlightenment of our Brains.[7]

LITTLE IS KNOWN of this group, other than it practised a daily group meditation using the Great Invocation and the Mantram of Unification printed on the last page of *The Reappearance of the Christ*.[8]

There is ever a continuity of purpose along esoteric Ashramic lines and, while the Group of Nine continued, there emerged quite independently although very loosely connected, a group of twelve known as Twelves.[9]

The Twelves model of advanced group meditation along the lines of white magic exists largely due to the efforts of its founder Steven Chernikeeff, whose valuable memoir *Esoteric Apprentice* details the purpose and methods of an experiment conducted for almost twenty years to 2000, providing the only known resource of its kind following in this tradition.[10] As a result, Twelves makes for an interesting case study.

Steven Chernikeeff was a teenager when he first read the Bailey teachings, having segued into the Ageless Wisdom via Christian Spiritualism, a faith he adopted for a phase hoping for an explanation as to why he kept hearing a bell ringing intermittently and consistently, a bell no one else could hear.[11] It is known in Spiritualist circles as the astral bell. It was this bell that propelled him on a quest for understanding. After coming across the Bailey books, Chernikeeff contacted Jan Nation at the Lucis Trust, who offered guidance and answers to his myriad questions.

Chernikeeff then became friends with another young seeker Robert Adams, who was a good friend of Sir John Sinclair. Unbeknownst to the two young men, Sinclair was at that time in Marian Walter's Group of Nine.

The pair spent many hours in Adam's dedicated meditation

room created out of his garden shed. They meditated together every Saturday. It was there, in 1981 when Chernikeeff was twenty-three years old, that the two friends received first contact with an Initiate from the ashram of the Brotherhood of the Star.[12] Over the course of the following four years, Chernikeeff received instructions that would form the foundation for Twelves.

Chernikeeff enjoys the faculty of higher telepathy in which, in deep meditation, he receives and intuits impressions. When a disciple is thus aligned, they can become a servant on the outer planes and also on the inner planes esoterically, helping the ashram do its work. Such contact is ever a combination of felt purpose, energetic stimulation or charge, an inpouring of energy, and the impression of ideas that are intuited and then slowly clothed, all bound up with a sense of duty, obligation and service. Having succumbed to and dispelled his own glamour around this, Chernikeeff notes the ordinary aspect. When such contact and energising occurs and proceeds, it just is, and it is vital that it is left as it is and not dressed up in astral clothes, inflating the personality, the sense of self. As Chernikeeff states and demonstrates throughout his book, ruthless humility is required for those able to engage in such contact.

How does anyone know if any of what Chernikeeff and others like him say, is true? It isn't about truth, but reality in consciousness, on the inner planes, and eventually, and without knowing how or why, the disciple comes to arrive at this inner knowing, which is an acceptance that at a certain point, from a certain angle, this is the inner reality of consciousness.

In his book, Chernikeeff goes to great lengths to explain the significance and potency of a group formation involving twelve participants. This quote from the Master Morya in the Agni Yoga stream sums up why the number was chosen:

 People do not want to understand group work, which multiplies the forces. The dodecahedron is one of the most perfect structures, with a dynamic power that can resist many assaults. A group of twelve, systematically united, truly can master even cosmic events. It must be understood that the enlarging of such a group can weaken it undermining the dynamic force of its structure.[13]

IN ESSENCE, twelve is a powerful, complete, strong number and considering the work involved, necessary. As a safe number, Twelves can resist the 'Forces of Darkness [that] are always seeking to disrupt those who work with Light.'[14]

Twelves is an extension of Triangles work. The purpose of Twelves is to help 'dispel glamour and thoughtforms' to assist 'planetary healing and transformation' and the 'Forces of Spiritual Change'. The method, in essence, is soul-infused energy work conducted in groups. Participants work on the plane of illumination to help clear the astral plane. One idea for Twelves is to work along Ray lines in 'thoughtform destruction, clearing of energy lines, building of lighted thoughtforms, healing and lastly creating energetic space for other work to be undertaken'. Twelves is essentially 'focused, laser-like work piercing the old and redundant thoughtforms of yesteryear and opening channels of light'.[15]

Chernikeeff and Adams had before them an important task. Before long, Dr Peter Maslin joined the pair, moving down from Scotland to be physically close to the work and enable the group to grow.

The Twelves Group expanded to around two-hundred members and in 1994 after twelve years of preparation, the first Twelves formation was held on Wesak in a room in Glastonbury, England. The meditation proceeded under the guidance of Chernikeeff, who played the role of focaliser outside of the group. After preparing the space and some protective work, the group spent some time in triangles, practicing the OM and readying themselves. Then, each triangle took up their positions in the Twelve formation. An energetic merging occurred, and the group experienced a vortex of energy surging into the inner circle formed by the group.

The experience of the Twelves meditation was immersive, intense, profound and long-lasting. 'Some saw light, some heard bells and some were overcome with a fragrance of such beauty they could hardly talk about it.'[16]

The initial Twelves group held physical Twelves meditations until 1999. During that time, there were some tensions, both within the group as various personalities were faced with having to adjust to one another, within the lives of participants challenged to fit Twelves into busy lives, and without, as partners and those not involved took issue with the commitment. Partly due to the deaths of Peter Maslin and Robert Adams the group then disbanded. Chernikeeff acknowledges the initial Twelves was experimental and preparatory. 'It is certainly not a question of, "Did we succeed or didn't we?" but more of, "What did we do, how did we do it and what is to be learned?"'[17]

A new phase of the Twelves work commenced in 2018, considered to be the implementation phase in which a new group of Twelves participants connect remotely and group cohesion is fostered through social media. Some of the original Twelves have also returned to participate. Of concern for Chernikeeff and participants is anticipation of the 2025 Conclave of the Spiritual Hierarchy, a key date in the Bailey calendar, one in which the survival of humanity is understood to be decided. This awareness lends a sense of urgency and a felt need to expand Twelves. At the time of writing the third edition of this biography (January 2021) Twelves has a few hundred members and several Twelves meditating in group formation.

Obstacles to Twelves expansion, then as now, lie in both the usual issues with time and commitment, and in the strained relations between traditionalists in the Theosophical Society and the

Bailey community, and those Agni Yoga followers who take Helena Roerich's view of Bailey. This is a problem that extends throughout the Ageless Wisdom community, thwarting the expansion of esoteric work that could be practised along white magic lines. Adherents wherever they are found are apt to hold on to the essential purity of the teachings, and this attachment to purity tends to foster crystallisation and a rejection of other teachings. Esoteric groupwork such as Triangles and Twelves actualises the core purpose of the Ageless Wisdom that came through Alice Bailey. The books were not given to study alone, as Chernikeeff demonstrates, they were given to encourage action.

CONCLUDING REMARKS

*A*lice Bailey gifted humanity a canon of esoteric thought; she was born into a family of water engineers and she sought to provide the texts that would usher in the new Age of Aquarius, the water bearer. Quite literally, she was a thought engineer.

Born with a mystical disposition, she quickly adopted an orthodox Christian view imbued with evangelical passion. Her righteous convictions sustained her for many years, until they were beaten out of her through a series of private and public humiliations and through her husband's fists, although that was never his intention. She was ripe for change when she found Theosophy, and she embraced it with passion, giving her entire life to it. The result is a body of work that continues to inspire.

In her lifetime, Alice Bailey was a tour de force, a trailblazer following in and advancing the Theosophical tradition, and creating organisational structures to foster fresh, innovative ways of esoteric practice. She blended the inner with the outer work, forming the Triangles network, World Goodwill, *The Beacon* magazine, the Lucis Trust and, above all, her Arcane School, all of them global organisations working to this day to foster goodwill and right relations. How many have graduated from her school and quietly gone on and applied what they have learned in their sphere of influence cannot ever be known. Most esoteric students remain private, not least because the exoteric world does not understand, and even today, esotericists will be ridiculed and shunned.

The core project the Tibetan embarked on in the early 1930s was to usher in discipleship in the New Age. While the New Group of World Servers went ahead with its outreach programme seeding Units of Service around the globe, it was the Tibetan's Seed Groups that formed the heart of his experiment. The letters to these groups make for fascinating reading and provide real insight into the challenges of spiritual growth.

Alice Bailey wanted esoteric knowledge and training to be available to all and not to an exclusive elite. There can be no doubt that the occultist deserves acknowledgement for making a substantial foundational contribution to the New Age movement, one warranting the title of 'mother'. She put her writings and her organisations out into the world in the same determined fashion with which she previously did her orthodox Christian views. For thirty years, she was surrounded by a cohort of dedicated co-workers who gave over their lives to promulgating her ideas and continuing her organisations after her death.

Early influencers helped to shape and promote the emergence of the New Age, initiating numerous foundations, networks, educational organisations, meditation retreats, all designed to develop soul-connectedness and further goodwill and right relations. Among her co-workers can be found adept negotiators, mediators, scholars, writers, artists, sophisticated thinkers and theorists, healers, light workers, psychologists and astrologers. Thought builds on thought, and DK's original thought-form has been greatly expanded and re-languaged to suit the moment. In this fashion, Alice Bailey's contribution is enormous. She was a catalyst, a butterfly causing a vast seismic shift, one by no means fully realised, but significant enough to represent a serious voice of change towards human and planetary betterment.

Attacks both from within and without dogged Alice Bailey from the outset. Purist Theosophists and Helena Roerich condemned her. Her own student Olga Fröbe turned on her with lasting consequences. After her death, many more launched attacks or cast Alice Bailey in a poor light. With regard to history, unfair portrayals matter, feeding into attitudes to Bailey's corpus upheld by sections of academia. It matters because such controversies and prejudices do Alice Bailey an injustice and prevent humanity from having any sort of balanced and general view of a woman who made a significant contribution to humanity, helping to shape current worldviews and inspire a raft of alternative thinking. Without due acknowledgement, a body of work designed to represent the highest attainment humanity can strive for is relegated to the dustbin.

There have been internal difficulties too, centred on the Arcane School and its leadership. The first split when Marian Walter broke away resulted in the removal of papers from the Lucis Trust and the ensuing discord. The idea of continuity central to the teachings requires cohesion amongst the core group within the Bailey community, those at the heart, and it is here that tensions still exist that hamper the ever-present opportunity. Yet as this biography has shown, such continuity does exist elsewhere – esoterically evinced through Triangles to Nines to Twelves – and while splits are always upsetting, perhaps they were necessary. It is clear that out of each of the three strands, the Lucis Trust, the School for Esoteric Studies and the University of the Seven Rays, much has been achieved and developed.

It is the responsibility of the worldwide Bailey community to advance the teachings, through studying, applying, teaching, speaking, lecturing, writing and, above all, publishing across a range of fields including psychology, astrology and within the scholarly field of Western Esotericism that Alice Bailey and the

Tibetan's teachings will reach those receptive in various circles and even the wider public.

Despite the Edwardian language and some outdated opinions, the Bailey books continue to attract students today, some as young as fifteen, others in the twenties and thirties, those of an esoteric disposition searching for wisdom. That the teachings resonate and draw in minds in the twenty-first century demonstrates the agelessness of what is taught.

Western esotericism has always been controversial, laced with allegations of fraud and deception, its very secrecy and elitism and abstruse knowledge garnering the suspicions of outsiders. Such suspicions are warranted. Perhaps it is better to understand Western esotericism as an energetic overlay, one pointing towards a greater ineffable mystery of existence and leave it at that.

Part of this overlay is the conviction held by Alice Bailey and other Theosophists of her era, including Annie Besant and Rudolph Steiner, that Christ would reappear and the Hierarchy would externalise to usher in a new age of spiritual enlightenment. From an energetic point of view, this belief concentrates the will, providing a point of focus and a sense of purpose, a motivational device, providing role models, exemplars for humanity to strive towards. The Ageless Wisdom arrives at a defining moment in its history as we approach the critical year of 2025, when a centennial Conclave of the Spiritual Hierarchy will occur:

 Thus, a great and new movement is proceeding and tremendously increased interplay and interaction is taking place. This will go on until A.D. 2025. During the years intervening between now and then very great changes will be seen taking place, and at the General Assembly of the Hierarchy–held as usual every century–in 2025 the date in all

probability will be set for the first stage of the
externalisation of the Hierarchy.[1]

WHATEVER BELIEF THE READER HOLDS, the idea of spiritual
assistance at a time when the world is riven with crises and the
planet is dying, could not be more apposite. In the light of this,
students of the Ageless Wisdom might ask themselves what they
would wish to advance: esoteric knowledge, an esoteric way of
knowing, or esoteric activism.

AN INCOMPLETE LIST OF GROUPS
INSPIRED BY THE AGELESS WISDOM

CANADA

- Alliance Group, Ottawa, Canada
- Center for Esoteric Studies, Ontario, Canada
- Healing from the Soul Group, Montreal, Canada
- Northern School of Esoteric Wisdom, Canada
- IDEAL: Institute for the Development of Education, Arts & Leisure, B.C., Canada
- Institute for Personal Development, Quebec, Canada

SOUTH AMERICA

- Fundación Lucis, Argentina
- Grupo Logos, Buenos Aires, Argentina
- House of the Pax Culture, Santa Fe, Argentina
- Litoral Group, Santa Fe, Argentina
- Bolivian Unit of Service, Cochabamba, Bolivia
- Casa Assagioli, Brasil
- Centro Caraívas, Pirenópolis, Goiás, Brazil

- Crystal Nucleus, Brasilia, Brazil
- Cultura Espiritual, Brasil
- CUMES Urusvati Center for Meditation, Study and Service, Brasilia, Brasil
- Encontro Espiritual, Brasil
- Federação Morya, Brasil
- Fundacão Cultural Avatar, Brasil
- Kwan Yin Group, Sao Paulo, Brasil
- Psychosynthesis Center, Sao Paulo, Brasil
- Saint Paul Group, Sao Paulo, Brasil
- Spiritual Culture Foundation -University of Light, Belo Horizonte, Brasil
- Unidade de Serviço para Educação Integral, Brasil
- Urusvati House, Sao Paulo, Brasil
- Synthesis in Aquarius, Tijuana, Mexico
- Escuela de Ciencias Esotéricas, Venezuela
- Federación Morya Hispanoamericana, Venezuela
- Fundaser, Venezuela
- New Thought Foundation, Caracas, Venezuela

EUROPE

- Center for Esoteric Astrology, Aarhus, Denmark
- Center for the Inner Dimensions of Life, Copenhagen, Denmark
- Golden Circle, Denmark
- GRO Group, Lejre, Denmark
- Kentaur Training and Publishing, Copenhagen, Denmark
- One Earth, Copenhagen, Denmark
- Sophia's Rose, Copenhagen, Denmark
- Soul Therapy, Copenhagen, Denmark
- The Golden Circle, Denmark

- Transformation Now, Copenhagen, Denmark
- Living Ethics Germany, Munich, Germany
- Banner of Peace Association, Rome, Italy
- Centro Studi Urania, Rome, Italy
- Community of Living Ethics, Citta'della Pieve, Italy
- Cultural Association of Triangles and World Goodwill, Rome, Italy
- Namaskar, Catania, Italy
- Parvati Studies Center, Turin, Italy
- Space INEH Italy, Turin, Italy
- Uriel Study and Research Center for the Will to Good, Collesano, Italy
- Urusvati Research Institute, Turin, Italy
- The Academy of Wisdom Teaching Europe, Leeuwarden- The Netherlands
- GEM- Grupo de Estudos Maitreya, Lisbon, Portugal
- Merry Human Life Society, Barcelona, Spain
- Sun Group, Fuengirola, Spain
- Sunhealing Group, Fuengirola, Spain
- Bjare Culture and Meditation Center, Bastad, Sweden
- Mandala Group, Malmo, Sweden
- School of the Esoteric Way, Stockholm, Sweden
- Sun in the Earth Group, Vaxjo, Sweden
- Institute for Planetary Synthesis, Geneva, Switzerland
- Ankh Spiritual Development Foundation, Kiev, Ukraine
- Centre Eurasia, Odessa, Ukraine
- Esoteric Enlightenment Center, Lviv, Ukraine
- Khortitske Society of Humanitarian Development, Zaporozhie, Ukraine
- School of Ageless Wisdom, Zhytomir, Ukraine

UNITED KINGDOM

- Centre of Light, Reading, UK
- Findhorn, Inverness, UK
- International Network of Esoteric Healing, Emsworth, UK
- Sundial House Group, East Sussex, UK
- Wisdom Study Group, Reading, UK

INDIA

- Darjeeling Goodwill Center, Darjeeling, India
- Himalayan Community of Living Ethics, Kalimpoong, India
- The Pranic Healers, India

MIDDLE EAST

- Hechal Center for Universal Spirituality, Jerusalem, Israel

ASIA-PACIFIC

- Path Centre, Australia
- The Triangle Centre, New Zealand
- Southern Lights Centre, Akaroa, New Zealand
- Prana World, Philippines
- World Pranic Healing Foundation, Philippines.

UNITED STATES OF AMERICA

- White Mountain Education Association, Prescott,

Arizona
- Arcana Workshops, Los Angeles, California

- Dove Healing Alliance, Aptos, California
- Esoteric & Astrological Studies, Art, Science & Research Institute, California
- International Foundation for Integral Psychology, Los Angeles, California
- Meditation Mount, Ojai, California
- Nature of the Soul, Los Angeles, California
- Pathways to Peace, San Francisco, California
- The Center for Visionary Leadership, San Rafael, California
- Wisdom Impression Publishers, Whittier, California
- Synthesis Foundation, Denver, Colorado
- JJ Esoteric Foundation, Naples, Florida
- Soul Group of SW Florida
- International Network of Esoteric Healing N. America, Indianapolis, Indiana
- Sirius Community, Shutesbury, Massachusetts
- Spirit Fire, Leyden, Massachusetts
- Esoteric Healing Twin Cities, Minnesota
- Intuition in Service, Olivebridge, New York
- Path of Light, Ashland, Oregon
- Wisdom Research, Dayton, Oregon
- Institute for the Advancement of Service, Alexandria, VA
- Ageless Wisdom Study Group, Washington, DC
- New Fusion Group, Washington, DC
- Truthseekers Network, Washington, DC
- NW School for Religious and Philosophical Studies, Spokane, Washington

INTERNATIONAL

- World Service Intergroup

- Seed Groups International
- Twelves Advanced Meditation Group

For a list of worldwide Goodwill groups, visit the Lucis Trust's "Worldwide Network" page on their website.

ABOUT THE AUTHOR

Isobel Blackthorn was born in Farnborough, Kent, England, and has spent much of her life in Australia. Isobel holds a PhD in Social Ecology from the University of Western Sydney for her ground-breaking study of the texts of theosophist Alice A. Bailey. She is the author of *The Unlikely Occultist: A biographical novel of Alice A. Bailey* and numerous fictional works. A prolific novelist, she is currently working on a trilogy of esoteric thrillers.

NOTES

INTRODUCTION

1. *Introduction*
   Alice A. Bailey, *The Unfinished Autobiography* (Albany, NY: Lucis Trust, 1951), p.1.
2. Olav Hammer, *Claiming Knowledge: Strategies of Epistemology from Theosophy to the New Age* (Leiden: Brill, 2000), p. xiii.
3. See Wouter J. Hanegraaff, *New Age Religion and Western Culture: Esotericism in the Mirror of Secular Thought* (Albany, NY: State University of New York Press, 1998).
4. Bailey's Arcane School (established in 1923), is a non-sectarian international school of esoteric training by correspondence. Men of Goodwill, established in 1932, is a non-government organization recognized by the United Nations. The Lucis Trust was incorporated in 1922, as a tax-exempt, religious, education corporation. The Lucis Publishing Company, a non-profit organization owned by the Lucis Trust continues to keep Bailey's texts in print. Finally, Triangles is a network under the auspices of the Lucis Trust, and described by its own literature as 'a service activity for men and women of goodwill who believe in the power of thought. Working in groups of three, they establish right human relationships by creating a worldwide network of light and goodwill' (Triangles Pamphlet). Bailey's intention underpinning these organizations was not simply to promote her own views, but to help to improve the human condition. See <https://www.lucistrust.org/> Accessed 3 September 2017.
5. Alice A. Bailey, *A Treatise on White Magic: or The Way of the Disciple*, (New York: Lucis Trust, 1991), p. 603.
6. Wouter J. Hanegraaff, "A Dynamic Typological Approach to the Problem of "Post-Gnostic" Gnosticism," in *ARIES*, 16: 5-43.
7. Lee Irwin, "Western Esotericism, Eastern Spirituality, and the Global Future," *Esoterica*, Vol III, 2001: 1-47.
8. Antoine Faivre, *Theosophy, Imagination, Tradition: Studies in Western Esotericism*, (Albany: State University of New York Press, 2000).
9. Peter Washington. *Madame Blavatsky's Baboon: Theosophy and the Emergence of the Western Guru*, (London: Secker and Warburg, 1993), p. 19. Also see Bruce F. Campbell. *Ancient Wisdom Revived: A History of the Theosophical Movement*, (Los Angeles: University of California Press, 1980; Jill Roe. *Beyond Belief: Theosophy in Australia 1879-1939*, (Sydney: New South Wales University Press, 1986); and Jocelyn Godwin. *The Theosophical Enlightenment*, (Albany: SUNY,1994).
10. Campbell, *Ancient Wisdom*, pp. 88-90, and Washington, *Blavatsky's Baboon*, pp. 79-82.

11. See Charles J. Ryan. *H.P. Blavatsky and the Theosophical Movement: A Brief Historical Sketch*, (San Diego: Point Loma); Campbell, op. cit.; and Kevin Tingay. "Madame Blavatsky's Children: Theosophy and its Heirs" in S. Sutcliffe and M. Bowman (eds), *Beyond New Age: Exploring Alternative Spirituality*, (Edinburgh: Edinburgh University Press, 2000).

12. It is difficult to examine theosophical texts with any sympathy without some provisional acceptance of the possibility that a hierarchy of masters may exist. Indeed, following Olav Hammer's assertion that 'the existence of the Masters is…an indispensable prerequisite if the teachings are to have any validity', whilst other aspects of Bailey's work may be regarded as peripheral, the notion of the masters forms a pivotal axis through her work. Quotation from Olav Hammer, *Claiming Knowledge: Strategies of Epistemology From Theosophy to the New Age*, (Leiden: Brill, 2001).

13. Bailey, *The Unfinished Autobiography*, p. 256.
    1 An Emerging Evangelist

1. AN EMERGING EVANGELIST

1. Ibid., p.16.

2. Birth certificate, Alice Harriet Hollinshead, Volume 09a, p. 319, Huddersfield Union, General Register Office.

3. Birth certificate, Alice Harriet Hollinshead, Volume 09a, p. 319, Huddersfield Union, General Register Office; "England and Wales Census, 1861," database with images, FamilySearch (https://family-search.org/ark:/61903/1:1:M7C4-1W8 : 24 October 2019), William Hollinshead, Huddersfield, Yorkshire, England, United Kingdom; from "1861 England, Scotland and Wales census," database and images, findmypast (http://www.findmypast.com : n.d.); citing PRO RG 9, The National Archives, Kew, Surrey.

4. Marriage certificate, Joseph Hollinshead and Elizabeth Swetmore, No. 605, General Register Office; 1861 Census, Ibid.

5. *The London Gazette*, 20 March 1863, p. 1609. and 24 March 1863, p. 1713.

6. *The London Gazette*, 27 June 1865, p. 1865. And 2 October 1868, p. 5223.

7. Louise appears to have been a twin, but her sister Blanche was absent when the 1871 census was taken on 2nd April. "England and Wales Census, 1871", database with images, FamilySearch (https://family-search.org/ark:/61903/1:1:VRN9-H1B : 29 September 2019), William Hollinshead, 1871.

8. "England and Wales Census, 1871", database with images, FamilySearch (https://familysearch.org/ark:/61903/1:1:KZGD-CH2 : 24 April 2019), Alice H Hollinshead in entry for Ann Hollinshead, 1871.

9. Death certificate, William Hollinshead, No. 398, District of St. Neots, General Registry Office.

10. Marriage certificate, Alice Harriet Hollinshead and Frederic Foster Bateman, No. 397, General Registry Office; Marriage banns, Alice Harriet Hollinshead and Frederic Foster Bateman, Diocese of London, 17 January 1879, cited on Ancestry.com, July 2019.

11. See "George Bower." *Grace's Guide to British Industrial History*, 2019, Web. 23 October 2019. <https://www.gracesguide.co.uk/George_Bower>

12. Jill Eastwood, "La Trobe, Charles Joseph (1801-1875)." *Australian Dictionary of Biography*, 2019, Web. 15 August 2019. <http://adb.anu.edu.au/biography/la-trobe-charles-joseph-2334>

13. See "La Trobe Family Tree." *The C J La Trobe Society*, 2013, Web. 10 January 2017. <https://www.latrobesociety.org.au/family-tree.html>

14. Peter Russell, "John Frederic La Trobe-Bateman (1810–1889) Water Engineer", in *Transactions of the Newcomen Society*, Volume 52, 1980, 1: 119-138. Published online: 31 Jan 2014.

15. Sir William Fairbairn, *The Life of Sir William Fairbairn*, edited and completed by William Pole (London: Longmans, Green, 1877).

16. William Fairbairn La Trobe-Bateman, *Memories Grave and Gay of William Fairbairn La Trobe-Bateman*
    with a foreword by the Right Rev. Bishop Gore, edited by Mildred La Trobe-Bateman. (London: Longmans, Green and Co., Ltd., 1927), p. xviii.

17. Birth certificate, Alice Ann Bateman, Uppermill, Saddleworth, Vol. 9a, p253, General Registry Office.

18. See "England and Wales Census, 1881," database with images, FamilySearch (https://familysearch.org/ark:/61903/1:1:Q27R-NLMC : 11 December 2017), Alice A Bateman in household of Captain Bateman, Saddleworth, Yorkshire, West Riding, England; from "1881 England, Scotland and Wales Census," database and images, findmypast (http://www.findmypast.com : n.d.); citing p. 39, Piece/Folio 4364/23, The National Archives, Kew, Surrey; FHL microfilm 101,775,223., and "England and Wales Census, 1881," database with images, FamilySearch (https://familysearch.org/ark:/61903/1:1:Q273-6K5B : 10 December 2017), John F Bateman, St Margaret And St John The Evangelist Westminster, London, Middlesex, England; from "1881 England, Scotland and Wales Census," database and images, findmypast (http://www.findmypast.com : n.d.); citing p. 29, Piece/Folio 117/54, The National Archives, Kew, Surrey; FHL microfilm 101,774,339.

19. William Fairbairn La Trobe-Bateman, *Memories Grave and Gay*, op. cit.

20. Frederic Foster Bateman, "St. Lawrence Bridge and Manufacturing Scheme: Engineer's report 18th January, 1882", *HathiTrust Digital Library*, 2008, Web. 2 July 2019. <https://babel.hathitrust.org/cgi/pt?id=aeu.ark:/13960/t03x8n71j&view=1up&seq=8>

21. At the time of writing, no birth certificate had been located for Lydia.

22. *The Unfinished Autobiography*, p. 20.

23. *The Unfinished Autobiography*, p. 21.

24. Death certificate: Alice Harriet Hollinshead, 3 October 1886, Newton Abbot, Torquay, Volume 5b, p. 99, General Registry Office.

25. *The Unfinished Autobiography*, p. 19.

26. In her autobiography, Alice Bailey makes the following remark: 'The Fairbairns did not belong to the so-called aristocracy of birth which is so much prized. Perhaps this was the salvation of the Bateman – Hollinshead – La Trobe stock.' P. 19.

27. H.E. Malden (ed.), "Parishes Frensham" in, *A History of the County of Surrey*, 1906, 2: 591-92; and Bill Price, *Charles Darwin: Origins and Arguments*, (London: Oldcastle Books, 2009).

28. *The Unfinished Autobiography*, p. 27.

29. *The Unfinished Autobiography*, p. 25.

30. Ibid.

31. John Barnes, *La Trobe: Traveller, Writer, Governor*, (Sydney: Halstead Press, 2017).

32. See John Barnes, ibid., and Daniel Thomas, "Bateman, Edward La Trobe (1815-1897)." *Australian Dictionary of Biography*, Volume 3 (MUP) 1969, Web. 3 February 2017. <http://adb.anu.edu.au/biography/bateman-edward-la-trobe-2951>

33. *The Unfinished Autobiography*, p. 27.

34. Ibid., p. 16.

35. Ibid., p. 14. For further inquiry into melancholia and mysticism see William James, *Varieties of Religious Experience*, (London: Longman, Green, and Co, 1902), Lectures VI and VII; and Evelyn Underhill, *Mysticism: A study in the nature and development of man's spiritual consciousness*, (New York: E.P. Dutton, 1930), a seminal work in the exploration of the mystical state of consciousness.

36. *The Unfinished Autobiography*, p. 23; and "John Frederic La Trobe Bateman." *Grace's Guide to British Industrial History*, 2018, Web. 10 June 2019 (1889, Institution of Civil Engineers: Obituaries).

37. *The Unfinished Autobiography*, p. 25.

38. Ibid., p. 28.

39. "Person Page 1513." *The Peerage*, 2019, Web. 12 July 2019. <http://thepeerage.com/p1513.htm#i15128>

40. *The Unfinished Autobiography*, p. 29.

41. Ibid.

42. Ibid., p. 31.

43. Ibid., p. 31.

44. Ibid., p. 14.

45. Ibid., p. 21.

46. Ibid., p. 36.

47. It is entirely possible to gain much of value in the Bailey books while suspending judgement on the existence of the Spiritual Hierarchy, as I found when undertaking my doctorate, a process in which I was required to take such steps in order to retain scholarly detachment.

48. *The Unfinished Autobiography*, p. 39. Interestingly, the meditation room at the United Nations bears some similarity with this vision, a matter explored in Isobel Blackthorn, *The Unlikely Occultist: a biographical novel of Alice A. Bailey*, (Japan: Next Chapter, 2018).

49. Ibid., pp. 39-40.

50. Ibid., p. 40.

51. Ibid., p. 41.

52. Alice Bailey, "Friday Talk", 30 April, 1943, p. 3. *School of Esoteric Studies*, 2019, Web. 24 September 2019. <http://www.esotericstudies.net/aabtalks/aab04-23-43.pdf>

53. *The Unfinished Autobiography*, p. 41.
54. Ibid., p. 43.
55. Lydia Dorothy La Trobe-Bateman Parsons, *A Vision of Immortality*, (Sydney: Wentworth Press, 2016).

    Also see "A Vision of Immortality [Poem]. *Internet Archive*, 2014, Web. 3 February 2017.
    <https://archive.org/details/visionofimmortal00parsiala/page/n7>
56. See Lydia Dorothy La Trobe-Bateman in *The Peerage*. <http://www.thepeerage.com/p1516.htm>
57. This was a matter she would later have to defend, at least to herself. She was barred from giving talks at universities because she lacked a degree. (see *The Unfinished Autobiography*, p. 218.) In the 1930s she strove to gain credibility for her works in the scholarly milieu. She was unsuccessful.

2. ELISE SANDES' SOLDIERS' HOMES

1. *2 Elise Sandes' Soldiers Homes*
   The Unfinished Autobiography, p. 48.
2. Ibid., p. 50.
3. From the Protestant point of view, good works both saved the souls of others and paved the way to personal salvation. Consequently, Christianity had long association with social work. See Robert Morris, *Rethinking Social Welfare: Why care for a Stranger?* (New York: Longman Inc., 1986); and Frank .K. Prochaska, *Women and Philanthropy in Nineteenth-Century England* (London: Clarendon Press, 1980).
4. See Maggie Andrews and Janis Lomas, *Hidden Heroines: The Forgotten Suffragettes*, (Marlborough: Crowood Press, 2019).
5. *The Unfinished Autobiography*, p. 77.
6. Ibid., p. 53.
7. Ella Potter and Winifred Matheson, *Elise Sandes and Theodora Schofield: Twenty-one years of Unrecorded Service for the British Army, 1913-1934*, (Edinbugh: Marshall, Morgan and Scott, 1935), p. 12.
8. *The Unfinished Autobiography*, p. 54.
9. Ibid.
10. Ibid., p. 54.
11. Ibid., pp. 55-6.
12. Ibid., p. 59.
13. Elise Sandes had family connections in India and had become well aware of the difficulties facing the soldiers stationed there. The military had made requests for homes to draw the men away from brothels, wet canteens and opium dens. See Potter and Matheson, *Elise Sandes and Theodora Schofield*, pp. 129-136.
14. *The Unfinished Autobiography*, pp. 63-4.
15. Neil Charlesworth, "British Rule and the Indian Economy, 1800-1914", in *Studies in Economic and Social History*, (London: Palgrave, 1981).

    Ian Stone, "Canal Irrigation in British India: Perspectives on Technological Change in a Peasant Economy", cited at <http://catdir.loc.gov/cat-dir/samples/cam034/84003200.pdf>

For Kitchener reforms see E. S. Grew, *Field-Marshall Lord Kitchener: his life and work for the empire*, (London: Gresham Publishing Company, 1916), pp. 29-30.

16. The British army were stationed there to defend the Bolan Pass, which, along with the Khyber Pass further north, was a strategic gateway through the mountains and therefore an invasion route from the north.
17. *The Unfinished Autobiography*, p. 70.
18. Ibid., pp. 148-9.
19. Ibid., p. 75.
20. Ibid., p. 76.
21. Ibid., p. 76.
22. Alice Bailey, "Friday Talk", 30 April 1943, p. 2. PDF at *School for Esoteric Studies*, 2019, Web. 24 September 2019. <http://www.esotericstud-ies.net/aabtalks/aab04-30-43.pdf>
23. *The Unfinished Autobiography*, p. 79.
24. Ibid., p. 82.
25. Ibid.
26. Ibid., p. 83.
27. Ibid., p. 84.
28. Ibid., p. 85.
29. Ibid., p. 85.
30. Ibid., p. 87.
31. Ibid., pp. 88-9.
32. Ibid., p. 89.
33. Ibid.
34. Ibid., p. 95.
35. Ibid., p. 96.
36. Ibid.
37. "England and Wales Birth Registration Index, 1837-2008," database, Family-Search (https://familysearch.org/ark:/61903/1:1:2XJ3-GZG : 1 October 2014), Walter Henry Evans, 1880; from "England & Wales Births, 1837-2006," database, findmypast (http://www.findmypast.com : 2012); citing Birth Registration, Guisborough, Yorkshire, England, citing General Register Office, Southport, England.

3 Dark Times as Mrs Evans

3. DARK TIMES AS MRS EVANS

1. *The Unfinished Autobiography*, p. 54.

Also see "Endynamited by Christ' Sandes Soldiers' homes", *History Ireland*, 2019, Web. 4 October 2019.

<https://www.historyireland.com/20th-century-contemporary-histo-ry/endynamited-by-christ-sandes-soldiers-homes/>

The Arbuthnot-Holmes and Rowan-Hamilton families have strong roots in Ireland. In mentioning these names in her autobiography, Alice Bailey makes it known to the reader that members of the landed gentry were gathered closely around her at the time.

2. *The Unfinished Autobiography*, p. 66.

3. Ibid., p. 101.

4. Ibid., p. 103.

5. See "Lane Theological Seminary". *Ohio History Central*, Web. 12 January 2017. <http://www.ohiohistorycentral.org/w/Cincinnati,_Ohio>

6. Despite my best efforts, I have been unable to establish contact with the person who knows the actual address. In early 2019, he informed me that he has in his possession documentary evidence.

7. "Lane Theological Seminary". *Ohio History Central*, Web. 12 January 2017. <http://www.ohiohistorycentral.org/w/Cincinnati,_Ohio>

8. *The Unfinished Autobiography*, p. 107.

9. see Trevor Ravenscroft, *The Spear of Destiny: The Occult Power Behind the Spear which pierced the side of Christ* (Cape Neddick, ME: Samuel Weiser, 1982), and Nicholas Goodrick-Clarke, *The Occult Roots of Nazism: Secret Aryan Cults and their Influence on Nazi Ideology* (New York: New York University Press, 1993).

10. *The Unfinished Autobiography*, p. 139.

11. Alice A. Bailey, *The Rays and The Initiations* (New York: Lucis Trust, 1972), p. 593.

12. see Gary w. Trompf, "Macrohistory in Blavatsky, Steiner and Guénon," in *Western Esotericism and the Science of Religion*, eds. Antoine Faivre and Wouter Hanegraaff (Leuven, Belgium: Peeters, 1998), pp. 269-296.

13. Arthur E. Powell, *The Solar System*, (Borodino Books, 2018).
    Joscelyn Godwin, *Atlantis and the Cycles of Time: Prophecies, Traditions, and Occult Revelations*. (Inner Traditions/Little Bear, 2010).

14. Ibid.

15. Alice A. Bailey, *Problems of Humanity* (New York: Lucis Trust, 1983), pp. 105-6.

16. Ibid., p. 107.

17. *The Unfinished Autobiography*, p. 104.

18. Ibid., p. 105.

19. Passenger list: Dorothy Bailey, Westernland 1931, 5043 New York, New York Passenger and Crew Lists, 1909, 1925-1957, vol 10899-10901, familysearch.org

20. *The Unfinished Autobiography*, p. 108.

21. see Richard Johnson, "Changing Attitudes About Domestic Violence," *Law and Order* 50 (2002): 60-65.

22. Marriage Certificate: Lydia Dorothy La Trobe-Bateman, 22 July 1911, Windsor, Vol 2c, Page1007, General Register Office.

23. *The Unfinished Autobiography*, p. 109.

24. Ibid.

25. Ibid., p. 28.

26. Ibid., p. 111.

27. See a number of photos of Reedley at "Reedley: An historical sketch". *The City of Reedley: The world's first fruit basket*, 2019, Web. 4 October 2019. <http://www.reedley.com/history/pdfs/Historical-Photos.pdf> and an image of Reedley in 1910 at "General View of Reedley, California". 2009,

Web. 4 October 2019. <https://oac.cdlib.org/ark:/13030/kt9t1nd07p/?brand=oac4>

28. *The Unfinished Autobiography*, p. 110.
29. Ibid., p. 111.
30. Ibid., p. 112.
31. Ibid., p. 112.
32. Ibid., p. 112.
33. "California Birth Index, 1905-1995," database, FamilySearch (https://family-search.org/ark:/61903/1:1:VG2N-7R5 : 27 November 2014), Mildred K Evans, 03 Aug 1912; citing Fresno, California, United States, Department of Health Services, Vital Statistics Department, Sacramento.
34. *The Unfinished Autobiography*, p. 112.
35. Ibid., p. 113.
36. Ibid., p. 114.
37. "California Birth Index, 1905-1995," database, FamilySearch (https://family-search.org/ark:/61903/1:1:VL1H-3MX : 27 November 2014), Ellison A Evans, 24 Jan 1914; citing Fresno, California, United States, Department of Health Services, Vital Statistics Department, Sacramento.
38. *The Unfinished Autobiography*, p. 115.
39. Ibid., p. 117.
40. Ibid.
41. Ibid., p. 119.
42. Ibid.
43. Alice A. Bailey, *The Externalisation of the Hierarchy* (New York: Lucis Trust, 1989), p. 87.
44. Bailey, *Problems of Humanity*, p. 102.
45. *The Unfinished Autobiography*, p. 145.
46. "Concerning the Ageless Wisdom Writing on the Jewish People". *Lucis Trust*, 2019, Web. 7 October 2019. <https://www.lucistrust.org/arcane_school/talks_and_articles/concerning_the_ageless_wisdom_writings_on_the_jewish_people>

From the same piece: "Some people wonder why, when human history is replete with examples of "man's inhumanity to man", the Tibetan seemed to single out the Jews for special criticism. Everything that the Tibetan wrote needs to be studied in the context of the entire body of teachings which promote goodwill, tolerance and mutual respect. Comments on the Jewish people must be read in their entirety, which includes mention of the splendid contribution of the Jewish people in many departments of human life. Criticism of separative tendencies in Zionism must be read in the context of biting comments on the subterfuge of the Vatican, materialism in the Christian churches, and "churchianity" in general. He was also outspoken in his opposition to American isolationism, Soviet totalitarianism, fascism, Nazism and the great evil embodied by Hitler and his closest associates, and to pacifism during the World War—all of which compromised the essential oneness of humanity and the spirit of responsible freedom.

It is that spirit of love and of inclusive identification which seeks to evoke the understanding and cooperation of the esoteric group in healing the fundamental human problem of separatism. Many people of goodwill are working diligently to find a solution. However, the unique aspect of esoteric teaching is that it challenges the student to penetrate to the causal level of all human problems, where the spiritual origins of the problems can be identified and lasting solutions can be precipitated into human consciousness. Perhaps that is why the Tibetan was unstinting in his criticism of Zionism, which sought to solve the problem of the stigmatisation of the Jewish people by giving them their own homeland rather than working for their integration into existing nations."

47. Ibid., p. 122.
48. Ibid.
49. Ibid., p. 123.
50. Ibid., p. 125.
51. Ibid., p. 125.
52. Ibid., p. 15.
53. Ibid., p. 126.
54. Ibid., p. 127.
55. Ibid., p. 123.
56. See "The Canneries". *Cannery Row*, 2015, Web. 9 October 2019. <http://cannneryrow.com/our-story/the-canneries/>
57. *The Unfinished Autobiography*, p. 128.
58. Ibid.
59. Ibid., p. 130.
60. Ibid., p. 132.
61. Ibid.
    4 An Esoteric Conversion

4. AN ESOTERIC CONVERSION

1. *The Unfinished Autobiography*, p. 134.
2. Ibid.
3. Ibid., pp. 134-5.
4. Ibid., p. 135.
5. Ibid., p. 136.
6. Ibid., p. 137.
7. Ibid.
8. Ibid., p. 138.
9. I adopted this method when researching the Bailey books for my doctoral thesis. See Isobel Wightman, *The Texts of Alice A Bailey: An Inquiry into the role of Esotericism in Transforming Consciousness*, PhD Thesis, (University of Western Sydney, 2006).
    <https://researchdirect.westernsydney.edu.au/islandora/object/uws%3A3753>
10. *The Unfinished Autobiography*, p. 139.
11. Annie Besant, *Initiation: The Perfecting of Man* (Chicago: Theosophical Press, 1912).
12. *The Unfinished Autobiography*, p. 140.

380 | NOTES

13. see Steven J. Sutcliffe, *Children of the New Age: A History of Spiritual Practices* (London: Routledge, 2003), p. 35.

14. Rudolph Steiner, The Way of Initiation or How to Attain Knowledge of the Higher Worlds (London: Theosophical Publishing, 1908).

15. To assert that the soul is consciousness appears simplistic and wrong. In Bailey's view, seated in the mind, consciousness is a kind of inner seeing. The mind and its physical counterpart, the brain, is a vast storehouse of data accumulated through sensory experience and systematised as knowledge. Consciousness is the part of us that is aware, that knows and experiences. To use the language of phenomenology, it is the intentional observer. We can perceive through our senses, and through an inner subjective eye, one that turns inwards in reflection. From a Theosophical perspective, the soul makes use of consciousness in order to fulfil the purposes of the particular incarnation.

16. William James, *Varieties of Religious Experience: A Study in Human Nature* (New York: Penguin, 1985), p. 197.

17. New Age guru and author of *Integral Theory*, Ken Wilber, describes consciousness as a spectrum, like the colour bands of a rainbow. By altering our state of consciousness, through meditation and even drugs, we can explore the whole spectrum and not be limited to ordinary waking consciousness. Yet delving into different kinds of awareness is not the same as expanding consciousness. If anything, such introspection can lead to a contraction, a sucking inwards, into the self.

18. Alice A. Bailey, *Esoteric Psychology: Volume II* (New York: Lucis Trust, 1988), p. 12.

19. Alice A. Bailey, *From Bethlehem to Calvary: The initiations of Jesus,* (New York: Lucis Trust, 1989), p. 105.

In Bailey's scheme there are nine initiations in all, and the first two are preparatory or threshold initiations. The third (also known as the first) occurs when the soul gains control of all three vehicles of the personality. From there, at each initiatory stage, a more fully realised spiritual consciousness grows. Of importance to humanity are the first four initiations.

20. Bailey states that 'there is no initiation possible without a preceding revelation, and yet each initiation leads to a subsequent revelation.' The former is generated by the disciple's own contemplative efforts, the latter is in some manner conferred. Alice A. Bailey, *Discipleship in the New Age: Volume II* (New York: Lucis Trust, 1986), p. 417.

21. Robert A. Segal, "Jung's Psychologising of Religion" in *Beyond New Age: Exploring Alternative Spirituality*, eds. Steven Sutcliffe and Marion Bowman (Edinburgh: Edinburgh University Press, 2000), p. 73.

22. Annie Besant, *Esoteric Christianity* (New York: John Lane, 1902).

23. Bailey, *From Bethlehem to Calvary*, p. 3.

24. Bailey, *Esoteric Psychology Vol II*, pp. 14-15.

Since the first initiation concerns the body, in Bailey's worldview it is not surprising that the new spirituality of the New Age contains a strong focus on physical techniques of alignment, including various forms of yoga, body alignment techniques, chakra balancing and reflexology.

25. Alice Bailey, *The Rays and The Initiations*, p. 577.

26. Alice A. Bailey, *The Destiny of the Nations* (New York: Lucis Trust, 1990), p. 138.
27. Alice A. Bailey, *Esoteric Psychology: Volume I* (New York: Lucis Trust, 1971), pp. 328-9.
28. This blast of light is known in Eastern mysticism as kundalini. Alice Bailey is at pains to stress that at the third initiation, the energy blasts through the crown chakra and descends to the root chakra. Many can mistake a similar but lesser experience, when the kundalini force flows in through the heart.
29. Bailey, *From Bethlehem to Calvary*, p. 128.

As with all stage models, there is a strong tendency inherent in us to map ourselves to the model and the model to ourselves. The potential for inflation is ever there. Who wouldn't want to consider themselves a fair way down the path? Bailey is far from alone in depicting a model of expanding or evolving human consciousness. Jung drew on the metaphor of the sun, Clare Graves who inspired Spiral Dynamics, postulated levels of human existence, Fowler came up with stages of faith, Wilber with his spectrum of consciousness. All stage models are teleological and progressive, from lesser to greater, all are ranking systems. And all stage models are seductive, as soon as we place ourselves inside it, locate our position or status, we have tacitly accepted the model's validity.

5 Krotona

5. MOVING TO KROTONA

1. Hadley Meares, "The Creation of Beachwood Canyon's Theosophist "Dreamland", *Curbed: Los Angeles*, 2014, Web. 15 February 2017. <http://la.curbed.com/2014/5/22/10099768/the-creation-of-beachwood-canyons-theosophist-dreamland-1>
2. See "Warrington, Albert Powell", *The Theosophical Encyclopedia*, 2013, Web. 20 October 2019. <http://theosophy.ph/encyclo/index.php?title=Warrington,_Albert_Powell>
3. Annie Wood Besant, *Avataras* (Whitefish, MT: Kessinger Publishing, 2007).
4. "The Krotona Institute of Theosophy". *The Theosophical Encyclopedia*, 2013, Web. 20 October 2019. <http://theosophy.ph/encyclo/index.php?title=Krotona_Institute_of_Theosophy,_The>
5. Kevin Star, The Dream Endures: California Enters the 1940s (Americans and the California Dream), Oxford University Press, 2002, p 198.
6. Hadley Meares, "The Creation of Beachwood Canyon's Theosophist "Dreamland", *Curbed: Los Angeles*, op. cit.
7. Ibid.
8. In 1918, Dorothy, and presumably also Mildred, attended the School of the Open Gate, a Theosophical school near Krotona established by Mary Gray. <https://theosophy.wiki/en/School_of_the_Open_Gate>

Dorothy is quoted in Mary Gray, "School of the Open Gate". The Messenger, May 1919, p. 364. PDF. *The International Association for the Preservation of Spiritualist and Occult Periodicals*, Web. 22 November 2019. <http://www.iap-

sop.com/archive/materials/theosophic_messenger_all/messenger_v6_n12_may_1919.pdf>

"One day I was up in the hills by myself. I could hear the birds sing. I seemed to know Just what they said. This is what they were calling: "Who are you? Who are you?" And I sang, " I am, I am. Who are y o u f " The birds answered, "I am the Spirit." Dorothy Evans, aged 8"

9. *The Unfinished Autobiography*, p. 154.

10. Ibid., p., 155.

11. see Chögyam Trungpa, *Cutting Through Spiritual Materialism* (Boulder, Colorado: Shambhala, 2002).

   6 Foster Arrives

6. FOSTER BAILEY ARRIVES

1. *The Unfinished Autobiography*, p. 156.

2. See "Bailey, Ebenezer Foster 1820". *World Cat. Identities*, 2019, Web. 17 October 2019.

   <http://worldcat.org/identities/lccn-n88257578/>

   Ebenezer Bailey, "A historical sketch of the C.C. Sunday school" in George A. Hitchcock, *A history of the Calvinistic Congregational Church and Society Fitchburg, Massachusetts*, (Fitchburg: Authorised by vote of the society, 1902). Cited at *HathiTrust Digital Library*, Web. 12 March 2017.

   <https://catalog.hathitrust.org/Record/100437576>

   Information on Uncle Harrison Bailey can be found in Charles Warren, *History Of The Harvard Law School And Of Early Legal Conditions In America*, Volume 1, Palala Press, 2015, p 139.

   Also see Dorothy S Kimball, "Massachusetts Home Missionary Society". *Annual report of the Massachusetts Home Missionary Society.* (Boston: Press of T.R. Marvin, 1844).

   Leonard A. Morrison and Stephen Paschall Sharples, *History of the Kimball Family in America from 1634 to 1897 and of Its Ancestors the Kemballs or Kemboldes of England With an Account of the Kembles of Boston*, (Massachusetts, Nabu Press, 2010).

   "Cora Isabel Wheeler Bailey". *Find a Grave*, 2013, Web. 12 February 2017.
   <https://www.findagrave.com/memorial/119327687/wheeler>

   Irene Weinmann, "Descendants of Thomas Kimball". *Genealogy*, 2019, Web. 1 October 2019.

   <http://www.genealogy.com/ftm/w/e/i/Irene-Weinmann/BOOK-0001/0088-0024.html>

3. The Theosophical Society became heavily involved in the support of First World War servicemen. Foster Bailey may have joined the society through their various campaigns. See Janet Kerschner, "Theosophy in Times of War", *The Theosophical Society in America*, Web. 6 October 2019. (originally published in *Quest*, Summer 2009).

   <https://www.theosophical.org/publications/quest-magazine/42-publications/quest-magazine/1678-theosophy-in-times-of-war>

   Membership Ledger Cards Roll 1. [Microfilm record] Theosophical

Society in America Archives. Cited at "Foster Bailey", *Theosophical Wiki*, 2018, Web. 7 October 2019. <https://theosophy.wiki/en/Foster_Bailey>

4. "United States World War I Draft Registration Cards, 1917-1918", database with images, FamilySearch (https://familysearch.org/ark:/61903/1:1:KZJS-JX2 : 24 August 2019), Foster Bailey, 1917-1918.

   In World War One, the United States Air Force was not a separate branch of the military but rather, it formed part of the United States Army.

5. "Foster Bailey (1888)", BIRLS Death File, U.S. Department of Veterans Affairs, 1850-2010. "Beneficiary Identification Records Locator Subsystem (BIRLS) Death File. Washington, D.C.: U.S. Department of Veterans Affairs." *Fold 3*, 2019, Web. 15 October 2019. <https://www.fold3.com/record/622325168-foster-bailey-1888>

6. *The Unfinished Autobiography*, p. 156. It is likely Alice Bailey confused the United States Air Force and Army in this paragraph.

7. Gordon Pugh, interview conducted by Rose Bates. "Rose Bates: Alice Bailey's Grandson's Memories & Photos". Video of talk at *Seven Ray Institute* Conference 2019, <https://youtu.be/YYDf1cTb6WY>

8. During this period, monthly editions of the sectional magazine *The Messenger* contain a report titled "War Work", summarizing the efforts of the society.

   Laura Slavens Wood, "War Work", The Messenger, pp. 279-280. PDF. *The International Association for the Preservation of Spiritualist and Occult Periodicals*, Web. 22 November 2019.

   <http://www.iapsop.com/archive/materials/theosophic_messenger_all/messenger_v6_n9_february_1919.pdf>

9. *The Unfinished Autobiography*, p. 156.

10. Spellings of names and dates given are at times unreliable in *The Unfinished Autobiography*. In a later chapter, she gives the dates of a Spiritual Summer School project one year later than when they were held.

11. Foster Bailey, *Reflections* (New York: Lucis Trust, 1979), p. 91.

12. Ibid., p. 92.

13. *The Unfinished Autobiography*, p. 14.

14. Membership Ledger Cards Roll 1. [Microfilm record] Theosophical Society in America Archives, cited at Cited at "Foster Bailey", *Theosophical Wiki*, 2018, Web. 7 October 2019. <https://theosophy.wiki/en/Foster_Bailey>

15. *The Unfinished Autobiography*, pp. 160-1.

16. Ibid., p. 163.

    7 The Tibetan

7. THE TIBETAN

1. *The Unfinished Autobiography*, p. 163.

2. Alice A. Bailey, *Letters on Occult Meditation*, (New York: Lucis Trust, 1993), p. 133.

3. Ibid., p. 133 and p. 134.

4. Alice A. Bailey, *Letters on Occult Meditation*, (New York: Lucis Trust, 1922), p.139.

5. I have not seen the letters in question in any form despite numerous requests to do so. I was told about them by a reliable source who stated in an email to me that they were part of their collection of materials and that they had sighted them.

6. *Externalisation of the Hierarchy,* p. 631.

7. It is disappointing that the Lucis Trust has so far chosen to veil the truth of the true date by removing the contrary evidence in *Letters on Occult Meditation,* presumably in order to not draw into question the authenticity of the April 1948 pamphlet, rather than reveal the precise date of the very first letter for the sake of the historical record. Astrologers are currently forced to rely on the 19 November 1919 date. The best that can be said about that date is it marks some sort of symbolic beginning, one entirely lacking any known foundation.

8. B P Wadia was on a tour of Theosophical lodges and he was scheduled to arrive at Krotona for Christmas. See Albert Warrington, "From the National President", *The Messenger,* p. 204. PDF. *The International Association for the Preservation of Spiritualist and Occult Periodicals,* Web. 22 November 2019.

    <http://www.iapsop.com/archive/materials/theosophic_messenger_all/messenger_v7_n7_december_1919.pdf>

    The details of Alice Bailey's submission to B P Wadia is taken up in the next chapter along with the various references.

9. Maureen Temple Richmond, "Great Esotericists: Alice A. Bailey (1880–1949), Twentieth-Century Sirian Channel", *The Esoteric Quarterly,* Winter 2018, pp. 100-1. <http://www.esotericquarterly.com/>

10. *The Unfinished Autobiography,* p. 165.

11. Alice A. Bailey, *Initiation, Human and Solar,* (New York: Lucis Trust, 1992), p. 57., and *The Externalisation of the Hierarchy,* p. 522. In the latter work, in a letter dated January 1946, the Tibetan claims to have passed through the fifth initiation 'ninety years ago', putting the occurrence in about 1856. However, it appears Alice Bailey became unreliable in taking down dates given by the Tibetan in her later years. The 1875 date given in the former work should be regarded more reliable.

12. Gordon Pugh, interview conducted by Rose Bates. "Rose Bates: Alice Bailey's Grandson's Memories & Photos". Video of talk at *Seven Ray Institute* Conference 2019, <https://youtu.be/YYDf1cTb6WY>

13. *The Unfinished Autobiography,* p. 164.

14. Ibid., p. 167.

15. See Hugh Major, *The Lantern in the Skull,* (New Zealand: Attar Books, 2019).

16. *The Unfinished Autobiography,* p. 166.

17. These chapters and the section of *A Treatise on Cosmic Fire* appear in 1921 issues of *The Theosophist.* See the following chapter for full citations.

18. This version can be found at <alicebaileyarchives.com>

19. Bailey, *Initiation, Human and Solar,* p. 71.

20. Ibid., pp. 53-59.

21. Alice Bailey, "Friday Talk", 17 March 1944, p. 7. PDF at *School for Esoteric Studies,* 2019, Web. 24 September 2019. <http://www.esotericstudies.net/aabtalks/aab03-17-44.pdf>

22. *The Unfinished Autobiography,* p. 164.

8. A TEAPOT TEMPEST

1. J Gordon Melton "The Theosophical Communities and their Ideal of Universal Brotherhood" in *America's Communal Utopias* ed. Donald E. Pitzer (Berkeley: University of North Carolina Press, 1997), p. 410.

2. "Board of Trustees: Minutes of meeting". *The Messenger*, October 1919, p. 155. PDF, *The International Association for the Preservation of Spiritualist and Occult Periodicals*, Web. 22 November 2019. <http://www.iapsop.com/archive/materials/theosophic_messenger_all/messenger_v7_n5_october_1919.pdf>

3. Ibid., p. 155.

4. Ibid., and,
   "Board of Trustees: Minutes of meeting". *The Messenger*, October 1918, p. 153. PDF, *The International Association for the Preservation of Spiritualist and Occult Periodicals*, Web. 22 November 2019.
   <http://www.iapsop.com/archive/materials/theosophic_messenger_all/messenger_v6_n5_october_1918.pdf>

5. "National Publicity Department", *The Messenger*, April 1919, pp. 344-345. PDF, *The International Association for the Preservation of Spiritualist and Occult Periodicals*, Web. 22 November 2019.
   <http://www.iapsop.com/archive/materials/theosophic_messenger_all/messenger_v6_n11_april_1919.pdf>

6. "Mr. Warrington Re-elected". *The Messenger*, April 1919, p. 346. PDF, *The International Association for the Preservation of Spiritualist and Occult Periodicals*, Web. 22 November 2019. <http://www.iapsop.com/archive/materials/theosophic_messenger_all/messenger_v6_n11_april_1919.pdf>

7. "Board of Trustees: Minutes of Meeting held May 24th, 1919". *The Messenger*, August 1919, p. 85. PDF, *The International Association for the Preservation of Spiritualist and Occult Periodicals*, Web. 22 November 2019.
   <http://www.iapsop.com/archive/materials/theosophic_messenger_all/messenger_v7_n3_august_1919.pdf>

8. *The Unfinished Autobiography*, p. 160.

9. "Board of Trustees: Minutes of meeting". *The Messenger*, October 1919, p. 154. PDF, *The International Association for the Preservation of Spiritualist and Occult Periodicals*, Web. 22 November 2019. <http://www.iapsop.com/archive/materials/theosophic_messenger_all/messenger_v7_n5_october_1919.pdf>

10. Bailey, *Letters on Occult Meditation*, (1993), pp. 123-138.

11. Ibid., p. 134.

12. Ibid.

13. *The Unfinished Autobiography*, p. 159.

14. Sarah Grand, "Femininities", in Ann Hellman ed., *New Woman Strategies*, (Manchester: Manchester University Press, 2004).

15. see Olav Hammer, "Schism and Consolidation: the case of the theosophical movement," *Sacred Schisms: How Religions Divide* eds. James R. Lewis and Sarah M. Lewis (Cambridge: Cambridge University Press, 2009), p. 202.

16. Kevin Tingay, "Madame Blavatsky's Children: Theosophy and Its Heirs", *in* Steven Sutcliffe and Marion Bowman, (eds), *Beyond New Age: Exploring Alternative Spirituality*, (Edinburgh: Edinburgh University Press, 2000), pp. 37-50.

17. *The Unfinished Autobiography*, pp. 159-160.

18. *The Unfinished Autobiography*, p. 159.

19. See Dallas Tenbroeck, "B. P. Wadia - A Life of Service to Mankind", *Eclectic Theosophical History*, Web. 7 October 2019. <http://www.katinkahesselink.net/his/dtb_2.htm>

20. *The Unfinished Autobiography*, p. 169.

21. Ibid., p. 167.

22. Alice Evans, "Initiation and the Solar System". *The Theosophist: A magazine of Brotherhood, Oriental Philosophy, Art, Literature and Occultism, Vol XLII, Part I: October 1920 to March 1921*, February 1921, pp. 457-472; and March 1921, pp. 575-582. PDF, *The International Association for the Preservation of Spiritualist and Occult Periodicals*, Web. 22 November 2019.

    Alice A. Evans-Bailey, "Cosmic and Systemic Law". *The Theosophist: A magazine of Brotherhood, Oriental Philosophy, Art, Literature and Occultism, Vol XLII, Part II: April 1921 - September 1921*, September 1921, pp. 576-593. PDF, *The International Association for the Preservation of Spiritualist and Occult Periodicals*, Web. 22 November 2019. <http://www.iapsop.com/archive/materials/theosophist/theosophist_v42_n1-n12_oct_1920-sep_1921.pdf>

    Alice A. Evans-Bailey "Cosmic and Systemic Law" (Part 2). *The Theosophist: A magazine of Brotherhood, Oriental Philosophy, Art, Literature and Occultism, Vol XLIII, April 1921 – September 1921*. pp. 164-177. PDF. *The International Association for the Preservation of Spiritualist and Occult Periodicals*, Web. 22 November 2019. <http://www.iapsop.com/archive/materials/theosophist/theosophist_v43_n1-n12_oct_1921-sep_1922.pdf>

23. Alice. A. Bailey, *A Treatise on Cosmic Fire*, (New York: Lucis Trust, 1989), pp. 567-586.

24. *The Unfinished Autobiography*, p. 167.

25. Little is mentioned of the Order of the Star of the East even on dedicated Krishnamurti websites. According to the Tibetan, the experiment was brought to an end by the Hierarchy during the 1925 Conclave. 'One of the first experiments He [the Christ] made as He prepared for this form of activity was in connection with Krishnamurti. It was only partially successful. The power used by Him was distorted and misapplied by the devotee type of which the Theosophical Society is largely composed, and the experiment was brought to an end; it served, however, a most useful purpose.' *Discipleship in the New Age, Vol II*, p. 171.

26. See Phil Hine, ""A thousand kisses darling": Sex, scandal and spirituality in the life of Charles Webster Leadbeater – IV" 9 April 2013. *Enfolding.org*, 2019, Web. 29 November 2019. <http://enfolding.org/a-thousand-kisses-darling-sex-scandal-and-spirituality-in-the-life-of-charles-webster-leadbeater-iv/>

    John Cooper, *The Theosophical Crisis In Australia: The Story of the Breakup of the Theosophical Society in Sydney from 1913 to 1923,* Masters thesis. (Sydney: The University of Sydney, 1986).

The Martyn letter, Cooper, ibid, p. 187.

Gregory John Tillet, *Charles Webster Leadbeater 1854-1934: A Biographical Study,* (Sydney: University of Sydney, Department of Religious Studies, 1986), p. 653.

27. *The Unfinished Autobiography,* p. 171.

28. Gregory John Tillett, op. cit., p. 653.

29. see Olav Hammer, *Claiming Knowledge,* op cit.; Sir John R. Sinclair, *The Alice Bailey Inheritance* (Wellingborough: Turnstone, 1984).

30. see Kurt Leland, *Rainbow Body: A History of the Western Chakra System from Blavatsky to Brennan* (Lake Worth, Fl: Ibis Press, 2016).

31. Bailey, *Initiation, Human and Solar,* p. 2.

32. Alice Evans, "A Vision of Krotona's Future" *The Messenger,* February 1920, pp. 257-262, PDF. *The International Association for the Preservation of Spiritualist and Occult Periodicals,* Web. 22 November 2019. <http://www.iapsop.com/archive/materials/theosophic_messenger_all/messenger_v7_n9_february_1920.pdf>

33. Steven Parfitt, "Working Men Pass Through all the Stages of Union: The Role of District Assembly 82 of the Knights of Labor in the Formation of the American Railway Union", *Australasian Journal of American Studies,* Vol. 29, No. 2 (December 2010), pp. 24-44.

34. Robert Bonnell and Leatrice Kreeger-Bonnell, "Memories of L.W. Rogers", *Quest,* 92:6 (Nov.-Dec. 2004), pp. 224-226. <https://www.theosophical.org/publications/quest-magazine/1509>

35. Robert Kelsey Walton, "The Mock in the League for Democracy", *The Messenger,* May 1920, pp 404-406. PDF. *The International Association for the Preservation of Spiritualist and Occult Periodicals,* Web. 22 November 2019. <http://www.iapsop.com/archive/materials/theosophic_messenger_all/messenger_v7_n12_may_1920.pdf>

36. Louis Rogers, "By the National President", *The Messenger,* June 1920 pp. 429-434. *The International Association for the Preservation of Spiritualist and Occult Periodicals,* Web. 22 November 2019. <http://www.iapsop.com/archive/materials/theosophic_messenger_all/messenger_v8_n1_june_1920.pdf >

37. Louis Rogers, 'By the National President', *The Messenger,* July 1920, pp. 458 *The International Association for the Preservation of Spiritualist and Occult Periodicals,* Web. 22 November 2019. <http://www.iapsop.com/archive/materials/theosophic_messenger_all/messenger_v8_n2_july_1920.pdf>

38. Ibid., pp. 458-9.

39. Louis Rogers, "By the National President", *The Messenger,* September 1920, p. 532. *The International Association for the Preservation of Spiritualist and Occult Periodicals,* Web. 22 November 2019.<http://www.iapsop.com/archive/materials/theosophic_messenger_all/messenger_v8_n4_september_1920.pdf>

40. Letter: Louis Rogers to Foster Bailey, 3 August 1920. Louis Rogers, "By the National President", *The Messenger,* September 1920, p. 530; Louis Rogers, ibid., p. 533. PDF. *The International Association for the Preservation of Spiritualist and Occult Periodicals,* Web. 22 November 2019.

<http://www.iapsop.com/archive/materials/theosophic_messenger_all/messenger_v8_n4_september_1920.pdf>

41. Bailey, *Letters on Occult Meditation*, p. 44.
42. *The Unfinished Autobiography*, p. 178.
43. Ibid.
    9 Breaking Away

9. BREAKING AWAY

1. *The Unfinished Autobiography*, p. 180.
2. Ibid., p. 13.
3. See Olav Hammer and Mikael Rothstein, *Handbook of the Theosophical Current*, (Leiden: Brill, 2013), p. 29.
4. see Jocelyn Godwin, *The Handbook of the Theosophical Current* (Leiden: Brill, 2013), p. 29; and "Harold W. Percival". *The Word Foundation: Publishers of thinking and destiny*, Web. 28 November 2019.
    <https://thewordfoundation.org/about-the-author/>
5. "Massachusetts Births and Christenings, 1639-1915," database, Family-Search (https://familysearch.org/ark:/61903/1:1:FHHJ-TVC : 11 March 2018), Ernest Salisbury Suffern, 10 Jan 1880; citing Boston, Suffolk, Massachusetts, 10775; FHL microfilm 594,916. And "New York Marriages, 1686-1980," database, FamilySearch (https://family-search.org/ark:/61903/1:1:F63Z-G3X : 10 February 2018), Ernest Salisbury Suffern and Georgia Louise Greene, 06 Apr 1904; citing reference ; FHL microfilm 1,556,703.
6. See Bradley's of South Derry, "Suffern: Suffern". *Geneanet*, Web. 28 November 2019. <https://gw.geneanet.org/belfast8?lang=en&v=SUFFERN&m=N>
7. *The Unfinished Autobiography*, pp. 179-81.
8. Letter: Ernest Suffern to Annie Besant, 25 April 1922, *Dawn: A magazine devoted to the Promotion of Universal Brotherhood*, pp. 22-23. *Katinka Hesselink*, Web. 28 November 2019. < http://theosophy.katinkahesselink.net/dawn/Vol-1-5-DAWN.htm>
    The Committee of 1400 campaign occurred during a scandal involving allegations of child sex abuse launched at Charles Leadbeater in Sydney, Australia, and exposed by Mr Martyn. The preface to this letter states, 'Mr. Suffern, like Mr. Martyn, was aware of certain serious scandals and has been for a long time past trying to interest Mrs. Besant in the good name of the Society, as will be gathered from his letter. Dawn has obtained permission to publish this, as it shows that Australian members are not alone in striving to have the Society to which they belong made clean and kept clean.'
9. see "Election Explanation", *The Messenger*, March 1921, p. 631. PDF. *The International Association for the Preservation of Spiritualist and Occult Periodicals*, Web. 22 November 2019. <http://www.iapsop.com/archive/materials/theosophic_messenger_all/messenger_v8_n10_march_1921.pdf>
    Ernest S. Suffern, *An appeal to the members of the American section of the*

Theosophical Society for administrative reform, 1921, Dr John Cooper Theosophy Collection, National Library of Australia.

<http://catalogue.nla.gov.au/Record/3097882>

Louis Rogers, "To the Members", The Messenger, April 1921, p. 653. PDF. *The International Association for the Preservation of Spiritualist and Occult Periodicals*, Web. 22 November 2019.

<http://www.iapsop.com/archive/materials/theosophic_messenger_all/messenger_v8_n11_april_1921.pdf>

10. William McGuire, "The Arcane Summer School" in *Spring: An Annual of Archetypal Psychology and Jungian Thought*, 1980: 149.
11. Leah Rae Lake: Unpublished memoir, "Adventures in Heaven and Hell", Chapter 14.
12. *The Unfinished Autobiography*, p. 188.
13. Ibid., p. 189.
14. Dallas Tenbroeck "B. P. Wadia - A Life of Service to Mankind 1881 – 1903", *Katinka Hesselink*, Web. 28 November 2019. <http://www.katinkahesselink.net/his/dtb_2.htm>
15. Alice Bailey, "Friday Talk", 24 November 1944, p. 7. PDF at *School for Esoteric Studies*, 2019, Web. 24 September 2019. <http://www.esotericstudies.net/aabtalks/aab11-24-44.pdf>
16. Alice A. Evans-Bailey, "H.P.B. and her Work", *The Theosophist: A magazine of Brotherhood, Oriental Philosophy, Art, Literature and Occultism, Vol XLIII, October 1921 - March 1922*, March 1922, pp 570-582. PDF, *The International Association for the Preservation of Spiritualist and Occult Periodicals*, Web. 22 November 2019 <http://www.iapsop.com/archive/materials/theosophist/theosophist_v43_n1-n12_oct_1921-sep_1922.pdf>
17. "International Election". *The Messenger*, April 1921, p. 650. PDF. *The International Association for the Preservation of Spiritualist and Occult Periodicals*, Web. 22 November 2019. <http://www.iapsop.com/archive/materials/theosophic_messenger_all/messenger_v8_n11_april_1921.pdf>
18. "L. W. Rogers" *Theosophy Wiki*, 2019, Web. 29 November 2019. <http://theosophy.ph/encyclo/index.php?title=America,_Theosophy_in>

10. A TREATISE ON COSMIC FIRE

1. *10 A Treatise on Cosmic Fire*
   The Unfinished Autobiography, p. 236.
2. Antoine Faivre, Access to Western Esotericism, (New York: SUNY Press, 1994), pp. 10-11.
   Pierre A. Riffard, Dictionnaire de l'ésotérisme, Paris: Payot, 1983, p. 34.
3. Alice A. Bailey, *A Treatise on Cosmic Fire* (New York: Lucis Trust, 1989), p. 572.
4. In Eastern mysticism these are known as atma, buddhi and manas or Shiva/Vishnu/Brahma.
5. Robert Ellwood describes involution in plain language as the process whereby spirit/consciousness takes on denser and denser forms 'in order to explore more fully what the pair can do together'. Involution is an outward

journey from the Source. Evolution is the return to Source. Robert Ellwood, *Theosophy: A modern expression of the wisdom of the ages.* (Wheaton: Quest, 1986), pp 58-961.

6. Bailey, *Cosmic Fire*, p. 7.
7. Under the third solar Logos, creation existed under the law of economy. The first solar Logos will exhale under the law of synthesis.
8. *Cosmic Fire*, p. 152.
9. Ibid., p. 437.

   In Bailey's scheme, since our solar Logos is operating through the second Ray of love-wisdom, all the Rays in our solar system are sub-Rays of this ray, animated by their corresponding cosmic Ray. The Rays absorb and transmit through the centres or chakras of the planetary Logos and through humanity, itself dominated by the fourth Ray.
10. Robert Ellwood, *Theosophy: A Modern Expression of the Wisdom of the Ages* (Wheaton: Theosophical Publishing House, 1986).

    11 A Secret Doctrine Class

11. A SECRET DOCTRINE CLASS

1. *The Unfinished Autobiography*, pp. 190-1.
2. Ibid.
3. *The Unfinished Autobiography*, p. 190.
4. *The Unfinished Autobiography*, p. 191.
5. "History". *Lucis Trust*, 2019, Web. 29 November 2019. <https://www.lucistrust.org/about_us/history>
6. Constance Cumbey, *The Hidden Dangers of the Rainbow: The New Age movement and our coming age of barbarism* (Shreveport: Huntington House, 1983), p. 49.
7. *Hidden Dangers*, 20.
8. The website <www.isobelblackthorn/alicebaileyarticles.com> provides a feast of material on the New World Order conspiracy theory, its history and how conspiracists view Alice Bailey.
9. *The Unfinished Autobiography*, p. 199.
10. "The Beacon magazine". *Lucis Trust*, 2019, Web. 29 November 2019. <https://www.lucistrust.org/books/the_beacon_magazine>
11. "Our Contemporaries". *The London Forum*, February 1934, p. 131. PDF. *The International Association for the Preservation of Spiritualist and Occult Periodicals*, Web. 22 November 2019. <http://www.iapsop.com/archive/materials/occult_review/london_forum_v59_n2_feb_1934.pdf>

    "Our Contemporaries". *The London Forum*, June 1934, p. 420. PDF. *The International Association for the Preservation of Spiritualist and Occult Periodicals*, Web. 22 November 2019.

    <http://www.iapsop.com/archive/materials/occult_review/london_forum_v59_n6_jun_1934.pdf >
12. see "The Beacon 1922 – continuing, New York, Lucis Trust, Foster Bailey". "Union Index of Theosophical Periodicals". *Theosophical Society of Australia,*

2018, Web. 29 November 2019. <http://www.austheos.org.au/indices/BEACON.HTM>

13. "Dane Rudhyar - An illustrated biographic sketch, Part 3, The Early Hollywood Years: 1920-1924". *Rudhyar Archival Project*, 2004, Web. 29 November 2019. <https://khaldea.com/rudhyar/bio3.shtml>

14. see "The Beacon 1922 – continuing, New York, Lucis Trust, Foster Bailey". "Union Index of Theosophical Periodicals". *Theosophical Society of Australia*, 2018, Web. 29 November 2019. <http://www.austheos.org.au/indices/BEACON.HTM>

15. Jacob Bonggren, "Key to Occult Chromotherapy". *The Beacon*, October 1923, p. 97: and

   Letter: Jacob Bonggren, quoted in "Dr Bonggren's Authority". *Canadian Theosophist*, Vol XXIII, February 1943, p. 390. *Katinka Hesselink*, Web. 28 November 2019. <http://theosophy.katinkahesselink.net/canadian/Vol-23-12-C-Theosophist.htm>

16. Jacob Bonggren, "Testing the Faithful", *The Theosophist* December 1923, p. 395, PDF. *The International Association for the Preservation of Spiritualist and Occult Periodicals*, Web. 22 November 2019. <http://www.iapsop.com/archive/materials/theosophist/theosophist_v45_n1-n12_oct_1923-sep_1924.pdf>; also quoted in a discussion on Alice Bailey in *The High Country Theosophist*, May 1997, p. 20. <http://www.hctheosophist.com/archives/pdf/hc199705.pdf>

17. Book review: "Letters on Occult Meditation". The Occult Review, December 1922, p. 396. PDF. *The International Association for the Preservation of Spiritualist and Occult Periodicals*, Web. 22 November 2019.
   <http://www.iapsop.com/archive/materials/occult_review/occult_review_v36_n6_dec_1922.pdf>

12. THE ARCANE SCHOOL

1. *12 The Arcane School*
   The Unfinished Autobiography, p. 175.

2. The emergence of *learning from* and experiential learning as pedagogical tools in education training in universities occurred in the 1990s, the result of the influence of humanistic psychology in education that occurred in the 1970s. Interestingly, Alice Bailey initiated her own version for adults in the 1920s. She did not set out to create a new teaching and learning method within andragogy or pedagogy. Rather, in her methods exists an implicit striving towards similar goals.

   See Professor of Adult and Community College Education Malcom S. Knowles, who writes extensively on this topic.

3. Ibid., p. 190.
4. Ibid., p. 263.
5. Ibid., p. 281.
6. Ibid., pp. 249-50.
7. Ibid., pp. 194-5.
8. Ibid., p. 281.

9. Ibid., p. 282.
10. Alice Bailey, "Friday Talk", 12 May 1944, p. 3. PDF at *School for Esoteric Studies*, 2019, Web. 24 September 2019. <http://www.esotericstudies.net/aabtalks/aab05-12-44.pdf>
11. Foster Bailey, *Reflections*, (New York: Lucis Trust, 1979), p. 95.
12. *The Occult Review*, April 1923, p. 193. PDF. *The International Association for the Preservation of Spiritualist and Occult Periodicals*, Web. 22 November 2019.
    < http://www.iapsop.com/archive/materials/occult_review/occult_review_v37_n4_apr_1923.pdf>
13. Foster Bailey, *Reflections*, 93-4.
14. *The Unfinished Autobiography*, 193.
15. *The Unfinished Autobiography*, 194.
16. *The Unfinished Autobiography*, 198.
17. Anthony, D., and Ecker, B., 1987, The Anthony Typology: A Framework for Assessing Spiritual and Consciousness Groups, pp 35-91, *in*, Wilber, K., Anthony, D., and Ecker, B., (eds), *Spiritual Choices*, Paragon House, New York, p84.
18. *The Unfinished Autobiography*, 195.
19. It is unclear when Foster Bailey resigned as secretary of the Theosophical Society of New York and in her autobiography there is no further mention of his involvement with Ernest Suffern in this regard.
20. 140 Cedar Street is situated close to Ground Zero, part of the area devastated by the World Trade Center buildings collapse on 9 September 2001, now the location of the 9/11 St Nicholas National Shrine at the World Trade Center. See advert in *The Occult Review*, April 1923, p. 193. PDF. *The International Association for the Preservation of Spiritualist and Occult Periodicals*, Web. 22 November 2019.
    < http://www.iapsop.com/archive/materials/occult_review/occult_review_v37_n4_apr_1923.pdf>

13. SOME INFLUENTIAL FRIENDS

1. Book review: "Raja Yoga: Or, conquering the internal nature by Swami Vivekananda". *Occult Review*, November 1922, p. 318. PDF. *The International Association for the Preservation of Spiritualist and Occult Periodicals*, Web. 22 November 2019.
    <http://www.iapsop.com/archive/materials/occult_review/occult_review_v36_n5_nov_1922.pdf>
2. *13 Some Influential Friends*
    "Hawaii, Honolulu Passenger Lists, 1900-1953," database with images, FamilySearch (https://familysearch.org/ark:/61903/1:1:QVR9-P9KH : 16 March 2018), Dorothy Bailey, 1928; citing Ship , NARA microfilm publication A3422 (Washington D.C.: National Archives and Records Administration, n.d.).
3. see *New York State's prominent and progressive men: an encyclopaedia of contemporaneous biography, Volume 3* (New York: New York Tribune, 1902)

4. Alan Robert Ginsberg, *The Salome Ensemble: Rose Pastor Stokes, Anzia Yezierska, Sonya Levien, and Jetta Goudal* (Syracuse, NY: Syracuse University Press, 2016), pp. 35-7.

Images and a description of the house can be found at: "Stamford island home holds rich history". *Stamford Advocate*, 3 August 2016, Web. 29 November 2019.

<http://www.stamfordadvocate.com/local/article/Stamford-island-home-holds-rich-history-9107954.php#photo-10704021>

5. In 2016, the island was home to John A. Morgan, great-grandson of JP Morgan of banking fame.

Ginsberg, *The Salome Ensemble,* p. 36.

6. The Arcane School and the Lucis Trust took offices on the top floor of Salmon Tower in 1928. Prior to this time, their offices were located at 140 Cedar Street, New York, which would have been where the Spinoza group met.

7. "History of the Biosophical Institute". *The Biosophical Institute: a foundation for peace*, 2019, Web. 29 November 2019. <https://biosophical.org/history-of-the-biosophical-institute/>

8. At the time of writing, the property was listed for sale at nine million dollars. "Stamford island home holds rich history". Op. cit.

9. *The Unfinished Autobiography*, p. 205.

10. William McGuire, "The Arcane Summer School" in *Spring: An Annual of Archetypal Psychology and Jungian Thought*, 1980: 153.

11. *The Unfinished Autobiography*, p. 206.

12. Ibid., p. 207.

13. Ibid.

14. *The Unfinished Autobiography*, p. 20.

15. Victor Fox is RVB in the *Discipleship in the New Age Vols I* and *II* letters: Rapid Reaction, Vision, The Breath.

16. Bally Knockarocker, "Serious minded Yanks meet Titles and are entertained". *Variety* magazine. May 1928, Web. 29 November 2019. <https://archive.org/stream/variety91-1928-05/variety91-1928-05_djvu.txt>

17. *The Unfinished Autobiography*, p. 211.

18. Grand Duke Alexander of Russia "The Nature of the Soul" in *The Beacon* February 1930, pp. 242-249.

19. Charles Lazenby, *The Work of the Masters*, (New York: The Path Publishing Co., 1917).

20. Alice A. Bailey, From Bethlehem to Calvary, (New York: Lucis Trust, 1989), p. 181. She quotes Edward Carpenter, *Pagan and Christian Deeds: Their Origin and Meaning*, (New York: Harcourt, Brace and Company, 1921), pp. 217-218.

21. Liz Stanley, "Epistemological Issues in Researching Lesbian History" in Hilary Hinds, Ann Phoenix, Jackie Stacey (eds.), *Working Out: New Directions for Women's Studies, Psychology Press*, p. 167.

22. *The Canadian Theosophist,* Vol. 69 No. 5 Toronto, Nov.-Dec., 1988, p. 102. *Katinka Hesselink,* Web. 28 November 2019. <http://theosophy.katinkahesselink.net/canadian/Vol-69-5-Theosophist.htm>

23. Ibid. p. 105.

24. "Path, (the Pub)". *Theosophy World: resource centre*, Web. 29 November 2019. <https://www.theosophy.world/encyclopedia/path-pub>

25. "The Path 1925-1949 (incomplete) Sydney, The Independent TS". *The Theosophical Society of Australia*, 2011, Web. 29 November 2019. <http://www.austheos.org.au/indices/PATHAU.HTM>

26. Rare edition, privately held. A new edition has been released by Forgotten Books, 2018.

    14 A Spiritual Summer School

14. A SPIRITUAL SUMMER SCHOOL

1. see Deirdre Bair, *Jung: A Biography* (Ney York: Little, Brown and Company, 2003), p. 412, and Hans Thomas Hakl, *Eranos: an alternative intellectual history of the twentieth century,* trans. Christopher McIntosh, (Montreal: McGill-Queen's University Press, 2013), pp. 12-16.

2. Bair, *Jung*, p. 412.

3. Hakl, *Eranos*, p. 33.

4. Bair, *Jung*, p. 412.

5. Bair, *Jung*, p. 413.

6. William McGuire, *Bollingen: And Adventure in collecting the Past*, (Princeton: Princeton University Press, 1989), p. 22.

7. Bair, *Jung*, p. 413.

8. Hakl, *Eranos*, p. 16.

9. William McGuire, "The Arcane Summer School" in *Spring: An Annual of Archetypal Psychology and Jungian Thought*, 1980: 155.

10. Olga Fröbe Kapteyn, "Know Thy Self", *The Beacon*, May 1929, p. 31.

11. *The Unfinished Autobiography*, p. 217.

12. Alice A. Bailey, *The Soul and Its Mechanism* (New York: Lucis Trust, 1987), p. 10.

13. Alice A. Bailey, *From Intellect to Intuition*, (New York: Lucis Trust, 1987).

14. *The Unfinished Autobiography*, p. 220.

15. Ibid.

16. Ibid., p. 222.

17. Ibid., p. 222.

18. Ibid., p. 223.

19. Goodrick-Clarke, *The Occult Roots of Nazism*, op. cit., pp. 24-25.

20. Ibid., p. p. 223.

21. Ibid., p. 224.

22. McGuire, "Summer School", p. 150.

23. Ibid., p. 151.

24. *The Unfinished Autobiography*, p. 225.

25. Ibid.

26. McGuire, "Summer School", pp. 152-3.

27. *The Unfinished Autobiography*, p. 242.

28. *The Unfinished Autobiography*, p. 225.

29. Bair, *Jung*, op. cit., p. 413.

30. Hakl, *Eranos*, op. cit., p. 49.

31. McGuire, "Summer School", p. 153.
32. Ibid., p. p. 154.
33. Ibid., p. 155.
34. The full story of the Spiritual Summer School is dramatically portrayed in my novel, *The Unlikely Occultist: A biographical novel of Alice A Bailey.*
35. "England and Wales Marriage Registration Index, 1837-2005," database, FamilySearch (https://familysearch.org/ark:/61903/1:1:QV8C-4FKZ : 8 October 2014), Dorothy M M E Bailey and null, 1934; from "England & Wales Marriages, 1837-2005," database, findmypast (http://www.findmypast.com : 2012); citing 1934, quarter 3, vol. 2A, p. 3597, Faversham, Kent, England, General Register Office, Southport, England.
36. "England and Wales Marriage Registration Index, 1837-2005," database, FamilySearch (https://familysearch.org/ark:/61903/1:1:QV8D-M9JV : 8 October 2014), Ellison A Bailey and null, 1936; from "England & Wales Marriages, 1837-2005," database, findmypast (http://www.findmypast.com : 2012); citing 1936, quarter 2, vol. 2A, p. 2738, Tonbridge, Kent, England, General Register Office, Southport, England.
37. "England and Wales Birth Registration Index, 1837-2008," database, FamilySearch (https://familysearch.org/ark:/61903/1:1:QVQF-1J12 : 1 October 2014), Elizabeth A Leahy, 1938; from "England & Wales Births, 1837-2006," database, findmypast (http://www.findmypast.com : 2012); citing Birth Registration, Tonbridge, Kent, England, citing General Register Office, Southport, England.
38. "England and Wales Death Registration Index 1837-2007," database, FamilySearch (https://familysearch.org/ark:/61903/1:1:QVZ8-Q7BB : 4 September 2014), Arthur Ronald W Leahy, Apr 1994; from "England & Wales Deaths, 1837-2006," database, findmypast (http://www.findmypast.com : 2012); citing Death Registration, Chichester, Sussex, England, General Register Office, Southport, England.
39. Letter: Alice Bailey to Mildred (Billy) 20 April 1949. Held by Rose Bates.
40. "England and Wales Birth Registration Index, 1837-2008," database, FamilySearch (https://familysearch.org/ark:/61903/1:1:QVQD-143H : 1 October 2014), Gordon M Pugh, 1936; from "England & Wales Births, 1837-2006," database, findmypast (http://www.findmypast.com : 2012); citing Birth Registration, Tonbridge, Kent, England, citing General Register Office, Southport, England.
    (Gordon married and had four children, a son and triplet daughters. – Rose Bates interview, op. cit.)
41. Bair, *Jung*, p. 414.
42. Hakl, *Eranos*, p. 31.
43. Ibid.
44. Bair, *Jung*, p. 470.
45. Hakl, *Eranos*, p. 302.
46. Alice Bailey, "Friday Talk", 1 December 1944, p. 3. PDF at *School for Esoteric Studies*, 2019, Web. 24 September 2019. <http://www.esotericstudies.net/aabtalks/aab12-01-44.pdf>
47. Hakl, *Eranos*, p. 12.
48. Hakl, *Eranos*, p. 27.

49. Hakl, *Eranos*, p. 278.

50. Olav Hammer, *Claiming Knowledge: Strategies of Epistemology from Theosophy to the New Age* (Leiden: Brill, 2003), pp. 65-66.

Sean O'Callaghan, "The Theosophical Christology of Alice Bailey". Olav Hammer and Mikael Rothstein eds., *Handbook of the Theosophical Current*, (Leiden: Brill, 2013), pp. 93-112.

51. Mark Christensen, "From the publisher". Lee Penn, *False Dawn: The United Religions Initiative, Globalism and the Quest for a One-World Religion*, (USA, Sophia Perennis, 2017), *Amazon*, 2019, Web. 14 December 2016, <https://www.amazon.com/False-Dawn-Religions-Initiative-Globalism/dp/159731000X>

52. Penn, *False Dawn*, p. 5.

53. Charles Upton, "Editor's Forward", in *False Dawn,* Lee Penn, pp. 3-4.

54. A discussion of Lee Penn's book, along with detailed material concerning the conspiracy theories surrounding Alice Bailey can be found at <www.isobelblackthorn.com/alicebaileyarticles>

15 The New Group of World Servers

15. THE NEW GROUP OF WORLD SERVERS

1. *The Unfinished Autobiography*, p. 234.

2. Ibid., pp. 230-1.

3. Alice A. Bailey, *Discipleship in the New Age: Volume I*, (New York: Lucis Trust, 1989), pp. 35-40.

4. McGuire, "Summer School", p. 153.

5. "Disciples Who Participated in DK's group work experiments". PDF. *Internet Arcano*, 2019, Web. 29 November 2019. <http://www.internetarcano.org/wp-content/uploads/downloads/2010/02/DINAgroups.pdf>

Also see *Discipleship in the New Age, Vol I and II.*

6. "Disciples Who Participated in DK's group work experiments", op. cit.

7. *Discipleship in the New Age: Volume I*, p. 157.

8. See Letters to Ernest Suffern, LTSK, in *Discipleship in the New Age Vol I*, pp. 595-620, and Vol II, pp. 724-733.

9. *The Unfinished Autobiography*, p. 234.

10. *The Unfinished Autobiography*, p. 235.

11. Alice A. Bailey, *Esoteric Psychology: Volume II*, (New York: Lucis Trust, 1988), p.120.

12. Bailey, *Externalization*, p. 463.

13. Known examples are the Institute of Planetary Synthesis. *Institute of Planetary Synthesis*, Web. 10 November 2019. <https://www.ipsgeneva.com/en/>; The Planetary System. *The Planetary System*, 2019, Web. 10 November 2019. <http://blog-en.theplanetarysystem.org/>; and Twelves, *Twelves*, 2019, Web. 10 November 2019. <http://www.twelvestar.org/>

14. An example of the World Goodwill movement is Sydney Goodwill. Sydney Goodwill, 2019, Web. 10 November 2019. <https://sydneygoodwill.org.au/>

16 Upsets with Helena Roerich

16. UPSETS WITH HELENA ROERICH

1. Sina Fosdick, *My Teachers: Meetings with the Roerichs, Diary Leaves 1922-1934*, (Prescott, AZ: White Mountain Education Association, 2015, Kindle edition). Chapter "America 1922-1923", entry March 23, 1923.
2. Ibid., "India 1928", entry 21 September 1928.
3. Svetoslav Roerich: Pamphlet, "Museum of Religion and Philosophy", p. 4. PDF, held by Agni Yoga Society.
4. Sina Fosdick, *My Teachers: Meetings with the Roerichs,* op. cit., Chapter "America 1929-1930", entry 25 November 1929.
5. Helena Roerich: Letter to New York Agni Yoga group, 9 February 1931, Document No156, p. 92, "E.I. Roerich Epistolary Archive". Roerich Museum, 2019, Web. 31 October 2019. <http://roerichsmuseum.ru/index.php/museum/arkhiv/256-pisma-eir>
6. Ibid.
7. See *The Temple of the People*, 2019, Web. 1 November 2019. <https://www.templeofthepeople.org/>
8. Alice A. Bailey, *A Treatise on White Magic*, p. 429.
9. Helena Roerich: letter to co-workers of the Latvian Roerich Society on the 23rd of August 1934, cited in Lars Adelskogh, "Helena Roerich – A False Messenger of the Planetary Hierarchy", pp. 6-7. PDF, 2019, Web. 2 November 2019.
    <http://livskunskap.dyndns.org/hylozoik/english/Helena%20Roerich%20a%20false%20messenger
    %20of%20the%20planetary%20hierarchy.pdf>
10. John F. Nash, review of *Nicholas & Helena Roerich: The Spiritual Journey of Two Great Artists and Peacemakers*, by Ruth A. Drayer, (Wheaton, IL: Quest Books, 2003/2005), in *The Esoteric Quarterly*, 2015, Web. 4 November 2019. <http://www.esotericquarterly.com/issues/EQ10/EQ1004/EQ100415-End.pdf>
11. Nicholas Roerich: Letter to Alice Bailey, 13 July 1938, p. 2, held by Agni Yoga Society.
12. Ibid.
13. Helena Roerich: Letter dated 16th of September 1951, Moscow, International Roerich Centre, volume 9., cited in Lars Adelskogh, "Helena Roerich – A False Messenger of the Planetary Hierarchy", p7. Op. cit.
14. Ibid.
15. Alice Bailey, "Friday Talk", 28 May 1943, p. 2. PDF at *School for Esoteric Studies*, 2019, Web. 24 September 2019. <http://www.esotericstudies.net/aabtalks/aab05-28-43.pdf>
16. Alice Bailey, "Friday Talk", 19 May 1944, p. 1. PDF at *School for Esoteric Studies*, 2019, Web. 24 September 2019. <http://www.esotericstudies.net/aabtalks/aab05-19-44.pdf>
17. Daniel Entin: Letter to Olga and Andrei, 19 July 2012, "Message board", *Agni Yoga Forum*, 2019, Web. 30 November 2019. <http://agni-yoga-forum.de/>

17. HEADQUARTERS AT TUNBRIDGE WELLS

1. *17 Headquarters at Tunbridge Wells*
   See "Ospringe Place", British Listed Buildings, 2019, Web. 1 December 2019.
   <http://www.britishlistedbuildings.co.uk/en-175928-ospringe-place-faversham-kent/comments#.WKy7QRJ951c>
2. Alice Bailey: letter to Arcane School students, July 1949, unpublished and privately held.
3. Ian Gordon-Brown ed., "World Goodwill Bulletin", 1958, listed in *The New Scientist,* 5 February 1959, p. 300.
4. A 38 Broadwater Down search on the prewar register can be accessed here: <https://www.findmypast.co.uk/>
5. Soloppgangen, "When the Army Came to Stay in WW2" posted on "WW2 People's War: An archive of World War Two memories – written by the public, gathered by the BBC". *BBC,* 2003, Web. 2 December 2019. <https://www.bbc.co.uk/history/ww2peopleswar/stories/50/a2077850.shtml>
6. Alice's granddaughter Elizabeth A. Leahy went on to marry Lieutenant-Colonel Jeremy Richard Parbury Cumberlege in 1960 in Midhurst, Sussex. They had a son Marc Arthur Richard Cumberlege, who married Mary Helen Bury and they have two children, Edward and Nicholas. See "England and Wales Marriage Registration Index, 1837-2005," database, Family-Search (https://familysearch.org/ark:/61903/1:1:QVDY-BTTD : 8 October 2014), Elizabeth A Leahy and null, 1960; from "England & Wales Marriages, 1837-2005," database, findmypast (http://www.findmypast.com : 2012); citing 1960, quarter 2, vol. 5H, p. 959, Midhurst, Sussex, England, General Register Office, Southport, England; and 'Person Page 49732". *The Peerage: A genealogical survey of the peerage of Britain as well as the royal families of Europe,* 2019, We. 2 December 2019. <http://www.thepeerage.com/p49733.htm#i497321>
7. "History Command and Staff College, Quetta". *Command and Staff College, Quetta, Pakistan,* 2015, Web. 2 December 2019. <https://cscquetta.gov.pk/Hist_college.php>
8. Bailey, Esoteric Psychology Vol I, pp. 150-1.
9. Svetoslav Roerich: "Pamphlet, Museum of Religion and Philosophy", p. 10, held by Agni Yoga Society.
10. "Co-Freemasonry", *Theosophy World: Resource Centre,* 2019, Web. 7 December 2019. <https://theosophy.world/fr/node/1623>
11. "Disciples Who Participated in DK's group work experiments", op. cit.
12. PDF: Grand Lodge AUM Original Documents and Statement, uploaded to public Facebook group, August 2020.
13. Svetoslav Roerich: "Pamphlet, Museum of Religion and Philosophy", p. 10, held by Agni Yoga Society.
14. Brian Taves, *Talbot Mundy, Philosopher of Adventure: A Critical Biography,* (Jefferson, NC: McFarland & Company, 2006), p. 158.
15. Keith Bailey, unpublished transcript of undated interview with Kathy Newburn for Seven Rays Institute, c2005. Privately held.

   18 Some Competition

18. SOME COMPETITION

1. Sutcliffe, *Children of the New Age*, op. cit., pp. 34-51.
2. Nicholas Goodrick-Clarke, *The Western Esoteric Traditions: A Historical Introduction*, (Oxford: Oxford University Press, 2008).
   Gareth Knight, *Dion Fortune and the Inner Light*, (Loughborough: Thoth Publications, 2000).
   Alan Richardson, *Priestess: The Life and Magic of Dion Fortune*, new and revised ed. (Loughborough: Thoth Publications, 2007).
3. "I AM movement". *Encyclopedia Britannica*, 2019, Web. 10 October 2019. <https://www.britannica.com/topic/I-AM-movement#ref66356>
4. "The First Ascended Master Organisation". *Light of Christ Truth*, 2018, Web. 10 October 2019. <http://lightofchristtruth.com/Asc_masters/IAM_Mvt.html>
5. See Gerald B. Bryan, *Psychic Dictatorship in America*, (Lulu, 2017); and Charles Samuel Braden, *These also Believe: A study of modern American cults & minority religions*, (London: Macmillan, 1949).
6. Bailey, *The Rays and The Initiations*, p. 16.
   19 The Reappearance of the Christ

19. THE REAPPEARANCE OF THE CHRIST

1. In 2000 the Lucis Trust changed 'Christ' to 'the Coming One' to accommodate the beliefs of multiple faiths.
2. Bailey, *Discipleship in the New Age, Vol II*, p. 149.
3. For the earlier versions, see *Discipleship in the New Age, Vol I*, p. 62 and p. 536. For an extensive analysis on the meaning and nature of the prayer, see Starling David Hunter, *The Compass of Light Vol 1 and II*, (Lulu, 2006). There are at least six known volumes in this series.
4. Morag Zwartz, *The New Age Gospel: Christ or Counterfeit*, (Melbourne: Parenesis, 1987), p. 8.
5. Zwartz, *The New Age Gospel*, pp. 65-6.
6. Bailey, *The Externalization of the Hierarchy*, p. 263.
7. Bailey, *Cosmic Fire*, pp. 564-6.
8. Alice A. Bailey, *Discipleship in the New Age: Vol II*, p. 313.
9. Ibid., pp. 279-280.
10. Alice A. Bailey, *The Reappearance of the Christ* (New York: Lucis Trust, 1996), p. 40.
11. Ibid., p. 149.
12. Ibid., pp. 144-147.
13. Ibid., p. 155.
14. Ibid., p. 158.
15. It is also possible to hold two or more contradictory ideals at once without realising, referred to as cognitive dissonance.
16. Bailey, *Glamour: A World Problem*, (New York: Lucis Trust, 1988), pp. 130-1.

17. In 2007, a Zurich team conducted using complexity theory modelling to unravel who owned the world's major corporations discovered that only 147 global corporations run the world. Described by the authors as a 'super entity', even this network of mostly banks, is comprised of a knot of mutual ownership, investment and representation on boards of directors. See "Revealed: The capitalist network that runs the world". *New Scientist*, 22 October 2011, Web. 13 October 2019.
    <https://www.newscientist.com/article/mg21228354-500-revealed-the-capitalist-network-that-runs-the-world/>
18. Bailey, *Glamour*, p. 72.
19. Bailey, *Externalization*, p. 219.
20. Bailey, *Externalization*, p. 233.
       20 Health in Decline

20. HEALTH IN DECLINE

1. Gordon Pugh, interview conducted by Rose Bates. "Rose Bates: Alice Bailey's Grandson's Memories & Photos". Video of talk at *Seven Ray Institute* Conference 2019, <https://youtu.be/YYDf1cTb6WY>
2. Ibid.
3. Bailey, *Externalisation*, pp. 623-31.
4. Alice Bailey, "Friday Talk", 17 September 1943, p. 1. PDF at *School for Esoteric Studies*, 2019, Web. 24 September 2019. <http://www.esotericstudies.net/aabtalks/aab09-17-43.pdf>
5. Sinclair, *The Alice Bailey Inheritance*, op. cit., p. 74.
6. Obituary: "Mildred Pugh", *Nevada State Journal*, Reno, Nevada, 27 December 1969.
7. Gordon Pugh, interview conducted by Rose Bates. "Rose Bates: Alice Bailey's Grandson's Memories & Photos". Video of talk at *Seven Ray Institute* Conference 2019, <https://youtu.be/YYDf1cTb6WY>
8. Alice Bailey, "Friday Talk", 5 March 1943, p. 2. PDF at *School for Esoteric Studies*, 2019, Web. 24 September 2019. <http://www.esotericstudies.net/aabtalks/aab03-05-43.pdf>
9. Ibid.
10. Alice Bailey, "Friday Talk", 5 March 1943, p. 1. Op. cit.
11. Alice Bailey, "Friday Talk", 10 November 1944, p. 3. PDF at *School for Esoteric Studies*, 2019, Web. 24 September 2019. <http://www.esotericstudies.net/aabtalks/aab11-10-44.pdf>
12. Ibid.
13. Alice Bailey, "Friday Talk", 1 December 1943, p. 7. PDF at *School for Esoteric Studies*, 2019, Web. 24 September 2019. <http://www.esotericstudies.net/aabtalks/aab12-01-44.pdf>
14. Alice Bailey, "Friday Talk", 14 January 1944, p. 8. PDF at *School for Esoteric Studies*, 2019, Web. 24 September 2019. <http://www.esotericstudies.net/aabtalks/aab01-14-44.pdf>

15. Alice Bailey, "Friday Talk", 2 April 1943, p. 5. PDF at *School for Esoteric Studies*, 2019, Web. 24 September 2019. <http://www.esotericstudies.net/aabtalks/aab04-02-43.pdf>
16. Alice Bailey, "Friday Talk", 7 January 1944, p. 1. PDF at *School for Esoteric Studies*, 2019, Web. 24 September 2019. <http://www.esotericstudies.net/aabtalks/aab01-07-44.pdf>
17. Alice Bailey, "Friday Talk", 31 March 1944. PDF at *School for Esoteric Studies*, 2019, Web. 24 September 2019. <http://www.esotericstudies.net/aabtalks/aab03-31-44.pdf>
18. Mary Bailey, *A Learning Experience*, (New York: Lucis Trust, 1990), p. 15.
19. Alice Bailey, "Friday Talk", 5 November 1943, p. 1. PDF at *School for Esoteric Studies*, 2019, Web. 24 September 2019. <http://www.esotericstudies.net/aabtalks/aab11-05-43.pdf>
20. Alice Bailey, "Friday Talk", 18 May 1945, p. 1. PDF at *School for Esoteric Studies*, 2019, Web. 24 September 2019. <http://www.esotericstudies.net/aabtalks/aab05-18-45.pdf>
21. Alice Bailey, "Friday Talk", 20 April 1945, p. 15. PDF at *School for Esoteric Studies*, 2019, Web. 24 September 2019. <http://www.esotericstudies.net/aabtalks/aab04-20-45.pdf>
22. Bailey, *Discipleship in the New Age, Vol II*, p. 148.
23. Bailey, *The Rays and The Initiations*, p. 237.
24. Bailey, *Externalization*, p. 190.
25. Bailey, *Externalization*, p. 191.
26. Bailey, *The Rays and The Initiations*, p. 747.
27. Alice A. Bailey, *Telepathy and the Etheric Vehicle* (New York: Lucis Trust, 2001)), pp. 4-5.
28. Bailey, *Externalization*, p. 448.
29. Transcript of interview with Gordon Pugh, conducted by Rose Bates, in which he states that Alice Bailey and Eleanor Roosevelt corresponded with some regularity. Also see "Rose Bates: Alice Bailey's Grandson's Memories & Photos". Video of talk at *Seven Ray Institute* Conference 2019, <https://youtu.be/YYDf1cTb6WY>
30. Bailey, *Glamour*, p. 163.
31. Bailey, *Problems of Humanity*, pp. 176-178.
32. Alice A. Bailey, *The Destiny of the Nations*, p. 174.
33. Ibid., p. 179.
34. Bailey, *Externalization*, p. 342.
35. It should be noted that there is some speculation within the Alice Bailey community regarding how much of the material taken down in these final years came through purely from the Tibetan and how much was her own thinking. Her detractors are quick to demolish the entire corpus on the strength of a few perhaps ill-conceived opinions concerning the use of the atomic bomb, Zionism and the Jewish people, and on race that were expressed by a woman who was distressed and infirm and anxious to complete the work before her death, an occultist with all of the various assumed opinions of her era and class. These contentious remarks circulate widely on the internet and the author has chosen to omit them from the current work. Such opinions are in no way representative of her opus.

36. Bailey, *The Rays and The Initiations*, pp. 679-680.
37. Ibid., p. 681.
38. Bailey, *Externalization*, p. 640.
39. Bailey, *Externalization*, p. 626.
40. Bailey, *The Unfinished Autobiography*, p. ix.
41. Resume: Frank Hilton F.C.I.I. unpublished PDF, School for Esoteric Studies, privately held. Cited 13 September 2019.
42. Alice Bailey: letter to Arcane School students, July 1949, unpublished and privately held.
43. Ibid.
44. *The Unfinished Autobiography*, p. x.
    21 Applicants at the Portal

21. APPLICANTS AT THE PORTAL

1. Bailey, *Discipleship in the New Age, Vol II*, p. 84.
2. Ibid.
3. Mary Bailey, *A Learning Experience*, p. 85.
4. Mildred Pugh: Goodwill Study Sets I-IV, Rose Bates collection. <www.alice-baileyarchives.com>
5. Foster Bailey: Letter to Mildred 25 April 1949. Rose Bates collection. Ibid.
6. Mildred Bailey: Letters privately held. These details of Mildred's role in those years were divulged to me in a telephone conversation and a Facebook message exchange in October 2019. Access to these letters is restricted.
7. Ibid.
8. Bailey, *Externalisation of the Hierarchy*, p. 641.
9. Mary Bailey, *A Learning Experience*, p. 86.
10. Bailey, *The Unfinished Autobiography*, p. 302.
11. Bailey, *Discipleship in the New Age, Vol II*, p. 86.
12. Foster Bailey: letter, February 1971, in Mary Bailey, *A Learning Experience*, p. 15.
13. Alice Bailey, "Friday Talk", 4 January 1946, p. 4. PDF at *School for Esoteric Studies*, 2019, Web. 24 September 2019. <http://www.esotericstudies.net/aabtalks/aab01-04-46.pdf>
14. "United States Census, 1900," database with images, *FamilySearch* (https://familysearch.org/ark:/61903/1:1:MMBR-RDM : accessed 24 September 2019), Marian Bath in household of Edwin H Bath, Center Township Muncie city Ward 4, Delaware, Indiana, United States; citing enumeration district (ED) 36, sheet 11B, family 267, NARA microfilm publication T623 (Washington, D.C.: National Archives and Records Administration, 1972.); FHL microfilm 1,240,367.
15. "New York, New York Passenger and Crew Lists, 1909, 1925-1957," database with images, *FamilySearch* (https://familysearch.org/ark:/61903/1:1:24L4-FNK : 12 March 2018), Marian Bath Walter, 1939; citing Immigration, New York, New York, United States, NARA microfilm publication T715 (Washington, D.C.: National Archives and Records Administration, n.d.).
    And "United States Census, 1940," database with

images, *FamilySearch* (https://familysearch.org/ark:/61903/1:1:KQSV-1JQ : 27 July 2019), Marian Walter in household of Leo Rohn Walter, Assembly District 12, Manhattan, New York City, New York, New York, United States; citing enumeration district (ED) 31-1000, sheet 18A, line 3, family 520, Sixteenth Census of the United States, 1940, NARA digital publication T627. Records of the Bureau of the Census, 1790 - 2007, RG 29. Washington, D.C.: National Archives and Records Administration, 2012, roll 2648.

16. Bailey, *Discipleship in the New Age, Vol I*, p. 638.
17. Ibid., pp. 643-4.
18. Bailey, *Discipleship in the New Age, Vol II*, p. 737.
19. Ibid., p. 738.
20. Ibid., p. 739.
21. Ibid.
22. Ibid., p. 740.
23. Ibid, p. 741.
24. Ibid, p. 745.
25. Ibid., p. 743.
26. Ibid., p. 746.
27. Ibid., p.749.
28. Letter from Regina Keller to Priscilla H., 11 November 1952 [unpublished]. Held by School for Esoteric Studies.
29. Extract from *The Rays and The Initiations*, p. 179, quoted in a letter from Frank Hilton to Marian Walter, 2 November 1950 [unpublished]. Held by School for Esoteric Studies.
30. Letter from Foster Bailey to Marian Walter, 26 June 1953 [unpublished]. Held by School for Esoteric Studies.
31. Ibid.
32. Marian Walter: "Applicants at the Portal", Study Set II, p. 31. (March 1952). PDF, *International Wisdom Synthesis Center*, 2019, Web. 20 October 2019. <www.monadmonadmonad.wordpress.com>
33. Regina Keller: letter to Priscilla, 11 November 1952 [unpublished]. Held by School for Esoteric Studies.
34. This matter is referred to in a letter dated 6 October 1952, and signed by Frank Hilton, Regina Keller, Joseph Lovejoy and Florence Garrigue [unpublished]. Held by School for Esoteric Studies.
35. Regina Keller: Letter to Priscilla, 11 November 1952 [unpublished]. Held by School for Esoteric Studies.
36. Regina Keller: letter to Priscilla, 11 November 1952 [unpublished]. Held by School for Esoteric Studies.
37. Letter from Foster Bailey to Marian Walter, dated 26 June 1953 [unpublished]. Held by School for Esoteric Studies.
38. It is claimed that there exists a letter from DK appointing Marian Walter head of Applicants at the Portal which Foster would presumably have been aware of. The author has not seen this letter but is assured it exists.
39. Letter from Regina Keller to Priscilla H, 28 June 1953 [unpublished]. Held by School for Esoteric Studies.
40. Bailey, *Discipleship in the New Age Vol I*, p. 571.

41. Also listed are Ayrel Bell, Michael Kaprilian, Hazel Rasmussen, Hilda Dean Going, Louise Crouse, E.O. Smith, Violet Cavell, Clarence Bush, Dorothy Blalock, Marie Marstbaum, Wei Tat, Dorothy Grayson, and Zeltie Todd. Based on a photograph given to Maureen Temple Richmond by Marion Crusselle of the Center for World Servers.

42. Marian Walter: Letter, October 1953, "Applicants at the Portal", Set III, p. 114. PDF, *International Wisdom Synthesis Center*, 2019, Web. 20 October 2019. <www.monadmonadmonad.wordpress.com>

43. Ibid., p. 115.

44. Ibid., p. 116.

45. Ibid., p. 123.

46. For example, a letter in Applicants at the Portal Study Set VIII is taken from the Tibetan's Ashram Series 33, dated April-August 1944.

47. Marian Walter: Letter to Applicants at the Portal, March 1952, in "Applicants at the Portal", Study Set II, p. 30. PDF, *International Wisdom Synthesis Center*, 2019, Web. 20 October 2019. <www.monadmonadmonad.wordpress.com>

48. Bailey, *The Rays and The Initiations*, pp. 511-3 corresponds to Applicants at the Portal Study Set II D, p. 48.

49. Marian Walter: Letter to Applicants at the Portal, Study Set III, October 1953, p. 115. PDF, *International Wisdom Synthesis Center*, 2019, Web. 20 October 2019. <www.monadmonadmonad.wordpress.com>

50. Marian Walter: Letter to Applicants at the Portal, February 1955, Study Set V, p. 246. Op. cit.

51. Ibid., p. 254.

52. Marian Walter: Letter to Applicants at the Portal, July 1955, Study Set VII, p. 373. Op. cit.

53. 'When man has taken the third initiation and consciously mounted the cardinal cross he is then released from the rule of Saturn and comes under the influence of Venus, ruler of the Hierarchy of Crocodiles.' (Applicants at the Portal Study Set VII, p. 417.) This should read:

    'When he has taken the third initiation and can consciously mount the Cardinal Cross, he is then released from the ruling of Saturn and comes under the influence of Venus, who is governor or ruler of the Hierarchy which is that of the Crocodiles.' (Alice A. Bailey, *Esoteric Astrology*, (New York: Lucis Trust, 1974), p. 163.)

    There is a difference between 'consciously mounted' and 'can consciously mount' and between a 'hierarchy of crocodiles' and 'the Hierarchy which is that of the Crocodiles', a reference to the Hindu myth of the legendary sea-creature Makara, half-terrestrial animal, half aquatic, and the glyph of Capricorn.

54. Marian Walter: Letter to Applicants at the Portal, July 1955, Study Set VII, p. 380.

55. Marian Walter: Letter to Applicants at the Portal, July 1955, Study Set VII, p. 371.

56. Ibid.

57. Mary Bailey, *A Learning Experience*, p. 80-1.
    22 The School for Esoteric Studies

22. THE SCHOOL FOR ESOTERIC STUDIES

1. Bailey, *The Rays and The Initiations*, p .759-60.
2. See "World Invocation Day". *Lucis Trust*, 2019, Web. 16 October 2019. <https://www.lucistrust.org/the_great_invocation/wid>
3. Mary Bailey, *A Learning Experience*, p. 74.
4. Mary Bailey, *Learning*, p. 86.
5. Ibid.
6. Bailey, *Discipleship in the New Age Vol I*, p. 169.
7. Ibid., p. 170.
8. Bailey, *Discipleship in the New Age Vol II*, p. 594.
9. Ibid.
10. Bailey, *Discipleship in the New Age Vol II*, p. 595.
11. Excerpt of Letter from Foster Bailey, 8 March 1954 [unpublished]. Held by School for Esoteric Studies.
12. Regina Keller: Letter to Foster Bailey, 27 April 1954, p.1 [unpublished]. Held by School for Esoteric Studies.
13. Regina Keller: Letter to Foster Bailey, 27 April 1954, p. 2 [unpublished]. Held by School for Esoteric Studies.
14. Ibid.
15. Regina Keller: Letter to Foster Bailey, 27 April 1954, pp. 2-8, [unpublished]. Held by School for Esoteric Studies.
16. Regina Keller: Letter to Foster Bailey, 30 April 1954 [unpublished]. Held by School for Esoteric Studies.
17. Foster Bailey: Letter to membership, 18 June 1954 [unpublished]. Held by School for Esoteric Studies.
18. Foster Bailey: Letter to Trustees, 7 March 1956 [unpublished]. Held by School for Esoteric Studies.
19. Regina Keller: Memorandum to Frank Hilton, 7 January 1954 [unpublished]. Held by School for Esoteric Studies.
20. Foster Bailey: Letter to Trustees, 17 February 1956 [unpublished]. Held by School for Esoteric Studies.
21. Foster Bailey: letter to Roberto Assagioli, 5 March 1956 [unpublished]. Held by School for Esoteric Studies.
22. Foster Bailey: letter to Trustees, 7 March 1956 [unpublished]. Held by School for Esoteric Studies.
23. Letter from Foster Bailey to 'friends', 24 April 1956 [unpublished]. Held by School for Esoteric Studies.
24. Foster Bailey: Letter to Regina Keller, 27 February 1962, [unpublished]. Held by School for Esoteric Studies.
25. "Mission and History of the School". *School for Esoteric Studies*, 2019, We. 12 November 2019. <http://www.esotericstudies.net/mission.html>
26. Regina Keller had also recorded and ptbed Alice Bailey's Friday talks (held 1943-1946), which have been made available on the School of Esoteric Studies' website.
27. "Mission and History of the School". *School for Esoteric Studies*, 2019, We. 12 November 2019. <http://www.esotericstudies.net/mission.html>

28. "History of Meditation Mount". *Meditation Mount*, 2019, Web. 23 November 2019. <https://meditationmount.org/history/>

29. Maureen Temple Richmond, *Studies in the Esoteric Astrology of Alice Bailey: Ray Analysis and Astrological Life Guidance Direct from the Master to an Advancing Disciple*, 2018, p. 19. PDF.

30. Foster Bailey: Letter to Frank Hilton, 30 June 1976, [unpublished]. Held by School for Esoteric Studies.

31. Foster Bailey: Letter to Frank Hilton, 11 May 1977, [unpublished]. Held by School for Esoteric Studies.

32. *The Esoteric Quarterly*, 2019, Web. 1 December 2019. <http://esotericquarterly.com/about/index.htm>

33. "Mission and History of the School". *School for Esoteric Studies*, 2019, We. 12 November 2019. <http://www.esotericstudies.net/mission.html>

34. Gail Jolley (executive director of the School for Esoteric Studies): Email to Isobel Blackthorn, 23 October 2019.
    23 Roberto Assagioli

23. ROBERTO ASSAGIOLI

1. Alice Bailey, "Friday Talk", 14 April 1944, p. 5. PDF at *School for Esoteric Studies*, 2019, Web. 24 September 2019. <http://www.esotericstudies.net/aabtalks/aab04-14-44.pdf>

2. Ibid.

3. "About Us". *Psychosynthesis Trust*, 2019, Web. 20 October 2019. <https://psychosynthesistrust.org.uk/about-psychosynthesis-trust/>

4. Kenneth Sørensen and Hanne Birkholm, "Roberto Assagioli – His Life and Work, a biography". *Kenneth Sørensen*, 02/06/2017, Web. 17 October 2019. <https://kennethsorensen.dk/en/roberto-assagioli-his-life-and-work/>

5. Ibid.

6. Al Mankoff, "Roberto Assagioli, Psychosynthesis, and the Esoteric Roots of Transpersonal Psychology". *Kenneth Sørensen*, 01/02/2019, Web. 17 October 2019. <https://kennethsorensen.dk/en/roberto-assagioli-psychosynthesis-and-the-esoteric-roots-of-transpersonal-psychology/>

7. Bailey, *Discipleship in the New Age Vol II*, p. 459.

8. Bailey, *Discipleship in the New Age Vol II*, p. 465.

9. Maureen Temple Richmond, *Studies in the Esoteric Astrology of Alice Bailey: Ray Analysis and Astrological Life Guidance Direct from the Master to an Advancing Disciple*, 2018, p. 19. PDF

10. "The Group for Creative Meditation: Another Roberto Assagioli Legacy", p. 5. PDF. *Meditation Mount*, 2019, Web. 18 October 2019. <https://meditationmount.org/wp-content/uploads/2017/01/History-of-Creative-Meditation.pdf>

11. Ibid., p. 3.

12. Al Mankoff, "Roberto Assagioli, Psychosynthesis, and the Esoteric Roots of Transpersonal Psychology". *Kenneth Sørensen*, 01/02/2019, Web. 17 October 2019. <https://kennethsorensen.dk/en/roberto-assagioli-psychosynthesis-and-the-esoteric-roots-of-transpersonal-psychology/>

13. "A Training Course in Creative Meditation". *Creative Group Meditation*, 2019, Web. 20 October 2109. <https://www.creativegroupmeditation.org/training-events>

14. A fuller biography of Ian Gordon-Brown can be found at: "Ian Gordon-Brown: in memory of a person on influence". *Laetus in praesens*, 12 December 2016, Web. 21 October 2019.
    <https://www.laetusinpraesens.org/guests/iangb/igb.php>

15. Barbara Somers, "Centre Profile: The Centre for Transpersonal Psychology". *Self & Society: An International Journal for Humanistic Psychology* Vol 26, 1998, Issue 5, 5 November 1998. <https://www.tandfonline.com/doi/abs/10.1080/03060497.1998.11085887?journalCode=rsel20>
    "History of CTP". *Centre for Transpersonal Psychology*, 2014, Web. 21 October 2019.
    <http://www.transpersonalcentre.co.uk/index.php/history-of-ctp>
    and "Ian Gordon-Brown 1925-1996". *Transpersonal Perspectives: the power of the transpersonal*, 2019, Web. 21 October 2019. <http://transpersonalperspectives.org/ian-gordon-brown-1925-1996/>

16. Nigel Wellings, Elizabeth Wilde McCormick, *Transpersonal Psychotherapy*, (New York: Sage, 2012), p. 2.
    24 The United Nations

24. THE UNITED NATIONS

1. Mary Bailey, *A Learning Experience*, pp. 81-2.
2. Foster Bailey wrote numerous articles in his lifetime. He also wrote the following volumes:
    Changing Esoteric Values. Tunbridge Wells, Kent: Lucis Press, 1955.
    The Spirit of Masonry (Tunbridge Wells, Kent: Lucis Press 1957), a compilation of DK teachings on masonry written down by Alice Bailey;
    Running God's Plan (New York: Lucis Press, 1972);
    Things to Come (New York: Lucis Press,1974);
    Reflections. (New York: Lucis Press, 1979).
3. See "About the Aquarian Age Community". *The Aquarian Age Community*, 2019, Web. 1 December 2019. <http://www.aquaac.org/about/about.html>
4. See Margaret McGurn, *Global Spirituality: Planetary Consciousness in the thought of Teilhard de Chardin and Robert Muller*, (World Happiness and Cooperation, 1981).
5. "Secretary-General's remarks at Memorial Service for Robert Muller". 11 March 2011. United Nations, Web. 15 December 2019. <https://www.un.org/sg/en/content/sg/statement/2011-03-11/secretary-generals-remarks-memorial-service-robert-muller-delivered>
6. Alice Bailey, *Education in the New Age*, (New York: Lucis Trust, 1987), p. x.
7. Ibid., p. 107.
8. A basic outline of the World Core Curriculum can be found at: "The World Core Curriculum". *UNESCO*, 2019, Web. 1 December 2019.
    <http://www.unesco.org/education/tlsf/mods/theme_c/popups/mod18t01s03.html>; and

"World Core Curriculum". *Robert Muller*, Web. 1 December 2019. <http://robertmuller.org/rm/R1/World_Core_Curriculum.html>

9. Gloria Cook is also the and author of *Trans-dimensional Daughter*, (Xlibris, 2014).

10. "Robert Muller Schools International". *The School of Ageless Wisdom*, Web. 1 December 2019. <http://www.theschoolofagelesswisdom.org/rms/>

11. Robert Muller, *New Genesis: Shaping a global spirituality* (New York: Doubleday, 1982); and "Biography". *Robert Muller*, Web. 1 December 2019. <http://robertmuller.org/rm/R1/Biography.html>

12. Donald Keys, *Earth At Omega: Passage to Planetization*, (Wellesley, MA: Branden publishing company, 1983), p. 81.

13. "Planetary Citizens". *Source Watch: The Center for Media and Democracy*, 2014, Web. 1 December 2019.
    <https://www.sourcewatch.org/index.php/Planetary_Citizens#cite_note-4>

14. See "Spirituality and the United Nations". *The Aquarian Age Community*, 2019, Web. 1 December 2019.
    <http://www.aquaac.org/un/sprtatun.html>

15. For some interesting speculations on the creation of the Meditation Room and Alice Bailey's possible influence, see my book, *The Unlikely Occultist: A biographical novel of Alice A. Bailey*.

16. U Thant, "The Making and Building of Peace". *The Beacon*, Vol 41 Issue 7, January/February 1966, p. 222.
    U Thant, "What Could We Build If We Worked Together". *The Beacon*, Volume 42 Issue 5, September/October 1967, p. 158.
    U Thant, "The United Nations and Human Rights". *The Beacon*, Volume 42 Issue 11, September/October 1968, p. 349.
    U Thant, "Trade, Aid and People". *The Beacon*, Volume 42 Issue 12, November/December 1968, p. 370.
    U Thant, "Message for Youth". *The Beacon*, Volume 43 Issue 12, November/December 1970, p 383.
    U Thant, "The United Nations: Crisis of Authority". *The Beacon*, Volume 44 Issue 2, March/April 1971, p. 56.
    U Thant, "The United Nations and the Human Environment". *The Beacon*, Volume 44 Issue 10, July/August 1972, p. 314.
    The above references were sourced from:
    "The Beacon 1922 – continuing, New York, Lucis Trust, Foster Bailey". "Union Index of Theosophical Periodicals". *Theosophical Society of Australia*, 2018, Web. 29 November 2019.
    <http://www.austheos.org.au/indices/BEACON.HTM>
    There is no indication that the Lucis Trust plans to digitise back copies of *The Beacon* and make them available for researchers online.

17. McLaughlin and Davidson, *Spiritual Politics: Changing the World From Inside Out*, (New York: Ballantine Books, 1994), p. 315.

18. McLaughlin and Davidson, *Spiritual Politics*, p. 317.

19. see *Spiritual Caucus at the United Nations*, 2019, Web. 1 December 2019. <http://www.spiritualcaucusun.org>

20. "Nancy B. Roof". *Kosmos: Journal for global transformation*, 2019, Web. 1 December 2019. <http://www.kosmosjournal.org/contributor/nancy-b-roof/>

21. see "Marcia S. Moore Collection, 1948-1999". *Concord Library*, 2016, Web. 1 December 2019. <https://concordlibrary.org/special-collections/fin aids/moore>; and "Robert and Eleanor Moore Collection, 1943-1963". *Concord Library*, 2016, Web. 1 December 2019. <https://concordlibrary.org/special-collections/fin_aids/moore_r_e>

22. Author, yoga teacher and astrologer Marcia Moore experimented with various psycho-stimulants. She experimented with ketamine with her fourth husband Howard Alltounian and died in mysterious circumstances in 1979 at age 50. Her body was discovered two years later in woods near her home in Washington. Suicide or an overdose were suspected but the cause of death remains unsolved. She was also the wife of well-known astrologer Louis S. Acker.

23. Robert S. Ellwood, *Islands of the Dawn: The Story of Alternative Spirituality in New Zealand* (Kolowalu: University of Hawaii Press, 1993).

24. See "United Nations Days & Years Meditation Initiative: Steve Nation". *Intuition in Service*, 2014, Web. 1 December 2019. <http://www.intuition-in-service.org/stevenation.cfm>

25. See Lifebridge Foundation, Web. 1 December 2019. <http://www.lifebridge.org/>; and

26. "Barbara Valocore". *Kosmos: Journal for global transformation*, 2019, Web. 1 December 2019.
<https://www.kosmosjournal.org/contributor/barbara-valocore/>
see "Upcoming Event – August". *Creative Group Meditation*, 2019, Web. 1 December 2019. <https://www.creativegroupmeditation.org/training-events/upcoming-event-31-8-2019>; and "Tara Stuart". *Kosmos: Journal for global transformation*, 2019, Web. 1 December 2019. <https://www.kosmosjournal.org/contributor/tara-stuart/>

27. "Avon Mattison". *Kosmos: Journal for global transformation*, 2019, Web. 1 December 2019.
<https://www.kosmosjournal.org/contributor/avon-mattison/>

28. see *The Source of Synergy Foundation*, 2009, Web. 1 December 2019. <http://sourceofsynergyfoundation.org/>
25 The New Age Movement

25. THE NEW AGE MOVEMENT

1. Alexander, K., "Roots of the New Age". Lewis, J.R., and Melton, G., (eds), *Perspectives on the New Age*, (State University of New York Press, Albany, 1992), pp. 30-47.
Bednarowski, M.F., "Literature of the New Age: A Review of Representative Sources". *Religious Studies Review*, Vol 17/3, 1991, pp. 209-216.

2. see Steven Sutcliffe, "Wandering Stars': Seekers and Gurus in the Modern World", *in*, Sutcliffe, S., and Bowman, M., (eds), *Beyond New Age: Exploring*

Alternative Spirituality, (Edinburgh: Edinburgh University Press, 2000) pp. 17-36.

Steven Sutcliffe, "Category Formation and the History of the 'New Age'". *Culture and Religion*, Volume 4 Issue 1, 2003, pp. 5-29.

Dick Anthony and Bruce Ecker, "The Anthony Typology: A Framework for Assessing Spiritual and Consciousness Groups". Ken Wilber, Dick Anthony and Bruce Ecker, (eds), *Spiritual Choices*, (New York: Paragon House, 1987), pp. 35-91.

Harold Bloom, *Omens of Millennium: The Gnosis of Angels, Dreams, and Resurrection*, (London: Fourth Estate, 1996).

Kevin Tingay, "Madame Blavatsky's Children: Theosophy and Its Heirs", *in* Steven Sutcliffe and Marion Bowman, (eds), *Beyond New Age: Exploring Alternative Spirituality*, (Edinburgh: Edinburgh University Press, 2000), pp. 37-50.

3. Marilyn Ferguson, *The Aquarian Conspiracy: Personal and Social Transformation in the 1980s* (London: Paladin, 1982), p. 23.

4. Marilyn Ferguson, *The Aquarian Conspiracy: Personal and Social Transformation in the 1980s*, (London: Paladin Grafton Books, 1980), p. 30.

5. see Kay Alexander, "Roots of the New Age". James Lewis and Gordon Melton (eds.), *Perspectives on the New Age*, (Albany: State University of New York Press, 1992), pp. 30-47.

6. Steven Sutcliffe, *Children of the New: A History of Spiritual Practices* (London: Routledge, 2003) p. 14.

7. Bailey, *From Intellect to Intuition*, p. 45.

8. Bailey, *A Treatise on White Magic*, p. 135.

9. Steven Sutcliffe and Marion Bowman (eds.), *Beyond the New Age: Exploring Alternative Spirituality*, op. cit.

10. Bailey, *Autobiography*, pp. 90-1.

11. Ibid., p. 89.

12. Ibid., p. 151.

13. Kurt Leland, *Rainbow Body: A History of the Western Chakra System from Blavatsky to Brennan* (Lake Worth, FL: Ibis Press, 2016), p. 94.

14. Leland, *Rainbow Body*, p. 131.

15. Ibid., pp. 215-9 and p. 385.

16. "Vera Stanley Alder". *Academic Dictionaries and Encyclopedias*, 2019, Web. 2 December 2019. <https://enacademic.com/dic.nsf/enwiki/9475828>

17. Ibid.

18. Bailey, *Discipleship in the New Age Vol I*, p. 131.

19. Leland, *Rainbow Body*, p. 224.

20. Ibid., p. 221.

21. Ibid., p. 225.

22. Ibid., pp. 357- 385.

23. Ibid., p. 385.

24. Ibid., p. 390.

25. Nicholas Campion, *The New Age in the Modern West: Counterculture, Utopia and Prophecy from the Late Eighteenth Century to the Present Day*, (London: Bloomsbury, 2015), p. 126.

26. See *The Lorian Association*, 2019, Web. 1 December 2019. <https://lorian.org/>

27. See "About the Findhorn Association". Findhorn Foundation, 2019, Web. 1 December 2019. <https://www.findhorn.org/aboutus/community/>

28. for a full account of a week at Findhorn see Sutcliffe, *Children of the New Age*, op. cit., pp.154-170.

29. Ibid., p. 139.

30. William Bloom (ed.), *Soulution: The Holistic Manifesto*, (California: Hay House, 2004); and William Bloom, *The New Age: An Anthology of Essential Writings* (London: Rider, 1991).

31. McLaughlin and Davidson, *Spiritual Politics*, p. 20.

32. Global Ecovillage Network, 2009, Web. 1 December 2019. <https://ecovillage.org/about/about-gen/>

33. *The Institute for Planetary Synthesis*, 2018, Web. 1 December 2019. <https://www.ipsgeneva.com/en/>

34. See *Hechal*, 2019, Web. 1 December 2019. <http://hechal.org/>

35. *Planetary Citizens: One Earth, One Humanity, One Destiny*, 2019, Web. 1 December 2019. <http://planetarycitizens.net/about-planetary-citizens/>
26 An Adversary and an Enthusiast

26. AN ADVERSARY AND AN ENTHUSIAST

1. One example is Darshan with the Messenger Elizabeth Clare Prophet, *The Work of the Adepts and the Teachings of the Seven Rays* which draws on Charles W. Leadbeater's *The Masters and the Path*

2. Phillip Charles Lucas, Foreword. Erin Prophet, *Prophet's Daughter: My Life with Elizabeth Clare Prophet Inside the Church Universal and Triumphant*, (Lanham, Maryland: Rowman and Littlefield, 2008), p. x.

3. "Teachings of the Ascended Masters", *Summit Lighthouse*, 2019, Web. 1 December 2019. <https://www.summitlighthouse.org/teachings-of-the-ascended-masters/>

4. Wikipedia provides a comparative tabulation of the seven rays and their various correspondences from Alice Bailey and The Summit Lighthouse on their Summit Lighthouse page. The two tables make for interesting reading. Evident in Prophet's version is her evangelism, each ray is 'of God'. Each ray has a location, a gemstone and a day of the week. Situating the two widely different streams and their respective tables together in a single discussion of the rays under the heading of New Age Teachings, with Leadbeater enjoying the higher ground of the preceding paragraph as having been a prime Theosophical mover, demotes Alice Bailey and suggests an equivalence of depth and integrity with Prophet. <https://en.wikipedia.org/wiki/Seven_rays#The_Summit_Lighthouse[51]>

5. Elizabeth Clare Prophet, *Pearls of Wisdom*, Vol. 19, no. 5.
   (Corwin Springs, MT: Summit University Press, 1976) cited in <http://www.alpheus.org/html/source_materials/krishnamurti/kh_on_k.html>

6. "Lady Master Clare de Lis". *The Hearts Center Community*, 2019, Web. 1 December 2019.

<https://www.heartscenter.org/TeachingsBlogs/AscendedMasters/ElizabethClareProphet-GuruMa/tabid/1159/Default.aspx#.XeM7HZMzZz8>
7. Bailey, *Esoteric Psychology, Volume II*, p. 347.
8. Ibid., p. 396.
9. Foundation for Inner Peace, 2019, Web. 1 December 2019. <http://www.acim.org/Scribing/about_scribes.html>
10. Olav Hammer, *Claiming Knowledge: Strategies of Epistemology from Theosophy to the New Age*, (Leiden: Brill, 2004), p. xiii.
11. "Benjamin Creme: a messenger of hope". *Share International*, 2019, Web. 1 December 2019.
    <http://www.share-international.org/background/bcreme/bc_main.htm>
12. Pastor Hal Mayer, "New Age Prophet Benjamin Creme Dies At Age 93", *Keep the Faith*, November 2016, Web. 1 December 2019. <https://ktfnews.com/new-age-prophet-benjamin-creme-dies-age-93/>
    27 Cedercrans and Laurency

27. CEDERCRANS AND LAURENCY

1. See "About Lucille". *Dakini Wisdom*, 2019, Web. 1 December 2019. <http://www.dakini-wisdom.com/AboutLucille.htm>
    Victor Dutro, "An Esoteric Profile" (Great Quest 02 DHY paper, 2014). PDF. *Morya Federation*, 2019, Web. 1 December 2019. <http://www.moryafederation.com/wp-content/uploads/2015/01/Lucille-Cedercrans1.pdf>
2. Zachary F. Lansdowne, "Cedercrans' Writings Compared to Bailey's Technique of Integration for the Seventh Ray". PDF. *The Esoteric Quarterly*, Spring 2015, pp. 39-63.
3. See Dutro, "An Esoteric Profile". op. cit.
4. Bailey, *Discipleship in the New Age Vol II*, p. 597.
5. Landsdowne, op. cit., p. 60.
6. Ibid.
7. "Introduction to the Works of Henry T. Laurency". *Laurency*, 2019, Web. 1 December. <https://www.laurency.com/introduc.htm>
8. Bailey, *A Treatise on White Magic*, p. 79.
9. Håkan Blomqvist, "The Henry T. Laurency esoteric legacy". *Håkan Blomqvist's Blog*, January 6, 2014, Web. 1 December 2019. <https://ufoarchives.blogspot.com/2014/01/the-henry-t-laurency-legacy.html>
10. Ibid.
11. Henry T. Laurency, *Knowledge of Life Three*, translated from the Swedish by Kent Hammarstrand and Lars Adelskogh, Sweden: Henry T. Laurency Publishing Foundation 2006), p. 3.
12. Ibid.

13. Lars Adelskogh, "Helena Roerich – A False Messenger of the Planetary Hierarchy". PDF. <http://livskunskap.dyndns.org/hylozoik/english/Helena%20Roerich%20a%20false%20messenger
%20of%20the%20planetary%20hierarchy.pdf>
28 Documents

28. DOCUMENTS

1. Bailey, *Discipleship in the New Age: Volume II*, p. 701.
2. Geoffrey Logie: interview with Isobel Blackthorn, October 2019.
3. Ibid.
4. see PDF: Grand Lodge AUM Original Documents and Statement, uploaded to a public Facebook group, August 2020.
5. Regina Keller: Letter to Priscilla, 11 November 1952 [unpublished]. Held by School for Esoteric Studies.
6. Keith Bailey: transcript of interview with Kathy Newburn. Op. cit.
7. Ibid.
8. Chris Adams, *The Grail Guitar: The Search for Jimi Hendrix's Purple Haze Telecaster*, (Lanham, Maryland: Rowman & Littlefield Publishers, 2016), pp. 191-194.
    And <https://keithbailey.net/parent-page/about/keith-bailey-biography/>
9. *Maitreya School and Healing Centre*, Web. 1 December 2019. <http://www.maitreyaschoolandhealingcentre.org.uk/>
10. "Cornford, Lily". *Kate Bush Encyclopedia*, 2019, Web. 1 December 2019. <https://www.katebushencyclopedia.com/cornford-lily>
11. Keith Bailey: transcript of interview with Kathy Newburn. Op. cit.
12. Ibid.
13. <http://www.grandlodgeaum.org/>
14. This information was given to the author by the AUM Grand Lodge. No such documents have been seen by the author.
15. *RWB Kevin Townley*, 2019, Web. 1 December 2019. <http://townley.mwglco.org/>
16. Circular posted at *Masonic Forum of Light*, 2005, Web. 1 December 2019. <http://staffs.proboards.com/thread/1372/dk-alice-bailey-russell>
17. PDF: Michael D. Robbins letter to Isobel Blackthorn dated 11 August 2020.
18. Geoffrey Logie: Message exchange with Isobel Blackthorn, 21 September 2019.
19. I have chosen to withhold the identities of members of The Polaris Project, a Yahoo forum that ran between 2005 -2010, to prevent further damage.
20. Stephen Pugh: private conversation with Isobel Blackthorn.
21. John Cobb: Message posted on The Polaris Project, c2005.
22. Two attempts were made to contact Michael Robbins by email.
23. Alice Bailey: Letter to Roberto Assagioli, February 1940, uncited and from an unverified source presumed to be the portion of the Marian Walter codicil papers currently in the possession of Michael Robbins and Keith Bailey.

24. This matter was aired on The Polaris Project.
25. Michael Robbins, "The Jewish Group: DK's letters to Roberto Assagioli". *Esoteric Astrologer*, 2019, Web. 1 December 2019. https://esotericastrologer.org/articles/the-jewish-group-service-unpublished-letters-of-dk-to-roberto-assagioli-fcd/>
26. Marian Walter, "Applicants at the Portal Study Set VII", p. 392. PDF, *International Wisdom Synthesis Center*, 2019, Web. 20 October 2019.
27. Michael Robbins, *Tapestry of the Gods Vol I*, (Arizona: University of the Seven Rays Publishing House, 1996), p. 20.
28. A deeper analysis is beyond the scope of the current work.
    29 Advancing the Teachings

29. ADVANCING THE TEACHINGS

1. See *School for the Study of the Seven Rays*, 2019, Web. 1 December 2019. <http://seven-rays.org/>
2. Kurt Abraham, *Threefold Method for Understanding the Seven Rays* (Cape May, NJ: Lampus Press, 1984).
3. "Michael Robbins, PhD". Seven Ray Institute and University of the Seven Rays, Web. 1 December 2019. <http://www.sevenray.org/robbins.html>
4. *Morya Federation: Esoteric Schools of Meditation, Study and Service*, 2019, Web. 1 December 2019. <http://www.moryafederation.com/>
5. *PIP II*, 2019, Web. 1 December 2019. <http://www.pipiionline.com/index_pip3c.asp>
6. Michael D. Robbins, *The Tapestry of the Gods: Volume I: The Seven Rays: An Esoteric Key to Understanding Human Nature*, (Phoenix: University of the Seven Rays, 1996), back cover matter.
7. *Shamballa School*, 2019, Web. 1 December 2019. <https://www.shamballaschool.org/>
8. "About Shamballa School". *Shamballa School*, 2019, Web. 1 December 2019. <https://www.shamballaschool.org/>; and *Highden Temple*, 2019, Web. 1 December 2019. <https://www.highdentemple.org/about-us>
9. See *Light-Weaver*, 2016. Web. 3 February 2020. <http://www.light-weaver.com/>
10. Douglas Baker, *Esoteric Psychology: The Seven Rays* and *The Seven Rays: Keys to the Mysteries*, (London: Aquarian Press, 1977).
    Also see *Douglas Baker: Home of Ancient Wisdom*, 2007, Web. 1 December 2019. <http://www.douglasbaker.com/>
11. Piero Ferrucci, *Inevitable Grace: Breakthroughs in Self-realization* (Los Angeles: Jeremy P. Tarcher, 1990).
12. David C. Borsos, "Cosmic Fire Studies and Academia – A Manifesto Part II: The Work". *Esoteric Quarterly*, 2017, Vol 13, p. 37.
13. Ibid., p. 55.
14. Steven Sutcliffe, *Children of the New Age*, (Abingdon, Routledge, 2003), p. 138.
15. The names and dates of the various presidents have been kindly supplied by Christine Morgan, President of the Lucis Trust.

16. Email from Christine Morgan to Isobel Blackthorn, January 2020: Letter as attachment: "2018 Financial Report" March 2019, Lucis Trust Headquarters Group.

17. Bette Stockbauer, "Africa and the Planetary Picture", *The Beacon*, 2019, Vol. 4, pp. 29-31; Anne Woodward, "The Paradoxical Utopia of Piet Mondrian", *The Beacon*, 2019, Vol. 4, pp. 17-20; Christine Aagaard , "Pluto and Global Economics". *The Beacon*, 2020, Vol 1, pp. 13-16.

18. <https://sydneygoodwill.org.au/>

19. Newsletter: "In Resonance with the Living Earth: A World Goodwill Seminar", Saturday 10 November 2018, Amba Hotel, Charing Cross, London, Lucis Trust.

20. Steve Nation: Letter to Isobel Blackthorn 7.20.2020.
    The keynote for 2019 was: *Let the Group Life be inspired by the Rules for Initiation: Know, Express, Reveal, Destroy and Resurrect.*

21. Newsletter: "An Invitation to Attend the Arcane School Conference London 15-16 June 2019", Lucis Trust.
    Steve Nation: Letter to Isobel Blackthorn 7.20.2020.

22. Letter to co-workers: "The Rise of the Group Hero". 2019 Festival Week of the New Group of World Servers, Lucis Trust. <https://www.lucistrust.org/about_us/lucis_trust/bi_annual_letter/2019_festival_week_letter?dm_t=0,0,0,0,0>

23. Bailey, *Discipleship in the New Age Vol II*, pp. 146-7.

24. "The Mantram of Unification". *Lucis Trust,* 17 January 2020. Web. <https://www.lucistrust.org/mantrams/the_mantram_unification>

25. "Humanity is One, And We are One with All.
    We seek to Love, not hate.
    We seek to Serve, and not exact due service.
    We seek to Heal, not hurt.
    Let pain bring due reward of Light and Love.
    Let the Soul control the outer form,
    And life and all events,
    And bring to light the Love That underlies the happenings of the time.
    Let Vision come and Insight.
    Let the future stand revealed.
    Let INNER UNION demonstrate and outer cleavages be gone.
    Let LOVE prevail.
    Let All People LOVE." – Facebook post, 23 December 2019.
    <https://www.facebook.com/olivia.hansen.906/posts/10218815727335865>
    30 Esoteric Astrology

30. ESOTERIC ASTROLOGY

1. Alice A. Bailey, *Esoteric Astrology* (New York: Lucis Trust, 1951).

2. Temple Richmond, "The Role of Alan Leo and Sepharial in the Development of Esoteric Astrology (Part I)", *Esoteric Astrology*, Summer 2005, p. 15.

3. Ibid., p. 13.

4. Ibid., p. 22.

5. See "Dane Rudhyar: Renaissance Man of the 20th Century". *Melanie Reinhart*, 2013, Web. 1 December 2019. <http://www.melaniereinhart.com/RUDHYARarticle.htm>
    Dane Rudhyar, *The Astrology of Personality* (New York: Lucis Publishing Company, 1936).
6. Dane Rudhyar, 'Biography', *The Free Dictionary*. Web. 14 July 2020. <https://encyclopedia.thefreedictionary.com/Dane+Rudhyar>
7. *Esoteric Astrology with Mermaid*, 2013, Web. 1 December 2019. <http://www.mermaid-uk.net/Esotericcontents.htm>
8. Jeffrey Wolf Green can be found at his website, *School of Evolutionary Astrology*, 2019, Web. 1 December 2109. <http://schoolofevolutionaryastrology.com/>
9. See *Esoteric Astrologer*, 2019, Web. 1 December 2019. <https://esotericastrologer.org/>
10. Phillip Lindsay, "The Hidden History of Humanity", 18 August 2017, Video, Web. 20 October 2019. <https://youtu.be/GbWMw249xY8>
11. Phillip Lindsay, "Capricorn Servers Week, 2025 and the Externalisation of the Hierarchy", October 2019, *Esoteric Astrologer*, 2019, Web. 1 December 2019. <https://esotericastrologer.org/newsletters/special-edition-news-letter-capricorn-servers-week-2025-the-externalisation-of-the-hierarchy/>
12. "Introduction to Esoteric Astrology". *Lynn Koiner: Astrological Research*, 2019, Web. 1 December 2019. <http://www.lynnkoiner.com/astrology-articles/introduction-to-esoteric-astrology>
13. Stephen D. Pugh, "Triple Sign Zodiacal Meditations", *The Esoteric Quarterly*, Fall 2012, pp. 53-65. His book, *The 72 Faces of Man: The Complete Sun Sign Guide to the Path of Initiation*, is available on Scribd.
14. Esoteric astrologer Phillip Lindsay asserts Dane Rudhyar's claim that Alice was born at 7.42am, which results in Leo Rising. See "Alice A. Bailey Horoscope: The Case for Leo Rising". *Esoteric Astrologer*, 2019, Web. 14 June 2020. <https://esotericastrologer.org/articles/alice-a-bailey-horoscope-the-case-for-leo-rising/>
15. Bailey, *The Unfinished Autobiography*, p. 183.
16. Stephen Pugh, Pisces Ascendant chart analysis, Esoteric Astrology group, <https://www.facebook.com/groups/486648064843029/search/?query=Pisces%20Rising&epa=SEARCH_BOX> accessed with his permission 11 October, 2019.

For interested astrologers, another indication of a Pisces Ascendant is the placement of Alice Bailey's Moon in Virgo. Virgo rules the digestive system, and pernicious anaemia is causally a digestive disorder. The ruler of the 6th House in the Pisces Rising chart is the Sun in Gemini, and Mercury as ruler of both Virgo and Gemini, is in Cancer/4th House, which rules the stomach. Pisces rising may also place Mars in the 6th house of health, in Leo, the sign associated with the heart. Mars is disposited by her Sun, which in turn is disposited by Mercury, which sits in mutual reception with her Moon, tying together the stomach and digestive system. With a Virgo Moon, this mutual reception between the Moon and Mercury dominates the chart, just as Alice Bailey's poor health dominated her life.

31 White Magic

31. WHITE MAGIC

1. Alice Bailey, *Letters on Occult Meditation*, p. 193.
2. *The Planetary System: Ideas, Formulas and Forms for a new Culture/Civilisation*, 2019, Web. 2 December 2019. <http://blog-en.theplanetarysystem.org/tps/>
3. John Rollo Sinclair, *The Other Universe*, (London: Rider, 1973), p. 115.
4. Dean Going: Letter to co-workers and close companions in Group of Nine, 1984. Held by *School for Esoteric Studies*, 2019, Web. 29 November 2019. <http://www.esotericstudies.net/>
5. Sir John R. Sinclair, *The Alice Bailey Inheritance*, 1984.
6. Ibid.
7. Marian Walter: Notes on Meditation of Soul Love, 1984, p. 3. Held by *School for Esoteric Studies*, 2019, Web. 29 November 2019. <http://www.esoteric-studies.net/>
8. Ibid.
9. There is an arithmetic progression from 3s (triangles) to 9s (three triangles) to 12s (four triangles). No group of 6 (two triangles) is known.
    See <http://twelvestar.org>
10. Steven Chernikeeff, *Esoteric Apprentice*, (BBR Publications, 2019).
11. Ibid., pp. 4-5.
12. Ibid., p. 9.
13. Helena Roerich, *Agni Yoga 1929*, p. 137.
14. Chernikeeff, *Esoteric Apprentice*, p. 94.
15. Ibid., p. 95
16. Ibid., p. 99.
17. Ibid., pp. 65-6.
    Concluding Remarks

32. CONCLUDING REMARKS

1. Bailey, *The Externalisation of the Hierarchy*, p. 562.

INDEX

Printed in Great Britain
by Amazon